Long-Term Outcomes of Military Service

Long-Term Outcomes of Military Service

THE HEALTH AND WELL-BEING OF AGING VETERANS

EDITED BY
Avron Spiro III
Richard A. Settersten Jr.
Carolyn M. Aldwin

AMERICAN PSYCHOLOGICAL ASSOCIATION
Washington, DC

Published by
American Psychological Association
750 First Street, NE
Washington, DC 20002
www.apa.org

APA Order Department
P.O. Box 92984
Washington, DC 20090-2984
Phone: (800) 374-2721; Direct: (202) 336-5510
Fax: (202) 336-5502; TDD/TTY: (202) 336-6123
Online: http://www.apa.org/pubs/books
E-mail: order@apa.org

In the U.K., Europe, Africa, and the Middle East, copies may be ordered from
Eurospan Group
c/o Pegasus Drive
Stratton Business Park
Biggleswade Bedfordshire
SG18 8TQ United Kingdom
Phone: +44 (0) 1767 604972
Fax: +44 (0) 1767 601640
Online: https://www.eurospanbookstore.com/apa
E-mail: eurospan@turpin-distribution.com

Typeset in Goudy by Circle Graphics, Inc., Columbia, MD

Printer: Sheridan Books, Chelsea, MI
Cover Designer: Naylor Design, Washington, DC

Library of Congress Cataloging-in-Publication Data
Names: Spiro, Avron, III, editor, author. | Settersten, Richard A., Jr., 1964-
  editor, author. | Aldwin, Carolyn M., editor, author.
Title: Long-term outcomes of military service : the health and well-being of aging veterans /
  edited by Avron Spiro III, Richard A. Settersten Jr., Carolyn M. Aldwin.
Description: Washington, DC : American Psychological Association, 2017. |
  Includes bibliographical references and index.
Identifiers: LCCN 2017014789 | ISBN 9781433828041 | ISBN 1433828049
Subjects: LCSH: Psychology, Military. | Veterans—Mental health—United States. |
  Post-traumatic stress disorder. | Combat—Psychological aspects. | War—
  Psychological aspects.
Classification: LCC U22.3 .L628 2017 | DDC 362.2086/970973—dc23
LC record available at https://lccn.loc.gov/2017014789

British Library Cataloguing-in-Publication Data
A CIP record is available from the British Library.

Printed in the United States of America
First Edition

http://dx.doi.org/10.1037/0000061-000

10 9 8 7 6 5 4 3 2 1

To Sergeant Avron "Sonny" Spiro Jr. and Colonel Francis J. Aldwin,
Veterans of World War II; and to all who have served our Nation
in times of war and peace, to their families,
and to those who serve them.

CONTENTS

CONTRIBUTORS

Carolyn M. Aldwin, PhD, Jo Anne Leonard Endowed Director, Center for Healthy Aging Research, and Professor, Human Development and Family Sciences, Oregon State University, Corvallis

Monika Ardelt, PhD, Associate Professor of Sociology, Department of Sociology and Criminology & Law, University of Florida, Gainesville

Soyoung Choun, PhD, Postdoctoral Fellow, Human Development and Family Sciences, Oregon State University, Corvallis

Abigail Tolhurst Christiansen, PhD, Director, Christiansen Counseling Services, Lafayette, IN

Joan M. Cook, PhD, Associate Professor, National Center for PTSD, VA Connecticut Healthcare System, and Department of Psychiatry, Yale School of Medicine, New Haven, CT

Eve Davison, PhD, Psychologist, National Center for PTSD, VA Boston Healthcare System, and Assistant Professor, Department of Psychiatry, Boston University School of Medicine, Boston, MA

Laura M. L. Distel, BA, Graduate Student, Clinical Psychology Doctoral Program, Loyola University Chicago, Chicago, IL

Glen H. Elder Jr., PhD, Odum Distinguished Research Professor, Department of Sociology, University of North Carolina, Chapel Hill

Anthony J. Faber, PhD, Professor of Family Studies, Southeast Missouri State University, Cape Girardeau

Meghann L. Fenn, Graduate Student, Human Development and Family Studies, Oregon State University, Corvallis

Gwenith G. Fisher, PhD, Associate Professor, Industrial/Organizational Psychology, Colorado State University, Fort Collins

Carol E. Franz, PhD, Associate Professor, Department of Psychiatry, University of California San Diego, San Diego

Bethany Godlewski, PhD Candidate, Human Development and Family Sciences, Oregon State University, Corvallis

Diane Highum Vaillant, MD, Orange, CA

Daniel H. Kabat, MS, Analyst, Department of Epidemiology, Mailman School of Public Health, Columbia University, New York, NY

Daniel W. King, PhD, Research Professor, Department of Psychiatry, Boston University School of Medicine, and Research Professor, Department of Psychology, Boston University, Boston, MA

Lynda A. King, PhD, Research Professor, Department of Psychiatry, Boston University School of Medicine, and Research Professor, Department of Psychology, Boston University, Boston, MA

Meredith A. Kleykamp, PhD, Associate Professor, Department of Sociology, University of Maryland, College Park

William S. Kremen, PhD, Professor, Department of Psychiatry, University of California San Diego, and Center of Excellence for Stress and Mental Health, VA San Diego Healthcare System, San Diego, CA

Ann T. Landes, PhD, Clinical Psychologist, Syracuse VA Medical Center, Syracuse, NY

Scott D. Landes, PhD, Assistant Professor of Sociology, Department of Sociology, Syracuse University, Syracuse, NY

Hyunyup Lee, MA, PhD Student, Human Development and Family Sciences, Oregon State University, Corvallis

Lewina O. Lee, PhD, Assistant Professor, Department of Psychiatry, Boston University School of Medicine, Boston, MA

Andrew S. London, PhD, Professor, Department of Sociology, Syracuse University, Syracuse, NY

Michael J. Lyons, PhD, Professor, Department of Psychological and Brain Sciences, Boston University, Boston, MA

Alair MacLean, PhD, Associate Professor, Department of Sociology, Washington State University Vancouver, Vancouver

Johanna C. Malone, PhD, Lecturer, Psychiatry, Harvard Medical School, Boston, MA, and Cambridge Health Alliance, Cambridge, MA

Sarah Mustillo, PhD, Professor, Department of Sociology, University of Notre Dame, South Bend, IN

William J. Oliver, MS, PhD Candidate, Department of Sociology, Syracuse University, Syracuse, NY

Crystal L. Park, PhD, Professor, Department of Psychological Sciences, University of Connecticut, Storrs

Anica Pless Kaiser, PhD, Clinical Research Psychologist, National Center for PTSD, VA Boston Healthcare System, and Research Assistant Professor, Department of Psychiatry, Boston University School of Medicine, Boston, MA

Claudia Recksiedler, PhD, Postdoctoral Researcher, Institute of Social Science, University of Lausanne, Switzerland

Paula P. Schnurr, PhD, Executive Director, National Center for PTSD, VA Medical Center, White River Junction, VT, and Professor, Department of Psychiatry, Geisel School of Medicine at Dartmouth, Hanover, NH

Richard A. Settersten Jr., PhD, Endowed Director, Hallie E. Ford Center for Healthy Children and Families, and Professor, Human Development and Family Sciences, Oregon State University, Corvallis

Merril Silverstein, PhD, Professor, Department of Sociology and Department of Human Development and Family Science, Syracuse University, Syracuse, NY

Avron Spiro III, PhD, Senior Research Career Scientist, VA Boston Healthcare System; Research Professor, Department of Epidemiology, Boston University School of Public Health; Research Professor, Department of Psychiatry, Boston University School of Medicine; and Associate Professor, Department of Health Policy and Health Services Research, Boston University Goldman School of Dental Medicine, Boston, MA

Robert S. Stawski, PhD, Associate Professor, Human Development and Family Sciences, Oregon State University, Corvallis

Jeanne Mager Stellman, PhD, Professor Emerita, Department of Health Policy & Management, Mailman School of Public Health, Columbia University, New York, NY

Steven D. Stellman, PhD, MPH, Department of Epidemiology, Mailman School of Public Health, Columbia University, New York, NY

Anna L. Tyzik, BS, Project Coordinator, Department of Epidemiology, Boston University School of Public Health, Boston, MA

George E. Vaillant, MD, Professor of Psychiatry, Harvard Medical School, Boston, MA

Shelley MacDermid Wadsworth, PhD, Professor, Department of Human Development and Family Studies, Purdue University, West Lafayette, IN

Robert J. Waldinger, MD, Clinical Professor of Psychiatry, Harvard Medical School, and Director, Laboratory of Adult Development, Massachusetts General Hospital, Boston

Joyce Wang, MPH, Research Public Health Analyst, RTI International, Waltham, MA

John Robert Warren, PhD, Professor, Department of Sociology, University of Minnesota, Minneapolis

Janet M. Wilmoth, PhD, Professor, Department of Sociology, Syracuse University, Syracuse, NY

Chenkai Wu, PhD, MPH, Assistant Professor, Department of Epidemiology and Community Health, New York Medical College, Valhalla

PREFACE

The seeds for this book were planted during the mid-1980s, when two of us (Avron Spiro III, Carolyn M. Aldwin) were working on the Normative Aging Study (NAS), a longitudinal study of aging men begun in the 1960s at the Boston Veterans Affairs (VA) Outpatient Clinic. We were conducting a study funded by the National Institute on Aging (R29-AG07465) to examine the effect of stress and coping processes on health and well-being. One of our hypotheses was the then-controversial idea that stress had positive as well as negative effects (Aldwin & Stokols, 1988). Because the NAS included many World War II and Korea-era veterans, what better acid test could there be than to examine the long-term positive and negative effects of combat experience? The NAS was an ideal sample, consisting of "normal" veterans, selected for good health at study entry, rather than the usual clinical, treatment-seeking sample characteristic of most previous research. We received funding from the VA Medical Research Service in 1989 and launched our studies of the effects of military service on health and well-being in aging veterans (Spiro, Schnurr, & Aldwin, 1994). We found that the effects of service could span many domains of functioning, be long-lasting, and be positive as well as negative.

Aging research was relatively new in the 1970s and 1980s, and much work focused on characterizing the aging process and differentiating normal from impaired aging. Almost all that we knew about aging was based on men and women who came of age in the 1940s and 1950s—those who were most likely to have served in World War II and Korea. However, few scholars were considering the impact of service and combat exposure on the aging process. This led us to the revelation that military service might be a "hidden variable" affecting the knowledge base on aging (Spiro et al., 1994). For example, we "know" that hearing loss increases with age, especially for men, but how much of that decline may have started with exposure to noise from weapons of war (Echt, Smith, Burridge, & Spiro, 2010)? In subsequent years, we collaborated with VA colleagues from the National Center for PTSD and elsewhere to study the effects of military service (e.g., Davison et al., 2016; Schnurr, Spiro, Aldwin, & Stukel, 1998). Spiro and Aldwin began collaborating with Settersten in 2006, when he edited a special issue of *Research on Aging* on the consequences of military service for aging and the life course.

During the 2009–2010 academic year, we three received funding from the National Institute on Aging to create a network focused on the "Lifespan Outcomes of Military Service" (R24-AG039343). Our mission was to advance a lifespan/life course perspective on the interdisciplinary study of the long-term effects of service on health and well-being in later life. To accomplish this, we created a national network of U.S. scholars (many of whom have authored chapters in this volume), identified existing longitudinal studies conducted in the United States and characterized their information on military service, and created a website to disseminate this information (http://health.oregonstate.edu/healthy-aging/military-life-course).

In the ensuing years, network members met at annual scientific meetings of the Gerontological Society of America (2011–2015) and at the Airlie House in northern Virginia (2014). During these meetings, many of the chapters in this volume were drafted, critiqued, and revised. Other contributions of the network include a special issue of *Research in Human Development* (Spiro & Settersten, 2012), and three articles in a special issue on aging veterans in *The Gerontologist* (Davison et al., 2016; Kang, Aldwin, Choun, & Spiro, 2016; Spiro, Settersten, & Aldwin, 2016).

This book is the capstone of the network's activity. We believe that the authors have done a remarkable job of providing new findings, insights, and opportunities for advancing the study of aging veterans. We hope that you, the reader, will agree, and will find in this volume some measure of the excitement, and honor, we feel for the study of aging veterans.

We would like to thank the National Institute on Aging for its generous support of our research network on Lifespan Outcomes of Military Service

(R24-AG039343), which allowed us to bring together this group of scholars and, ultimately, to create this book.

Next, we wish to express our deep appreciation to the members of that network, many of whom have authored chapters here, for their input and shared commitment to better understanding the long-term effects of military service from lifespan/life course perspectives.

Finally, we each wish to acknowledge particular people and institutions. Avron Spiro would like to thank his colleagues at the VA Boston Healthcare System, including the Massachusetts Veterans Epidemiology Research and Information Center and the National Center for PTSD, and elsewhere in the VA system, and those at Boston University, for their support and encouragement over many years on the importance of aging veterans.

Richard Settersten would like to acknowledge the support of the College of Public Health and Human Sciences at Oregon State University (OSU), and particularly the Hallie E. Ford Center for Healthy Children and Families, which he directs. We are especially grateful for the skilled assistance of Ms. Laura Arreola in preparing the manuscript for publication. Richard would also like to thank the OSU Center for the Humanities for a sabbatical fellowship, during which time this book was completed.

Carolyn Aldwin would like to thank Jo Anne Leonard Petersen for her support of the Center for Healthy Aging Research at OSU. Dr. Soyoung Choun also provided data management and analysis support for some of the chapters. Special thanks are due to Dr. Raymond Bossé, former Director of Psychosocial Research at the VA Normative Aging Study, without whom this work would never have been started.

REFERENCES

Aldwin, C., & Stokols, D. (1988). The effects of environmental change on individuals and groups: Some neglected issues in stress research. *Journal of Environmental Psychology, 8*, 57–75. http://dx.doi.org/10.1016/S0272-4944(88)80023-9

Davison, E. H., Pless Kaiser, A., Spiro, A., III, Moye, J., King, L. A., & King, D. W. (2016). From late-onset stress symptomatology (LOSS) to later-adulthood trauma reengagement (LATR) in aging combat veterans: Taking a broader view. *The Gerontologist, 56*, 14–21. http://dx.doi.org/10.1093/geront/gnv097

Echt, K. V., Smith, S. L., Burridge, A. B., & Spiro, A., III. (2010). Longitudinal changes in hearing sensitivity among men: The Veterans Affairs Normative Aging Study. *The Journal of the Acoustical Society of America, 128*, 1992–2002. http://dx.doi.org/10.1121/1.3466878

Kang, S., Aldwin, C. M., Choun, S., & Spiro, A., III. (2016). Combining lifespan and life course perspectives on combat exposure and PTSD symptoms in later life: Findings from the VA Normative Aging Study. *The Gerontologist, 56*, 22–31. http://dx.doi.org/10.1093/geront/gnv505.19

Schnurr, P. P., Spiro, A., III, Aldwin, C. M., & Stukel, T. (1998). Physical symptom trajectories following trauma exposure: Longitudinal findings from the Normative Aging Study. *Journal of Nervous and Mental Disease, 186*, 522–528. http://dx.doi.org/10.1097/00005053-199809000-00002

Spiro, A., III, Schnurr, P. P., & Aldwin, C. M. (1994). Combat-related PTSD symptoms in older veterans. *Psychology and Aging, 9*, 17–26. http://dx.doi.org/10.1037/0882-7974.9.1.17

Spiro, A., III, & Settersten, R. A., Jr. (Guest Eds.). (2012). Military service in the life course: Implications for later-life health and well-being. *Research in Human Development, 9*, 183–271. http://dx.doi.org/10.1080/15427609.2012.705551

Spiro, A., III, Settersten, R. A., Jr., & Aldwin, C. M. (2016). Long-term outcomes of military service in aging and the life course: A positive re-envisioning. *The Gerontologist, 56*, 5–13. Erratum at http://www.ncbi.nlm.nih.gov/pubmed/26888758

Long-Term Outcomes of Military Service

INTRODUCTION: UNDERSTANDING THE LONG-TERM OUTCOMES OF MILITARY SERVICE

AVRON SPIRO III, RICHARD A. SETTERSTEN JR.,
AND CAROLYN M. ALDWIN

This volume is the result of the efforts of a large number of people, a community of scholars committed to advancing lifespan/life course perspectives for understanding the long-term effects of military service on the health and well-being of veterans. Some of the contributors have been advocating this approach for over 3 decades; others have only recently become interested in understanding the multifaceted nature of service, its full range of outcomes as veterans and their families grow older, and how these outcomes differ across historical eras. As described briefly in this chapter, and detailed in subsequent ones, we are united in our conviction that veterans of World War II, Korea, and Vietnam are a large, important, and too often understudied

Preparation of this chapter was supported by a grant from the National Institute on Aging, R24-AG039343, and a Senior Research Career Scientist award from the Clinical Science Research and Development Service, U.S. Department of Veterans Affairs. The views expressed in this chapter are those of the authors and do not necessarily represent the views of the U.S. Department of Veterans Affairs or other support institutions.

http://dx.doi.org/10.1037/0000061-001
Long-Term Outcomes of Military Service: The Health and Well-Being of Aging Veterans, A. Spiro III, R. A. Settersten Jr., and C. M. Aldwin (Editors)

segment of the aging population, despite recent efforts to address this over-sight (e.g., Pruchno, 2016; Wilmoth & London, 2013, 2016).

Before orienting readers to the volume and the model that frames it, we offer some context in which to consider the issue of aging veterans and our rationale on why this issue is important to consider from a lifespan/life course perspective. We then provide an overview of the volume's organization and contents. Finally, we close with thoughts on a few critical issues confronting research and practice related to aging veterans.

PURPOSE OF THE BOOK

Military service can have profound effects on veterans' health and well-being across the lifespan—whether good, bad, or just plain ugly (Spiro, Settersten, & Aldwin, 2016). On the one hand, veterans are a select population, having been screened for physical, mental, and cognitive health at entry to the military—the "healthy soldier" effect (Seltzer & Jablon, 1974). On the other, many have been exposed to dangerous or hazardous conditions as a result of training or deployment, which can have profound short- and long-term effects. These effects, both positive and negative, exist (but are seldom studied) in multiple domains of functioning—in physical and mental health, and in social, family, and economic relations. As mentioned earlier, military service is a "hidden variable" that lurks beneath much of our knowledge of aging, especially among men. Continued inattention to the varied effects of service could also affect our knowledge of women's aging in the future, as women now comprise 15% to 20% of the U.S. Armed Forces (Reiber & LaCroix, 2016) and a comparable percentage of veterans (Spiro et al., 2016).

Demographic data illustrate the magnitude of the concern. In 2014, the U.S. civilian population aged ages 18 and older included over 244 million adults, of whom 9% were veterans (U.S. Census Bureau, 2016). Half (51%) of the U.S. population were women, but women comprised only 10% of veterans. Compared with the U.S. population, veterans are older, averaging about 64 years of age versus 49 years for nonveterans. Nearly half of veterans (49%) are 65 and older, versus 16% of the nonveteran population, a threefold difference. At age 55+, 68% of veterans are this age, compared with 33% of civilians, only a twofold difference.

During World War II, those in military service made up 12% of the U.S. population, including the 50% of men who were eligible for service (Segal & Segal, 2004); about 25% of these experienced combat. Since that time, the characteristics of the military, and of veterans, have changed. Women now make up about 20% of the active military and of older veterans; minorities account for about 35% of veterans ages 55+ since Vietnam, compared with 15% of veterans from prior conflicts (U.S. Department of Veterans Affairs [VA],

Office of the Actuary, 2015b). Further, older individuals are now being deployed. In recent conflicts, Reserve and National Guard troops, often older than those active duty service members, made up a significant proportion of those deployed (Institute of Medicine [IOM], 2013). Thus, the age structure of veterans is also changing, partially a function of changes in the age structure of the military, suggesting that the coming wave of aging veterans following the baby boomers will further challenge the already strained VA.

About 10% ($101 billion) of U.S. government health care spending is for the military and veterans (Khullar & Chokshi, 2016). The VA treated 9 million beneficiaries at a cost of $65 billion and in FY2015 also provided disability benefits ($2.5 billion) to over 4.1 million veterans as part of its $164 billion budget (VA, 2015a). The U.S. Department of Defense (whose FY2014 budget was $560 billion) spent $40 billion for health care for 10 million beneficiaries. Understanding the long-term effects of military service on health is critical to the financial future of the United States (Geiling, Rosen, & Edwards, 2012).

Military service can affect veterans' morbidity and mortality in many ways—for example, through exposure to tobacco smoking, which leads to premature mortality (Bedard & Deschênes, 2006), or through increased stress, which can lead to heart disease (Kubzansky, Koenen, Spiro, Vokonas, & Sparrow, 2007) and premature mortality (Aldwin, Jeong, Igarashi, & Spiro, 2014). Perhaps less obvious, military service can have long-term negative effects on social (e.g., family formation, dissolution, violence), economic (e.g., earnings/wealth), and psychological (e.g., depression, posttraumatic stress disorder [PTSD], suicide) outcomes. However, much less is known about these long-term outcomes and how they are affected by (and in turn affect) the course of aging. And as we have argued elsewhere (Spiro et al., 2016), and as various chapters in this volume illustrate, we know even less about positive outcomes that can result from service.

There is an urgent need to take an integrative, multidisciplinary approach to understanding the legacies of military service on the health and well-being of veterans and their families over time—how service can serve as a risk or protective factor for aging, how potentially negative effects of service could be offset or potentially positive effects enhanced, and how the losses and gains resulting from service might accumulate over the life course. The long-term outcomes of service are less often studied than the more immediate (and typically negative) ones, such as PTSD and traumatic brain injury among recent veterans (IOM, 2013).

This book was conceived to fill these voids. It provides a broader understanding of the spectrum of positive and negative effects of military service, and of their long-term impact, by examining past veterans in the hope of better understanding future generations. The intended audience includes academics, researchers, and practitioners interested in understanding how service affects veterans' lives over the long term. We hope that the volume is also of interest to those who are concerned with public policies and treatment of aging veterans and their families.

The chapters in this book are grounded in a combination of lifespan and life course perspectives on adult development and aging. These two complementary perspectives share a focus on the use of longitudinal data to address questions of change and long-term outcomes. The life course perspective is grounded in social theory and examines social institutions (e.g., military, work, families), social roles (e.g., employment, retirement), as well as cohort differences. The lifespan perspective, in contrast, is more grounded in psychological theory and examines health, well-being, and other outcomes in the individual's developmental context. We believe that the combination of these two perspectives provides a very strong theoretical framework for the research presented in this book, as well as for future research, and can offer valuable insights into programs and policies that recognize the long-term impacts of service.

Nowhere is this better illustrated than in the theoretical model shown in Figure 1, which situates the individual's life trajectory (lower arrow) within their sociohistorical context, indicated by the upper arrow representing American wartime eras. The middle section of the figure represents an individual's life course, including their military career. It is important to note that premilitary characteristics influence the process of joining the military but can also influence the outcomes of military service. Characteristics at entry are also important—for example, whether one enlists or is drafted, and at what rank. Military experiences are included in the central box, which identifies aspects of service that can lead to positive or negative outcomes in later life. However, postmilitary experience can also influence long-term outcomes, which are enumerated in the "pathways" box. These include homecoming experiences as well as material or social benefits (e.g., use of benefits from the GI Bill). The final box lists possible outcomes of the service. This figure is a useful framework when reading the chapters.

OVERVIEW OF THE BOOK

We asked authors to select one or more studies, preferably longitudinal, and use these data to assess the impact of military service on aspects of health or well-being in later life. We had originally hoped that all chapters would use longitudinal data, preferably from multiple studies, to compare and contrast experiences across different eras of service or different outcomes. Because of limitations in available data, this proved too ambitious. Only one chapter (Chapter 1) was able to compare similar measures across multiple studies. Still, over half the chapters used longitudinal or prospective data (see Table 1 for

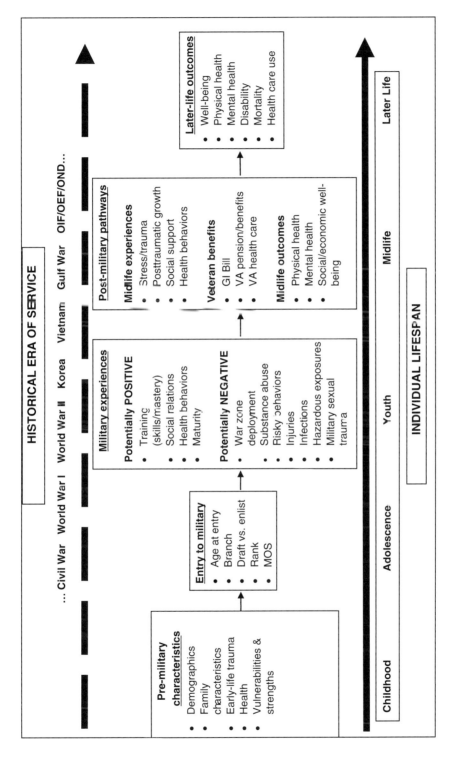

Figure 1. Model of long-term outcomes of military service. OIF/OEF/OND = Operation Iraqi Freedom/Operation Enduring Freedom/Operation New Dawn. From "Long-Term Outcomes of Military Service in Aging and the Life Course: A Positive Re-Envisioning," by A. Spiro III, R. A. Settersten, and C. M. Aldwin, 2016, *The Gerontologist, 57*, p. 7. Copyright 2016 by Oxford University Press. Reprinted with permission.

TABLE 1
Select Characteristics of Studies Used in This Volume

Chapter	Lead author	Data set(s)	Sample	Design	Era	N	Include women?	Include minorities?
1	Settersten	VA NAS	Veteran only	Cross-sect	WW2/K	1,099	no	yes
		Harvard Study of Adult Development	Veteran only	Cross-sect	WW2	145	no	no
2	Malone	Oakland	Veteran only	Cross-sect	WW2	61	no	?
		Berkeley	Veteran only	Cross-sect	WW2/K	103	no	?
		Harvard Study of Adult Development	Both V and non-V	Longit	WW2	83	no	no
3	Kabat	American Legion outreach	Veteran only	Cross-sect	VN	428	no	yes
		Women Veterans Memorial Project	Veteran only	Cross-sect	VN	1,285	yes	?
4	MacDermid Wadsworth	CPS: 1992, 1999, 2004	Both V and non-V	Reptd cross-sect	multiple	120,736	yes	yes
		DMDC Active Duty Survey: 1985, 1992, 1999	Military	Reptd cross-sect	multiple	148,004	yes	yes
5	MacLean	CPS (IPUMS): 1967–2010	Both V and non-V	Reptd cross-sect	multiple	?	no	yes
6	Silverstein	LSOG G2	Both V and non-V	Longit	multiple	314	no	?
		LSOG G3	Both V and non-V	Longit	multiple	758	yes	?

#	Author	Study	Population	Design	War	N		
7	Wilmoth	HRS Core: 1992–2012; HRS LB: 2006, 2008, 2010, 2012; HRS 2013 Veterans	Both V and non-V	Longit	multiple	16,347	no	yes
8	Lee	VN RPW; 1992 LOSS survey	Veteran only; Veteran only	Longit; Longit	VN; VN	567; 292	no; no	yes; yes
9	Aldwin	HRS LB: 2006, 2008	Both V and non-V	Cross-sect		3,412	no	yes
10	Landes	NHIS: 1997–2004; NDI: 1997–2006 linked	Both V and non-V	Longit	multiple	92,459	no	yes
11	Stawski	HRS: 1998–2010	Both V and non-V	Longit		7,020	no	yes
12	Franz	VETR; VETSA T1; VETSA T2	Veteran only	Longit	VN	1,237; 469; 387	no	yes
13	Vaillant	Harvard Study of Adult Development	Both V and non-V	Longit	WW2	248; 244	no	no

Note. VA NAS = Veterans Affairs Normative Aging Study; CPS = Current Population Survey; DMDC = Defense Manpower Data Center; IPUMS = Integrated Public Use Microdata Series; LSOG = Longitudinal Study of Generations; HRS = Health and Retirement Study; LB = Leave Behind; VN RPW = Vietnam repatriated prisoners of war; LOSS = late-onset stress symptomatology; NHIS = National Health Interview Survey; NDI = National Death Index; VETR = Vietnam Era Twin Registry; VETSA = Vietnam Era Twin Study of Aging; V = veteran; non-V = nonveteran; longit = longitudinal; cross-sect = cross-sectional; WW2 = World War II; K = Korea; VN = Vietnam.

descriptive information on the data sets used in the various chapters). This table and the information provided on our website (http://health.oregonstate.edu/ healthy-aging/military-life-course) are useful guides to longitudinal studies that can be used for further investigation.

This volume is organized into three parts and two online appendices. The chapters in Part I, Psychosocial Dynamics, examine how various psychological and social outcomes of military service were affected by different aspects of military service. The chapters in Part II, Health Dynamics, consider how service can alter trajectories of physical, mental, cognitive, and neurological health, as well as mortality. The chapters in Part III, Implications for Practice and Policy, review aspects of mental health and service use among older veterans and offer some summary implications gleaned from the chapters for practice and policy. The online appendices, available at http://pubs.apa.org/books/supp/spiro/, contain (a) a discussion of different ways of identifying periods of service based on age and birth cohort and (b) a short module of items that could be included in new or ongoing surveys to better assess aspects of military experience.

Part I, Psychosocial Dynamics

Chapters 1 through 6 focus on how military service matters for psychosocial development, family and other social relationships, and work and retirement. In Chapter 1, Settersten and his colleagues bring together data from four longitudinal studies to unearth the collective memories of World War II experience and assess the impact of service on veterans' lives. They find that the meaning and memory of wartime experiences depend on how embedded veterans are in supportive relationships and networks, and on how much they communicate with others about their experiences.

Malone and her collaborators in Chapter 2 examine the impact of combat exposure on ego development. Contrary to theories of stress-related growth, combat exposure is associated with lower levels of ego development in midlife. However, the effect is moderated by conscientiousness, which supports the idea that it could be a resilience factor related to successful aging (Friedman, Kern, Hampson, & Duckworth, 2014).

In Chapter 3, Kabat and his colleagues present data from some of the few studies that have included women (nurses) and minority veterans. As expected, exposure to combat or combat-related situations was the strongest predictor of PTSD among all groups, but sex and ethnicity influenced these relations. Thus, there may be important individual and group differences in the influence of social and personal factors on service and its outcomes in later life.

In Chapter 4, MacDermid Wadsworth and her collaborators take a life course perspective to examine the prevalence of marriage in military families, using data from two national surveys. They find that military service is a different marital context for men and women. For men, service appears to be a supportive context for marriage. For women, there is less support in military life for marriage.

In Chapter 5, MacLean and her collaborators examine trends in labor force participation among male veterans. Employment and retirement are shaped by changes in benefit policies and in economic and historical conditions. The advantages resulting from these benefits seem especially significant for minority veterans, who often have fared better than their nonveteran counterparts.

In Chapter 6, Silverstein and his colleagues examine nationalism and patriotism among World War II veterans and their baby-boom children. They trace how service shapes veterans' attitudes toward nationalism and patriotism—defined by support for an assertive U.S. foreign policy and pride in national virtues—and, in turn, how those attitudes are passed on to, and persist in, the next generation. Their findings lead them to the provocative and paradoxical idea that World War II veterans, through intergenerational transmission of these values, may actually have primed the antiwar movement of their children's generation.

Part II, Health Dynamics

Chapters 7 through 13 consider the impact of military service on various health outcomes—self-rated health (SRH), cognition, mental and physical health, and mortality. Chapter 7, by Wilmoth and her colleagues, examines the impact of service on changes in SRH. They find that combat veterans had better SRH from their 50s through 70s, but worse thereafter, and that specific aspects of military experience account for both level and rate of change in health during later life.

In Chapter 8, Lee and her collaborators report results from a longitudinal study of repatriated prisoners of war (RPW) from Vietnam. Comparisons with literature on prisoners of war from other eras offer some suggestions regarding the nature of resilience, coping, and growth following extreme adversity and may hold promise for other veterans.

In Chapter 9, Aldwin and her collaborators examine the long-term impact of military service on stress, well-being, and health in later life. The chapter drew on the hypothesis that military samples are useful for studying optimal, normal, and impaired aging. Veterans are generally healthier than civilians, and thus may be expected to age optimally, but combat veterans are exposed to both psychological and physical trauma that can accelerate aging. Distinguishing among combat and noncombat veterans from multiple war-time eras and civilians, they found, as hypothesized, that noncombat veterans reported higher levels of well-being than the other two groups; combat veterans reported higher levels of stress but nonetheless showed resilience in that there were no differences among the groups in biomarkers, body mass index, and eudaimonic well-being (Ryff, 1989).

In Chapter 10, Landes and his colleagues find that although Korea and Vietnam veterans were initially healthier than civilians, some effects of service, such as wartime service or adoption of smoking, can increase their mortality risk in later life.

In Chapter 11, Stawski and his colleagues examine the impact of military service on cognitive aging, focusing on episodic memory. Their findings suggest that the impact of service on cognitive functioning in late life is complex and that much more work is needed to identify individual and contextual differences in cognitive trajectories among veterans.

In Chapter 12, Franz and her collaborators use longitudinal data from the Vietnam Era Twin Study of Aging to examine the impact of combat exposure on midlife posttraumatic stress symptoms (PTSS) and the effect of PTSS on brain structures and on physical and mental health in later life. They find that combat exposure predicts higher PTSS at both midlife and later life but does not affect brain structures or health in later life; however, midlife PTSS predicted lower hippocampal volumes in later life, and impaired brain structures predicted worse physical and mental health later in life.

In Chapter 13, Vaillant and Highum Vaillant examine the role of PTSD on mortality, using data collected over 70 years from men in the Harvard Study of Adult Development (aka the Grant Study), largely World War II veterans. Those who were exposed to severe combat, especially those with symptoms of PTSD, had earlier mortality. PTSD may have mediated the effects of adverse military experiences.

Taken together, the chapters in Part II highlight the necessity of examining contextual factors in the long-term effects of service and hint at potential mediators and moderators, such as PTSD or PTSS and health behaviors, of long-term health outcomes.

Part III, Implications for Practice and Policy

Chapter 14, by Pless Kaiser and her collaborators, reviews the literature on mental health considerations and service use in later life adults and veterans. They present convincing evidence that older people in general, and older veterans in particular, underuse mental health services. Although older veterans exhibit more mental health symptoms, the literature addressing the efficacy of treatment for depression, anxiety, and PTSD in older veterans is sparse.

To conclude the volume, Settersten and his colleagues offer in Chapter 15 some reflections on this book and the broader implications for policy and practice regarding aging veterans. Among other things, they discuss strengthening veterans' social relationships and networks, fostering resilience and promoting physical health among veterans, intervening at strategic points of transition, building workforce capacity to serve aging veterans, and the need to improve both data and health care systems to better serve them.

When it comes to questions of policy and practice, too often the answer is "we don't know"—either because the data do not exist or because investigators did not consider possible differences by age, cohort, or other characteristics. As this book reveals, we know most about the long-term outcomes for veterans of World War II, Korea, and to a lesser extent, Vietnam. Our hope is that the information presented here will help the country to better serve these aging veterans and also motivate researchers to understand how current cohorts of veterans are aging, while also recognizing that they differ from today's older veterans in their greater gender and ethnic diversity, as well as combat-related disability and brain trauma.

Online Appendices

The volume includes two online appendices, offered in the belief that knowledge gained should be shared. These can be accessed via the APA website, at http://pubs.apa.org/books/supp/spiro/. First, we found little consensus among researchers as to when a particular conflict started (or ended), complicating the definition of wartime service, especially when period of service was not directly measured. For example, in Vietnam, should those who served just before the onset of major American involvement be considered Vietnam veterans? In Online Appendix A, Wilmoth and her colleagues offer recommendations for identifying the time periods for the different wars and conflicts. This will help researchers more systematically classify veterans and comparison civilians, especially in studies with limited information on service, as to specific conflicts and combat situations that have occurred in the 20th and 21st centuries.

All too often, studies neglect to assess military service altogether or, at best, include only one or two items about whether and perhaps when individuals served. Given the importance of differences in age trajectories among combat and noncombat veterans, and civilians, we strongly suggest that these studies should do a better job of assessing military experience. Thus, we developed a short module that could be included in new or ongoing surveys (included as Online Appendix B) to better assess key aspects of service. Most of the items were taken from existing surveys, thus allowing some degree of comparability with other people's data. Those interested in assessing other aspects of military service can refer to the VA Military Health History pocket card (https://www.va.gov/oaa/pocketcard/); we recommend that clinicians in particular consider this when assessing new adult patients.

CONCLUSION

As citizens, and researchers, we owe a debt of gratitude to our World War II– and Korea-era veterans. They not only risked their lives in the service of the American ideal, but they also are largely the cohort from whom we have learned a great deal about the aging process. Through their suffering, we learned that smoking causes lung cancer and a host of other ailments. They participated in experiments that have allowed us to transform what had been lethal diseases to more manageable chronic illnesses. The Vietnam veterans—the baby boomers—are aging differently, and it is clear that there is an increase in health disparities in aging in more recent cohorts (Antonucci et al., 2016). Although we are better at managing disease, the higher levels of PTSD and the likelihood of exposure to subsequent civilian trauma could accelerate the aging process (Schnurr, Spiro, Aldwin, & Stukel, 1998). The remarkable resilience of both the Vietnam RPWs and other combat veterans can provide salient examples of how individuals become resilient in the face of stress, and hopefully their lessons can be taught to others.

The current cohort of veterans, from the Gulf War, Iraq, and Afghanistan, similarly face a unique constellation of circumstances that will affect their aging processes. On the one hand, the mortality rates during deployment were low, compared with previous wars, but the disability rates were higher. These veterans experienced multiple deployments and higher levels of combat exposure than earlier cohorts. Of particular concern are traumatic brain injury and other adverse outcomes stemming from exposure to improvised explosive devices and other explosive devices, which may have unique effects on physiology, including neurophysiology (Trotter, Robinson, Milberg, McGlinchey, & Salat, 2015). Although the military has started programs to enhance the resilience of its soldiers and thus (hopefully) its veterans, much more carefully constructed research is needed to identify the strengths and vulnerabilities of the forthcoming veteran cohorts.

It's been a long journey since our first forays into the study of aging veterans 30 years ago. We hope that by providing these chapters, a lifespan/ life course perspective in which to view veterans' lives, more information on data that are available, and suggestions for collecting additional information on military service, more can and will be done by those interested in understanding the long-term effects of service on the aging veterans of today and tomorrow. Although old soldiers may never die, but just fade away, we hope that this volume will encourage others to study them before they do, both for their own sake and for what they might reveal about the next generation.

REFERENCES

Aldwin, C. M., Jeong, Y.-J., Igarashi, H., & Spiro, A., III. (2014). Do hassles and uplifts change with age? Longitudinal findings from the VA normative aging study. *Psychology and Aging, 29*, 57–71. http://dx.doi.org/10.1037/a0035042

Antonucci, T., Berkman, L., Börsch-Supan, A., Carstensen, L. A., Fried, L. P., Furstenberg, F. F., . . . Zissimopoulos, J. (2016). Society and the individual at the dawn of the twenty-first century. In K. W. Schaie & S. Willis (Eds.), *Handbook of the psychology of aging* (8th ed., pp. 41–62). San Diego, CA: Academic Press. http://dx.doi.org/10.1016/B978-0-12-411469-2.00003-0

Bedard, K., & Deschênes, O. (2006). The long-term impact of military service on health: Evidence from World War II and Korean War veterans. *The American Economic Review, 96*, 176–194. http://dx.doi.org/10.1257/000282806776157731

Friedman, H. S., Kern, M. L., Hampson, S. E., & Duckworth, A. L. (2014). A new life-span approach to conscientiousness and health: Combining the pieces of the causal puzzle. *Developmental Psychology, 50*, 1377–1389. http://dx.doi.org/10.1037/a0030373

Geiling, J., Rosen, J. M., & Edwards, R. D. (2012). Medical costs of war in 2035: Long-term care challenges for veterans of Iraq and Afghanistan. *Military Medicine, 177*, 1235–1244. http://dx.doi.org/10.7205/MILMED-D-12-00031

Institute of Medicine. (2013). *Returning home from Iraq and Afghanistan: Assessment of readjustment needs of veterans, service members, and their families.* Washington, DC: National Academies Press.

Khullar, D., & Chokshi, D. A. (2016). Toward an integrated federal health system. *JAMA, 315*, 2521–2522. http://dx.doi.org/10.1001/jama.2016.4641

Kubzansky, L. D., Koenen, K. C., Spiro, A., III, Vokonas, P. S., & Sparrow, D. (2007). Prospective study of posttraumatic stress disorder symptoms and coronary heart disease in the Normative Aging Study. *Archives of General Psychiatry, 64*, 109–116. http://dx.doi.org/10.1001/archpsyc.64.1.109

Pruchno, R. (2016). Veterans aging. *The Gerontologist, 56*, 1–4. http://dx.doi.org/10.1093/geront/gnv671

Reiber, G. E., & LaCroix, A. Z. (2016). Older women veterans in the Women's Health Initiative. *The Gerontologist, 56*(Suppl. 1), S1–S5. http://dx.doi.org/10.1093/geront/gnv673

Ryff, C. (1989). Happiness is everything, or is it? Explorations on the meaning of psychological well-being. *Journal of Personality and Social Psychology, 57*, 1069–1081. http://dx.doi.org/10.1037/0022-3514.57.6.1069

Schnurr, P. P., Spiro, A., III, Aldwin, C. M., & Stukel, T. A. (1998). Physical symptom trajectories following trauma exposure: Longitudinal findings from the Normative Aging Study. *Journal of Nervous and Mental Disease, 186*, 522–528. http://dx.doi.org/10.1097/00005053-199809000-00002

Segal, D. R., & Segal, M. W. (2004). America's military population. *Population Bulletin*, *59*, 3–40.

Seltzer, C. C., & Jablon, S. (1974). Effects of selection on mortality. *American Journal of Epidemiology*, *100*, 367–372. http://dx.doi.org/10.1093/oxfordjournals.aje.a112047

Spiro, A., III, Settersten, R. A., Jr., & Aldwin, C. M. (2016). Long-term outcomes of military service in aging and the life course: A positive re-envisioning. *The Gerontologist*, *56*, 5–13. Erratum at http://www.ncbi.nlm.nih.gov/pubmed/26888758

Trotter, B. B., Robinson, M. E., Milberg, W. P., McGlinchey, R. E., & Salat, D. H. (2015). Military blast exposure, ageing and white matter integrity. *Brain*, *138*, 2278–2292. http://dx.doi.org/10.1093/brain/awv139

U.S. Census Bureau. (2016). *Veteran status: 2014 American Community Survey 1-year estimates*. Retrieved from https://factfinder.census.gov/faces/tableservices/jsf/pages/productview.xhtml?src=bkmk

U.S. Department of Veterans Affairs. (2015a). *VA benefits and health care utilization*. Retrieved from http://www.va.gov/vetdata/docs/pocketcards/fy2015q4.pdf

U.S. Department of Veterans Affairs, Office of the Actuary. (2015b). *Veteran population projection model 2014* (VetPop2014). Washington, DC: Author.

Wilmoth, J. M., & London, A. S. (Eds.). (2013). *Life course perspectives on military service*. New York, NY: Routledge.

Wilmoth, J. M., & London, A. S. (2016). The influence of military service on aging. In L. K. George & K. Ferraro (Eds.), *Handbook of aging and the social sciences* (8th ed., pp. 227–250). Waltham, MA: Elsevier. http://dx.doi.org/10.1016/B978-0-12-417235-7.00011-1

I

PSYCHOSOCIAL DYNAMICS

1

TWO FACES OF WARTIME EXPERIENCE: COLLECTIVE MEMORIES AND VETERANS' APPRAISALS IN LATER LIFE

RICHARD A. SETTERSTEN JR., CLAUDIA RECKSIEDLER,
BETHANY GODLEWSKI, AND GLEN H. ELDER JR.

Why should we care about the subjective experience of aging veterans? Evidence suggests that veterans' recall (or reconstructions) of their military experiences may be more important than their actual experiences in predicting the health and well-being outcomes of their service. Coming to terms with wartime service—whether one was exposed to danger, participated in combat, or had other roles and responsibilities—is both an individual and a public health issue. Prior wartime eras are also part of the larger collective memory of nations and the people in them, and they continue to affect perspectives on peace, democracy, and defense.

Preparation of this chapter was supported by a grant from the National Institute on Aging, R24-AG039343. We also wish to acknowledge with gratitude the collaboration with Glen Elder of two former sociology graduate students—Cynthia Gimbel and Rachel Ivie (Sweat)—in the measurement of World War II memories from retrospective surveys of the Oakland and Berkeley study members and their spouses.

http://dx.doi.org/10.1037/0000061-002
Long-Term Outcomes of Military Service: The Health and Well-Being of Aging Veterans, A. Spiro III, R. A. Settersten Jr., and C. M. Aldwin (Editors)

In this chapter, we use data from four longitudinal studies to examine veterans' appraisals of military service and collective memories of war from the vantage point of later life. We probe their recollections of World War II and, to a lesser degree, the Korean War. Although much knowledge of aging is based on these cohorts, which were heavily marked by war, little attention has been paid to the long-term outcomes of their military experiences, and even less to subjective aspects of service.

COLLECTIVE MEMORIES OF WARTIME EXPERIENCE

Collective memories reflect the shared experiences of people who live in a specific historical time and place (Halbwachs, 1980). Periodic outbreaks of war across the 20th century have shaped the collective memories of populations. In the case of wartime experience, social rituals sustain collective memories. For example, the Fourth U.S. Marine Division, which fought on Iwo Jima, holds public assemblies to pay tribute to the unit's fallen comrades and share memories and emotions. Veterans' days, commemorations on anniversary dates, and the erection of national monuments also keep these experiences alive for younger generations.

Especially during epochs of rapid change, a birth cohort (a collection of people born the same year) is thought to be "distinctly marked by the [life] stage it occupies" when it encounters social change, such as war (Ryder, 1965, p. 846). People of the same age during a historical period often have a "common consciousness" or understanding of the period and its influence on them (Mannheim, 1928/1997). Experiences within cohorts, however, are likely differentiated by gender, social class, and other aspects of an individual's life history. Nonetheless, collective memories define the past in ways that have profound social and psychological implications for the present and future, such as our understanding of global and local conflicts, military intervention, and peace. And for veterans, personal memories are entangled with how they appraise their wartime experiences as they age.

VETERANS' APPRAISALS OF WARTIME EXPERIENCES

Veterans' recall of their wartime experiences determines their meaning and importance. Appraisal is part of the recollection process. To paraphrase W. I. Thomas's (with D. S. Thomas; Thomas & Thomas, 1928, p. 571) famous dictum: If veterans recall situations as real, they are real in their consequences. This suggests that behaviors can be guided more by individuals' perceptions of situations than by their "objective" circumstances. Present recollections represent constructions of the past, of what is cherished, harbored, or remembered.

Appraisal processes have long been central components of models of stress, adaptation, and coping (e.g., Aldwin, 2007). The severity of demands in an individual's environment, coupled with the availability of resources for coping with those demands, influences whether and how a person deems a situation to be stressful. For example, veterans' experiences varied significantly by the timing, duration, location, rank of service, and whether they saw combat. Furthermore, whether an adverse situation results in adverse outcomes depends on the effectiveness of an individual's coping strategies. For example, members of the armed forces are trained to experience combat and can access formal services and informal support networks. These factors could minimize negative appraisals and facilitate coping.

Veterans' recall and appraisal of service matters for how they adapt to life afterward. Recent findings have suggested that it may not be military experiences themselves that determine health and well-being as much as how veterans assess them (Settersten, Day, Elder, & Waldinger, 2012). For example, more positive assessments are related to greater resilience and better emotional health outcomes later in life and can mediate the relationship between service experiences and these outcomes. Optimism and positive appraisals can be seen as expressions of human agency (Hitlin & Elder, 2007), and appraisals of earlier or current life events affect future goals and expectations (Schafer, Ferraro, & Mustillo, 2011).

Although appraisals of military experiences are remarkably stable across as many as 40 years (Settersten et al., 2012), they can be further shaped by how often and with whom veterans revisit these experiences. The process of actively sharing war-related experiences with family members and former service mates may reinforce the centrality of service in the identities and personal life stories of veterans and family members, whether as points of pride or difficulty.

Veterans' appraisals of wartime service therefore determine how service is integrated into their lives and the potential effects it might have—or be perceived as having—with the passing of time. We draw on four longitudinal studies that contain similar questionnaire items and assemble a comprehensive portrait of both general and specific appraisals of military service from World War II– and Korean War–era veterans. These items have their origin in Glen Elder's 1985 retrospective life history survey of participants in the Berkeley Growth and Guidance Studies and the Oakland Growth Study. They were subsequently included in a 1988 survey of the Harvard Study of Adult Development (the Grant Study) and a 1990 survey of the VA Normative Aging Study. Data from these four studies are not only historically concurrent but also reflect different samples of veterans from the World War II and Korean War eras, which were similar in the nature of warfare, selection into service, and GI provisions, but distinct from the eras thereafter. As such, we have a unique opportunity to compare the perspectives of a diverse set of veterans. Unfortunately, there are no comparable data for assessing Vietnam veterans, who are now close to the ages of these veterans when they reported on their experiences.

GOALS

First, we are interested in understanding how veterans recalled and appraised their wartime service in both broad and specific terms:

1. Broadly, we ask how aging veterans evaluate earlier military experiences within the context of their lives. We examine evaluations of service as (a) the best period, (b) the worst period, (c) one of the most influential periods, and (d) a turning point in life, as well as (e) whether service was more of an advantage than a disadvantage, and (f) its lifetime costs and benefits.
2. Specifically, we ask how aging veterans evaluate their military experiences with respect to a range of desirable experiences (e.g., making lifelong friends, facilitating independence, achieving self-discipline and dependability, finding direction and purpose in life) and undesirable experiences (e.g., delaying careers, disrupting marriage, being lonely for loved ones, losing friends and health).

We examine how both types of appraisals (broad and specific) differ by four objective aspects of service: age at service, length of service, whether the veteran saw combat, and where the veteran served (Europe, Pacific, or stateside). In addition, we examine how appraisals differ by the presence of meaningful service-related relationships and communication, such as whether they keep in touch with service mates, are members of veteran organizations, or talk often with spouses about military experience. Social relationships offer an outlet for processing service experiences, and military organizations serve as a symbol of the veteran's sustained identity and engagement with service and as a unifying representation of veterans to the general public.

Second, for two of the studies (Berkeley and Oakland), we have the opportunity to explore collective memories of wartime by incorporating the memories of nonveterans, including women. A question asks respondents to report on any "vivid memories" of personal experience on the home front or war front.

THE STUDIES

VA Normative Aging Study

The Boston Veterans Administration Outpatient Clinic initiated the Normative Aging Study (NAS) in 1961 to examine aging processes in healthy men (Bossé, Ekerdt, & Silbert, 1984). Over 6,000 volunteers were recruited from the Boston area and screened between 1961 and 1970, and 2,280 men meeting stringent health requirements were ultimately enrolled. Although the sample covers a wide age range from men born between 1884 and 1945, the majority were born between 1915 and 1934 (89% were ages 30–59 years at study entry; Spiro, Schnurr, & Aldwin, 1994). Over 95% of NAS men were veterans, with the majority having served during wartime (ranging from World War I to Vietnam, but most in World War II or Korea).

Our analyses are based on respondents to a 1990 mail survey on military service (response rate, 83%) when men were between the ages of 43 and 91. Of the 444 completed surveys, 1,009 men were veterans and served either in World War II and/or the Korean War. The majority (59%) enlisted; a third were drafted. Nearly half (47%) served in the army and about a third (31%) in the navy. Well more than half (62%) ended service as noncommissioned officers or officers.

Harvard Study of Adult Development

This study began with 268 undergraduate men chosen from the Harvard College graduation classes of 1940 to 1944 (Vaillant, 1977) for their mental and physical fitness on the basis of deans' evaluations (Heath, 1945). Their birth years ranged from 1915 to 1924, but 71% were born between 1920 and 1922. Study members were examined in their sophomore year by an interdisciplinary team of internists, psychiatrists, psychologists, and anthropologists. In 1946, an extensive questionnaire was sent to all 224 surviving men who served in the military, which was followed by an in-depth interview (Monks, 1957). Major follow-ups occurred in early adulthood, midlife, and late life.

Our analyses are based on the initial 1946 questionnaire, as well as a 1988 questionnaire with retrospective accounts of military experiences, when most (71%) were between the ages of 66 and 68 years. We examine reports from 145 veterans who responded to the 1988 survey. All men served in World War II, and 29% served in the Korean War or between World War II and Korea. Forty percent (40%) enlisted and 16% were drafted, but a high proportion entered through ROTC, Reserves, or other routes (44%). Half served in the navy, and a third served in the army. Half served in the Pacific.

Berkeley Guidance and Growth Study

Researchers at the Institute on Human Development at the University of California, Berkeley, sampled every third birth for 18 months during 1928 to 1929 and collected annual data throughout childhood and adolescence (see Eichorn, Clausen, Haan, Honzik, & Mussen, 1981). In 1985, after three major adulthood follow-ups, the male participants and the husbands of female participants were sent a questionnaire about military experiences.

Our analyses are based on 103 male veterans (two females were excluded). About half (52%) enlisted and a third (35%) were drafted. Nearly half of the Berkeley men (48%) served in the army and 21% in the navy. Given their younger age, only 39% of the Berkeley men served at the end of World War II; 40% of these men were in the Pacific, and another 40% were stateside. Of the Berkeley men, 53% served in Korea.

Oakland Growth Study

Participants from the Oakland Growth Study were born during 1920 to 1921 and were followed through the 1930s and adulthood with the same frequency as the Berkeley sample (see Eichorn et al., 1981). Our analyses are based on 61 male veterans (five female veterans were excluded). More than half (57%) enlisted and a quarter (26%) were drafted. Given that the Oakland men were older than the Berkeley men, 95% served during World War II, most (59%) in the Pacific.

Reports on World War II memories were also obtained from the Berkeley and Oakland studies on 158 nonveteran women and 145 male veterans who responded to a question on vivid memories of personal experience on the home front and war front.

For all four of these studies, we draw on data from a common historical time (1985–1990) and from common ages in the lives of these veterans (from their late 50s to late 60s). Information on veterans' service experiences for the four studies can be found in Table 1.1.

FINDINGS

Veterans' Broad Evaluations of Military Service in the Context of Their Lives

Table 1.2 displays participants' reflections on military service in the context of the life course. Overall, participants' evaluations were fairly positive across studies. Veterans' endorsements of service as the "best time of their

TABLE 1.1
Descriptive Statistics of Veterans' Service Experiences

Indicator	NAS (N = 1,009) 1990	Grant (N = 145) 1988	Berkeley (N = 103) 1985	Oakland (N = 61) 1985
Age at survey, M (SD)	67.4 (5.9)	67.5 (1.6)	58.3 (3.4)	64.9 (2.3)
Age at service, M (SD)	21.2 (4.3)	22.2 (1.6)	21.8 (3.0)	22.8 (2.4)
Branch of service, %				
Army	47.0	33.6	47.5	34.4
Navy	31.1	50.3	21.4	39.3
Coast Guard	2.5	0.7	2.9	4.9
Marines	6.9	1.4	6.8	3.3
Air Force	17.9	14.0	17.5	13.1
Length of service, M (SD)	2.9 (1.5)	3.3 (1.3)	3.3 (4.2)	4.0 (3.9)
3 years or less, %	74	66	82	55
4–10 years, %	25	33	15	41
11–30 years, %	0	1	2	3
Service location, %				
Stateside	28	25	42	18
Europe	28	25	16	16
Pacific	44	50	40	59
Combat exposure, %	34	47	28	62
Keep in touch with service mates[a]	29	54	31	53
Active member of military organization,[b] %	48	22	28	41
Talk with spouse about service, %	59[c]	38[d]	27[d]	43[d]

Note. NAS = Normative Aging Study.
[a]Question was phrased, "Are there any friends from your service days that you keep in touch with on a regular basis?" We combined "yes" responses for "casual" and "close" friendships and created a dichotomous variable (1 "yes," 0 "no"). [b]Examples included Veterans of Foreign Wars, American Legion, or National Guard. [c]For NAS, the original items were scaled 0 (not applicable), 1 (never), 2 (used to but stopped), 3 (occasionally), and 4 (frequently). To make data comparable, items have been dichotomized with 0–2 = 0 (never) and 3–4 = 1 (ever). [d]For Grant, Berkeley, and Oakland, the original items were scaled 1 (often), 2 (seldom), and 3 (never). To make data comparable, items have been dichotomized with 2–3 = 0 (never) and 1 = 1 (ever).

lives" and "more of an advantage" were consistently above 5.5 on a 10-point scale. Similarly, in each study, about half or more (48%–67%) said that the benefits of service were greater than the costs.

However, the fact that these overall evaluations are positively skewed should not lead us to overlook the realities that there were also explicitly negative evaluations and that military experience can be a double-edged sword, at once a best and worst time. Within studies, sizable percentages saw service as one of the worst periods of their lives (with 17%–30% of men in the upper third of the distribution). Indeed, average endorsements of the "worst period" item were only slightly lower than average endorsements of the "best period" item. In addition, between 33% and 53% said the costs were greater than or equal to the benefits.

TABLE 1.2
Reflections on Military Service in the Context of the Life Course

Indicator	NAS (N = 1,009) 1990	Grant (N = 145) 1988	Berkeley (N = 103) 1985	Oakland (N = 61) 1985
"Military service was one of the best periods of my life," M (SD)[a]	5.5 (2.1)	6.1 (2.2)	5.9 (2.5)	5.9 (2.3)
High agreement (≥ 7), %	52	49	42	44
Low agreement (≤ 3), %	8	15	8	9
"Military service was one of the worst periods of my life," M (SD)[b]	4.6 (2.0)	4.7 (2.3)	5.1 (2.5)	5.0 (2.4)
High agreement (≥ 7), %	29	17	22	23
Low agreement (≤ 3), %	13	35	30	34
"Military service was one of the most influential events of my life," M (SD)[c]	5.6 (2.5)	—	5.0 (2.5)	6.0 (2.4)
High agreement (≥ 7), %	57	—	31	39
Low agreement (≤ 3), %	13	—	37	18
"Military service was more of an advantage than a disadvantage," M (SD)[d]	5.6 (3.1)	7.5 (2.0)	6.9 (2.2)	7.3 (2.2)
High agreement (≥ 7), %	62	71	63	69
Low agreement (≤ 3), %	20	4	9	8
"Military service was a turning point[e] in my life," %				
No	—	34	39	39
Yes	—	66	54	54
Lifetime costs and benefits of wartime experience,[f] %				
"Costs are greater"	—	9	12	12
"About equal"	—	24	35	41
"Benefits are greater"	—	67	50	48

Note. NAS = Normative Aging Study.
[a]Rated on a scale from 1 (worst) to 10 (best). [b]Rated on a scale from 1 (best) to 10 (worst). [c]Rated on a scale from 1 (least influential) to 10 (most influential). [d]Rated on a scale from 1 (definite disadvantage) to 10 (definite advantage). [e]A "turning point" is a time when "life events can change the direction and quality of our lives." [f]Question was phrased, "How would you weigh the lifetime costs and benefits of your wartime experiences?"

In each study, at least half of the veterans said that military service was a turning point—an experience that changed the direction and quality of their life. Similarly, in judging whether service was among the most influential events in shaping who they would eventually become, veterans' average endorsements were between 5 and 6 on a 10-point scale. Unfortunately, these items do not reveal whether the nature of the turning point or influence was positive or negative. It is likely to be both. Either way, for many of these men, service stood out as a significant life event. And yet, it is surprising that many men nonetheless said that service was not a turning point (34%–39%) or not a very influential event in terms of the person they became (13%–37% were in the bottom third of responses).

In comparing studies, it is clear that the Harvard men had more positive evaluations. Remember, however, that these men served exclusively in World War II and were less exposed to the brutalities of war: They held higher rank and were not likely to see combat, whereas most of the Oakland men served in the Pacific, which tended to be the most violent theatre. In contrast, the Berkeley men were almost entirely Korean-era veterans, though some were involved at the end of World War II and called back into Korea. Entering service at an older age was generally associated with more negative appraisals across all four studies, whereas serving for an extended period of time was linked to more positive appraisals of war-related experiences. (Because of space limitations, analyses are not shown but are available on request.)

Veterans' Specific Evaluations of Service: Desirable and Undesirable Experiences

Table 1.3 provides the percentages of men who reported particular desirable and undesirable experiences related to military service. In the Grant, Berkeley, and Oakland studies, veterans simply indicated whether they had the experience. In NAS, the format was altered such that veterans indicated *how much* they had the experience. We grouped *somewhat* and *a lot* into "yes," and *not at all* and *a little* into "no." One item ("appreciate peace more") was not available in the Berkeley and Oakland studies, resulting in 13 rather than 14 desirable items.

Consistent with the findings on the broader appraisals, a comparison of the top and bottom halves of Table 1.3 reveals that reports of desirable experiences were far more frequent than undesirable experiences. One can also see that the NAS veterans generally had much higher reports of desirable experiences, though this may reflect the difference in response format.

Four desirable experiences were cited by at least half of the men in each study: (a) acquiring a broader perspective on life and the world, (b) coping with adversity, (c) becoming self-disciplined and dependable, and (d) gaining independence. Two other desirable experiences were mentioned by just under half of men: learning cooperation and teamwork, and having rewarding memories. And yet, the average number of desirable experiences ranged from only 4.9 to 5.9 for the NAS, Berkeley, and Oakland studies; it was much higher for the Grant Study, at 9.7. Most men therefore did not see more than a handful of desirable experiences, the bulk of which were captured in the six experiences just noted. Entering the military at older ages, experiencing combat, keeping in touch with service mates, and talking with one's spouse

TABLE 1.3
Reported Desirable and Undesirable
Experiences of Military Service

Indicator	NAS[a] (N = 1,009) 1990	Grant (N = 145) 1988	Berkeley (N = 103) 1985	Oakland (N = 61) 1985
Desirable experiences, %				
Broader perspective	75	75	67	70
Coping with adversity	78	53	48	73
Self-discipline, dependability	81	50	60	74
Independence	79	54	69	58
Lifelong friends	26	31	22	36
Education	54	34	3	25
Value life more	76	26	25	36
Feel positive about self	79	39	34	44
Proud to be an American	84	24	31	48
Clearer direction and purpose	65	28	27	27
Better job skills and options	47	26	26	12
Rewarding memories	68	46	42	48
Learning cooperation, teamwork	75	47	50	58
Appreciate peace more	83	41	—	—
Undesirable experiences, %				
Separation from loved ones	46	36	35	57
Disrupted my life	29	36	40	48
Delayed career behind age mates	26	38	35	46
Waste of time, boredom	11	37	28	31
Economic problems for family	12	6	9	12
Lonely for my family	19	20	13	37
Combat anxiety, apprehensions	11	16	13	24
Hurt my marriage	2	2	0	2
Misery, discomfort	14	13	25	24
Loss of friends	11	14	16	2
Lost my good health	6	5	3	2
Drinking problems	4	1	4	5
Bad memories or nightmares	7	2	12	9
Death or destruction	15	10	12	27
Count of desirable experiences[b], M (SD)	9.7 (3.9)	5.6 (3.2)	4.9 (3.1)	5.9 (3.4)
Count of undesirable experiences[c], M (SD)	2.1 (2.3)	2.3 (1.9)	2.8 (1.9)	3.5 (2.1)

Note. NAS = Normative Aging Study.
[a]For NAS, the original items were scaled 0 (*not at all*), 1 (*a little*), 2 (*somewhat*), and 3 (*a lot*). To make data comparable, items have been dichotomized such that 2–3 = 1 (*yes*) and 0–1 = 0 (*no*). [b]Based on the 13 common items (excludes "appreciate peace more"). [c]Based on the 14 items listed.

about service were associated with reporting desirable experiences (analyses available on request).

In contrast, for undesirable experiences, none of the items was mentioned by at least half of veterans in any of the studies. Across the board, the item most often endorsed—by at least 35%—was "separation from loved ones" (from 35% to 57%). This was followed by "disrupted my life," which was endorsed by at least about 30% (from 29% to 48%), and "delayed career, behind age mates," which was endorsed by at least 25% of veterans (from 26% to 46%). We also find significant endorsements of "waste of time, boredom" (from 28% to 37%) in the Grant, Berkeley, and Oakland studies. The remaining negative experiences were infrequently mentioned. The average number of undesirable experiences was two or three (ranging from two to four).

Significant correlations between the positive and negative items, however, suggest that those who cited positive experiences were also likely to cite negative experiences (Oakland, $r = .30$; Berkeley, $r = .26$; Grant, $r = .27$; in NAS, the corresponding figure, while significant, is only .07). So, although the profiles were largely positive, dark sides of service were in many men found alongside the bright sides. In contrast to reports of desirable experiences, none of the objective measures of service or communication with family members or peers consistently predicted the reporting of negative experiences (analyses available on request). This is probably because it is more difficult to acknowledge and discuss negative experiences.

Vivid Memories of the Home Front and War Front

Using the Berkeley and Oakland studies, we are able to gain insight into larger, collective memories of war. In the 1985 follow-up, both women and men were asked to think back to World War II and respond to the question "Does any vivid memory of personal experience on the home front and war front stand out?" Two thirds replied with one or more memories that fit four themes: (a) mobilization experiences on the home front, (b) loss, (c) separation, and (d) direct participation in military action, which we describe next.

But first, how can it be that nearly a third of men and women claimed no vivid recollection of their wartime experiences? Because members of these cohorts were adolescents or adults during the war, they should remember something about it. Research has shown that people are especially likely to recall memories from the second and third decades of life (Glück & Bluck, 2007)—the so-called reminiscence bump. However, for a variety of reasons, memories of major collective events—wartime or otherwise—may not always be vivid or even accessible to those who experienced them (Corning & Schuman, 2015). The same is true of personal life events, especially sad, traumatic, and involuntary memories (Berntsen & Rubin, 2002). In our case, the war may have simply lost its significance in light of more recent events or the passage of time. As one veteran explained, "It is something in the past and is no longer relevant—we live for the future." For others, memories of war may be so painful that they are repressed or difficult to recollect. As another veteran recounted, he does not talk about the war because he does "not wish to dwell on [a] sad, terrifying part of my young life."

What differentiates those who have vivid memories from those who do not? Exposure to wartime trauma represents a likely source of vivid memories of the war. This trauma may have been experienced as exposure to combat or as the loss of a close friend or family member. Loss was a common experience. Approximately 12% of the men and women reported the loss of a family member in World War II. Many more reported the loss of friends—nearly three out of five men and two out of five women. However, loss of family or friends is no more common among adults who had vivid war memories than among those who reported no such memories. At least in these samples, personal loss during World War II was not predictive of notable wartime memories.

Exposure to combat did identify men who have vivid memories of war. Among men who served in World War II, nine out of 10 veterans of heavy combat reported such memories. This compares with 58% of all other veterans, the noncombatants as well as those with exposure to light combat. For veterans of heavy combat, memories of war may be made more salient by attending military reunions, where they relive experiences with former service mates. When memories are shared, the distant past becomes relevant to present concerns.

The most common memory (mentioned by 47% of those who had memories) portrayed some aspect of *home-front mobilization*, such as blackouts, scrap drives, rationing, and the feeling of togetherness. One woman recalled, "test for blackouts, air raid warning tests, rationing, scrap metal drives, buying war stamps and bonds, everyone pulling and working together for the good of the country. Felt strong patriotism . . ." Forty-seven percent (47%) of those who said they had memories of World War II mentioned these types of experiences. Of course, because the Bay Area was a hub of wartime mobilization and industry, Berkeley and Oakland subjects felt the daily presence of war in their lives.

A quarter (26%) of those with memories of World War II recalled the *loss of a significant relationship*, either family member or friend. One woman observed, "My brother was an army pilot and was killed in the South Pacific in 1944. I can still relive that time vividly. My mother perhaps suffered most, but it was an extremely painful time for our family." A former Marine with service in the South Pacific recalled the enduring sorrow of "losing close friends, the ease of dying and killing, the first landing and [his] first wound." Another woman reported "losing [former] classmates to death, producing a vivid memory of fear and sadness," and still another noted "the loss of childhood companions."

A major impact of war mobilization was *separation from loved ones*: husbands from wives, parents from children. Nineteen percent (19%) of those who reported memories recalled separation from family and friends; this recollection was almost exclusively concentrated among women, who were most often the ones "left behind." One third reported painful separations that lasted several years. One woman said, "My husband was gone overseas for four years—it was hard to bring up our son alone." A woman who was an expectant bride when her husband left for overseas remembered that it was a "God-send to have my parents around me as it was a long two and a half years."

Seventeen percent (17%) of those who reported memories recalled *participation in the war*, but these memories were common among older men. Veterans of heavy combat were most likely to recall participation. One veteran remembered "being fired upon as open targets and the feeling that there was nowhere to hide," and another "the terror of being forced, against one's free will, to kill or be killed." Still another observed that his most vivid memory was "giving a Purple Heart to a soldier who had just lost both arms and both legs and had a torn hole in his intestines, and then later visiting him several times before he was transferred to the U.S."

DISCUSSION

There are few systematic investigations of how veterans appraise their military service, or of collective memories of wartime, and how they might matter for aging. We assembled data from four different samples of World War II and Korean War veterans, which contained the same items and were gathered at roughly the same historical time (1985–1990) and ages (from their late 50s to late 60s). For two of the studies (Berkeley and Oakland), we also examined responses to a question posed to both veterans and nonveterans about vivid home-front and war-front memories.

Over and again, we found two simultaneous and seemingly oppositional faces of war experience—one positive and even transformative, the other painful and even traumatic. As veterans in later life reflected on service within the context of lives, many endorsed it as a best time and one that brought advantages and benefits. And yet, many also endorsed it as a worst period, emphasizing the significant costs carried in the body and psyche. Both bright and dark sides of military service exist within individual veterans.

Deeper insights into these two faces of war were obtained by examining a range of specific desirable and undesirable experiences. Here, the picture was more skewed in a positive direction, particularly for those who entered at younger ages and served longer. The more negative reports from those who served at older ages were not surprising, given that careers and families were already established, and they were more likely to leave behind spouses and children. The fact that those who served longer had more positive reports was at first surprising, but for these veterans, military life seemed to be even more central to their identities because of their longer personal and institutional investments. Additionally, the process of actively sharing war-related experiences with spouses and former service mates likely reinforced the centrality of service in the identities and life stories of veterans and family members.

Most veterans reported developing a broader perspective on their lives and on the world, learning to cope with adversity, becoming self-disciplined and dependable, and gaining independence. This is consistent with notions of stress-related growth. Few of the other positive items were widely endorsed.

Only four negative items were endorsed by sizable percentages of veterans: separation from loved ones, disruption to life plans and progress, delayed careers, and feeling as if time had been wasted. The stronger profile of positive reports was surprising because, in these samples, sizable proportions of veterans served in the more violent Pacific theatre and saw combat (28%–62%); they were likely to have fired a weapon or been fired on, to have killed someone, and to have been exposed to dead and wounded Americans and enemies. These men were generally successful in their lives and, presumably, at dealing with the negative effects of combat.

Another possible explanation for the fact that negative reports were relatively infrequent could relate to the fact that data were gathered up to 4 decades after the experience, thus reflecting a long-term perspective of survivors rather than a short-term perspective of an entire population. For example, Elder and Clipp (1988a, 1988b) showed that veterans who were involved in heavy combat were at great risk for emotional and behavioral problems shortly after the war. In the long run, however, they appeared to be more resilient and less helpless compared with men who saw no or light combat. Thus, appraisals for men with heavy combat exposure may become more positive over time through the reevaluation and integration of war-related experience into their broader life trajectory. This tendency to see an experience in more positive terms as with greater distance from it would seem typical of all veterans, not only those who saw combat (but perhaps especially so for them). It would also likely be heightened in middle and later life, as individuals are inclined to look back on their lives and make meaning of the past. Research on the long-term outcomes of service demands an exploration of a spectrum of possible positive effects, not just negative effects (for illustrations, see Spiro, Settersten, & Aldwin, 2016).

In examining women's and men's "vivid memories" of the home front and war front during World War II, we again unearthed two very different experiences. For some, the war meant engagement in a popular national venture much bigger than oneself. For others, the war meant the trauma of permanently broken ties, repeated separations, and a tragically dismembered social world. For this question, however, the women and men who remembered the positive aspects of war generally failed to report memories of negative aspects.

This one-sided nature of recollection was reinforced by the fact that nearly a third of the men and women claimed no vivid memories of wartime experiences. And for the two thirds who did, memories were sometimes extraordinarily painful. The most common memories related to aspects of home-front mobilization. But difficult memories of personal loss and separation were present for many. Memories of direct participation in war were also common. Not surprisingly, these differences reflect life stage differences: Oakland men, who were older and served mostly in World War II, were more likely to recall participation, whereas Berkeley subjects, who were adolescent boys and girls during wartime, were more likely to remember contributing to the war effort at home. Women, in contrast, were more likely to recall war losses and separation, as they were the ones left behind and coping with the potential loss of husbands, brothers, and fathers.

Memories of wartime losses have implications for contemporary understandings of peace, war, and national defense (see also Chapter 6, this volume). Remembered losses of family members or friends could foster activities among survivors meant to preserve the meaning of their sacrifices. Examples include political vigilance regarding national priorities on military strength and defense, along with efforts to ensure remembrance through memorial times, places, and structures. As Halbwachs (1980) put it, "to forget a period of one's life is to lose contact with those who then surrounded us" (p. 30).

Memories of loss also highlight the tragic waste of lives in war. Remembering the human costs of war can reinforce a dedication to disarmament and world peace. Memories of fallen soldiers and family members, and other sacrifices made on both battle sites and home fronts, become part of historical and family narratives passed down across generations through social exchanges. For example, 85% of the men in the Berkeley and Oakland studies reported that their fathers, uncles, brothers, and cousins had served in the military, which made families a key context for acknowledging and processing military experiences.

The special climate of World War II, in particular, may have led men to provide more positive reports. World War II veterans returned home as heroes and resumed or built their lives in a vibrant economy and with generous GI benefits (indeed, a majority of veterans in these studies reported using GI benefits for education [42%–72%] and housing [40%–70%]). These factors, too, reinforce the American master narrative about the essential role that these veterans played in ensuring the safety and vitality of the United States and the world during the last century (Settersten, 2006), thereby keeping appraisals elevated. And unlike many other countries, the United States, apart from Pearl Harbor in Hawaii, was largely devoid of physical evidence of wartime battles and devastation. Halfway around the globe in either direction, soldiers in the Pacific and European theaters of war returned to ravaged cities and landscapes, and to constant reminders of the war's toll on human lives. In these circumstances, it may have been easier for American veterans to appraise their experiences and outcomes more positively.

CONCLUSION

We turned our attention to subjective aspects of military service because research has suggested that it may not be objective experiences that matter in shaping aging outcomes as much as how veterans assess their experiences. Coming to terms with wartime service—whether one was exposed to danger, in combat, or had other roles and responsibilities—is a developmental issue in its own right, one that potentially brings protections and risks, depending on how it is understood. For our purposes, W. I. Thomas's famous aphorism becomes, "If veterans *remember* past events and experiences as real, they are real in their consequences." Appraisals are part of the recollection process, and how individuals—and societies—interpret the past has profound social and psychological implications for the present and future.

We should keep in mind that World War II and Korean War veterans may have been in a relatively favorable situation compared with veterans of Vietnam and more current conflicts because of high public endorsement and pride in service, as well as positive reception, economic opportunity, and GI benefits on their return. Our findings also highlight the influence of social privilege on more positive wartime evaluations, as Grant men, especially, were relatively sheltered from adverse experiences. More recent generations may face less rosy prospects because of the controversial nature of military intervention, as well as targeted recruitment and high representation of soldiers from underprivileged socioeconomic backgrounds.

Thus, major data collection efforts related to veterans' aging should pay greater attention to gathering subjective perspectives on military experience. Because more positive later life appraisals are associated with membership in veteran organizations and talking with spouses and service mates, veteran organizations might prioritize opportunities that encourage veterans to share their experiences and facilitate continued contact among service mates. This offers an important avenue for interventions to improve the health and social integration of veterans. Because past wars continue to influence the politics of peace today, and because current conflicts will influence the politics of peace in the future, we must continue to probe the long-term outcomes of war for human lives and societies.

REFERENCES

Aldwin, C. M. (2007). *Stress, coping, and development: An integrative approach* (2nd ed.). New York, NY: Guilford Press.

Berntsen, D., & Rubin, D. C. (2002). Emotionally charged autobiographical memories across the life span: The recall of happy, sad, traumatic, and involuntary memories. *Psychology and Aging, 17*, 636–652. http://dx.doi.org/10.1037/0882-7974.17.4.636

Bossé, R., Ekerdt, D. J., & Silbert, J. E. (1984). The Veterans Administration Normative Aging Study. In S. A. Mednick, M. Harway, & K. M. Finello (Eds.), *Handbook of longitudinal research* (Vol. 2, pp. 273–289). New York, NY: Praeger.

Corning, A., & Schuman, H. (2015). *Generations and collective memory*. Chicago, IL: University of Chicago Press. http://dx.doi.org/10.7208/chicago/9780226282831.001.0001

Eichorn, D., Clausen, J., Haan, N., Honzik, M., & Mussen, P. (Eds.). (1981). *The past and present in middle life*. New York, NY: Academic Press.

Elder, G. H., Jr., & Clipp, E. C. (1988a). Combat experience, comradeship and psychological health. In J. Wilson, Z. Hard, & B. Kahana (Eds.), *Human adaptation to extreme stress: From the Holocaust to Vietnam* (pp. 131–156). New York, NY: Plenum. http://dx.doi.org/10.1007/978-1-4899-0786-8_6

Elder, G. H., Jr., & Clipp, E. C. (1988b). Wartime losses and social bonding: Influences across 40 years in men's lives. *Psychiatry, 51*, 177–198.

Glück, J., & Bluck, S. (2007). Looking back across the life span: A life story account of the reminiscence bump. *Memory & Cognition, 35*, 1928–1939. http://dx.doi.org/10.3758/BF03192926

Halbwachs, M. (1980). *The collective memory*. New York, NY: Harper and Row.

Heath, C. W. (1945). *What people are: A study of normal young men*. Cambridge, MA: Harvard University Press.

Hitlin, S., & Elder, G. H., Jr. (2007). Time, self, and the curiously abstract concept of agency. *Sociological Theory, 25*, 170–191. http://dx.doi.org/10.1111/j.1467-9558.2007.00303.x

Mannheim, K. (1997). The problem of generations. In M. A. Hardy (Ed.), *Studying aging and social change: Conceptual and methodological issues* (pp. 22–65). Thousand Oaks, CA: Sage. (Original work published 1928)

Monks, J. P. (1957). *College men at war*. Portland, ME: Anthoensen Press.

Ryder, N. B. (1965). The cohort as a concept in the study of social change. *American Sociological Review, 30*, 843–861. http://dx.doi.org/10.2307/2090964

Schafer, M. H., Ferraro, K. F., & Mustillo, S. A. (2011). Children of misfortune: Early adversity and cumulative inequality in perceived life trajectories. *American Journal of Sociology, 116*, 1053–1091. http://dx.doi.org/10.1086/655760

Settersten, R. A., Jr. (2006). When nations call: How wartime military service matters for the life course and aging. *Research on Aging, 28*, 12–36. http://dx.doi.org/10.1177/0164027505281577

Settersten, R. A., Jr., Day, J., Elder, G. H., Jr., & Waldinger, R. J. (2012). Men's appraisals of their military experiences in WWII: A 40-year perspective. *Research in Human Development, 9*, 248–271. http://dx.doi.org/10.1080/15427609.2012.705558

Spiro, A., III, Schnurr, P. P., & Aldwin, C. M. (1994). Combat-related posttraumatic stress disorder symptoms in older men. *Psychology and Aging, 9*, 17–26. http://dx.doi.org/10.1037/0882-7974.9.1.17

Spiro, A., III, Settersten, R. A., Jr., & Aldwin, C. (2016). Long-term outcomes of military service in aging and the life course: A positive re-envisioning. *The Gerontologist, 56*, 5–13. http://dx.doi.org/10.1093/geront/gnv093

Thomas, W. I., & Thomas, D. S. (1928). *The child in America: Behavior problems and programs.* New York, NY: Knopf.

Vaillant, G. E. (1977). *Adaptation to life.* Boston, MA: Little, Brown.

2

MIDLIFE EGO DEVELOPMENT OF WORLD WAR II VETERANS: CONTRIBUTIONS OF PERSONALITY TRAITS AND COMBAT EXPOSURE IN YOUNG ADULTHOOD

JOHANNA C. MALONE, LAURA M. L. DISTEL,
AND ROBERT J. WALDINGER

War is, for many, a life-changing event, yet the effects of combat on adult personality development are not well understood. Research has suggested that psychological functioning after military service is associated with specific risk and resilience factors, and how these relate to each other and to adult personality requires further elucidation (Ardelt, Landes, & Vaillant, 2010; Elder & Clipp, 1989; Jennings, Aldwin, Levenson, Spiro, & Mroczek, 2006; Lee, Vaillant, Torrey, & Elder, 1995; Miller, Greif, & Smith, 2003). The psychological effects of combat exposure are often studied in relation to development of particular forms of psychopathology (e.g., Bollinger, Riggs, Blake, & Ruzek, 2000; Ikin, Creamer, Sim, & McKenzie, 2010; Orsillo et al., 1996; E. Pietrzak, Pullman, Cotea, & Nasveld, 2012). However, less is known about the psychological effects of war among the many who do not develop significant

Preparation of this manuscript was supported by Grants R01-MH42248 and R01-AG034554, and funding from the W. T. Grant Foundation.

http://dx.doi.org/10.1037/0000061-003
Long-Term Outcomes of Military Service: The Health and Well-Being of Aging Veterans, A. Spiro III, R. A. Settersten Jr., and C. M. Aldwin (Editors)

psychopathology. In this chapter, using a measure of ego development, we examine how exposure to combat may impact an individual's subsequent global psychological functioning and habitual style of making meaning out of experience. In addition, we assess how personality traits assessed prewar may moderate the impact of combat severity on psychological maturity in midlife.

EGO DEVELOPMENT

This study uses unique longitudinal data to examine links between young men's combat experience in World War II and their psychological maturity at midlife (approximately age 55), as understood through the lens of ego development. Ego development is conceptualized as an individual's organizing frame of reference for understanding the self and the world—a frame that is subject to change based on new experiences across the lifespan (Hy & Loevinger, 2015; Loevinger, 1966; Loevinger & Blasi, 1976). According to this model, one's level of ego maturity shapes how one faces moral dilemmas, understands relationships, and reacts both cognitively and behaviorally when confronted with paradox or internal conflicts.

The lens of ego development affords an opportunity to understand factors that contribute to or hinder nonpathological maturation processes of adult development across the lifespan. Loevinger (1987, 1996; Loevinger & Blasi, 1976) viewed the ego as a "master trait" made up of four interrelated domains: character development (including moral development), cognitive style, interpersonal style, and conscious preoccupations. Each of these aspects of the self is thought to reorganize continually across development in relation to one's social and physical environment. For example, as individuals mature, they become less focused on being punished for doing something wrong and instead are motivated by internalized standards that increase self-regulation and modulate impulse control. Loevinger's model asserts that ego development occurs in an invariant sequence, with each stage being required as a foundation for the development of subsequent stages (see Table 2.1). In adulthood, these stages are thought to be relatively independent of chronological age and to be associated with particular challenges for functioning in the world (Hy & Loevinger, 2015; Loevinger, 1966).

COMBAT EXPOSURE AND EGO DEVELOPMENT

At present, there is little research on how combat exposure in young adulthood may impact ego development across the lifespan. Most available data are cross-sectional, combining concurrent assessments of personality with

TABLE 2.1
Loevinger's Stages of Ego Development

Stage	Character development	Interpersonal style	Conscious preoccupations
1. Impulsive	Driven by impulses, fearful, dys-regulated	Exploitative, dependent, egocentric	Bodily sensations
2. Opportunistic/ (self-protective)	Driven by self-interest and fear of being caught	Exploitative, manipulative, obedient, wary	Maintaining advantage and control, self-protection, "trouble"
3. Conformist	Conventional and moralistic, prone to shame and guilt, respect for the rules	Influenced by a need to belong or conform, loyal, cooperative	Appearance, and reputation focused, little attention to feelings
4. Conscientious/ conformist (self-aware)	Initial realization of standards, contin-gencies, allows exceptions to the rules	Interest in helping others becomes linked to inter-personal relatedness	A growing sense of the self being separate from the larger group, attention to feel-ings, problems, and adjustment
5. Conscientious	Internalized sense of the rules, more self-evaluation/ criticism, reflective	Intense, responsible	Long-term goals and achieve-ments, aware-ness of internal feelings/states, self-respect
6. Individualistic	Awareness of one's individuality, engages in unique self-expression	Mutual, tolerant of others, relation-ships are valued more than achievements	Aware of one's own internal conflicts, focused on expression of ideas, feelings, views of process and change roles
7. Autonomous	Developed capac-ity to cope with conflicts and tolerance of ambiguity	Respects the autonomy of both self and others with a view of relation-ships as interdependent	Focused on self-actualization, self-fulfillment, psychological causation, under-standing the self in a social context
8. Integrated	Wise, able to reconcile inner conflicts and actualize one's potentials	Empathic, strongly values individuality	Increasing sense of one's own full identity

Note. Data from Loevinger, 1966, 1976; Hauser, 1976; Hy & Loevinger, 1996.

MIDLIFE EGO DEVELOPMENT OF WORLD WAR II VETERANS   *39*

retrospective accounts of wartime experiences. Findings from this research present a mixed picture. Some studies have suggested that combat exposure is associated with less adaptive defense mechanisms and lower ego development (Silverstein, 1996), whereas others have suggested that the relationship between combat exposure and aspects of ego development in later life (e.g., wisdom) may be nonlinear. For example, Jennings et al. (2006) found that moderate combat exposure is associated with higher wisdom, whereas no combat exposure or more severe combat exposure is associated with lower levels of wisdom. (This research focused on wisdom defined by self-transcendence, which involves seeing beyond one's self in ways that allow increased empathy, understanding, and compassion.) One concern about such research is that retrospective assessments of combat exposure are filtered through the lens of the personality characteristics that they are posited to predict. The present study expands our understanding of this area by using prospective longitudinal data to examine midlife ego development of World War II veterans.

Most research examining the psychological sequelae of combat exposure has focused on the increased likelihood of posttraumatic stress disorder (PTSD), internalizing psychopathology (depression, anxiety), or externalizing psychopathology (antisocial behaviors, substance abuse; Dedert et al., 2009; Green, Grace, Lindy, Gleser, & Leonard, 1990; Kelley et al., 2013; Mott, Graham, & Teng, 2012; Sutker, Uddo, Brailey, Vasterling, & Errera, 1994). Combat exposure, which leads to PTSD, in turn, increases an individual's risk for many other Axis I disorders (Orsillo et al., 1996). Although studies generally show that more severe combat exposure is associated with increased symptomatology, a number of pre- and postdeployment variables have been identified as either risk or protective factors. These include experiences of childhood trauma, family stress both during and postdeployment, perceived adequacy of training, and personality characteristics prior to service (R. Pietrzak et al., 2010; Tracie Shea, Reddy, Tyrka, & Sevin, 2013).

A focus on ego development can provide new information about the range of normative (nonpathological) ways in which individuals exposed to combat can problem solve and make meaning of the world. Research has suggested that some stressful experiences facilitate the development of what Aldwin and Levenson (2004) called *stress-related growth*, in which the experience of combat may lead to a greater sense of mastery, enhanced self-esteem, and more adaptive coping skills (Aldwin, Levenson, & Spiro, 1994). However, other forms of stress may derail personality development because of an individual's need to defend against reexperiencing past trauma by using maladaptive coping mechanisms such as avoidance and hypervigilance that curtail psychological growth (Price, 2007; Silverstein, 1994; Wright, Foran, Wood, Eckford, & McGurk, 2012).

PERSONALITY TRAITS AND EGO DEVELOPMENT
FOR MEN WITH COMBAT EXPOSURE

In addition to examining the longitudinal relationship of combat exposure and midlife ego development, this study also took into account personality traits assessed prior to wartime service. This allowed us not only to control for preexisting personality traits but also to examine the interaction between personality traits and combat exposure in young adulthood in relation to midlife ego development.

The relationship between personality traits and ego development is an area of debate in the literature. Loevinger (1993, 1994) strongly asserted that five-factor model (FFM) traits were inadequate to capture the dynamic maturational processes involved in ego development. Other researchers have highlighted the potential overlap between the FFM trait Openness to Experience and ego development (Kurtz & Tiegreen, 2005; Lilgendahl, Helson, & John, 2013; McCrae & Costa, 1980). Costa and McCrae (1993) hypothesized that both Openness and higher levels of ego development entail a focus on understanding experience and include more intellectual curiosity, a nondogmatic approach to life, and greater sensitivity to feelings. In addition, longitudinal research has found that greater Openness to Experience in early adulthood predicts increasing levels of ego development over time (Lilgendahl et al., 2013).

Of particular relevance to this study is an important semantic distinction between the FFM trait of Conscientiousness and Loevinger's conscientious stage of ego development. Loevinger (1994) emphasized that the FFM trait of Conscientiousness is more strongly associated with a lower form of ego development—the conformist stage—characterized by an emphasis on concerns such as doing one's duty and following rules. In distinguishing between conformist and conscientious levels of ego development, she stated,

> Where the conformist feels guilty for breaking the rules, the conscientious person feels guilty when the consequences of his or her actions hurts another person. Achievements are cherished not merely in terms of recognition by others, which is important to conformists (and cannot be irrelevant to anyone); achievements are evaluated in terms of the conscientious person's own standard. (Loevinger, 1994, p. 5)

Overall, whereas certain personality traits are associated with psychological maturity (i.e., ego development; Kurtz & Tiegreen, 2005; Lilgendahl et al., 2013; McCrae & Costa, 1980), less is understood about how combat exposure and preexisting personality traits may interact to predict ego development at midlife. For some individuals, combat may heighten the sense that one must follow rules and conform to authority, which are essential in the military, whereas for others combat may prompt more complex approaches to life that acknowledge and accommodate moral ambiguity (i.e., grappling with negative and positive elements).

AIMS OF THE PRESENT STUDY

The present study uses longitudinal data to investigate the relationship between severity of combat exposure and midlife ego development. Unlike previous studies of ego development and combat exposure, we were able to account for the influence of prewar personality traits to examine whether combat exposure makes an independent contribution to midlife ego development. In addition, given that certain precombat personality traits may shape an individual's experience of combat, we also examined whether personality traits moderated the relationship between combat exposure and ego development. To further understand our quantitative findings, we also examined qualitative data from interviews and questionnaires.

METHOD

Participants

Participants were 83 men drawn from a sample of 268 non-Hispanic White male Harvard College sophomores (born between 1915 and 1924) in the Harvard Study of Adult Development (Heath, 1945; Vaillant, 2000; see also Chapters 1 and 13, this volume). Selection criteria for the full sample included absence of both physical and mental illness and satisfactory freshman academic record (Heath, 1945). The men from the overall sample were primarily of upper-class and upper-middle-class socioeconomic status; however, 50% were on scholarship and/or had to work during college. At the onset of the project, the men were assessed by internists, psychiatrists, psychologists, and anthropologists. Since the study began in 1938, men completed questionnaires approximately every 2 years, their medical records were obtained every 5 years, and they were interviewed by study staff approximately every 10 to 15 years.

For this study, we included only the 83 men for whom we had complete data on age 21 FFM personality traits, World War II combat exposure, and midlife Loevinger ego development. Using t-tests, we determined that these 83 men did not differ from the remaining men in the full sample with respect to level of midlife ego development, Combat Exposure Scale score, or any of the FFM traits with the exception of Neuroticism. Men in our included sample were higher on Neuroticism than those not included ($M = 15.89$, $SD = 6.41$ vs. $M = 13.74$, $SD = 6.39$; $t(154) = 2.09$, $p < .05$). Men included in our sample also did not differ from the remaining men with respect to level of education, warmth of childhood environment, social class in childhood, defense maturity in young adulthood, or social functioning in midlife.

Measures

Personality Traits

At the time of college completion and prior to military service, 252 participants were rated on 25 dichotomously scored (yes/no) personality characteristics by a study psychiatrist familiar with the complete data set of each participant. A previous study (Soldz & Vaillant, 1999) described how ratings were converted to the FFM trait personality (Neuroticism, Extraversion, Openness to Experience, Agreeableness, and Conscientiousness). These traits were predictably related to global adjustment, career, relationships, substance use, and both family history and childhood variables.

Combat Exposure

The Combat Exposure Scale (Lee et al., 1995) assesses exposure to specific combat experiences and the extent to which a person was exposed to sustained combat danger (Monks, 1957). It assesses both the intensity and frequency of an individual's combat experience. On the basis of men's responses to combat-related items *immediately* following military service, the following six questions were coded as present (1) or absent (0): (a) Being under enemy fire, (b) Firing at the enemy, (c) Killing anyone, (d) Seeing the allies killed or wounded, (e) Seeing the enemy killed or wounded, and (f) Being wounded. Added to these scores were points for sustained danger (0 = no days spent in danger levels 6 or 7; 1 = 1–21 days spent in danger levels 6 or 7; and 2 = 22 days or more spent in danger levels 6 or 7). Severity of danger was scored (0 = no days spent in danger levels 6 or 7; 1 = moderate [i.e., highest level of danger was 6]; 2 = severe [i.e., highest level of danger was 7]). In previous studies the Combat Exposure Scale was significantly correlated with PTSD symptoms following wartime service (Lee et al., 1995).

Ego Development

Ego development was assessed using the Washington University Sentence Completion Test (WUSCT; Loevinger, 1979; Loevinger & Wessler, 1970), which participants completed by mail in 1975 when they were approximately 55 years old. The measure has been widely used in other adult samples (see, e.g., Bauer, McAdams, & Sakaeda, 2005; Lilgendahl et al., 2013) and has demonstrated good reliability and validity (Cohn & Westenberg, 2004; Holt, 1980; Loevinger, 1979).

One hundred forty-one participants completed the measure, which asks respondents to complete 36 sentence stems (e.g., "Raising a family is . . ."). Two independent raters from Loevinger's laboratory who were blind to all other study data coded the WUSCT for all participants. This coding process entailed that each sentence be coded and matched to one of eight stages of adult ego development (see Table 2.1). A total protocol rating was derived from the 36 stems (see Hy & Loevinger, 2015). Reliability was strong (kappa = .72, $p < .001$).

Among the 83 men in the present sample, 14 were coded *conscientious/conformist*, 35 were coded *conscientious*, 22 were coded *individualistic*, eight were coded *autonomous*, and four were coded *integrated*. Previous research from our study using this measure has found positive associations between Loevinger's ego development and higher Eriksonian Psychosocial Development and Creativity (Vaillant & McCullough, 1987). In addition, Vaillant and McCullough (1987) found no relationship between ego development and IQ.

RESULTS

Quantitative Findings

Means, standard deviations, and correlations among these variables are presented in Table 2.2. As can be seen, Openness to Experience in college was positively related to midlife ego development, whereas combat exposure in World War II was inversely associated with ego development.

TABLE 2.2
Means, Standard Deviations, and Correlations

	1	2	3	4	5	6	7
1. Midlife ego development stage							
2. Neuroticism	−.05						
3. Extraversion	−.09	−.25*					
4. Openness	.30**	.03	.17				
5. Agreeableness	.06	−.21+	.01	−.17			
6. Conscientiousness	−.07	−.30**	−.04	−.14	.19+		
7. Combat Exposure Scale	−.21*	−.03	.17	.08	−.12	.10	
M	5.47a	15.89	26.87	29.83	32.77	34.34	3.14
SD	1.14	6.41	6.26	5.91	5.79	6.60	3.26

Note. $N = 83$.
aCorresponds to Loevinger conscientious stage. Note that personality was assessed in college, combat exposure during World War II, and ego development in midlife.
+$p < .10$. *$p < .05$. **$p < .01$.

We used hierarchical regression analyses to test the impact of young adult personality traits, the intensity of World War II combat experience, and the interaction of these variables on midlife ego development. In our initial model, we included all young adult FFM personality traits in Step 1, Combat Exposure Scale score in Step 2, and the interaction between each personality trait and the Combat Exposure Scale score in Step 3. In the final step of the model, only Openness to Experience, the Combat Exposure Scale, and the interaction between Conscientiousness and the Combat Exposure Scale independently accounted for a significant portion of the variance in midlife ego development (results not shown).

On the basis of these initial findings, we ran a reduced regression model including only those variables that made a significant contribution to the variance in ego development to obtain a more parsimonious model. These results are presented in Table 2.3. As before, we included Openness in Step 1 of the model, which accounted for 9% of the variance. In Step 2 of the model, we added the Combat Exposure Scale. Combat Exposure Scale was negatively associated with ego development. In Step 3 of the model, the interaction term between Conscientiousness and the Combat Exposure Scale was added. The addition of this interaction term in Step 3 again resulted in a significant increment in R^2, with the overall model accounting for 19% of the variance in ego development. In this final step of the model, both the main effects and the interaction term remained significant.

The pattern of results suggested that higher openness in young adulthood and lower levels of combat exposure in World War II were predictors of

TABLE 2.3

Final Stepwise Hierarchical Linear Regression Predicting Midlife Ego Functioning (Age 55) From College Traits (Age 21) (Step 1), Combat Exposure Scale (Step 2), and Interaction Term (Step 3)

	B	SE	β	R^2
Step 1				.09*
Openness	.06	.02	0.30**	
Conscientiousness	−.004	.02	−0.02	
Step 2				.15*
Openness	.06	.02	0.32**	
Conscientiousness	.001	.02	0.01	
Combat Exposure Scale	−.08	.03	−0.23*	
Step 3				.19*
Openness	.06	.02	0.33**	
Conscientiousness	.01	.02	0.05	
Combat Exposure Scale	−.08	.04	−0.24*	
Conscientiousness* Combat Exposure Scale	.01	.01	0.22*	

Note. N = 83. SE = standard error.
*p < .05. **p < .01.

higher ego maturity in midlife. However, conscientiousness moderated the impact of combat experience on midlife ego development such that for individuals high in conscientiousness, combat had no effect on ego development in midlife. However, those with low conscientiousness who were exposed to more intense combat had lower levels of ego development than others (see Figure 2.1).

Qualitative Findings

To better understand the significant interaction in our data, we next more closely examined the lives of four participants who could be characterized into four quadrants using high and low conscientiousness by high and low combat. Using a person-centered approach, we reviewed narrative responses on surveys and interviews (see, e.g., Singer & Ryff, 2001; Singer, Ryff, Carr, & Magee, 1998). We wanted to determine whether qualities of ego development might be observed from the ways in which they viewed their lives. In each description we first describe their personality style during college and their military experience. The descriptions also try to capture elements of the

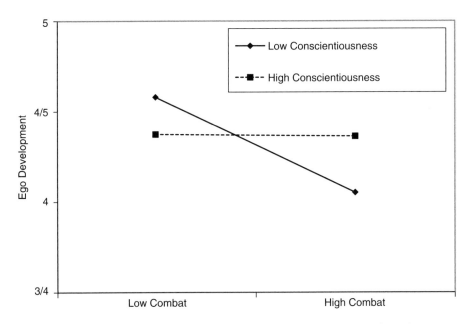

Figure 2.1. Midlife ego development outcomes based on World War II combat exposure and college conscientiousness (prewar). Ego development: 3/4 = conscientious/conformist (self-aware), 4 = conscientious, 4/5 = individualistic, 5 = autonomous.

ways that the participants were making sense of the world and living in the world as they entered midadulthood to highlight connections to their ego development.

- *Case 1—low conscientiousness and low combat exposure*: As an undergraduate, this participant was unenthusiastic about academics. The interviewer stated that he "has a very immature attitude toward his ideas of education and feels that the four years at Harvard should be mainly centered around having a good time and not doing any particular amount of work." Entering the war as an air combat intelligence officer, he did not have much exposure to battle, but the experience gave him "a greater sense of responsibility to help put into effect political or social ideas." These ideas were for greater participation of the United States in the United Nations organization and abatement of racial and religious discrimination. He saw a broader perspective on the world and developed a sense of social obligation and intellectual curiosity that he had previously lacked. He went on to actively participate in his community by becoming a teacher. His midlife ego development was classified as Integrated.

- *Case 2—low conscientiousness and high combat exposure*: As an undergraduate student, this man was described as extremely careless. He made many errors in his schoolwork, was constantly late to appointments, and often failed to complete his responsibilities. A notable example was during college when he purchased a pet that died the following week because of his neglect. The interviewers described him as "superficial, flighty and abstract." However, he also described himself as having a "rigid and positive moral and ethical code." He came from a military family and entered the war as part of the ROTC. He originally saw himself as becoming an artist, but after his experience as a ship navigator during World War II, he went into business. He reported having directly seen soldiers killed and also witnessing torture but was never injured himself. He tended to minimize his feelings about the war saying that he was "not very affected by the war" and reported that he became more religious during his time in the service. Later in his life he indicated having long-standing "survivor's guilt." In 1988 he said that he did not respond well to the return to civilian life, he felt guilty for surviving, he decided to "go into industry instead of arts and letters," and his wartime experience helped him "manage his life better." His midlife ego development was classified as Conscientious-conformist.

- *Case 3—high conscientiousness and low combat exposure:* This participant was described as "tidy," "well-integrated," and "self-driving" in his undergraduate years. He wanted to follow in his family's footsteps of owning a farm. He saw college as a "waste of time" and "impractical" and had little interest in the literature or the arts. He felt he could have used those years to do something more profitable. He went into the navy as a supply officer in a largely administrative job and described this experience as "satisfaction only in the sense that a degree of effectiveness and efficiency was reached, but never as completely as desired." After his time in the service, he found it hard to settle down and difficult to concentrate, and he felt unappreciated. He did not feel his military training experiences were helpful in his career and retrospectively saw the army as his "not too successful" first experience as a manager. His midlife ego development was classified as Conscientious-conformist.
- *Case 4—high conscientiousness and high combat exposure:* As an undergraduate this participant was described as a "self-driving," "neat," and "organized" man with "high intellectual maturity." He worked his way through his undergraduate degree because he came from a poor family. He was always intellectually curious and had a mind for philosophy. During the war he was exposed to combat, was wounded, and suffered severe injuries that affected him for the rest of his life. He also lost family members in the war. During the war he wrote that he was "undergoing a period of change and feeling within himself" that was resulting in self-reflection. He said that "so much is indefinite about the future that the work of today should be done well." He remained studious following the war and became a medical doctor with the goal of helping others. He said that he "wanted to do something constructive to make up for all the destruction I took part in" (killed others). By 1988 he had written two semiautobiographical stories about his war experience. In thinking about World War II he was able to simultaneously hold multiple perspectives, saying that it reinforced his pacifist attitudes but he also continued to doubt that Nazism could be resolved nonviolently. His midlife ego development was classified as Autonomous.

These cases illustrate how prewar personality in conjunction with combat exposure could influence ego development in midlife. Case 1 shows a man who had low conscientiousness and a positive experience during his time in the service with little exposure to combat. This meaningful experience was positive, and he ultimately grew into someone who was curious and actively engaged with the world in fulfilling ways. In contrast, in Case 2, a man with low conscientiousness who was exposed to severe combat appeared to lose connections to his creativity and expressiveness. He appeared to need more structure and was less open in his thinking to organize the traumas he experienced. In Case 3, the subject with high conscientiousness and low combat exposure appeared to have difficulty developing his self-identity. He appeared to try to live life with a sense of purpose that was more characterized by order and achievement. His experience in the war lacked significant meaning for him. Finally, in Case 4, the participant with high conscientiousness and high combat exposure appeared to draw on his strong organizational capacities and sense of motivation to make sense of his experience. Rather than resort to concrete explanations of what was good or bad, the participant was able to reflect on the actual ambiguities involved in his experiences of the war.

DISCUSSION

It is well documented that combat exposure increases risk for certain forms of psychopathology for some veterans (Ikin et al., 2010; Orsillo et al., 1996; Tracie Shea et al., 2013; Wright et al., 2012), whereas others go on to experience personal growth (Aldwin & Levenson, 2004; Aldwin et al., 1994; Jennings et al., 2006). Following combat, an individual must psychologically reconcile their participation in war. This may occur in ways that embrace the complexity of the experience (e.g., tolerating ambiguity) or in ways that reduce complexity (e.g., engaging in "black-and-white" thinking). This study expands our knowledge of postcombat psychological sequelae by using longitudinal data collected over 34 years to examine midlife ego development in World War II veterans, taking into account their personality traits assessed prior to deployment. In addition, we were able to assess whether predeployment personality traits buffered or amplified the impact of combat experience on later ego development.

Consistent with previous studies (e.g., Lilgendahl et al., 2013; McCrae & Costa, 1980), FFM Openness was associated with higher levels of midlife ego development. Greater combat exposure was associated with lower levels of midlife ego development even after controlling for FFM personality traits assessed prior to combat. This is consistent with findings from other studies using retrospective reports of combat experience that did not control for personality traits (Silverstein, 1996).

It is possible that functioning at a lower level of ego development after exposure to combat is adaptive. The more conventional approaches to life's challenges that emphasize the importance of rules, responsibility, conformity, loyalty, and cooperativeness may make it easier to make sense of combat experiences than an ego orientation that values unique self-expression, individuality, and an appreciation for ambiguity. Loevinger (1994) emphasized that higher stages of ego development were not necessarily superior but were more or less adaptive depending on one's specific context and experience.

The significant interaction between conscientiousness and combat exposure suggests that conscientiousness may have been a protective factor for midlife ego development in individuals exposed to more severe combat in World War II. Individuals with higher conscientiousness are more attentive to detail, careful, organized, and motivated by the desire to do something well (McCrae & Costa, 2003). High conscientiousness is also related to being more traditional and conventional (Bogg & Roberts, 2013). These qualities may have allowed individuals exposed to greater combat to make sense of the experience in a way that did not derail ego development. In addition, conscientiousness is associated with better emotional regulation (Javaras et al., 2012). This is consistent with research suggesting that conscientiousness may play a role in protecting an individual against the emotional trauma associated with combat (Clark & Owens, 2012).

Interestingly, for those higher in conscientiousness, ego development did not vary by combat exposure, suggesting that in the absence of the stressor of combat exposure conscientiousness did not necessarily promote growth (see Figure 2.1). However, in looking at the qualitative data for Case 4, it does appear that this conscientious man who experienced high levels of combat did experience stress-related growth. It would be valuable in future research to directly consider the relationship between stress-related growth, ego development, and personality traits.

Those with lower conscientiousness who were exposed to more intense combat had lower ego development in midlife. It could be that without access to the self-organizing and self-regulating capabilities associated with greater conscientiousness, these individuals would be more easily overwhelmed by the traumatic aspects of combat, which might hinder more adaptive ego development later in life. Conversely, because they are more likely to be nonconforming, rebellious, and nontraditional in ways that might facilitate higher levels of adult ego development, individuals lower in conscientiousness who are not exposed to intense combat might be better positioned to mature psychologically after military service. In sum, conscientiousness may provide a useful organizing structure for individuals exposed to a traumatic or stressful event such as combat, but it may hinder ego development in the absence of a serious stressor.

This study has both strengths and limitations that are important to note. The primary strength is the use of longitudinal data allowing for prospective examination of ego development approximately 30 years following combat exposure. No study to date has been able to look at ego development from such a perspective. Next, our study broadens and complements existing research on postcombat psychological functioning by focusing on ego development rather than a specific form of psychopathology. Understanding the links between combat exposure and subsequent meaning making may be beneficial not only for developing psychological interventions but also for assisting men as they reintegrate into their relationships, families, and vocations following deployment. It may be that revisiting the framework of meaning making captured by the construct of ego development could offer an expanded view of psychological health and functioning.

In terms of limitations, our study relies on a small sample of Caucasian men. The results are also specific to men who served in World War II and cannot be generalized to men who served in other wars that may have had different meanings both to individual soldiers and for the culture at large. In addition, we used a dimensional score of combat severity but did not assess other aspects of the individual's combat experiences. For example, how did individuals who saw peers die differ from those who killed opponents? Did chronic exposure to ongoing combat affect individuals differently than one intense and dangerous exposure? These more nuanced distinctions, which may be important to how one assigns meaning to experience, will need to be examined in future studies. Finally, our study was not able to assess ego development prior to service in World War II. Although we were able to control for preexisting personality traits, it would be useful in future studies to understand how precombat levels of ego development may change following combat.

This study suggests the possibility that exposure to combat in wartime may have an impact on midlife psychological maturity as indexed by ego development and that this link is both direct and indirect. Given that ego development is associated with how one makes meaning in the world, it may be an important tool for understanding the general psychological sequelae of combat.

REFERENCES

Aldwin, C. M., & Levenson, M. R. (2004). Posttraumatic growth: A developmental perspective. *Psychological Inquiry, 15*, 19–22.

Aldwin, C. M., Levenson, M. R., & Spiro, A., III. (1994). Vulnerability and resilience to combat exposure: Can stress have lifelong effects? *Psychology and Aging, 9*, 34–44. http://dx.doi.org/10.1037/0882-7974.9.1.34

Ardelt, M., Landes, S. D., & Vaillant, G. E. (2010). The long-term effects of World War II combat exposure on later life well-being moderated by generativity.

Research in Human Development, 7, 202–220. http://dx.doi.org/10.1080/15427609.2010.504505

Bauer, J. J., McAdams, D. P., & Sakaeda, A. R. (2005). Interpreting the good life: Growth memories in the lives of mature, happy people. *Journal of Personality and Social Psychology, 88,* 203–217. http://dx.doi.org/10.1037/0022-3514.88.1.203

Bogg, T., & Roberts, B. W. (2013). The case for conscientiousness: Evidence and implications for a personality trait marker of health and longevity. *Annals of Behavioral Medicine, 45,* 278–288. http://dx.doi.org/10.1007/s12160-012-9454-6

Bollinger, A. R., Riggs, D. S., Blake, D. D., & Ruzek, J. I. (2000). Prevalence of personality disorders among combat veterans with posttraumatic stress disorder. *Journal of Traumatic Stress, 13,* 255–270. http://dx.doi.org/10.1023/A:1007706727869

Clark, A. A., & Owens, G. P. (2012). Attachment, personality characteristics, and posttraumatic stress disorder in U.S. veterans of Iraq and Afghanistan. *Journal of Traumatic Stress, 25,* 657–664. http://dx.doi.org/10.1002/jts.21760

Cohn, L. D., & Westenberg, P. M. (2004). Intelligence and maturity: Meta-analytic evidence for the incremental and discriminant validity of Loevinger's measure of ego development. *Journal of Personality and Social Psychology, 86,* 760–772. http://dx.doi.org/10.1037/0022-3514.86.5.760

Costa, P. T., & McCrae, R. R. (1993). Ego development and trait models of personality. *Psychological Inquiry, 4,* 20–23. http://dx.doi.org/10.1207/s15327965pli0401_3

Dedert, E. A., Green, K. T., Calhoun, P. S., Yoash-Gantz, R., Taber, K. H., Mumford, M. M., . . . Beckham, J. C. (2009). Association of trauma exposure with psychiatric morbidity in military veterans who have served since September 11, 2001. *Journal of Psychiatric Research, 43,* 830–836. http://dx.doi.org/10.1016/j.jpsychires.2009.01.004

Elder, G. H., Jr., & Clipp, E. C. (1989). Combat experience and emotional health: Impairment and resilience in later life. *Journal of Personality, 57,* 311–341. http://dx.doi.org/10.1111/j.1467-6494.1989.tb00485.x

Green, B. L., Grace, M. C., Lindy, J. D., Gleser, G. C., & Leonard, A. (1990). Risk factors for PTSD and other diagnoses in a general sample of Vietnam veterans. *The American Journal of Psychiatry, 147,* 729–733. http://dx.doi.org/10.1176/ajp.147.6.729

Hauser, S. T. (1976). Loevinger's model and measure of ego development: A critical review. *Psychological Bulletin, 83,* 928–955. http://dx.doi.org/10.1037/0033-2909.83.5.928

Heath, C. (1945). *What people are.* Cambridge, MA: Harvard University Press.

Holt, R. R. (1980). Loevinger's measure of ego development: Reliability and national norms for male and female short forms. *Journal of Personality and Social Psychology, 39,* 909–920. http://dx.doi.org/10.1037/0022-3514.39.5.909

Hy, L. X., & Loevinger, J. (2015). *Measuring ego development* (2nd ed.). New York, NY: Psychological Press: Taylor Francis Group.

Ikin, J. F., Creamer, M. C., Sim, M. R., & McKenzie, D. P. (2010). Comorbidity of PTSD and depression in Korean War veterans: Prevalence, predictors, and impairment. *Journal of Affective Disorders, 125,* 279–286. http://dx.doi.org/10.1016/j.jad.2009.12.005

Javaras, K. N., Schaefer, S. M., van Reekum, C. M., Lapate, R. C., Greischar, L. L., Bachhuber, D. R., . . . Davidson, R. J. (2012). Conscientiousness predicts greater recovery from negative emotion. *Emotion, 12,* 875–881. http://dx.doi.org/10.1037/a0028105

Jennings, P. A., Aldwin, C. M., Levenson, M. R., Spiro, A., & Mroczek, D. K. (2006). Combat exposure, perceived benefits of military service, and wisdom in later life findings from the Normative Aging Study. *Research on Aging, 28,* 115–134. http://dx.doi.org/10.1177/0164027505281549

Kelley, M. L., Runnals, J., Pearson, M. R., Miller, M., Fairbank, J. A., & Brancu, M., the VA Mid-Atlantic MIRECC Women Veterans Workgroup, & the VA Mid-Atlantic MIRECC Registry Workgroup. (2013). Alcohol use and trauma exposure among male and female veterans before, during, and after military service. *Drug and Alcohol Dependence, 133,* 615–624. http://dx.doi.org/10.1016/j.drugalcdep.2013.08.002

Kurtz, J. E., & Tiegreen, S. B. (2005). Matters of conscience and conscientiousness: The place of ego development in the five-factor model. *Journal of Personality Assessment, 85,* 312–317. http://dx.doi.org/10.1207/s15327752jpa8503_07

Lee, K. A., Vaillant, G. E., Torrey, W. C., & Elder, G. H. (1995). A 50-year prospective study of the psychological sequelae of World War II combat. *The American Journal of Psychiatry, 152,* 516–522. http://dx.doi.org/10.1176/ajp.152.4.516

Lilgendahl, J. P., Helson, R., & John, O. P. (2013). Does ego development increase during midlife? The effects of openness and accommodative processing of difficult events. *Journal of Personality, 81,* 403–416. http://dx.doi.org/10.1111/jopy.12009

Loevinger, J. (1966). The meaning and measurement of ego development. *American Psychologist, 21,* 195–206. http://dx.doi.org/10.1037/h0023376

Loevinger, J. (1976). *Ego development.* San Francisco, CA: Jossey-Bass.

Loevinger, J. (1979). Construct validity of the Sentence Completion Test of Ego Development. *Applied Psychological Measurement, 3,* 281–311. http://dx.doi.org/10.1177/014662167900300301

Loevinger, J. (1987). *Paradigms of personality.* New York, NY: W. H. Freeman.

Loevinger, J. (1993). Measurement of personality: True or false. *Psychological Inquiry, 4,* 1–16. http://dx.doi.org/10.1207/s15327965pli0401_1

Loevinger, J. (1994). Has psychology lost its conscience? *Journal of Personality Assessment, 62,* 2–8. http://dx.doi.org/10.1207/s15327752jpa6201_1

Loevinger, J. (1996). In defense of the individuality of personality theories. *Psychological Inquiry, 7,* 344–346.

Loevinger, J., & Blasi, A. (1976). *Ego development: Conceptions and theories.* San Francisco, CA: Jossey-Bass.

Loevinger, J., & Wessler, R. (1970). *Measuring ego development: Construction and use of a sentence completion test* (Vol. 1). San Francisco, CA: Jossey-Bass.

McCrae, R. R., & Costa, P. T. (1980). Openness to experience and ego level in Loevinger's Sentence Completion Test: Dispositional contributions to developmental models of personality. *Journal of Personality and Social Psychology, 39,* 1179–1190. http://dx.doi.org/10.1037/h0077727

McCrae, R. R., & Costa, P. T., Jr. (2003). *Personality in adulthood: A five-factor theory perspective* (2nd ed.). New York, NY: Guilford Press.

Miller, M. W., Greif, J. L., & Smith, A. A. (2003). Multidimensional Personality Questionnaire profiles of veterans with traumatic combat exposure: Externalizing and internalizing subtypes. *Psychological Assessment, 15,* 205–215. http://dx.doi.org/10.1037/1040-3590.15.2.205

Monks, J. P. (1957). College men at war. *Memoirs of the American Academy of Arts and Sciences, 24,* iii–310. http://dx.doi.org/10.2307/25058514

Mott, J. M., Graham, D. P., & Teng, E. J. (2012). Perceived threat during deployment: Risk factors and relation to Axis I disorders. *Psychological Trauma: Theory, Research, Practice, and Policy, 4,* 587–595. http://dx.doi.org/10.1037/a0025778

Orsillo, S. M., Weathers, F. W., Litz, B. T., Steinberg, H. R., Huska, J. A., & Keane, T. M. (1996). Current and lifetime psychiatric disorders among veterans with war zone-related posttraumatic stress disorder. *Journal of Nervous and Mental Disease, 184,* 307–313. http://dx.doi.org/10.1097/00005053-199605000-00007

Pietrzak, E., Pullman, S., Cotea, C., & Nasveld, P. (2012). Effects of deployment on mental health in modern military forces: A review of longitudinal studies. *Journal of Military and Veterans' Health, 20,* 24–36.

Pietrzak, R. H., Johnson, D. C., Goldstein, M. B., Malley, J. C., Rivers, A. J., Morgan, C. A., & Southwick, S. M. (2010). Psychosocial buffers of traumatic stress, depressive symptoms, and psychosocial difficulties in veterans of Operations Enduring Freedom and Iraqi Freedom: The role of resilience, unit support, and postdeployment social support. *Journal of Affective Disorders, 120,* 188–192. http://dx.doi.org/10.1016/j.jad.2009.04.015

Price, J. P. (2007). Cognitive schemas, defense mechanisms and post-traumatic stress symptomatology. *Psychology and Psychotherapy: Theory, Research and Practice, 80,* 343–353. http://dx.doi.org/10.1348/147608306X144178

Silverstein, R. (1994). Chronic identity diffusion in traumatized combat veterans. *Social Behavior and Personality, 22,* 69–79. http://dx.doi.org/10.2224/sbp.1994.22.1.69

Silverstein, R. (1996). Combat-related trauma as measured by ego developmental indices of defenses and identity achievement. *The Journal of Genetic Psychology, 157,* 169–179. http://dx.doi.org/10.1080/00221325.1996.9914855

Singer, B., & Ryff, C. D. (2001). Person-centered methods for understanding aging: The integration of numbers and narratives. In R. H. Binstock & L. K. George

(Eds.), *Handbook of aging and the social sciences* (5th ed., pp. 44–65). San Diego, CA: Academic Press.

Singer, B., Ryff, C. D., Carr, D., & Magee, W. J. (1998). Linking life histories and mental health: A person-centered strategy. *Sociological Methodology, 28*, 1–51. http://dx.doi.org/10.1111/0081-1750.00041

Soldz, S., & Vaillant, G. E. (1999). The Big Five personality traits and the life course: A 45-year longitudinal study. *Journal of Research in Personality, 33*, 208–232. http://dx.doi.org/10.1006/jrpe.1999.2243

Sutker, P. B., Uddo, M., Brailey, K., Vasterling, J. J., & Errera, P. (1994). Psychopathology in war-zone deployed and nondeployed Operation Desert Storm troops assigned graves registration duties. *Journal of Abnormal Psychology, 103*, 383–390. http://dx.doi.org/10.1037/0021-843X.103.2.383

Tracie Shea, M., Reddy, M. K., Tyrka, A. R., & Sevin, E. (2013). Risk factors for post-deployment posttraumatic stress disorder in national guard/reserve service members. *Psychiatry Research, 210*, 1042–1048. http://dx.doi.org/10.1016/j.psychres.2013.08.039

Vaillant, G. E. (2000). Adaptive mental mechanisms. Their role in a positive psychology. *American Psychologist, 55*, 89–98. http://dx.doi.org/10.1037/0003-066X.55.1.89

Vaillant, G. E., & McCullough, L. (1987). The Washington University Sentence Completion Test compared with other measures of adult ego development. *The American Journal of Psychiatry, 144*, 1189–1194. http://dx.doi.org/10.1176/ajp.144.9.1189

Wright, K. M., Foran, H. M., Wood, M. D., Eckford, R. D., & McGurk, D. (2012). Alcohol problems, aggression, and other externalizing behaviors after return from deployment: Understanding the role of combat exposure, internalizing symptoms, and social environment. *Journal of Clinical Psychology, 68*, 782–800. http://dx.doi.org/10.1002/jclp.21864

3

PERCEIVED RACIAL, ETHNIC, AND GENDER DISCRIMINATION AMONG MALE AND FEMALE VIETNAM-ERA VETERANS AND PTSD SYMPTOMS LATER IN LIFE

DANIEL H. KABAT, STEVEN D. STELLMAN, AND JEANNE MAGER STELLMAN

Approximately 8.2 million Americans served in the armed forces during the Vietnam War era, including about 3.3 million who were deployed to Southeast Asia. About 720,000 Blacks and 340,000 Hispanics were in the military during the Vietnam era, with approximately 340,000 and 150,000, respectively, deployed to Vietnam (Kulka et al., 1988). A much smaller number of women, about 265,000, were in the military during the Vietnam era, and it is thought that approximately 11,000 were deployed to Vietnam. The military women primarily served in the Nurse Corps of each branch of the armed services. An unknown number of women also served in Vietnam in other government posts, as well as with nongovernment agencies such as the American Red Cross and the United Service Organizations (History.com, 2011).

Although a great deal of attention has been devoted to investigations of posttraumatic stress disorder (PTSD) and other psychiatric disorders stemming from wartime experiences, there is comparatively little research on

http://dx.doi.org/10.1037/0000061-004
Long-Term Outcomes of Military Service: The Health and Well-Being of Aging Veterans, A. Spiro III, R. A. Settersten Jr., and C. M. Aldwin (Editors)

the specific experience of Black and Hispanic Vietnam veterans. There are virtually no data on how perceived differential treatment by their superiors and peers during the war may have affected their postwar mental health. Similarly, little research exists on how perceptions of gender discrimination may affect long-term PTSD symptoms in deployed women, both military and civilian.

In its examination of Vietnam War veterans, the National Vietnam Veterans Readjustment Study (NVVRS) found a significantly higher prevalence of PTSD among Black and Hispanic veterans compared with White veterans (20.6% for Blacks and 27.9% for Hispanics, compared with 13.7% for Whites), although only comparisons between Hispanic and non-Hispanic soldiers remained significant after adjustment for confounders (Schlenger et al., 1992). Additional research on the NVVRS data by Dohrenwend, Turner, Turse, Lewis-Fernández, and Yager (2008) confirmed these two main findings and identified differing levels of combat exposure and average age at first deployment to Southeast Asia as the main reasons for the observed differences between Whites and Hispanics. Because the NVVRS had no measure for perception of discrimination, however, this was not examined in the Dohrenwend et al. study.

Other researchers have used NVVRS data to examine whether Hispanic veterans of differing national descents have similar rates of PTSD. Ruef, Litz, and Schlenger (2000) and Lewis-Fernández et al. (2008) found that the observed associations did not appear to be a function of combining heterogeneous cultural groups or of different modes of expression specific to Hispanic veterans. Studies in other veteran populations have also found similar higher levels of severity of PTSD symptoms in Black and Hispanic Vietnam veterans and have similarly concluded that other modeled covariates (e.g., income, education, cultural differences in modes of expression) could not explain the results (Green, Grace, Lindy, & Leonard, 1990; Ortega & Rosenheck, 2000; Penk et al., 1989).

Recent research in civilian survivors of the World Trade Center terrorist attacks has shown similar racial/ethnic differences in PTSD outcomes, with consistently higher PTSD prevalence in Hispanics compared with Blacks and Whites (Brackbill et al., 2009; DiGrande et al., 2008; Farfel et al., 2008). One possible explanation is that racial and ethnic discrimination may be responsible, at least in part, for the differences in PTSD outcomes. Studies have shown that perception of discrimination can have a potent negative impact on mental health outcomes (Kessler, Mickelson, & Williams, 1999; Williams, Neighbors, & Jackson, 2003; Williams, Yu, Jackson, & Anderson, 1997), and the experience of discrimination in a wartime environment may contribute additional stress beyond the stresses of combat and life-threatening situations. The role of perception of discrimination as a stressor in a wartime environment, however, has not been explored.

Gender differences in PTSD have also been observed in a number of studies, but little work has been done to link perceptions of gender discrimination to extent of PTSD symptomatology. Breslau (2002) concluded that the burden of PTSD on community samples is greater in women than in men and that this is likely to be the result of higher exposure to assaultive violence. Tolin and Foa (2002) explored gender differences in cognitive processing of traumatic events and concluded that women appear more likely to blame themselves for the trauma, to hold more negative views of themselves, and to view the world as more dangerous than do male trauma victims.

In this chapter we address the gaps in the existing literature and examine the ramifications of exposure to discrimination as a component of the Vietnam War experience. In particular, we address the following questions:

1. Is discrimination a distinct predictor of postwar PTSD symptomology, independent of other wartime stressors?
2. What can we learn from the experience of discrimination among Vietnam War veterans, and how might this knowledge be applied to improve the military experience of the current generation of men and women serving in the armed forces?

METHOD

To explore whether perceived discrimination (racial, ethnic, or gender) experienced during the Vietnam War is related to the extent of PTSD symptoms assessed 3 decades later (in 1998), we took advantage of two unique data sets. For the study of perceived racial and ethnic discrimination, we drew on responses from 428 veterans to a 1998 questionnaire mailed to all Vietnam veteran members of the American Legion in Puerto Rico and members from American Legion posts in Texas and New Mexico, known to have relatively high numbers of Black and Hispanic members. This outreach study was part of an effort to broaden representation of Black and Hispanic veterans in the Columbia University–American Legion longitudinal study of Vietnam Veteran Health (Koenen, Stellman, Stellman, & Sommer, 2003; Stellman, Stellman, & Sommer, 1988).

The 1998 survey replicated the original (1984) survey of Legionnaires, including questions about experiences during the Vietnam War, exposure to combat stresses, mental and physical health, use of Veterans Administration health services, community attitude and family support on returning home, and exposure to chemical herbicides. It also included five new questions about the perception of discrimination in a Likert-type format with response options from 1 (*not true*) to 4 (*very true*):

1. I believe race or ethnicity did affect a person's military career during the Vietnam War.
2. I was treated differently in the Armed Forces because of my race or ethnicity.
3. The places to which I was assigned were chosen in part because of my race or ethnicity.
4. I was given unpleasant duty assignments because of my race or ethnicity.
5. I was given dangerous duty assignments because of my race or ethnicity.

The last four items, which dealt with personal experiences, were summed into a perceived discrimination scale that was found to be highly reliable (Cronbach's $\alpha = 0.91$). The questionnaire was available in both English and Spanish. All Puerto Rican Legionnaires were sent the Spanish version, and Legionnaires in Texas and New Mexico could request a Spanish version if they preferred.

The 1,285 women in the present study were drawn from the members of the Vietnam Women's Memorial Project and included both military and civilian women. The women's questionnaire was similar to the men's, with additional sections specific to women's health and deployment conditions. Two questions that specifically addressed perceived gender bias had five response categories ranging from 1 (*never*) to 5 (*very often*) and asked "How often did you . . ."

1. Feel you were being mistreated because you were a woman?
2. Feel that your role was perceived as sexual rather than professional?

PTSD symptomology was assessed using the 18-item checklist that was developed for the men's surveys conducted in 1984 and 1998. These 18 items cover the three domains of PTSD symptoms: reexperiencing the traumatic event (e.g., having vivid recollections of military service, feeling like you were back in the service), decline in external involvement (feeling that it is not worth getting close to others, feeling like shutting the rest of the world away), and behavioral signs of distress (getting nervous when certain things reminded you of your military service, worrying about losing your temper and hurting someone). The questions in the checklist directly map to the diagnostic criteria for PTSD specified in the *Diagnostic and Statistical Manual of Mental Disorders* (third ed., rev.; DSM–III–R; American Psychiatric Association, 1987; Stellman et al., 1988), the revision in effect at the time the first survey was administered. The index shows a high degree of reliability (Cronbach's $\alpha = 0.94$; Koenen et al., 2003; Snow, Stellman, Stellman, & Sommer, 1988; Stellman et al., 1988).

A number of risk factors have been repeatedly associated with PTSD in veterans, the most important of which is exposure to combat situations (Kulka et al., 1988; Snow et al., 1988). We used an eight-item Likert-type scale that covered the extent of enemy fire and life-threatening situational exposures, with a total score ranging from 8 to 40. This instrument has been validated in a number of studies of Vietnam veterans (Figley, 1978; Frye & Stockton, 1982; Stellman et al., 1988). The questions were modified for women because they were not assigned to combat roles, but many did in fact, then as now, serve in heavy combat areas and were exposed to life-threatening situations. The women in the Nurse Corps were also likely to have been exposed to many soldiers who had been wounded or killed in combat.

Our longitudinal work with the larger Legion cohort has shown that community attitude on return from service was a significant predictor of PTSD symptoms (Koenen et al., 2003). Community attitude was assessed using the 5-point, Likert-scale question "What did you feel the attitude of your community (not including your immediate family and close friends) was on your discharge?" Responses could range from *very supportive* to *hostile*, and the same question was used for both men and women.

RESULTS

In the male cohort, the three racial/ethnic groups showed statistically significant differences in age, $F(2, 425) = 7.85$, $p < .01$, and mean age was 2 years lower for the Black and Hispanic male Legionnaires compared with non-Hispanic Whites ($M = 53.6$, 53.3, and 55.8 years, respectively; see Table 3.1). Group differences in education were also statistically significant, $\chi^2(4, n = 424) = 18.8$, $p < .01$. Nearly a quarter (22%) of White veterans had attended graduate or professional school compared with 13% of Black and 11% of Hispanic veterans, and nearly half (45%) of Black veterans completed high school education or less. The groups also varied significantly in current income, $\chi^2(12, n = 408) = 27.5$, $p < 0.01$. The proportion with incomes of $60,000 or more was 43.3% of White veterans, compared with 32.4% of Black and 17.6% of Hispanic veterans. Differences in marital status were not statistically significant, $\chi^2(6, n = 420) = 11.7$, $p = .06$.

White and minority veterans differed significantly in their mean discrimination score, $M = 6.7$ for Whites, 13.0 for Blacks and 11.2 for Hispanics, $F(2, 420) = 84.9$, $p < .01$. Examining the components of the score, fewer than one third (32%) of White veterans believed that race or ethnicity

TABLE 3.1
Demographic Characteristics of American Legion Veterans
Deployed to Vietnam, by Race and Ethnicity

	Non-Hispanic White (*n* = 112)	Non-Hispanic Black (*n* = 141)	Hispanic (*n* = 175)
Education, %			
High school graduate or less	22.3	44.9	33.9
Some college or college, vocational/ technical school graduate	55.4	42.0	55.2
Graduate or professional school	22.3	13.0	10.9
Income, %			
Less than $15,000	8.7	8.6	14.6
$15,000–$19,999	1.9	5.8	5.5
$20,000–$29,999	10.6	13.0	18.2
$30,000–$39,999	11.5	15.8	20.6
$40,000–$49,999	12.5	10.1	11.5
$50,000–$59,999	11.5	14.4	12.1
$60,000 or more	43.3	32.4	17.6
Marital Status, %			
Currently married	73.6	63.5	79.2
Never married	4.6	8.0	2.3
Divorced, separated, widowed	21.8	28.5	18.5

affected one's military career, compared with 82.1% of Black and 61.3% of Hispanic veterans. Although only a very small percentage of White veterans (8.9%) believed they were treated differently on the basis of race or ethnicity, just under half (47.1%) of Hispanics and over two thirds (68.6%) of Blacks reported that they experienced such discrimination.

The three veteran groups showed statistically significant differences in PTSD scores, M = 44.5 for Whites, 41.8 for Blacks, and 53.4 for Hispanics, $F(2, 406) = 16.23$, $p < .01$. Bonferroni-corrected t-tests showed that these differences were entirely explained by the much higher mean PTSD score among Hispanic veterans, $t(406) = 8.97$, $p < .01$ for Hispanics versus Whites, $t(406) = 11.66$, $p < .01$ for Hispanics versus Blacks. Despite all the other observed differences among the racial/ethnic groups, we found no significant differences in average combat scores, $F(2, 366) = 2.24$, $p > .1$.

Regression analyses were used to predict PTSD score symptoms as a function of perception of discrimination, combat exposure, and variables representing the veteran's perceived community and family support on return from Vietnam. Age and education were included as covariates. Results are reported separately for Blacks and Hispanics; the analysis was not carried out for Whites because their perceived discrimination was extremely low, with little variation. After adjustment for combat and other confounders, perception of discrimination was a significant predictor of more severe PTSD symptoms in Hispanics, $\beta = 0.7$, $p = .02$, but only marginally in Blacks, $\beta = 0.62$, $p = .08$. Though the variable was significant in predicting worse outcomes for Hispanics, it should be noted that the magnitude of the effect was small. Community attitude on return from Vietnam was also a significant predictor of PTSD (less support was associated with higher scores) for both Blacks, $\beta = 3.06$, $p < 0.01$, and Hispanics, $\beta = 5.89$, $p < .01$. Family support was significantly protective in Blacks, $\beta = 2.45$, $p = .03$, but not in Hispanics, $\beta = .13$, $p > 0.5$. Combat exposure was the strongest predictor of more severe PTSD symptoms among Blacks, $\beta = 1.0$, $p < .01$, and was also a significant predictor for Hispanics, $\beta = 0.72$, $p < .01$. Finally, education was a significant protective factor only in Hispanics, $\beta = -2.89$, $p < .01$. Age was unrelated to PTSD symptoms in both groups.

Demographic characteristics of the 1,285 women are shown in Table 3.2. Just over three fourths of the cohort (76%) served in the military, and the remainder were deployed as civilians. Military women were categorized into short-, medium-, or long-term career, on the basis of the number of years they served. Veterans were eligible for full military benefits once they completed 20 years of service, which was the reason for the choice of > 20 years as the cutoff for the career category; the short- and medium-term categories divided the requisite 20 years into two 10-year periods. The three military groups showed statistically significant differences in age at first deployment, $M = 24.1$ for short-term career, 31.0 for medium-term career, and 33.3 for career-military women, $F(3, 1221) = 165.94$, $p < .01$. As would be expected, career military women held the highest ranks. They were less likely to have been married (67.7% were never married) than short-term military (18.4%) or nonmilitary women (25.0%), and far fewer had children (8.2%) than did short-term military (62.6%) or nonmilitary women (48.7%). At the time of the survey, nonmilitary and career military women had considerably higher educational backgrounds, with nearly half having attended graduate school, but medium-term and career servicewomen had lower 1998 incomes.

The three service categories showed statistically significant differences in perceived family support after returning from Southeast Asia, $M = 2.48, 2.80$, and 2.29 for short-, medium-, and career-military, respectively, $F(2, 940) = 5.44$, $p < .01$. Perceived community support after returning from Southeast Asia also showed significant differences, $M = 3.18, 2.94$, and 2.66 for short-, medium-, and career-military, respectively, $F(2, 904) = 18.0$, $p < .01$, as did overall exposure to combat, $M = 18.38, 19.09, 17.19$ for short-, medium-, and career-military respectively, $F(2, 909) = 9.99$, $p < .01$. We also found significant differences in perceived gender discrimination based on military category, $M = 3.22, 3.19$, and 2.87 for short-, medium-, career-military, respectively, $F(3, 1274) = 36.40$, $p = .01$. It is worth noting that, though higher rank appears to have provided

TABLE 3.2
Demographic Characteristics of Civilian
and Military Women Deployed to Vietnam

		Years of military service		
	Nonmilitary $n = 308$	Short term (< 10 years) $n = 550$	Medium term (10–19 years) $n = 59$	Career (≥ 20 years) $n = 368$
Rank, %				
Enlisted		3.3	3.4	2.5
Lieutenant		44.4	6.8	2.5
Captain, Lieutenant (navy)		41.6	13.6	0.3
Major, Lieutenant Colonel, Lieutenant Commander		3.5	44.1	14.4
Lieutenant Colonel (army), Commander		5.3	23.7	49.7
Captain (navy), Colonel, or higher		2.0	8.5	30.7
Marital Status, %				
Never married	25.0	18.4	50.9	67.7
Married	49.7	60.2	28.8	17.9
Divorced or widowed	24.0	20.9	18.6	13.0
Children, %				
Had children	48.7	62.6	22.0	8.2
No children	51.3	37.4	78.0	91.8
Education, %				
High school or less	2.3	1.5	1.7	2.5
Some college or vocational school	6.2	19.4	20.3	14.2
College graduate	42.5	39.0	42.4	35.5
Graduate school	49.0	10.1	35.6	47.8
Income, %				
Under $20,000	4.0	2.1	7.0	1.8
$20,000–$29,999	6.4	3.2	15.8	6.2
$30,000–$39,999	11.5	7.4	17.5	19.7
$40,000–$49,999	8.0	12.0	14.0	19.1
$50,000–$59,999	12.1	17.7	7.0	16.5
$60,000 or more	57.9	57.5	38.6	36.8

some protection for medium- and career-military women, no group was completely immune to gender-based discrimination.

Regression analyses, adjusting for age, income, and category of military service, showed several significant predictors of PTSD, including greater exposure to combat, $\beta = 0.85$, $p < .01$; worse perception of community attitude on return from Vietnam, $\beta = 2.45$, $p < .01$; worse perception of family support on return from Vietnam, $\beta = 1.42$, $p < .01$; and greater perceived gender discrimination, $\beta = 1.75$, $p < 0.01$. Neither age nor military service was a significant predictor of PTSD symptoms. Note that income was a protective factor, $\beta = -1.30$, $p < 0.01$.

DISCUSSION

As expected, our findings demonstrated that combat stress was the strongest predictor of higher PTSD symptoms in all groups of veterans. However, it is important to note that perceptions of racial/ethnic discrimination were also significantly associated with higher PTSD symptoms in Hispanic veterans and were marginally significant in Black veterans. Previous research has shown that family and community support plays an important role in the development and persistence of PTSD, both in military (Koenen et al., 2003) and civilian populations (Brackbill et al., 2009), and we demonstrate that these associations are equally predictive in minority and female veteran populations.

Perceptions of racial/ethnic discrimination in the male veterans, and gender discrimination in the female veterans, were predictive of PTSD symptomology, independent of exposure to combat stress and other factors known to be important to PTSD outcomes. The extent of perceived gender discrimination among the women is noteworthy, especially because so many of them were high-ranking career officers. Although our results were not statistically significant for the Black cohort, it is important to note that the regression coefficients for discrimination among Blacks and Hispanics are nearly the same, and lack of statistical significance in the Black cohort could simply reflect inadequate power due to smaller sample size. Overall, our findings are consistent with those of the NVVRS (Kulka et al., 1988).

Our results are also consistent with other reports showing that individuals who reported lifetime and/or day-to-day exposure to discrimination also reported significantly worse mental health (Kessler et al., 1999; Williams et al., 1997), and these outcomes may be further worsened by other risk factors (e.g., low socioeconomic status, worse access to health care). Even in high-combat veterans—individuals who reported that they often saw comrades die, killed enemy combatants, and felt that they were in immediate danger of death—the perception that superiors and peers treated them differently because of their racial or ethnic background remains a significant factor in their mental health 25+ years after their military service.

One primary role that discrimination might play in the pathway between wartime experience and negative health outcomes is that of exacerbating fears about an already dangerous environment. Though the specifics of the discrimination experienced by minority men and White women serving in the military were undoubtedly different (primarily an experience of being treated as an expendable "other" in the case of the former; being treated as a combination second-class citizen/sex object in the case of the latter), one can see that both might feel a similar lack of support from soldiers outside their minority group.

The fundamental lack of respect that comes with discrimination, as well as associated traumatic experiences (inappropriate language/unwanted touching/harassment/rape in the case of women, racist language/insults/violence in the case of minority men), creates a hostile environment for the victims that could exacerbate fears both in combat and noncombat situations. Whereas individuals who felt a general sense of camaraderie and support might find momentary relief from the stresses of combat during between-action times, those who saw others around them as a potential threat (or at the very least did not feel that they could be completely safe) might live in a state of constant hypervigilance, without any respite. The institutionalized nature of this discrimination (e.g., complaining to superiors without any effect, experiencing racism/harassment from superiors) would only serve to worsen the perception that peers cannot be trusted and that one has no support in a highly dangerous environment. In this way these additional stressors might materially change the character of the already extreme wartime experience. Besides adding another layer of trauma and stress to normal combat stresses, experience of discrimination might change the fundamental understanding of one's place in the war zone and rob an individual of the basic support that might help one to cope with the expected combat stresses.

The issue of reporting perceptions of racism is somewhat more complex. Over the past 20 years, research in social psychology has described two different responses to discrimination: *vigilance*, or being inclined to identify ambiguous or nondiscriminatory experiences as discrimination, and *minimizing*, or the tendency to overlook genuine instances of discrimination as not truly discriminatory (Kaiser & Major, 2006). An individual's social context (i.e., prior experiences of racism and discrimination) has been shown to engender a vigilance response (Stangor et al., 2003). Under this model, young Black and Hispanic men growing up in the culture of the 1950s and 1960s would be more likely to identify wartime events (e.g., a dangerous unit assignment) as evidence of racial discrimination even if, objectively, no such discrimination had occurred. It should also be noted, however, that the recognition of discrimination is a psychologically taxing process that involves abandoning a fundamental notion that the world is a safe, fair place (Jost & Banaji, 1994). For individuals who were already in a dangerous environment, especially those who served in Southeast Asia and were exposed to moderate and high levels of combat stress, the recognition of apparently discriminatory practices may have been overwhelming. It is difficult to know whether the populations examined in this study tended toward one mechanism over another, but the clear observed relationships between perception of discrimination, reporting of combat stress, and experiences of posttraumatic stress symptoms suggest that there were genuine differences in experience and subsequent outcomes comparing minority soldiers with their White counterparts. It is also difficult to determine whether the experiences of the relatively small survey sample are representative of the experiences of the broader minority Vietnam veteran population—as we state, such data are not available—but it seems reasonable to assume that many other minority veterans may have experienced similar discrimination as those surveyed.

CONCLUSIONS

Much has changed since the Vietnam War era, both in terms of military policy and broader American societal norms. Discrimination based on race or gender is widely seen as unjust, and instances of alleged prejudice are met with public outrage. Women and men of color hold positions today that would have been thought unlikely or impossible in the mid-1970s—military generals and the President of the United States. Yet for all these progressive steps, there are many deeper prejudices that have not changed. More subtle and insidious forms of racism and sexism are part of everyday life for women and minorities, and America remains plagued by the same injustices it has worked to ameliorate for decades. With this in mind, it seems that the question of discrimination as a source of traumatic stress for the men and women who serve in the military is as pertinent today as it was 40 years ago. More recent studies have shown that race- and gender-based discrimination are still an important facet of the military experience for minority and female soldiers and that the experience of discrimination remains associated with poorer mental health (Foynes et al., 2013, 2015). Even with the increased media coverage of modern warfare, the battlefield often remains far separated from American soil and society. There is enormous potential for acts of prejudice and violence to go unreported and unaddressed. Men and women living in these places, coping with the ever-present dangers of injury and death, are in the same fragile psychological space as their Vietnam-era predecessors, and it is here that a cruel word or an unwanted touch may do the most damage. The military has a duty to foster an environment in which such acts of discrimination or harassment can be safely reported, where they are met with the same outrage as would be found anywhere else in American society. It is a traumatic enough experience to face hate from the enemy in front of you; it is that much worse to face it from the comrade next to you.

REFERENCES

American Psychiatric Association. (1987). *Diagnostic and statistical manual of mental disorders* (3rd ed., rev.). Washington, DC: Author.

Brackbill, R. M., Hadler, J. L., DiGrande, L., Ekenga, C. C., Farfel, M. R., Friedman, S., . . . Thorpe, L. E. (2009). Asthma and posttraumatic stress symptoms 5 to 6 years following exposure to the World Trade Center terrorist attack. *JAMA, 302*, 502–516. http://dx.doi.org/10.1001/jama.2009.1121

Breslau, N. (2002). Gender differences in trauma and posttraumatic stress disorder. *The Journal of Gender-Specific Medicine, 5*, 34–40.

DiGrande, L., Perrin, M. A., Thorpe, L. E., Thalji, L., Murphy, J., Wu, D., . . . Brackbill, R. M. (2008). Posttraumatic stress symptoms, PTSD, and risk factors among lower Manhattan residents 2–3 years after the September 11, 2001 terrorist attacks. *Journal of Traumatic Stress, 21*, 264–273. http://dx.doi.org/10.1002/jts.20345

Dohrenwend, B. P., Turner, J. B., Turse, N. A., Lewis-Fernández, R., & Yager, T. J. (2008). War-related posttraumatic stress disorder in Black, Hispanic, and majority White Vietnam veterans: The roles of exposure and vulnerability. *Journal of Traumatic Stress, 21*, 133–141. http://dx.doi.org/10.1002/jts.20327

Farfel, M., DiGrande, L., Brackbill, R., Prann, A., Cone, J., Friedman, S., . . . Thorpe, L. (2008). An overview of 9/11 experiences and respiratory and mental health conditions among World Trade Center Health Registry enrollees. *Journal of Urban Health, 85*, 880–909. http://dx.doi.org/10.1007/s11524-008-9317-4

Figley, C. R. (1978). *Stress disorders among Vietnam veterans*. New York, NY: Brunner/Mazel.

Foynes, M. M., Shipherd, J. C., & Harrington, E. F. (2013). Race and gender discrimination in the Marines. *Cultural Diversity & Ethnic Minority Psychology, 19*, 111–119. http://dx.doi.org/10.1037/a0030567

Foynes, M. M., Smith, B. N., & Shipherd, J. C. (2015). Associations between race-based and sex-based discrimination, health, and functioning: A longitudinal study of Marines. *Medical Care, 53*(Suppl. 1), S128–S135. http://dx.doi.org/10.1097/MLR.0000000000000300

Frye, J. S., & Stockton, R. A. (1982). Discriminant analysis of posttraumatic stress disorder among a group of Viet Nam veterans. *The American Journal of Psychiatry, 139,* 52–56. http://dx.doi.org/10.1176/ajp.139.1.52

Green, B. L., Grace, M. C., Lindy, J. D., & Leonard, A. C. (1990). Race differences in response to combat stress. *Journal of Traumatic Stress, 3,* 379–393. http://dx.doi.org/10.1002/jts.2490030307

History.com. (2011). *Women in the Vietnam War.* Retrieved from http://www.history.com/topics/vitenam-war/women-in-the-vietnam-war

Jost, J. T., & Banaji, M. R. (1994). The role of stereotyping in system-justification and the production of false consciousness. *British Journal of Social Psychology, 33,* 1–27. http://dx.doi.org/10.1111/j.2044-8309.1994.tb01008.x

Kaiser, C. R., & Major, B. (2006). A social psychological perspective on perceiving and reporting discrimination. *Law & Social Inquiry, 31,* 801–830. http://dx.doi.org/10.1111/j.1747-4469.2006.00036.x

Kessler, R. C., Mickelson, K. D., & Williams, D. R. (1999). The prevalence, distribution, and mental health correlates of perceived discrimination in the United States. *Journal of Health and Social Behavior, 40,* 208–230. http://dx.doi.org/10.2307/2676349

Koenen, K. C., Stellman, J. M., Stellman, S. D., & Sommer, J. F., Jr. (2003). Risk factors for course of posttraumatic stress disorder among Vietnam veterans: A 14-year follow-up of American Legionnaires. *Journal of Consulting and Clinical Psychology, 71,* 980–986. http://dx.doi.org/10.1037/0022-006X.71.6.980

Kulka, R. A., Schlenger, W. E., Fairbank, J. A., Hough, R. L., Jordan, B. K., Marmar, C. R., & Weiss, D. S. (1988). *Contractual report of findings from the national Vietnam Veterans Readjustment Study: Vol. I. Executive summary, description of findings, and technical appendices.* Research Triangle Park, NC: Research Triangle Institute.

Lewis-Fernández, R., Turner, J. B., Marshall, R., Turse, N., Neria, Y., & Dohrenwend, B. P. (2008). Elevated rates of current PTSD among Hispanic veterans in the NVVRS: True prevalence or methodological artifact? *Journal of Traumatic Stress, 21,* 123–132. http://dx.doi.org/10.1002/jts.20329

Ortega, A. N., & Rosenheck, R. (2000). Posttraumatic stress disorder among Hispanic Vietnam veterans. *The American Journal of Psychiatry, 157,* 615–619. http://dx.doi.org/10.1176/appi.ajp.157.4.615

Penk, W. E., Robinowitz, R., Black, J., Dolan, M., Bell, W., Dorsett, D., . . . Noriega, L. (1989). Ethnicity: Post-traumatic stress disorder (PTSD) differences among black, white, and Hispanic veterans who differ in degrees of exposure to combat in Vietnam. *Journal of Clinical Psychology, 45,* 729–735. http://dx.doi.org/10.1002/1097-4679(198909)45:5<729::AID-JCLP2270450507>3.0.CO;2-H

Ruef, A. M., Litz, B. T., & Schlenger, W. E. (2000). Hispanic ethnicity and risk for combat-related posttraumatic stress disorder. *Cultural Diversity & Ethnic Minority Psychology, 6,* 235–251. http://dx.doi.org/10.1037/1099-9809.6.3.235

Schlenger, W. E., Kulka, R. A., Fairbank, J. A., Hough, R. L., Kathleen Jordan, B., Marmar, C. R., & Weiss, D. S. (1992). The prevalence of post-traumatic stress disorder in the Vietnam generation: A multimethod, multisource assessment of psychiatric disorder. *Journal of Traumatic Stress, 5*, 333–363. http://dx.doi.org/10.1002/jts.2490050303

Snow, B. R., Stellman, J. M., Stellman, S. D., & Sommer, J. F., Jr. (1988). Post-traumatic stress disorder among American Legionnaires in relation to combat experience in Vietnam: Associated and contributing factors. *Environmental Research, 47*, 175–192. http://dx.doi.org/10.1016/S0013-9351(88)80040-9

Stangor, C., Swim, J. K., Sechrist, G. B., DeCoster, J., Van Allen, K. L., & Ottenbreit, A. (2003). Ask, answer, and announce: Three stages in perceiving and responding to discrimination. *European Review of Social Psychology, 14*, 277–311. http://dx.doi.org/10.1080/10463280340000090

Stellman, J. M., Stellman, S. D., & Sommer, J. F., Jr. (1988). Social and behavioral consequences of the Vietnam experience among American Legionnaires. *Environmental Research, 47*, 129–149. http://dx.doi.org/10.1016/S0013-9351(88)80038-0

Tolin, D. F., & Foa, E. B. (2002). Gender and PTSD: A cognitive model. In R. Kimerling, P. Ouimette, & J. Wolfe (Eds.), *Gender and PTSD* (pp. 76–97). New York, NY: Guilford Press.

Williams, D. R., Neighbors, H. W., & Jackson, J. S. (2003). Racial/ethnic discrimination and health: Findings from community studies. *American Journal of Public Health, 93*, 200–208. http://dx.doi.org/10.2105/AJPH.93.2.200

Williams, D. R., Yu, Y., Jackson, J. S., & Anderson, N. B. (1997). Racial differences in physical and mental health: Socio-economic status, stress and discrimination. *Journal of Health Psychology, 2*, 335–351. http://dx.doi.org/10.1177/135910539700200305

4

USING A LIFE COURSE PERSPECTIVE TO EXAMINE THE PREVALENCE OF MARRIAGE IN MILITARY FAMILIES

SHELLEY MacDERMID WADSWORTH, SARAH MUSTILLO, ANTHONY J. FABER, AND ABIGAIL TOLHURST CHRISTIANSEN

One of the defining moments of modern U.S. military history occurred in 1973 when the U.S. military became an all-volunteer force (Chambers, 1987). Since then, the armed forces have had to compete with civilian employers to recruit high-quality personnel, and because they are very expensive to train, to retain them (Segal & Segal, 1999). Longer careers have increased the prevalence of married personnel and parents in the military population, and today spouses, children, and adult dependents of active duty service members constitute a population of 3 million, outnumbering service members (Office of the Deputy Assistant Secretary of Defense, Military Community and Family Policy, 2014).

The past 20 years have seen substantial increases in programs and policies to support military families, which are most often defined as the spouses, children, and adult dependents of service members. The U.S. Department of Defense (DoD) directives on Family Readiness (1342.22, effective as of

http://dx.doi.org/10.1037/0000061-005
Long-Term Outcomes of Military Service: The Health and Well-Being of Aging Veterans, A. Spiro III, R. A. Settersten Jr., and C. M. Aldwin (Editors)

2012), Child Development programs (6060.02, effective as of 2014), and Education Activity (1342.20, effective as of 2007) specify an extensive list of required programs and services aimed at supporting families, including deployment supports such as family-support groups and deployment cycle training, relocation assistance, child care at subsidized rates, education, care for family members with special needs, programs to improve spouses' access to jobs and careers, counseling, and financial planning assistance.

As the presence of families in the U.S. military has increased, so too have the demands of military service. After the end of the Cold War, the number of troops persistently deployed increased (Levy, Thie, Sollinger, & Kawata, 2000); between 1991 and 1996 the U.S. Army deployed about twice as many personnel each year as it had during 1975 to 1989. From 1997 to 2000 the number of units deployed over 120 days per year more than doubled (Polich & Sortor, 2001). This increase in "tempo" was intensified by a one-third reduction in the size of the force (from 2.1 million active-duty troops in 1986 to 1.4 million in 2003; Defense Manpower Data Center, 2017). The United States is currently in the longest war in its history, deploying over 2 million service members over the past 15 years (Institute of Medicine, 2013).

Now that families are such a prominent part of military culture, the prevalence and stability of military members' marriages is seen by some military leaders as an indicator of the health of the force. Over the past 15 years, multiple studies have examined marriage patterns in the military, focusing in particular on the implications of wartime deployments for marital stability (Karney, Loughran, & Pollard, 2012). Studies have shown, for example, that the impact of deployments depends on whether marriages occur prior to or following deployment, how early in marriage deployments occur, their duration and content, and other factors (Negrusa, Negrusa, & Hosek, 2016). The focus of the current study, however, is on the period immediately prior to the recent war.

During the 1990s, the prevalence of marriage among military members fell to a 2-decade low (Office of the Under Secretary of Defense, Personnel and Readiness, 2014), raising concern among policymakers who viewed it as a negative indicator of the well-being of the military population. Figure 4.1 shows historical trends in marital status among military members and civilians of comparable age. The prevalence of marriage in the general population among 18- to 44-year-olds fell from 61.3% to 50.9% during the period shown, but the opposite pattern was seen among military members. In 1980, only 46.6% of military members in this age group were married, 15 percentage points less than in the general population at that time. Over the next decade, the marriage gap between military members and the general population narrowed, closing in 1990. After peaking at 57.4% in 1994, levels in the mili-

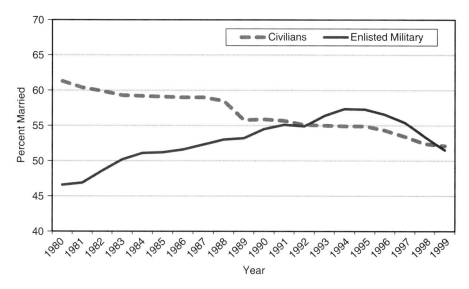

Figure 4.1. Prevalence of current marriage among military members and among 10- to 44-year-olds in the population, 1980–2002. Data come from *Population Representation in the Military* (2012), Table D-14. Retrieved from http://prhome. defense.gov/portals/52/Documents/POPREP/poprep2011/appendixd/d_14.html.

tary then fell steadily, to 48.2% in 2001, about twice the percentage-point decline in the population, where the prevalence of current marriage fell from 54.9% to 50.9% (Office of the Under Secretary of Defense, Personnel and Readiness, 2014).

What might explain these changes in military patterns? Given rising age at first marriage and falling marriage rates among young people in the general population, were the declines in the military simply echoing civilian trends (Fields & Casper, 2001; Teachman, 2009)? Did they reflect some systematic change in the composition of the military? Or were marriage declines a negative signal about the health of the force? In this study, we use the life course perspective to help us understand changes in the prevalence of marriage in the military and general populations between 1985 and 1999. A defining feature of the life course perspective is its recognition of the importance of multiple dimensions of time in helping us to understand human behavior. The passage of time during our lives, and the lives of those around us, as well as the broad sweeps of historical change, influence our opportunities to marry, have children, and pursue careers (Bengtson & Allen, 1993). We paid specific attention to the life course variables of historical time, individual time, and family time.

Historical time refers to macrolevel events and trends that punctuate the lives of large groups. We measure historical time as birth cohort in this study because it positions individuals in time relative to major changes in society. For example, members of the 1940–1949 birth cohort entered the military during the 1960s, in the aftermath of the Korean War, when there was a draft, and strict limits on women in the forces. Members of the 1970–1979 birth cohort entered an all-volunteer military force in the 1990s that was about to downsize, where almost all jobs were open to women, and significant numbers of troops were deployed to Kosovo, Bosnia, and the Persian Gulf. Because a clear prediction for military marriage patterns was difficult to distill from the juxtaposition of rising intensity of military service, expanding opportunities for women, and increasing emphasis on programs to support families, we based our hypotheses on patterns in the general population, where marriage rates have been falling (Schoen & Standish, 2000):

Hypothesis 1: The prevalence of marriage will decline over time.

Hypothesis 2: Members of more recent birth cohorts, such as the 1960s and 1970s cohorts, will be less likely to be married than members of earlier cohorts, such as the 1940s and 1950s cohorts.

Individual time refers to the lifespan of an individual and is indicated in this study by chronological age. From trends in the general population, we know that the vast majority of individuals marry and that the likelihood of being married increases steeply with age, even though the age at first marriage has risen by about 4 years since 1985, to 27 for women and 29 for men (U.S. Census Bureau, 2016). Thus, we expect the likelihood of being married to increase with age, possibly with declines later in life because of divorce.

Hypothesis 3: The probability of being married will rise with age.

Family time refers in this study to the presence or absence of children in the home. Although they do not always co-occur and their sequence varies, marriage and parenthood often go hand in hand. Military life carries both incentives and disincentives for marriage, and most military members are young and work long hours with unpredictable schedules. Other disincentives to marriage include frequent moves and family separations, not to mention dangerous work assignments that can be very challenging (Segal & Segal, 2004). Both men and women report difficulties combining marriage, family, and military service. In focus groups with men and women conducted by the DoD Advisory Committee on Women in the Services, the most common reason for deciding to leave the military was family and personal life (Mutter et al., 2003). Respondents reported concerns about family stability, finding adequate time to spend with family, and starting a family in the military. In contrast, incentives for marriage include subsidies, benefits, and job security, as well as the need to be able to deploy even if children are in the home. We focused on these factors and patterns in the general population civilian patterns to form the following prediction:

Hypothesis 4: Parents will be more likely to be married than nonparents.

It is well known that military policies have treated men and women differently. In the mid-19th century, the U.S. Army prohibited men from enlisting if they were married or had children (Goldman, 1976). A century later, fathers were included in the drafts for World War II and the Korean conflict (Hill, 1949; Schumm, Rice, Bell, & Schuman, 1996). For women, marriage, motherhood, or simply being female have been barriers to advancement. In 1951 an executive order authorized discharging women in the services who became pregnant, adopted a child, or had a stepchild in their home. This executive order was repealed first by the Air Force in 1971 and then the rest of the services in 1976 after a U.S. Court of Appeals ruling (Women's Research and Education Institute, 2004). After a 2% cap on the proportion of women in the enlisted ranks was lifted in 1967, the next 3 decades saw significant expansion in women's career opportunities (Harrell, Beckett, Chien, & Sollinger, 2002).

In 2013, the DoD rescinded the Combat Exclusion Rule prohibiting women from serving in combat units (U.S. Department of Defense, 2013). Mothers are no longer compelled to leave the military; DoD regulations now state that women "*may* be separated from military service due to pregnancy or childbirth *unless* retention is determined to be in the best interests of the Service" (emphasis ours; DoD Instruction 1332.14). Female officers are about 10% less likely than males to stay in the service, even though junior female officers expressed more interest in doing so than males in the 2002 Status of Forces Survey. By 2013, the proportion of women rose to 14.9% of the active duty force (Office of the Deputy Assistant Secretary of Defense, Military Community and Family Policy, 2014). Given that gender remains a defining feature of military life, with women still the focus of some job restrictions, we expected the proportion of military members who were married to be smaller among women than men.

Hypothesis 5: Women will be less likely than men to be married.

To the extent that groups differ in their experiences of military life, we anticipated significant differences in patterns for men and women. For example, given the substantial differences between their positions in the military, we expected that patterns for men and women might be quite different across age or cohort. Finally, because we knew that marriage patterns could be affected by individuals' personal characteristics and experiences, we tested whether our findings for life course variables were robust to background variables such as ethnicity; income; or in the case of military members, years of service.

Hypothesis 6: Marriage patterns across age or cohort will differ for men and women.

METHOD

Data for this study came from the 1985, 1992, and 1999 panels of the U.S. Census Bureau and U.S. Bureau of Labor Statistics' Current Population Survey (CPS) and the 1985, 1992, and 1999 panels of the Defense Manpower Data Center's Active Duty Survey (ADS). Both surveys focused on respondents' demographic, employment, health, and social characteristics. The CPS is a monthly study of a national probability sample of over 60,000 U.S. households that began in the 1930s. From each household, one noninstitutionalized, nonmilitary individual age 15 or older (typically the homeowner or renter) is chosen as the reference person. Response rates are generally around 90%. We restricted our sample to those age 18 to 55 who were employed full time, yielding 43,900 participants in 1985, 43,375 participants in 1992, and 41,291 participants in 1999. Data were weighted to ensure representativeness by age, sex, race, ethnicity, area of residence, and nonresponse.

The DoD has conducted surveys of active duty personnel regularly since 1969. Stratified random sampling designs and data weighting were used to produce representative samples of all active duty military personnel serving in the U.S. Armed Forces with at least 6 months of active duty service and below the rank of general or admiral; members of the Coast Guard were not included in the present analyses because they are subject to different family-related policies than DoD personnel. The response rates for the 1985, 1992, and 1999 surveys were 71%, 66%, and 51%, respectively. Restricting the sample by age yielded 88,943 participants in 1985, 59,930 participants in 1992, and 33,189 participants in 1999.

Participants

After removing cases with missing data, the combined CPS analysis sample included 120,736 participants, whereas the military sample consisted of 148,604 military members. Descriptive information about the samples is shown in Table 4.1. The average age increased in both the military and civilian samples, whereas the percentage of those who were parents fell across surveys. The proportion of married sample members fell in the general population but rose slightly in the military samples. The average length of military service was 7 to 10 years, rising slightly across the surveys. Both the civilian and military samples became more ethnically diverse.

Measures

Our dependent variable was marital status (1 = married, 0 = not married) at the time of the survey. The married category included those married for the

TABLE 4.1
Descriptive Statistics for Each Survey Year[a]

	Civilian (from Current Population Survey)						Military (from DMDC Active Duty Survey)					
	1985 n = 43,900		1992 n = 43,375		1999 n = 41,291		1985 n = 88,943		1992 n = 59,930		1999 n = 33,189	
Variables	M (SD) or %	Range	M (SD) or %	Range	M (SD) or %	Range	M (SD) or %	Range	M (SD) or %	Range	M (SD) or %	Range
Year of birth	1950 (9.6)	1930–1967	1955 (9.3)	1937–1974	1961 (9.7)	1944–1981	1957 (7.0)	1930–1967	1963 (7.2)	1937–1974	1969 (7.6)	1950–1981
Age	34.8 (9.6)	18–55	36.8 (9.3)	18–55	38.3 (9.7)	18–55	27.8 (7.0)	18–55	28.6 (7.2)	18–55	29.5 (7.6)	18–49
Marital status[b]	64%	—	63%	—	60%	—	62%	—	63%	—	65%	—
Gender[c]	41%	—	43%	—	43%	—	9%	—	12%	—	15%	—
Parent status[d]	49%	—	46%	—	44%	—	51%	—	46%	—	44%	—
White	83%	—	80%	—	75%	—	73%	—	74%	—	67%	—
Hispanic	5%	—	6%	—	8%	—	6%	—	5%	—	10%	—
Black	9%	—	10%	—	12%	—	16%	—	17%	—	14%	—
Other	3%	—	4%	—	5%	—	5%	—	4%	—	10%	—
Military rank[e]	—	—	—	—	—	—	7.3 (4.6)	1–20	6.7 (4.8)	1–20	7.1 (5.0)	1–20
Years of service[f]	—	—	—	—	—	—	2.7 (1.9)	1–9	2.8 (1.9)	1–9	3.0 (2.0)	1–9

Note. DMDC = Defense Manpower Data Center.
[a]Data for each year are weighted to accurately represent the population at the time. [b]Marital status: 1 = married, 2 = not married. [c]Gender: 1 = female, 0 = male. [d]Parent status: 1 = children, 0 = no children. [e]Military rank: 1 = E1 (e.g., Private), 20 = O6 (e.g., Colonel). [f]Years of service: 1 = 4 years or less, 3 = 31+ years.

first time as well as those who had remarried, or were married but separated. The unmarried category included those who had never married and those who were divorced or widowed.

In terms of life course variables, individual time was represented by age, which was self-reported in both samples. Period in both data sets was the year of the survey. Historical time was indexed by cohort, which comprised aggregated groups of birth years (1930–1939, 1940–1949, 1950–1959, 1960–1969, 1970–1986). Family time was represented as the presence or absence of children under the age of 18 living in the home (parent = 1, nonparent = 0).

In addition to the life course variables, we examined demographic (gender, ethnicity, family income) and military factors (rank, years of service). *Gender* was dummy coded with male as the reference group. Three dummy-coded variables for *ethnicity* were created, with White as the referent: African American, Hispanic (Spanish, Hispanic, Latino) and other (Asian, American Indian, Pacific Islander, and other races). For the CPS sample, family income was coded into 14 categories, adjusted for inflation: 1 = less than $5,000 to 14 = $75,000 or more. *Military rank*, which corresponds closely to income, was coded according to paygrade and ranged from E1 (1, equivalent to the enlisted rank of private in the army) to O6 (20, an officer rank equivalent to a colonel in the army). *Years of service* was represented by nine options: 4 years or less, 5–6 years, 7–10, 11–14, 15–16, 17–20, 21–25, 26–30, and 31 years or more.

Analyses

It is difficult to disentangle effects of age, period, and cohort in regression models because they are mathematically dependent—knowing the value of any two reveals the value of the third. To deal with this, we used an hierarchical cross-classified random effects model (Yang, 2008, 2010; Yang & Land 2006), which provides unbiased and efficient results for data of this type. We also included nonlinear (quadratic) terms for time and grouped birth years into 10-year cohorts to reduce the mathematical dependence. Because the outcome is binary (e.g., married, not married), results are presented as odds ratios or the odds of being married, such that values greater than 1 indicate that a variable is associated with increased odds of being married, and a value less than 1 indicates reduced odds.

The models we tested included tests of variation across period (i.e., survey years) and cohort (i.e., birth year), as well as group comparisons according to both linear and curvilinear trends for age (i.e., age and age^2) and gender, and interactions between gender and the age variables. For both the general and military populations, Model 1 tested effects for age (linear and nonlinear), sex, and the interaction between sex and age. Model 2 tested additional variables including parent status and its interaction with sex, as well as controlled for ethnicity and family income for the general population and ethnicity, years of service, and military rank for the military sample (see Table 4.2).

RESULTS

Figure 4.2 displays the predicted probabilities of being married, separately for men and women, by period, age, and cohort, using results from Model 1 in Table 4.2. Panels A, B, and C on the left side of the figure focus on the general population; Panels D, E, and F on the right side focus on active duty military personnel.

Model 1

We first present results for period and cohort, followed by the other variables.

Period

In both the general and the military populations, there was a significant effect for period, indicating that the odds of being married varied significantly by year of the survey. In both samples, there was a slight downward trend across the years of the surveys, consistent with Hypothesis 1 (see Panel A in Figure 4.2). In the general population, controlling for age, the prevalence of marriage hovered around 70% for men and 60% for women. In the military population (see Panel D in Figure 4.2), the trend was flat for men, hovering around 75%, and declining among women from about 58% to 47% across survey years.

Cohort

In both populations, the odds of being married varied significantly by cohort. Consistent with Hypothesis 2, there was an overall pattern of declining prevalence of marriage across birth cohorts. That is, individuals born in the 1930s were more likely to be married than individuals born in the 1970s, regardless of when data were collected. Consistent with Hypothesis 6, however, this pattern differed by gender, especially in the military sample. The gender gap in the probability of being married was larger for earlier cohorts, narrowing substantially among more recent cohorts. In the general population (see Panel B of Figure 4.2), the prevalence of marriage declined across

TABLE 4.2
Hierarchical Cross-Classified Random Effects Model of Marriage

| | Current Population Survey data N = 120,736 | | | | Active Duty Survey data N = 148,604 | | | |
| | Model 1 | | Model 2 | | Model 1 | | Model 2 | |
	EC	SE	EC	SE	EC	SE	EC	SE
Random effects								
Period	0.166***	0.069	0.026	0.016	0.042	0.023	0.026	0.016
Cohort	0.042	0.023	0.113	0.046	0.166	0.069	0.113	0.046
Chi-squared	591.45***		1434.65***		618.25***		52.26***	
Fixed effects								
Age	1.110***	0.002	1.103***	0.003	1.177***	0.002	1.068***	0.003
Age^2	0.995***	0.0001	0.998***	0.0001	0.993***	0.0001	0.997***	0.0001
Female	0.598***	0.011	1.136***	0.029	0.338***	0.006	0.753***	0.016
Female by age	0.961***	0.001	0.958***	0.002	0.884***	0.002	0.926***	0.002
Female by age^2	1.002***	0.0001	1.001***	0.0002	1.002***	0.0002	1.000	0.0002
Parent	—		20.375***	0.093	—		19.568***	0.455
Female by parent	—		0.176***	0.006	—		0.236***	0.008
Hispanic	—		0.946	0.029	—		1.038	0.031
Black	—		0.492***	0.013	—		0.691***	0.014
Other race	—		0.966**	0.037	—		0.908***	0.028
Family income	—		1.224***	0.003	—		—	
Years of service	—		—		—		1.114***	0.008
Paygrade	—		—		—		1.014***	0.008

Note. EC = exponentiated coefficient; SE = standard error.
**p < .01; ***p < .001.

CURRENT POPULATION SURVEY   ACTIVE DUTY SURVEY

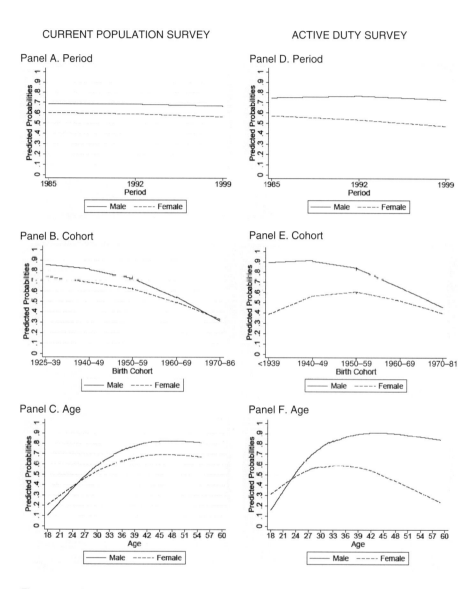

Figure 4.2. Percentage married by period, cohort, and age for men and women by survey. Data are from the 1985, 1992, and 1999 panels of the U.S. Census Bureau and U.S. Bureau of Labor Statistics' Current Population Survey and the 1985, 1992, and 1999 panels of the Defense Manpower Data Center's Active Duty Survey.

cohorts for both men and women, but more rapidly for men. For example, in the 1930–1939 cohort, 85% of men and 72% of women were married, declining to 75% of men and 65% of women by the 1950 to 1959 cohort. For the most recent cohort, however, the probabilities were equal, at 39%.

In the military population (see Panel E of Figure 4.2), 90% of men but only 40% of women born before 1939 were married. It remained high for men across the 1940–1949 and 1950–1959 cohorts, then declined to 47% by the 1970–1981 cohort. For women, the probability increased across the 1940–1949 and 1950–1959 cohorts to a maximum of 60%, then declined to 40% among the 1970–1981 cohort.

Age

In Model 1, there was a significant effect for age in both the civilian and military samples but the effect was nonlinear, providing support for Hypothesis 3. As shown in Panels A and D in Figure 4.2, the percentage of married individuals rose dramatically during the 20s and leveled off in the 40s. However, this varied by gender. In the civilian sample, women at age 18 were almost twice as likely as men to be married (19% vs. 10%). At age 26, the probabilities were similar for men and women, but at later ages, women were slightly less likely to be married. In the military sample, the effect was quite dramatic, with women far less likely to be married, starting around age 23. Whereas the highest probability of being married at any age was 90% for men, the peak for women was 60% (see Panel F of Figure 4.2).

Model 2

Model 2 included the full set of predictors, incorporating parental status and ethnicity for both populations, family income in the civilian model, and years of service and military rank in the military model. All of the effects reported previously for Model 1 remained significant in Model 2 (i.e., period, cohort, age and age^2, sex, and the sex-by-age interaction) except that the interaction between sex and age^2 fell from significance in Model 2. Thus, all but one of the effects observed in Model 1 remained significant with the inclusion of parenthood and demographic variables. Our presentation of results focuses on the findings unique to Model 2.

Age

In the general population, each additional year of age was associated with an 11% increase in the odds of being married for men, but the significant quadratic term indicated that the increase was nonlinear and tapered off at older ages, once again consistent with Hypothesis 4. Controlling for other variables, women were more likely than men to be married ($OR = 1.136$). This finding differs from that in Model 1, where women were less likely than men to be married ($OR = .598$), indicating that when parental status and demographic variables were taken into account, the gender gap in marriage in the general population narrowed.

In the military population, there also were significant age effects. The odds of being married for women, controlling for other variables, were about 25% lower than for men, and this gap increased over time, as shown by the significant interaction between female and age and the nonsignificant interaction between female and age^2. This gender gap was only about half as large, however, as that observed in Model 1, where women were 66% less likely to be married than men. These gender patterns differed between Models 1 and 2. In Model 1, patterns in both the military and civilian samples were consistent with Hypothesis 5, with women less likely to be married than men. In Model 2, the gender gap in the military narrowed by half, and the gap in the civilian population reversed, with women slightly *more* likely than men to be married.

Parenthood

As Model 2 shows, both civilians and military members were approximately 20 times more likely to be married if they were parents, consistent with Hypothesis 4. However, once again, this varied by gender, as predicted by Hypothesis 6. In the civilian population, fathers were about 20 times more likely to be married than men without children, but mothers were 83% *less* likely to be married than women without children. Black individuals in the general population were about half as likely as White individuals to be married ($OR = 0.492$). In the military, fathers were almost 20 times more likely to be married than men without children, but the interaction between female and parent showed that mothers were about 76% less likely to be married than women without children.

Demographic Characteristics

In the general population, the odds of being married were higher when income was higher, and lower when participants were non-Hispanic Black service members or service members of other races ($OR = 0.492$ and 0.966, respectively). In the military sample, each additional increment in years of military service was associated with about a 14% increase in the odds of being married, and each paygrade higher was associated with a 1.4% increase in the odds. Non-Hispanic Black service members and service members of other races were less likely to be married than White service members ($OR = 0.691$ and 0.908, respectively).

DISCUSSION

Why did the prevalence of marriage decline in the military in the late 1990s? To a large extent, the decline echoed what was happening in the general population. The overall declines in marriage were largely cohort and period effects, as parent status and age (especially young age) both were positively related to marriage. On their own, these patterns do not suggest that declines in marriage should be alarming to military policymakers.

On the other hand, the results make it clear that the military was a very different marital context for men and women during the time period covered by this study. For men, military service appeared to be a supportive context for marriage. Prevalence of marriage among men was very high, especially when they were fathers. For women, the supportiveness of military life for marriage was less clear. Today's expanding opportunities for women in the military also may increase the likelihood of deployment and family separation, which could be problematic for women who bear traditional responsibilities as primary caregivers for children. Perhaps this is why married women in the military today are 6 times more likely than men to be married to other military members (MacDermid Wadsworth, 2014). To the extent that women marry other service members in large numbers, and deployments become longer and less predictable, military duties may become harder to coordinate. To the extent that women marry civilians, it may have been—and continues to be—difficult to find partners willing or able to tolerate the challenges to their own careers. Perhaps it is harder to find someone willing to be a "trailing husband" than a "trailing wife." It is also possible that single mothers may be drawn to stay in the military because the job security, pay, and benefits (e.g., health care, housing, child care) far exceed what many private employers would provide, particularly for those in enlisted ranks who mostly have high school educations.

The purpose of this study was to examine marriage patterns among military members as a function of historical time, individual time, family time, and gender. With regard to historical time, we predicted that the prevalence of marriage would decline over time, and indeed we saw small declines across survey years in both samples. We also predicted that declines in marriage would be evident across birth cohorts, with individuals in more recent cohorts less likely to be married than those born in earlier years. Cohort differences were of particular interest in this study because of the rising intensity of military duties and different treatment of men and women by military policies. Once again, our results were consistent with this prediction. Our third hypothesis predicted that the odds of marriage would rise with age. We did find this pattern, but only until about age 40, after which the odds level off.

We hypothesized that marriage patterns would differ for men and women, and this hypothesis was consistently supported. In most instances, women were less likely to be married than men, but the results related to this gender gap differed depending on whether income and ethnicity were included in our models. When income and ethnicity were *not* taken into account, women were less likely to be married than men in both samples. Comparisons by historical period showed that in the general population, there was a consistent gender gap of about 10 percentage points, with men more likely than women to be married. In the military population, the gender gap was about 15 percentage points and grew slightly across periods because of declines in the prevalence of married women in the samples. Relative to the general population, the odds of being married in the military population were about 5 percentage points higher for men and about 11 percentage points lower for women across periods. When income and ethnicity *were* considered, the gender gap narrowed by half in the military and reversed in the general population, with women slightly more likely to be married than men.

The nature of this gender gap also varied across birth cohorts. In the earliest cohort, the gender gap in marriage prevalence was 10% in the general population but 50% in the military population. In more recent cohorts, the gender gap narrowed in both populations, closing completely in the general population.

Another striking gender-related pattern was high prevalence of marriage among young military women, with 30% married before age 25, twice the percentage of men. These percentages were high relative to the general population, among whom only 19% of women and 10% of men were married by that age. Given that only 7.6% to 11.1% of members were married at entry between 1976 and 2012 (Office of the Under Secretary of Defense, Personnel and Readiness, 2014), significant numbers of military members married early in their careers. Research by Teachman and colleagues (Lemmon, Whyman, & Teachman, 2009) showed that military pay and benefits—some offered only to married couples—constitute significant incentives for marriage among active-duty personnel. With the legalization of same-sex marriage and the budget constraints imposed by the federal sequester, all military policies related to compensation and benefits are under scrutiny, which may weaken or remove these incentives in the future.

These early marriages may partly explain elevated rates of marital dissolution in the military relative to the population. Adler-Baeder, Pittman, and Taylor (2006) compared the prevalence of divorce and remarriage among military members with that in the population, finding that the percentage of military members divorced by age 30 was almost double that in the population. By age 40, rates for men had almost converged, but military women remained almost 20% more likely than civilian women to have experienced divorce.

Further investigation revealed that this relationship was more evident among men. Prevalence continued to rise with age, to over 80% among men age 50 and older in the general population, and 90% among men age 40 and older in the military. Why might men in the military be more likely to be married than civilians of comparable age? One possibility is that the education, employment, and benefits (e.g., health care, pension) that accompany even the most junior military positions (unlike many civilian jobs) are attractive resources to bring to marriage.

There was a strong positive association between parenthood and marriage among men. Regardless of period or cohort, military fathers were striking for their very high prevalence of marriage—over 90%—a level slightly higher than among comparable civilian fathers, and substantially higher than military or civilian women. Mothers in the military were more likely to be married than mothers in the general population when younger than 25, but progressively less likely to be married than civilian mothers at older ages. The demands of military jobs may make marriage particularly important for parents, who must ensure that children can be cared for during sometimes long and unpredictable work hours, as well as family separations due to training or deployments. Civilian mothers were about 18% as likely as fathers to be married; in the military, the percentage was 24%.

Men and women were more similar in more recent cohorts, but more different in recent periods and when older. Why were women in the military less likely than men to be married? One obvious possibility is that women who choose the nontraditional occupation of military service are less interested in marriage. Comparison of civilian and military women in the National Longitudinal Survey of Youth offers mixed evidence: Despite scoring lower on traditional family values, military women in that sample married earlier and "more pervasively" (Lundquist & Smith, 2005, p. 11) than civilians. Enlisted women were more likely to prefer childlessness but if they wanted children, to want the same number as civilian women.

Limitations

This study has several limitations. First, the data came from repeated cross-sectional surveys, not panel studies of the same individuals over time. Thus, we could not track the decisions of individual participants to enter or leave marriages or to have children. Instead, our results document patterns of group behavior within the general and military populations, and we cannot make inferences about the behaviors and motivations of individual members. Similar to patterns in the general population, the response rates to the military surveys fell noticeably over time, raising concerns about potential response bias. These concerns are partially addressed by the wide variety of administrative data used by the Defense Manpower Data Center to weight the collected data to be representative of the entire military population, including not only characteristics of military service but also personal and family demographic characteristics. Changes in the composition of the military over time may not have been fully captured by the demographic characteristics we studied, which may be particularly important given the occurrence of the first Gulf War in the early 1990s. Finally, our focus on marriage excluded nonmarital relationships, an increasingly important omission over time.

Future Directions

This study focused on the prevalence of marriage in large groups at specific points in time, but research has yet to thoroughly examine the marital *careers* of military members, meaning the unfolding of transitions related to marriage, child bearing, child rearing, divorce, and remarriage over the course of their military careers. Clear understanding of marital careers requires longitudinal data, which also would permit examination of the timing of exits from the military relative to early marriages, long deployments, dissatisfaction with quality of life, and marital dissolution. Such analyses are even more important given the potential impact of the past 15 years of war on the marital relationships and prospects of military personnel.

We focused in this study only on the likelihood that military members were married, which offers a very limited view of service members' relationships. Over time, adults in the United States have increasingly delayed or eschewed marriage in favor of cohabitation, meaning that the prevalence of marriage is becoming less useful as a meaningful indicator of health of the force. In addition, marital *status* provides no information about relationship *quality*, which is probably far more important for understanding the well-being and functioning of service members and their partners. Special efforts will likely be required to develop an adequate understanding of relationships involving military members who are members of sexual minority groups.

Findings from studies such as this can inform military policies, particularly given the degree to which marriage has historically been a "gate" to certain military benefits. The substantial differences between men's and women's experiences regarding marriage, which continue to be evident in more recent studies, suggest that it may be wise to consider the possible role of policies in shaping those differences. In addition, to the extent that the quality and stability of relationships are or should be indications of the health of the force, continued examination of men's and women's experiences as a function of historical, individual, and family time may prove enlightening.

REFERENCES

Adler-Baeder, F., Pittman, J. F., & Taylor, L. (2006). The prevalence of marital transitions in military families. *Journal of Divorce & Remarriage, 44,* 91–106. http://dx.doi.org/10.1300/J087v44n01_05

Bengtson, V. L., & Allen, K. R. (1993). The life course perspective applied to families over time. In P. G. Boss & W. J. Doherty (Eds.), *Sourcebook of family theories and methods: A contextual approach* (pp. 469–504). New York, NY: Plenum Press. http://dx.doi.org/10.1007/978-0-387-85764-0_19

Chambers, J. W. (1987). *To raise an army: The draft comes to modern America.* New York, NY: Free Press.

Defense Manpower Data Center. (2017). Active duty military strength historical reports 1954–1993 and 1994–2012. Retrieved from https://www.dmdc.osd.mil/appj/dwp/dwp_reports.jsp

Fields, J., & Casper, L. M. (2001). America's families and living arrangements: Population characteristics. *2000 Current Population Reports* (pp. 20–537). Washington, DC: U.S. Census Bureau.

Goldman, N. L. (1976). Trends in family patterns of U.S. Military Personnel during the 20th century. In N. L. Goldman & D. R. Segal (Eds.), *The social psychology of military service* (pp. 119–134). Beverly Hills, CA: Sage.

Harrell, M. C., Beckett, M. K., Chien, C. S., & Sollinger, J. (2002). *The status of gender integration in the military: Analysis of selected occupations.* Santa Monica, CA: Rand.

Hill, R. (1949). *Families under stress.* New York, NY: Harper & Brothers.

Institute of Medicine. (2013). *Returning home from Iraq and Afghanistan: Assessment of readjustment needs of veterans, service members and their families.* Washington, DC: National Academies Press.

Karney, B. R., Loughran, D. S., & Pollard, M. S. (2012). Comparing marital status and divorce status in civilian and military populations. *Journal of Family Issues, 33,* 1572–1594. http://dx.doi.org/10.1177/0192513X12439690

Lemmon, M., Whyman, M., & Teachman, J. (2009). Active-duty military service, cohabiting unions, and the transition to marriage. *Demographic Research, 20,* 195–208. http://dx.doi.org/10.4054/DemRes.2009.20.10

Levy, C. M., Thie, H., Sollinger, J. M., & Kawata, J. H. (2000). *Army PERSTEMPO in the post cold war era.* Santa Monica, CA: Rand.

Lundquist, J. H., & Smith, H. L. (2005). Family formation among women in the U.S. military: Evidence from the NLSY. *Journal of Marriage and Family, 67,* 1–13. http://dx.doi.org/10.1111/j.0022-2445.2005.00001.x

MacDermid Wadsworth, S. M. (2014, May). *Family structure issues.* Presentation as part of the panel on psychological and social aspects of health and well-being at the Women in Combat conference, Falls Church, VA.

Mutter, C. A., Aspy, C. L., Duniphan, J. P., Ford, B. F., Hamre, J. P., Horner, H., . . . Silberman, R. (2003). *Defense Department Advisory Committee on Women in the Services (DACOWITS) 2003 report.* Washington, DC: U.S. Department of Defense.

Negrusa, S., Negrusa, B., & Hosek, J. (2016). Deployment and divorce: An in-depth analysis by relevant demographic and military characteristics. In S. MacDermid Wadsworth & D. Riggs (Eds.), *War and family life* (pp. 35–54). New York, NY: Springer. http://dx.doi.org/10.1007/978-3-319-21488-7_3

Office of the Deputy Assistant Secretary of Defense, Military Community and Family Policy. (2014). *2013 demographics: Profile of the military community.* Arlington, VA: Author.

Office of the Under Secretary of Defense, Personnel and Readiness. (2014). *Population representation in the military services, 2012.* Washington, DC: U.S. Department of Defense. Retrieved from https://www.cna.org/pop-rep/2012/

Polich, J. M., & Sortor, R. (2001). *Deployments and Army personnel tempo.* Santa Monica, CA: Rand.

Schoen, R., & Standish, N. (2000). *The footprints of cohabitation: Results from marital status life tables for the U.S., 1995.* University Park: Pennsylvania State University, Population Research Institute.

Schumm, W. R., Rice, R. E., Bell, D. B., & Schuman, P. M. (1996). Marriage trends in the U.S. Army. *Psychological Reports, 78,* 771–784. http://dx.doi.org/10.2466/pr0.1996.78.3.771

Segal, D. R., & Segal, M. W. (1999). Changes in the American armed forces: Implications for military families. In P. McClure (Ed.), *Pathways to the future: A review of military family research* (pp. 1–10). Scranton, PA: Military Family Institute.

Segal, D. R., & Segal, M. W. (2004). America's military population. *Population Bulletin, 59,* 1–40.

Teachman, J. (2009). Military service, race, and the transition to marriage and cohabitation. *Journal of Family Issues, 30,* 1433–1454. http://dx.doi.org/10.1177/0192513X09336338

U.S. Census Bureau. (2016). *Figure MS-2: Median age at first marriage: 1890 to present.* Retrieved from https://www.census.gov/content/dam/Census/library/visualizations/time-series/demo/families-and-households/ms-2.pdf

U.S. Department of Defense. (2013). *Defense department rescinds direct combat exclusion rule; services to expand integration of women into previously restricted occupations and units* [News release 037-13]. Retrieved from http://archive.defense.gov/releases/release.aspx?releaseid=15784

Women's Research and Education Institute. (2004). *Chronology of significant legal and policy changes affecting women in the military: 1947–2003.* Washington, DC: Author.

Yang, Y. (2008). Social inequalities in happiness in the United States, 1972 to 2004: An age-period-cohort analysis. *American Sociological Review, 73,* 204–226. http://dx.doi.org/10.1177/000312240807300202

Yang, Y. (2010). Aging, cohorts, and methods. In R. Binstock & L. K. George (Eds.), *The handbook of aging and the social sciences* (7th ed., pp. 17–30). Amsterdam, the Netherlands: Elsevier/Academic Press.

Yang, Y., & Land, K. C. (2006). A mixed models approach to the age-period-cohort analysis of repeated cross-section surveys: Trends in verbal test scores. *Sociological Methodology, 36,* 75–97. http://dx.doi.org/10.1111/j.1467-9531.2006.00175.x

5

LABOR FORCE PARTICIPATION AMONG OLDER VETERANS

ALAIR MacLEAN, MEREDITH A. KLEYKAMP,
AND JOHN ROBERT WARREN

This chapter examines whether veterans tend to leave the labor force earlier than nonveterans, and if this difference has changed over the last four and a half decades among men who were eligible to serve from before World War II to the Vietnam era. We use Current Population Survey (CPS) data from 1967 to 2010 to describe trends in work among men at middle age and older. The results suggest that today men generally are more likely than in the past to have left the labor force between the ages of 55 and 69. Trends toward increasing rates of retirement appear to have slowed for all ages and possibly reversed for those ages 60 to 69 starting in the early 2000s. Veterans as a group were more likely to leave the labor force at younger ages than nonveterans; however, this effect was seen primarily among those who came of age before 1934 and between 1964 and 1974 (the pre–World War II and Vietnam eras) and not among the members of intervening cohorts. Veterans differ most from nonveterans when labor force participation rates are highest. This difference

http://dx.doi.org/10.1037/0000061-006
Long-Term Outcomes of Military Service: The Health and Well-Being of Aging Veterans, A. Spiro III, R. A. Settersten Jr., and C. M. Aldwin (Editors)

may stem from veterans' access to a consistent set of benefits over the 50-year period that afford them opportunities for early retirement even when macro-social conditions are less favorable for other workers.

In fall 2013, the U.S. Congress proposed reducing funds for military pensions. Journalists, politicians, and activists decried the move as an attempt to renege on promises that had been made to compensate military retirees for their sacrifices, and the proposal ultimately did not succeed (Lowrey, 2014). Although this proposed policy change led to public outrage, researchers and journalists have rarely explored questions related to military retirement or the broader question of veterans' labor force participation at older ages.

Much is known, however, about the broad trends regarding how long men continue to participate in the labor force or, said another way, the ages at which men retire. The term *labor force* refers to people who are either working or who are unemployed and looking for work. Until the middle of the 20th century, it was unusual for people to retire (Warner, Hayward, & Hardy, 2010). At the turn of that century, more than two thirds of men continued working past age 65. Around that time, men increasingly began to retire. By the mid-1940s, 90% of men between the ages of 55 and 64 were still in the labor force, but just 47% of those older than 65 were (Costa, 1998, 1999). By 1998, 68% of those between the ages of 55 and 64 were still in the labor force, but only 17% of men older than 65 were. This trend toward retirement at younger ages appears to have slowed in the 1990s (Costa, 1998, 1999), and now men have started to work past traditional retirement ages at greater rates (Tang, Choi, & Goode, 2013).

Scholars have demonstrated that a number of factors, such as gender, age, attitudes, income, and education, affect when and how people retire (Wang & Shi, 2014). These individual characteristics interact with meso-level traits, such as the attributes of the organizations in which people work, as well as political and economic factors at the macrolevel (Wang & Shi, 2014). Yet little is known about the impact on retirement of early life experiences such as military service.

Accordingly, this chapter examines the rates at which men, particularly veterans, leave the labor force early, that is, between the ages of 55 and 69, and how those rates have changed over the past four and a half decades. Over that period, men have had different chances both of military service when they were younger and of remaining in the labor force when they were older. The chapter builds on the life course concepts of the timing of events in people's lives, as well as that of location in time and place (Elder & Johnson, 2002). It describes how the timing of withdrawal from the labor force, or retirement, has changed and why. It also assesses how veterans may differ from non-veterans in the chances that they will retire and how those relative chances may have varied according to location in historical time, or cohort membership.

It assesses whether there have been cohort differences in the shares of both types of men who left the labor force at particular ages. It extends previous research looking at retirement at relatively young ages, between 55 and 69, to veterans. It compares veterans to nonveterans in different age categories and across different cohorts.

The chapter proceeds according to the following plan. First, it reviews research and theory regarding retirement, focusing on early retirement, among American workers more broadly. Next, it examines how veterans may be expected to differ from those broad trends. It then presents the data and analyses regarding labor force participation among men who became eligible to serve in cohorts across the 4 decades stretching from the years before World War II through the Vietnam era. Briefly, the findings suggest that there have been changes in the overall likelihood that men would leave the labor force and in the position of veterans relative to nonveterans, with men who became eligible to serve before World War II and in the Vietnam era military occupying a distinct position compared with those who came of age in the World War II, Korean, and post-Korean Cold War eras. The findings demonstrate that veterans were not consistently more likely than nonveterans to retire early, but they appear to have been less susceptible to overall trends in retirement.

FACTORS INFLUENCING RETIREMENT TRENDS

According to the age stratification perspective, people engage in particular activities and roles in ways that are age graded (Riley, Kahn, & Foner, 1994). Theorists have argued that people adopt different roles through the life course according to their age. In the ideal type, people gain education when they are young, and retire and live lives of leisure when they are old. They work and form families when they are between these two extremes (Riley et al., 1994).

History of Retirement in the United States

In the larger historical picture, however, Americans have only recently begun to retire. Up until the 1940s, more than half of American men remained in the labor force after age 65 (Costa, 1998). Scholars have observed that retirement is not a one-time event but a process in which people imagine, plan, and then finally leave the labor force (Beehr, 2014). Indeed, people may not stay permanently retired. They may take "bridge jobs," or they may return to the labor force after leaving (Warner et al., 2010). Accordingly, there are at least eight different ways that researchers have measured retirement status, including nonparticipation in the labor force, which is the measure used in the following analyses (Wang & Shi, 2014).

The concept of retirement has thus changed dramatically over the last century and a half, in part because of changes in both the average length of people's lives and the public and private funds available to people who stop working. The first pensions were introduced for Union army veterans of the Civil War, but these required veterans to establish that they had been disabled because of their military service (Costa, 1998; Skocpol, 1993). In the 1920s and 1930s, poor people began to be able to receive funds to enable them to stop working at older ages from state-level programs that were the precursor to the Social Security system. During the Depression, the federal government expanded these programs to provide pensions to everyone who worked and paid into the system (Costa, 1998).

The Policy Context

As mentioned previously, people retire because of a combination of individual, mesolevel, and macrolevel factors. Previous research has demonstrated that people leave or persist in the labor force at older ages in part because of macrolevel factors. For example, workers are more likely to leave the labor force when social security benefits are more generous (Henretta & Lee, 1996).

In addition to these governmental benefits, former workers began to be able to draw pensions from private employers around the start of Social Security, under what are called *defined benefit plans*. Under these plans, they were guaranteed a certain level of income regardless of market forces (Wang & Shultz, 2010). More recently, private employers have begun to shift from these defined benefit pensions to *defined contribution plans*, in which workers invest in third-party plans that are subject to market risks and then can draw on this money in retirement (Clark & Strauss, 2008). Under defined contribution plans, then, retirees do not have a guaranteed level of income. Scholars have argued that this shift from defined benefit to contribution has made leaving the labor force less attractive to and more risky for workers (Clark & Strauss, 2008; Shuey & O'Rand, 2004).

At the same time, as workers began to see retirement as less financially viable because of the shift to defined contribution pension plans, they also were no longer required to stop working at age 65. Since the 1940s, workers had been required to retire at age 65 in the majority of government jobs and in about a third of jobs with private employers (Barker & Clark, 1980). In 1978, Congress updated the Age Discrimination in Employment Act, which had been passed a decade earlier, to prohibit mandatory retirement for federal workers and raise the age at which private employers could require workers to retire from 65 to 70. In 1986, the law was amended again to remove any upper age limit (Lahey, 2010).

Individual Finances

People retire on the basis of both factors that make retirement attractive and factors that make working difficult, which can vary historically. According to previous research, they retire early because of a number of sometimes competing factors related to wealth, unemployment, and health. The findings are mixed and sometimes contradictory regarding the impact on retirement of wealth. According to some research, wealthier workers are more likely to retire at younger ages in the United States and the Netherlands (Beehr, Glazer, Nielson, & Farmer, 2000; Bloemen, 2011). Indeed, older Americans appear to have postponed retirement if they lost wealth during the recent economic downturn (McFall, 2011). According to other research, however, workers did not choose to retire on the basis of increases and decreases in their own wealth between 1980 and 2009, but instead because of increases in the external unemployment rate (Coile & Levine, 2007, 2011a, 2011b). Overall, these findings suggest that people with higher socioeconomic status may retire earlier than those with lower socioeconomic status.

Other scholars, however, have produced findings that suggest that people with lower socioeconomic status may leave the labor market earlier, especially if they have relatively poor prospects for finding work. People retire at younger ages if they have recently been unemployed (Bould, 1980). They are also more likely to do so when aggregate unemployment rates are high than when such rates are low (Coile & Levine, 2007, 2011a, 2011b). They may be responding to the likelihood of losing a job and not being able to find another. In contrast to the findings regarding wealth, these results suggest that people with lower status may retire earlier than those with higher status.

Health

Researchers have also produced contradictory findings regarding the impact of health on early retirement. People are more likely to retire early if they are in poor health, at least partly because their health limits their ability to continue working (de Wind et al., 2013; Kubicek, Korunka, Hoonakker, & Raymo, 2010). Among married workers who grew up in the 1950s, those who were in better health worked till they were older (Kubicek et al., 2010). Yet, in a qualitative study of Dutch retirees, respondents had also planned to retire early to be able to enjoy their retirement if they were in good health (de Wind et al., 2013).

Thus, people may be more likely to retire early for either positive or negative reasons. With respect to positive stimuli, they may retire at younger ages because they have access to better pension plans or greater individual wealth. On the negative side, they may leave the labor force sooner if they are in worse health or have recently been unemployed.

HOW RETIREMENT MIGHT DIFFER ACCORDING
TO MILITARY SERVICE

The following section describes how people may differ in labor force participation at older ages based on veteran status. Little is known about retirement among veterans, though more is known about the characteristics and policies that may influence their labor force participation more generally. Previous research on the impact of service on other outcomes suggests potentially conflicting conclusions regarding how one might expect such service to relate to retirement. Veterans may continue working later or stop earlier than nonveterans because of factors associated with preservice characteristics, physical health, socioeconomic success, or military pensions, and the impact of at least some of these factors may vary by cohort.

Veterans and Early Retirement

Apparently only one article examines whether veterans are more likely to retire early, and it focuses not on behavior but on plans. According to this article, among 40- to 64-year-old men in 1984, veterans were more likely than nonveterans to plan to leave the labor force, which the authors speculated is because veterans have access to more generous governmental benefits (Holtmann, Ullmann, Fronstin, & Longino, 1994). Because there is little previous research on this topic, we present relatively general and competing predictions regarding the chances that veterans will retire early.

Veterans have had different average characteristics before their service because of selection into the military, which has varied across cohorts. They have alternately been positively or negatively selected into the armed forces. For example, World War II veterans enlisted with more advantages in terms of health and family background than men who did not serve during that war (Angrist & Krueger, 1994). By contrast, Vietnam veterans entered the armed forces with fewer advantages, on average, than their peers who did not serve (Conley & Heerwig, 2012). Service members have also differed demographically from civilians, and these differences have changed over time. Whites were more likely than Blacks to enlist during the Korean and post-Korean eras, whereas Blacks were more likely to do so during the Vietnam War (MacLean, 2011). Thus, veterans have had different characteristics depending on when they became eligible to serve, which may be associated with greater or lesser chances that they will retire.

Different Military Experiences

In addition, some service members have served during war, whereas others have served during peace, leading to different risks of seeing combat and being injured, which can affect health and socioeconomic attainment. People who serve during wartime are at risk of getting injured, either mentally or physically, with long-term effects (Elder, Clipp, Brown, Martin, & Friedman, 2009). Combat veterans, in turn, are more likely to be disabled and unemployed than veterans who did not experience combat (MacLean, 2010). If they have worse health on average, these men may also be more likely to retire early.

Veterans' Socioeconomic Trajectories

Men have had more or less success in the labor market if they served in the military, which may influence the age at which they retire. Veterans were more likely than nonveterans to be employed, for example, among men who served during the early part of the contemporary volunteer era, which began in 1973 (Angrist, 1998). Among others who have served more recently, however, they were less likely (Kleykamp, 2013). Few scholars have, however, evaluated such success at relatively older ages or among older cohorts. As just described, people are more likely to retire if they have been recently unemployed; thus, we expect the chances of early retirement among veterans to vary across cohorts.

Veterans also seem to have had different levels of earnings depending on when they served. Men earned more if they served during World War II than if they did not (Teachman & Tedrow, 2004). Research on earnings among Vietnam veterans has produced mixed findings, with some researchers showing that these men earned less (Angrist, 1990) and others showing that they earned more than their nonveteran counterparts (Teachman, 2004). These findings suggest that the association of military service with different outcomes likely varies across cohorts. If veterans have more socioeconomic success than nonveterans, on average, then they may be more likely to leave the labor force at younger ages.

Military Pensions

Veterans, however, may have had consistent chances of retirement over the last 50 years because military pensions have varied little. Although retirement plans and pensions have changed more for people who retire from private institutions, service members have had benefits that have changed less if they retire from the armed forces. Since the end of World War II, Congress has rarely changed the retirement benefits available to those who served in the armed forces. American veterans have been provided with some post-service income since at least the colonial era (U.S. Department of Defense, Office of the Actuary, 2007). After the Civil War, they received pensions if they were disabled. During the draft era, stretching from World War II to the

Vietnam era, the government extended these pensions to veterans who were not disabled. In general, service members who retire after serving at least 20 years receive a guaranteed portion of their income for life (U.S. Department of Defense, Office of the Actuary, 2007). Thus, for example, a person who retires after 20 years receives 50% of the income they would have earned if they remained in the armed forces. Service members who leave the armed forces before serving 20 years and become veterans do not receive these benefits. Veterans may therefore retire at younger ages, on average, than non-veterans, because at least some of them have had access to more consistent packages of benefits, in particular a defined benefit pension that is becoming less frequently available to individuals in the private sector (Kleykamp & Hipes, 2014).

They may, however, be affected by the factors that cause people to retire early for more negative reasons. They may leave the labor force because they have worse health on average or are more likely to be unemployed. There are few data available on what fraction of veterans have access to different kinds of benefits including retirement pensions available to those serving 20 or more years and/or disability compensation, which varies based on the severity of any service-connected disabilities. Our own tabulations of CPS Veteran Supplement data suggests that less than 15% of veterans of recent All-Volunteer Force cohorts served for 20 or more years, making them eligible for retirement pensions, whereas 8% to 9% of veterans from Vietnam and Korean War cohorts served for 20 or more years (King et al., 2010). The Congressional Budget Office estimated that in 2013, 16% of Vietnam veterans and 22% of Gulf War veterans were receiving some VA disability compensation (Bass & Golding, 2014). Rising rates of disability compensation receipt have been associated with reduced labor force participation among older veterans (Autor, Duggan, Greenberg, & Lyle, 2016; Coile, Duggan, & Guo, 2015).

METHODS

We used data from the 1967 to 2010 CPS to assess patterns of retirement, or labor force participation, among men ages 55 to 69. The CPS is conducted monthly and consists of rotating panels of 60,000 households (U.S. Census Bureau, 2006). The data are accessed through the Integrated Public Use Microdata Series (King et al., 2010).

Because the CPS does not include a direct measure of retirement, researchers using these data have examined related questions by looking at labor force participation. To sharpen the focus on early retirement, the following analyses are based on the inverse measure, which captures the share of men not in the labor force (Coile & Levine, 2011b). Men may, of course, be included in this category even if they are not formally retired. They could also report neither working nor looking for work at one time, but later reenter the labor force. Thus the measure presents a proxy for retirement, albeit a strong one, because the data are provided by relatively older men ages 55 and up.

The samples are limited to men because the survey only began to ask women if they served in the military in 1984. The analyses focus on early retirement, or retirement before or shortly after the normative age of 65, by looking at men in 5-year age ranges: 55 to 59, 60 to 64, and 65 to 69. We separate men into two basic categories: veterans (those who had served on active duty in the armed forces) and nonveterans (those who did not).

The analyses present differences between veterans defined by cohorts based on the year that respondents turned 18, thus becoming eligible to serve in the military (see Online Appendix A, available at http://pubs.apa.org/books/supp/spiro/). This measure allows us to compare veterans with nonveterans of roughly comparable ages. Among veterans who served in the postdraft era that began in 1974, only the oldest turned 55 in 2011. The analyses therefore focus on men who were eligible to serve during the draft era. The measure of cohort is based on the years in which respondents turned 18 and captures patterns of service among veterans applied to all respondents. It combines the CPS definitions of dates of wars with the modal years during which veterans reported serving in the military to generate a variable measuring CPS potential service cohort. It categorizes all respondents based on the year they turned 18 into the era during which they would potentially have served, allocating them to one of five service eras: pre-World War II (< 1934), World War II (1934–1947), Korean War (1948–1954), post-Korean Cold War (1955–1963), and Vietnam War (1964–1974).

FINDINGS

We calculated the rates at which respondents reported that they were not in the labor force by the years in which men turned 18. Figures 5.1 and 5.2 present these retirement rates according to 5-year age groups (55–59, 60–64, and 65–69) and by year. Figure 5.3 presents these same rates but this time by cohorts in which the respondents were eligible to serve in the military (pre-World War II, World War II, Korean War, post-Korean Cold War, and Vietnam War).

Figure 5.1 contains the percentage of men not in the labor force by age and year, which shows an increase in early retirement followed by a plateau or decline among men depending on age. Between 1967 and 1985, men had increasingly retired by their late 60s; the proportions of these men who were no longer in the labor force increased from 55% to 75%. These shares

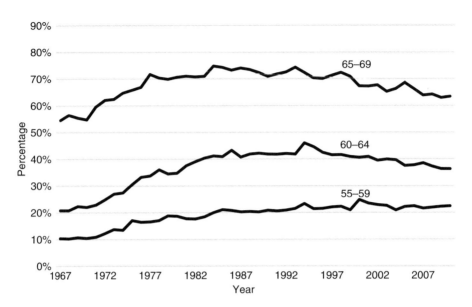

Figure 5.1. Percentage of men not in the labor force by age and year. Data from 1967–2010 Current Population Surveys, men between the ages of 55 and 69.

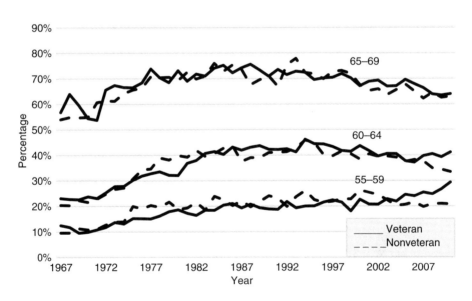

Figure 5.2. Percentage of men not in the labor force by age, year, and veteran status. Data from 1967–2010 Current Population Surveys, men between the ages of 55 and 69.

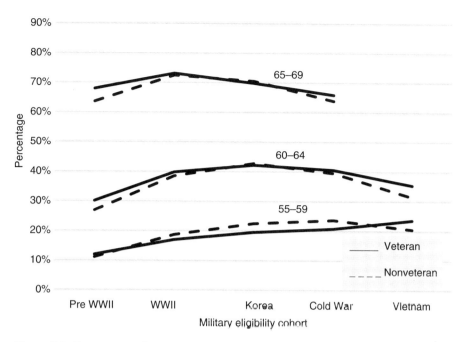

Figure 5.3. Percentage of men not in the labor force by age, military eligibility cohort, and veteran status. Data from 1967–2010 Current Population Surveys, men between the ages of 55 and 69. WWII = World War II.

remained above 70% during the 1990s, at which point they began to decline. In the most recent year, men had retired at these ages at a somewhat lower rate of 65%. Among men between the ages of 60 and 64, the share who were not in the labor force doubled in the 3 decades between 1967 and 1997, rising from 20% to over 40%. In the early 2000s, the share declined somewhat, with the rate for the most recent years under 40%. Similarly, the share of men who were not in the labor force between the ages of 55 and 59 also doubled from 10% in the late 1960s, to more than 20% in the 2000s. Among men in this age group, the share retired has plateaued, remaining slightly above 20%.

Figure 5.2 presents these trends separately for veterans and nonveterans. Both groups follow the same general pattern described previously, with first an increase and then a plateau or decline in the shares not in the labor force. According to the figure, veterans were neither consistently more nor less likely than nonveterans to retire at any of the age categories throughout the period. This finding contradicts the prediction that these men would leave the labor force at younger ages. Veterans were more likely to be retired at both the beginning and end of 4 decades than nonveterans, particularly between the ages of 55 and 64. They were less likely to have left the labor force between the ages of 55 and 64 in the mid-1970s. These findings suggest that although there is no general pattern, there may be fluctuations by cohort in the relative chances that veterans will retire at particular ages.

Figure 5.3 presents the data organized by cohorts on the basis of when respondents were potentially eligible to serve in the military. Among those who became eligible to serve before World War II, veterans were slightly more likely than nonveterans to retire in all age categories. Although Vietnam veterans are not yet observed when they are between the ages of 65 and 69, they were more likely to have left the labor force than their nonveteran counterparts at the younger ages. Among those who became eligible to serve in the Korean and post-Korean Cold War eras, veterans were less likely to have retired in the youngest age category. These findings indicate that the relative chances of retirement among veterans have varied by cohort.

DISCUSSION

According to the preceding analyses, veterans were more likely than nonveterans to have left the labor force at older ages among those eligible to serve during the pre-World War II and Vietnam eras and less likely to do so in the intervening Korean War and Cold War eras. Veterans were not consistently more or less likely, across the four and a half decades, to have retired between the ages of 55 and 69 than nonveterans. These findings contradict the one previous analysis of veteran retirement that suggested that they were more likely to at least plan to retire early (Holtmann et al., 1994). They suggest that the association of service with retirement has varied across cohorts.

Veterans were less susceptible than nonveterans to the overall trends in retirement. When the odds of early retirement were higher, there were fewer differences on average between veterans and nonveterans. However, when those odds were relatively low, veterans were more likely than nonveterans to retire early. Taken together, these findings may reflect the fact that at least some veterans had access to a more consistent set of benefits than did nonveterans, which may have supported their earlier retirement than their nonserving peers. Alternatively, they may indicate that veterans have had rates of ill health and unemployment that lead them to leave the labor force at a more consistent rate. The availability of service-connected disability compensation may combine both influences, allowing those who might continue working with health problems to retire early because of income supports.

These same patterns may not hold in the future for men who have grown up since the end of the Vietnam War. Among these men, at least some veterans may hold a relatively privileged position with respect to retirement. They will continue to have access to relatively generous retirement benefits, specifically a defined benefit pension, whereas nonveterans will increasingly have to draw on pensions that have shifted to the lower defined contribution plans (Kleykamp & Hipes, 2014).

The preceding analyses are limited in that they measure retirement indirectly. They cannot, therefore, evaluate whether cross-sectional labor force patterns represent trends in permanent or only temporary retirement. People may increasingly come to move in and out of the labor force at older ages, suggesting a new "phased retirement" (Pleau & Shauman, 2013; Purcell, 2000). Future research should extend the preceding analyses on cohort experiences to examine whether veterans are more or less likely to experiences these shifts in participation during this portion of the life course.

Future research should examine whether veterans retire because of the same combination of factors as do nonveterans. Veterans may, for example, be more or less sensitive to changes in unemployment, both their own and the overall rate, or to changes in Social Security benefit. They may also be more or less likely than men who never served to retire because of ill health.

Nevertheless, our findings suggest that military service during the draft era was not consistently associated with trends in early retirement. Rather, veterans appear to follow the broad trends in labor force participation at older ages seen among nonveterans. With the exception of those who grew up before World War II and during the Vietnam War, they were not more likely to retire early. Thus, as with other outcomes, Vietnam veterans may have had different later lives compared with their nonveteran counterparts than did those of other cohorts. To derive policy recommendations from these empirical findings, future research should examine whether such differences stem from positive consequences of service, such as the relatively generous pension plans, or those that are negative, including poor health and unemployment, or a combination of the two, such as the extension of service-connected disability status to prevalent chronic health conditions (Autor et al., 2016).

REFERENCES

Angrist, J. D. (1990). Lifetime earnings and the Vietnam era draft lottery: Evidence from Social Security administrative records. *The American Economic Review*, 80, 313–336.

Angrist, J. D. (1998). Estimating the labor market impact of voluntary military service using social security data on military applicants. *Econometrica*, 66, 249–288. http://dx.doi.org/10.2307/2998558

Angrist, J. D., & Krueger, A. B. (1994). Why do World War II veterans earn more than nonveterans? *Journal of Labor Economics*, 12, 74–97. http://dx.doi.org/10.1086/298344

Autor, D., Duggan, M., Greenberg, K., & Lyle, D. (2016). The impact of disability benefits on labor supply: Evidence from the VA's Disability Compensation Program. *American Economic Journal. Applied Economics, 8*(3), 31–68. http://dx.doi.org/10.1257/app.20150158

Barker, D. T., & Clark, R. L. (1980). Mandatory retirement and labor-force participation of respondents in the Retirement History Study. *Social Security Bulletin, 43*(11), 20–29, 55.

Bass, E., & Golding, H. (2014). *Veterans' disability compensation: Trends and policy options.* Washington, DC: Congress of the United States, Congressional Budget Office. Retrieved from https://www.cbo.gov/sites/default/files/113th-congress-2013-2014/reports/45615-VADisability_2.pdf

Beehr, T. A. (2014). To retire or not to retire: That is not the question. *Journal of Organizational Behavior, 35,* 1093–1108. http://dx.doi.org/10.1002/job.1965

Beehr, T. A., Glazer, S., Nielson, N. L., & Farmer, S. J. (2000). Work and nonwork predictors of employees' retirement ages. *Journal of Vocational Behavior, 57,* 206–225. http://dx.doi.org/10.1006/jvbe.1999.1736

Bloemen, H. G. (2011). The effect of private wealth on the retirement rate: An empirical analysis. *Economica, 78,* 637–655. http://dx.doi.org/10.1111/j.1468-0335.2010.00845.x

Bould, S. (1980). Unemployment as a factor in early retirement decisions. *American Journal of Economics and Sociology, 39,* 123–136. http://dx.doi.org/10.1111/j.1536-7150.1980.tb01622.x

Clark, G. L., & Strauss, K. (2008). Individual pension-related risk propensities: The effects of socio-demographic characteristics and a spousal pension entitlement on risk attitudes. *Ageing & Society, 28,* 847–874. http://dx.doi.org/10.1017/S0144686X08007083

Coile, C., Duggan, M., & Guo, A. (2015). Veterans' labor force participation: What role does the VA's Disability Compensation Program play? *The American Economic Review, 105,* 131–136. http://dx.doi.org/10.1257/aer.p20151062

Coile, C. C., & Levine, P. B. (2007). Labor market shocks and retirement: Do government programs matter? *Journal of Public Economics, 91,* 1902–1919. http://dx.doi.org/10.1016/j.jpubeco.2007.01.005

Coile, C. C., & Levine, P. B. (2011a). The market crash and mass layoffs: How the current economic crisis may affect retirement. *The B.E. Journal of Economic Analysis & Policy, 11*(1). Advance online publication. http://dx.doi.org/10.2202/1935-1682.2568

Coile, C. C., & Levine, P. B. (2011b). Recessions, retirement, and Social Security. *The American Economic Review, 101*(3), 23–28. http://dx.doi.org/10.1257/aer.101.3.23

Conley, D., & Heerwig, J. (2012). The long-term effects of military conscription on mortality: Estimates from the Vietnam-era draft lottery. *Demography, 49,* 841–855. http://dx.doi.org/10.1007/s13524-012-0103-2

Costa, D. L. (1998). The evolution of retirement: Summary of a research project. *The American Economic Review*, 88, 232–236.

Costa, D. L. (1999, May). *Has the trend toward early retirement reversed?* Paper presented at the First Annual Joint Conference for the Retirement Research Consortium, Washington, DC.

de Wind, A., Geuskens, G. A., Reeuwijk, K. G., Westerman, M. J., Ybema, J. F., Burdorf, A., . . . van der Beek, A. J. (2013). Pathways through which health influences early retirement: A qualitative study. BMC *Public Health, 13,* Article 292. Retrieved from https://bmcpublichealth.biomedcentral.com/articles/10.1186/1471-2458-13-292

Elder, G. H., Jr., Clipp, E. C., Brown, J. S., Martin, L. R., & Friedman, H. S. (2009). The lifelong mortality risks of World War II experiences. *Research on Aging, 31,* 391–412.

Elder, G. H., Jr., & Johnson, M. K. (2002). The life course and aging: Challenges, lessons, and new directions. In R. A. Settersten, Jr. (Ed.), *Invitation to the life course: Toward new understandings of later life* (pp. 49–81). Amityville, NY: Baywood.

Henretta, J. C., & Lee, H. (1996). Cohort differences in men's late-life labor force participation. Work and Occupations, 23, 214–235. http://dx.doi.org/10.1177/0730888496023002005

Holtmann, A. G., Ullmann, S. G., Fronstin, P., & Longino, C. F., Jr. (1994). The early retirement plans of women and me: An empirical application. *Applied Economics, 26,* 591–601. http://dx.doi.org/10.1080/00036849400000029

King, M., Ruggles, S., Alexander, J. T., Flood, S., Genadek, K., Schroeder, M. B., . . . Vick, R. (2010). Integrated Public Use Microdata Series, Current Population Survey (Version 3.0) [Machine-readable database]. Minneapolis: University of Minnesota.

Kleykamp, M. (2013). Unemployment, earnings and enrollment among post 9/11 veterans. *Social Science Research, 42,* 836–851. http://dx.doi.org/10.1016/j.ssresearch.2012.12.017

Kleykamp, M., & Hipes, C. (2014). Social programs for soldiers and veterans. In D. Béland, C. Howard, & K. J. Morgan (Eds.), *The Oxford handbook of US social policy* (pp. 565–584). New York, NY: Oxford University Press.

Kubicek, B., Korunka, C., Hoonakker, P., & Raymo, J. M. (2010). Work and family characteristics as predictors of early retirement in married men and women. *Research on Aging, 32,* 467–498. http://dx.doi.org/10.1177/0164027510364120

Lahey, J. N. (2010). International comparison of age discrimination laws. *Research on Aging, 32,* 679–697. http://dx.doi.org/10.1177/0164027510379348

Lowrey, W. (2014, February 12). Senate votes to restore cuts to military retirees. *Washington Post.*

MacLean, A. (2010). The things they carry: Combat, disability, and unemployment among U.S. men. *American Sociological Review, 75,* 563–585. http://dx.doi.org/10.1177/0003122410374085

MacLean, A. (2011). The stratification of military service and combat exposure, 1934–1994. *Social Science Research, 40,* 336–348. http://dx.doi.org/10.1016/j.ssresearch.2010.04.006

McFall, B. H. (2011). Crash and wait? The impact of the Great Recession on retirement planning of older Americans. *The American Economic Review, 101*(3), 40–44. http://dx.doi.org/10.1257/aer.101.3.40

Pleau, R., & Shauman, K. (2013). Trends and correlates of post-retirement employment, 1977–2009. *Human Relations, 66,* 113–141. http://dx.doi.org/10.1177/0018726712447003

Purcell, P. J. (2000). Older workers: Employment and retirement trends. *Monthly Labor Review, 123*(10), 19–30.

Riley, M. W., Kahn, R. L., & Foner, A. (1994). *Age and structural lag: Society's failure to provide meaningful opportunities in work, family, and leisure.* New York, NY: Wiley.

Shuey, K. M., & O'Rand, A. M. (2004). New risks for workers: Pensions, labor markets, and gender. *Annual Review of Sociology, 30,* 453–477. http://dx.doi.org/10.1146/annurev.soc.30.012703.110534

Skocpol, T. (1993). America first social security system: The expansion of benefits for Civil War veterans. *Political Science Quarterly, 108,* 85–116. http://dx.doi.org/10.2307/2152487

Tang, F., Choi, E., & Goode, R. (2013). Older Americans employment and retirement. *Ageing International, 38,* 82–94. http://dx.doi.org/10.1007/s12126-012-9162-3

Teachman, J. D. (2004). Military service during the Vietnam era: Were there consequences for subsequent civilian earnings? *Social Forces, 83,* 709–730. http://dx.doi.org/10.1353/sof.2005.0021

Teachman, J. D., & Tedrow, L. M. (2004). Wages, earnings, and occupational status: Did World War II veterans receive a premium? *Social Science Research, 33,* 581–605. http://dx.doi.org/10.1016/j.ssresearch.2003.09.007

U.S. Census Bureau. (2006, October). *Current Population Survey: Design and methodology* (Technical Paper 66). Retrieved from https://www.census.gov/prod/2006pubs/tp-66.pdf

U.S. Department of Defense, Office of the Actuary. (2007). *Valuation of the military retirement system.* Washington, DC: Author.

Wang, M., & Shi, J. (2014). Psychological research on retirement. *Annual Review of Psychology, 65,* 209–233. http://dx.doi.org/10.1146/annurev-psych-010213-115131

Wang, M., & Shultz, K. S. (2010). Employee retirement: A review and recommendations for future investigation. *Journal of Management, 36,* 172–206. http://dx.doi.org/10.1177/0149206309347957

Warner, D. F., Hayward, M. D., & Hardy, M. A. (2010). The retirement life course in America at the dawn of the twenty-first century. *Population Research and Policy Review, 29,* 893–919. http://dx.doi.org/10.1007/s11113-009-9173-2

6

NATIONALISM AND PATRIOTISM AMONG WORLD WAR II VETERANS AND THEIR BABY-BOOM CHILDREN

MERRIL SILVERSTEIN, ANDREW S. LONDON,
AND JANET M. WILMOTH

Because of factors that select individuals into military service and the socialization experiences that occur during the active-duty period, there are good reasons to expect that veterans will express heightened patriotic feelings and a preference for assertive foreign policy relative to nonveterans. However, empirical evidence provides a mixed picture about whether military service—particularly during times of war—induces support or wariness in relation to involvement in future wars and enhances or suppresses patriotic fervor. The magnitude of World War II and its consequences—including the Holocaust, and the bombing of Hiroshima and Nagasaki, which ushered in the atomic age—may have amplified the enhancement or suppression of nationalism–patriotism among those who served in that era.

In this chapter, we examine how World War II–era veteran status shapes men's nationalistic and patriotic values, and how those values are passed on to, as well as persist among, their children, who form part of the baby-boom

http://dx.doi.org/10.1037/0000061-007
Long-Term Outcomes of Military Service: The Health and Well-Being of Aging Veterans, A. Spiro III, R. A. Settersten Jr., and C. M. Aldwin (Editors)

cohort. In the parental generation, we distinguish between veterans who served during World War II, veterans of other periods, and nonveterans. We assess men's values toward nationalism and patriotism at a time of political tumult—during the Vietnam War—25 to 30 years after the end of World War II. In this same era, we examine similar values among these men's adolescent and young-adult children who are members of the baby-boom cohort. Finally, we examine the stability of nationalism–patriotism in this younger cohort as it reaches midlife during the first decade of the 21st century.

ATTITUDES TOWARD NATIONALISM–PATRIOTISM IN RELATION TO VETERAN STATUS

The nature of the relationship between individuals and the countries in which they reside is parsimoniously defined in terms of expressions of nationalism and patriotism (Blank & Schmidt, 2003)—two related but independent components of the more general concept of national identity. Kosterman and Feshbach (1989) discussed nationalism as support for an aggressive or dominant posture toward other countries, and patriotism as commitment to the ideals or virtues represented in the core values of the nation.

The literature that addresses veteran status and attitudes toward nationalism and patriotism is inconclusive as to whether there is a relationship and its direction. Many studies find little or no difference between veterans (including those exposed to various foreign wars) and nonveterans with respect to a wide range of specific political attitudes toward domestic and foreign policy issues (Bachman & Jennings, 1975; Grote, Frieze, & Schmidt, 1997; Jennings & Markus, 1976, 1977; London, Wilmoth, & Dutton, 2017; Phillips, 1973; Segal & Segal, 1976). However, using a nationally representative sample, Schreiber (1979) found that World War II–era veterans were less likely than nonveterans to think that the United States should take an activist role in world affairs. This result held even after controlling for education and age, and serves as the most important touchstone for the current study.

Research on veterans from eras other than World War II is instructive, but findings are also inconclusive. Supporting the hypothesis that wartime service would strengthen an anti-interventionist stance, evidence from a quasi-experimental study showed that Vietnam-era college-bound males who held low 1969 draft lottery numbers—which increased their probability of serving during the Vietnam War—became more antiwar relative to those with higher draft lottery numbers (Erikson & Stoker, 2011). However, among Vietnam War–era veterans, other findings indicate a positive relationship between military service and international assertiveness as a policy preference (Frey-Wouters & Laufer, 1986). Vietnam veterans expressed more support than nonveterans for military preparedness (Ivie, Gimbel, & Elder, 1991), as well as stronger endorsement of the Persian Gulf War (Grote, Frieze, & Schmidt, 1997). More recent research using nationally representative data and compares veterans to nonveterans, while controlling for a broad range of demographic and premilitary characteristics, has reported that veterans have more confidence in the military; favor more spending on the military, armaments, and defense; favor less spending on foreign aid; and see more beneficial consequences of patriotic feelings (London et al., 2017).

Taken together, findings in this research area seem especially sensitive to the particular outcome constructs and measures used, the period of military service considered, and the types of control variables applied. Although veterans tend to support the military and particular wars more than nonveterans, they appear to offer weaker support for the conditions and policies that may lead to war.

MILITARY VETERANS, EDUCATION, AND NATIONALISM–PATRIOTISM

The political values of veterans, particularly those who served during World War II, are also likely to be influenced by the access to education that they were afforded through the Servicemen's Readjustment Act of 1944 (i.e., the original GI Bill; Mettler, 2005). Education benefits were used by millions of returning veterans and are generally credited with fueling the postwar expansion of the American middle class. This legislation offered veterans education/training benefits, home, farm, and business loan guarantees, as well as unemployment compensation. The educational benefit was generous and provided financial support for higher education to veterans in a historical period when financial aid for college attendance for nonveterans was not widely available. By one account, 40% to 50% of veterans used GI Bill education and training benefits as of 1950 (Mettler, 2005). Stanley (2003) estimated that the GI Bill benefit covered 52% to 83% of the cost of attending a university, depending on the type of institution (private versus public) and the number of children the beneficiary had.

GI Bill benefits allowed World War II–era veterans to achieve substantially higher years of education and college completion than nonveterans (Bound & Turner, 2002; Fredland & Little, 1985; Stanley, 2003; Turner & Bound, 2003). Although Black veterans from the South were unable to fully access benefits for which they were eligible, the World War II–era GI Bill had positive effects on the education of veterans from a broad range of backgrounds (Mettler, 2005), particularly men from socioeconomically disadvantaged families (Sampson & Laub, 1996).

With regard to other periods of military service, there is some evidence that the educational outcomes of Korean War–era veterans were similar to those of World War II–era veterans (Stanley, 2003). However, research is clear that those who served during the Cold War and the Vietnam War did not experience the same benefit to their educational attainment as veterans in earlier periods (Bennett & McDonald, 2013). For various reasons, veterans' uptake of GI Bill educational benefits after the Korean War was relatively low (Bennett & McDonald, 2013; MacLean, 2005).

Considerable research documents that educational attainment is negatively associated with expressions of patriotism and nationalism (Coenders & Scheepers, 2003; de Figueiredo & Elkins, 2003; Haubert & Fussell, 2006) and support for the military (Davis & Sheatsley, 1985; Frey-Wouters, & Laufer, 1986). Ishio (2010) found that among Whites, having an advanced degree reduced patriotism, controlling for other social factors. The author explained this finding by suggesting that higher education promotes critical thinking that leads to the questioning of government policy. Such an interpretation is consistent with other explanations for the negative association between education and nationalist attitudes, such as the notion that "educational institutions are more likely to emphasize cosmopolitan values and humanistic commitments than a sense of collective identity aligned with national borders and boundaries" (Straughn & Andriot, 2011, p. 557). These findings form the basis for our expectation that higher educational achievement among World War II–era veterans would suppress their values of patriotism and nationalism.

GENERATIONAL CHANGE AND CONTINUITY IN NATIONALISM–PATRIOTISM

There is ample evidence that the historical decline in patriotism and support for military assertiveness is based on cohort differences in the unanimity with which the public legitimized international conflicts. In *Bowling Alone*, Robert Putnam (2000) paid some attention to the heightened patriotism of those exposed to the World War II era, calling it a "Zeitgeist of national unity and patriotism" (p. 267). Putnam demonstrated that patriotism was highest among those born before 1934 and declined substantially and monotonically across subsequent cohorts. Compared with World War II–era veterans, Vietnam-era veterans were less likely to favor spending on the military and to think that a strong defense was important.

This suggests a veteran-cohort effect of diminished public support for nationalistic goals based on historical exposure to the particular war in question (Schreiber, 1979).

On the other hand, research has shown substantial intergenerational continuity *within families* in core social values, including religious attitudes (Bengtson, 2013), gender role ideology (Min, Silverstein, & Lendon, 2012), and antiwar activism (Dunham, 1998). That is, communication and socialization occurring between parents and children *within* family lineages induce stability in social attitudes across generations that may run counter to inter-cohort change in those same attitudes.

Finally, we note that military service itself is likely to be reproduced across generations. Considerable evidence documents that the likelihood of enlisting in the armed forces and pursuing a career in the military is higher among individuals who had a parent who served in the military (Faris, 1984; Kilburn & Klerman, 1999). For example, the U.S. Department of Defense (2011) estimated that 57% of active-duty military personnel in 2011 were children of active-duty service members or veterans.

HYPOTHESES

We predict that veterans, particularly those who served in World War II, will be more wary of interventionist policies and partisan ideals than nonveterans. We expect that World War II veterans will express relatively weaker nationalistic and patriotic values than other veterans as a result of having taken greater advantage of education benefits afforded by the GI Bill and achieving higher levels of education as a result. Their experiences during the war, as well as the horrors of the Holocaust and the atomic bombings of Hiroshima and Nagasaki, may also have induced wariness of future military intervention.

Because social values are commonly transmitted across generations, we further predict that the nationalistic and patriotic values of veterans will be communicated to their children and that these values will shape these children's outlooks throughout their lives. In making these predictions, we focus on transmission across generations within families, something that is rarely considered because of the documented ideological chasm between the political attitudes of the World War II and Vietnam generations at the cohort level. The data set we use is especially well positioned to address our research questions because of its multigenerational and longitudinal design, with the potential to illuminate what may be a hidden political connection between the "Greatest Generation" and the "Protest Generation."

DATA

Sample

This study uses data from the Longitudinal Study of Generations (LSOG). The LSOG began in 1971 with 2,044 respondents, who were members of 418 three-generation families (see Bengtson & Schrader, 1982, for further details). Grandfathers and their spouses (G1) were selected via a multistage stratified random sampling procedure from a population of 840,000 individuals enrolled in Southern California's first large HMO. Adult children (G2) and grandchildren (G3) of the selected grandparents were also invited to participate in the survey. Grandchildren ranged in age from 16 years to 26 years. Response rates exceeded 70% in each generation. Seven follow-up surveys were administered up to 2005. Data have been collected via a mail-back paper survey, except in 2005 when about half of G3s responded via a web survey and about half via a mail-back paper survey.

The sample for our analysis consists of 314 (G2) fathers with a mean age of 45.55 years ($SD = 5.37$) and 758 of their (G3) children with a mean age of 19.09 years ($SD = 2.59$) when both generations were surveyed in 1971. Because testing intergenerational transmission is one of our aims, the data were restructured to consist of 758 father–child dyads. Of these dyads, 55% were father–daughter and 45% were father–son. Survey reports from G3 children ($n = 369$) in 2005 were matched to these earlier data for the purpose of examining the stability of patriotic and nationalistic values among these G3 children from young adulthood to middle age.

Measures

We measured nationalism–patriotism as strength of agreement with the following three statements:

1. What we need in this country is more patriotism.
2. The United States should be ready to answer any challenge to its power anywhere in the world.
3. The United States should use its military power to maintain peace in the world.

Agreement was rated as *strongly disagree* (1), *disagree* (2), *agree* (3), or *strongly agree* (4).

To compare the strength of nationalism–patriotism across veteran statuses and generations, we created an additive scale of agreement with the three statements above. Cronbach's alpha reliability coefficients were moderate but acceptable, .77 for fathers in 1971, .60 for children in 1971, and .70 for children in 2005. In our multivariate models, the three measures were considered as manifest indicators of the latent construct of nationalism–patriotism.

Veteran status of G2 fathers was ascertained in 1971 by asking whether they served in the military and, if yes, the years in which they served. Respondents were allowed to cite up to three tours of duty. On the basis of established criterion used by the U.S. Department of Veterans Affairs, we classified fathers who had at least one service period between 1941 and 1946 as World War II veterans (U.S. Code of Federal Regulations, 2014; see also Online Appendix A, available at http://pubs.apa.org/books/supp/spiro/). Veterans who served during other years and nonveterans formed two additional categories. Table 6.1 shows that more than half of fathers in the sample (60%) served in the military during World War II, 22% served in other periods, and 18% never served in the military. Because of a split questionnaire in 1971, 87 of the 314 fathers were not asked about their military service but were included in our analysis because their valid data contributed to the estimation of relationships among other variables in the model.

The education of fathers, which we conceptualized as a primary mediating variable in the relationship between military service and nationalistic/patriotic values, was measured with an ordinal 1–8 scale, where 1 = *less than 6 years of education* and 8 = *postgraduate education*. Supporting a possible mediating role of education, Table 6.1 shows that military veterans who served during World War II were more likely to have had at least some college education (70%), compared with those who served during other periods (64%) and those who never served in the military (55%).

Because period of military service is correlated with age, we also controlled for the age of fathers in predicting their nationalism–patriotism. In predicting nationalism–patriotism of children, we controlled for their age, gender, years of education, and military service history. Controlling for the veteran status of children is intended to account for the component

TABLE 6.1
Distribution of Veteran Status of Fathers, Achieved Education,
and Nationalism–Patriotism Score

Veteran status	n	%	% with some college or more	Mean (SD) nationalism– patriotism score
Served 1941–1946 (World War II)	137	60.4	70.1	2.68 (.81)
Served other years	50	22.0	64.0	2.88 (.81)
No service	40	17.6	55.0	3.11 (.67)
Total[a]	227	100.0	66.1	2.83 (.80)

[a]Due to a split questionnaire in 1971, 87 fathers were not asked about their military service.

of intergenerational transmission that emerges from the shared military exposure of some fathers and their children.

ANALYTIC PLAN

To examine the source, transmission, and persistence of nationalistic and patriotic attitudes related to paternal veteran status, we used structural equation modeling (SEM) with latent variables. SEM has several desirable properties for the purposes of this investigation, including the ability to (a) track causal pathways of influence across generations and over time, (b) account for measurement error in the main construct of interest, and (c) reduce bias due to missing data and nonresponse by using all available data. Because of the presence of siblings in the data (758 G3 children were nested within 474 G2 families), we estimated robust standard errors to account for family clustering. All exogenous variables are allowed to correlate with each other. Estimates are derived using a full information maximum likelihood approach with Mplus 6.1 software (Muthén & Muthén, 2011).

RESULTS

Descriptive Results

Table 6.1 shows the average strength of agreement across the three items by the veteran status of fathers. These values indicated that military service was associated with having weaker values of nationalism–patriotism, particularly among World War II veterans ($M = 2.68$, $SD = .81$) whose values were weakest compared with other veterans ($M = 2.88$, $SD = .81$) and nonveterans ($M = 3.11$, $SD = .67$). A multiple group analysis of variance (ANOVA) test revealed that these mean differences were statistically significant ($F = 5.17$, $df = 2$, $p < .001$) and suggested that military service in the largest conflict of the 20th century suppressed support for U.S. dominance and the ascribed importance of patriotism.

Comparing the strength of nationalism–patriotism across generations and over time, we found in 1971 that fathers more strongly endorsed values of nationalism–patriotism ($M = 2.83$, $SD = .80$) than their adolescent and young adult children ($M = 2.48$, $SD = .80$). However, the children increased their support for these values when they reached midlife in 2005 ($M = 2.64$, $SD = .69$). A repeated measures ANOVA test revealed significant differences among these three means ($F = 31.47$, $df = 2$, $p < .01$). This pattern supports both a cohort perspective based on experiential differences between World

War II participants and their baby-boom children and an aging perspective based on lifespan changes in these values in baby boomers. Because baby boomers in their youth tended to take liberal positions on most social and political issues, the strengthening of their nationalism–patriotism values over time might be attributed to the conservatizing influence of maturation or large-scale transformations in the sociopolitical Zeitgeist between the 1970s and the 2000s.

Model Building

Next, we examine the formation and intergenerational transmission of nationalism–patriotism using SEM. A simplified version of the model is shown in Figure 6.1, illustrating theoretically relevant paths (labelled *a–g*), with rectangles indicating observed variables and circles representing latent constructs (measurement errors, residual variances, and control variables are omitted, but their estimates can be found in Table 6.2). The structural paths that lead directly from veteran status to education (a, b) are hypothesized to be positive, with a > b. Fathers' education is proposed to have a negative relationship with nationalism–patriotism (e). The indirect effects of military

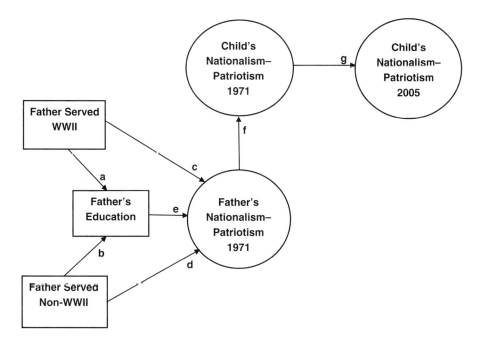

Figure 6.1. Structural model of nationalism–patriotism of fathers and children in relation to fathers' veteran status and education (latent variables shown in circles and observed variables shown in rectangles). WWII = World War II.

TABLE 6.2
Estimates for Model Summarized in Figure 6.1 ($N_{dyads} = 758$)

Parameter estimate	Unstandardized coefficient (*SE*)	Standardized coefficient	*p*
Measurement coefficients			
Fathers' nationalism–patriotism$_{1971}$ → X$_1$	1.00	.71	—
Fathers' nationalism–patriotism$_{1971}$ → X$_2$	.96 (.09)	.57	< .001
Fathers' nationalism–patriotism$_{1971}$ → X$_3$	1.17 (.09)	.67	< .001
Children's nationalism–patriotism$_{1971}$ → X$_4$	1.00	.56	—
Children's nationalism–patriotism$_{1971}$ → X$_5$	.96 (.09)	.49	< .001
Children's nationalism–patriotism$_{1971}$ → X$_6$	1.17 (.09)	.61	< .001
Children's nationalism–patriotism$_{2005}$ → X$_7$	1.00	.71	—
Children's nationalism–patriotism$_{2005}$ → X$_8$	.96 (.09)	.70	< .001
Children's nationalism–patriotism$_{2005}$ → X$_9$	1.17 (.09)	.80	< .001
Measurement error variance			
X$_1$	.37 (.05)	.49	
X$_2$	.73 (.07)	.67	< .001
X$_3$	.64 (.08)	.55	< .001
X$_4$	.69 (.05)	.68	< .001
X$_5$	.95 (.05)	.76	< .001
X$_6$	.74 (.05)	.63	< .001
X$_7$	.33 (.04)	.50	< .001
X$_8$	.33 (.03)	.52	< .001
X$_9$	.25 (.04)	.36	< .001
Structural coefficients			
WWII veteran → Fathers' education	1.01 (.43)	.31	.018
Non–WWII veteran → Fathers' education	−.29 (.39)	−.07	.463
Fathers' education → Fathers' nationalism–patriotism$_{1971}$	−.15 (.03)	−.39	< .001
WWII veteran → Fathers' nationalism–patriotism$_{1971}$	−.28 (.11)	−.22	.015
Non–WWII veteran → Fathers' nationalism–patriotism$_{1971}$	−.11 (.14)	−.07	.430
Fathers' nationalism–patriotism$_{1971}$ → Children's nationalism–patriotism$_{1971}$	.53 (.07)	.58	< .001
Children's nationalism–patriotism$_{1971}$ → Children's nationalism–patriotism$_{2005}$	.67 (.08)	.66	< .001

TABLE 6.2
Estimates for Model Summarized in Figure 6.1 (N_{dyads} = 758)   (*Continued*)

Parameter estimate	Unstandardized coefficient (*SE*)	Standardized coefficient	*p*
Residual variance			
Fathers' education	2.73 (.29)	1.06	< .001
Fathers' nationalism–patriotism$_{1971}$	.30 (.05)	.78	< .001
Children's nationalism–patriotism$_{1971}$	.18 (.03)	.57	< .001
Children's nationalism–patriotism$_{2005}$	.19 (.03)	.56	< .001

Note. $\chi^2(101) = 180.24$, $p < .001$; CFI = .91; TLI = .90; RMSEA = .03; age of fathers and education, age, gender, and veteran status of children are controlled in structural model. All exogenous variables are allowed to correlate as well as fathers' education and children's education. Measurement coefficients are constrained to be equal across the three latent factors. Robust standard errors (*SE*) are reported to account for family clustering. Reference group for *World War II* (*WWII*) *veteran* and *non–WWII veteran* is *No Military Service*. X_1, X_4, and X_7 = What we need in this country is more patriotism. X_2, X_5, and X_8 = The U.S. should use its military power to maintain peace in the world. X_3, X_6, and X_9 = The U.S. should be ready to answer any challenge to its power anywhere in the world.

service through greater education (a*e, b*e) are expected to be negative, with a*e < b*e. Direct effects of military service on nationalism–patriotism (c, d)—presumably deriving from combat exposure—are predicted to be negative, with c < d. The model further posits that fathers' values are transmitted to their children (f), who maintain those values into midlife (g).

Because it is important to know whether measurement coefficients of nationalism–patriotism (analogous to factor loadings) are consistent between fathers and children and between the 1971 and 2005 assessments, we conducted a comparative test of goodness of fit between a measurement model that imposed equality constraints on those coefficients and a measurement model that imposed no such constraints. This test (not reported) indicated statistical equivalence in the strength with which each measured item corresponded to its respective underlying construct and suggested that the meaning of the construct was similar for each generation and time period. Consequently, the results reported in Table 6.2 constrained corresponding measurement coefficients to be equal across the three latent constructs of nationalism–patriotism.

Model Results

In this section, we discuss the structural coefficients indicating the relationships between theoretically relevant variables. However, first we note that several goodness-of-fit statistics noted at the bottom of Table 6.2 indicate that the model provided a good fit with the observed data and thus reasonably represented the overall process as it was hypothesized.

Structural coefficients for the estimated model revealed a direct negative relationship between World War II–era service and attitudes toward nationalism–patriotism. In 1971, 25 years after World War II ended, veterans of World War II expressed weaker support than nonveterans for an assertive U.S. presence in the world and a need for more patriotism. That this result emerged with education controlled suggests that a strict mediating model in which education fully mediates the effect of military service could not be supported. However, a significant and negative indirect influence of World War II–era military service on nationalism–patriotism was indicated by multiplying the significant positive effect of World War II service on education and the significant negative effect of education on values of nationalism–patriotism ($b_{mediation} = -.153$; $p < .05$). Stated otherwise, the weaker values toward nationalism–patriotism found among men who served in the World War II era were partially explained by their greater educational achievement.

Examining the cross-generational transmission of values in 1971, we found evidence of a significant association between fathers and their children. The standardized coefficient ($B = .58$) indicated a robust intergenerational correlation between middle-aged fathers and their adolescent/young adult children at the family level of analysis; this result stood in contrast to the fact that the two generations showed mean differences at the group or cohort level of analysis. Additionally, values of nationalism–patriotism remained stable in these children from the initial 1971 assessment to the 2005 assessment when they reached midlife ($B = .66$).

Taken together, these findings suggest two main conclusions. First, World War II–era veterans were less nation-centric in their attitudes both directly as a result of their service and indirectly through their greater educational achievement. Second, these attitudes were transmitted to and subsequently retained by their children.

CONCLUSION

The results from our analysis confirmed our central hypothesis that World War II veterans would more weakly endorse values of patriotism–nationalism compared with nonveterans. The unique impact that World War II had on the worldviews of veterans more than a quarter century after the war is further supported by the finding that military veterans from other periods were no different than nonveterans. Although it is tempting to conclude from these findings that exposure to combat softened enthusiasm for policies that could lead to future wars, we have no direct information about the nature of veterans' military service experiences. Although such factors may have played a role, our findings indicate that World War II veterans derived their values in part from the long reach that higher education had in tempering their support for an interventionist U.S. policy and restraining unqualified patriotism. These findings speak to the unique advantages garnered by this generation of men who fueled the postwar economic expansion and were responsible for the baby boom of that era.

We also found that the attitudes of World War II veterans were transmitted to their adolescent and young-adult children, raising the intriguing possibility that the "Protest Generation" adopted antiwar attitudes from the "Greatest Generation" as a result of the latter's World War II–era service and subsequent access to higher education. This line of reasoning implies that the "generation gap" of the 1960s may have been overstated and that the seeds of political discontent over the Vietnam War among the youth of that time were sown within the families of World War II veterans. Such an interpretation is consistent with evidence regarding the impact of World War II on other social changes in the latter half of the 20th century. For example, the 1960s civil rights movement was fueled in part by the military's generally successful experiments with racial integration during World War II, including President Harry S. Truman's (1948) postwar Executive Order 9981, which required "equality of treatment and opportunity for all persons in the Armed Forces without regard to race, color, religion, or national origin" (Lutz, 2013).

Several limitations of our study deserve mention. First, the study does not include measures of place of deployment, exposure to combat, or whether veterans served in a theater of war. Although it is reasonable to assume that most World War II–era veterans in the study experienced the war in direct and visceral ways, we cannot ascertain the level of exposure to dangerous and stressful conditions. The mechanism by which service influences attitudes must therefore be inferred. Second, the sample is mostly derived from Southern California (where the aerospace industry provided unprecedented employment opportunities to skilled workers in the postwar period) and consists almost exclusively of White non-Hispanic families. Although it is difficult to know how these restrictions influence our findings, beyond possibly overstating the education benefit procured by veterans, some caution is advised in generalizing our results beyond our study population.

Military service and exposure to war conditions are fundamental life experiences that shape life pathways materially, socially, and psychologically. Consistent with the life course perspective (e.g., Elder, Shanahan, & Jennings, 2015), we found that the unique exposure of a particular cohort to a cataclysmic historical event at a critical period of development had consequences for worldviews that lasted into midlife. We also found that they were communicated to the next generation, possibly priming political discontent against a later war that turned unpopular. As such, we emphasize the importance of viewing the sociopolitical attitudes and values of veterans as structured by specific historical contingencies and embedded within family contexts. Curiously, we did not observe that the children of veterans were more likely to serve in the military than the children of nonveterans. In fact, we found the opposite for fathers and sons, which further illuminates the sometimes paradoxical ways that military experience, and the values it inculcates, produce reactivity, as well as resemblance, across family generations.

REFERENCES

Bachman, J. G., & Jennings, M. K. (1975). The impact of Vietnam on trust in government. *Journal of Social Issues, 31*, 141–155. http://dx.doi.org/10.1111/j.1540-4560.1975.tb01017.x

Bengtson, V. L. (2013). *Families and faith: How religion is passed down across generations.* New York, NY: Oxford University Press. http://dx.doi.org/10.1093/acprof:oso/9780199948659.001.0001

Bengtson, V. L., & Schrader, S. S. (1982). Parent-child relations. *Research Instruments in Social Gerontology, 2*, 115–186.

Bennett, P. R., & McDonald, K. B. (2013). Military service as a pathway to early socioeconomic achievement for disadvantaged groups. In J. M. Wilmoth & A. S. London (Eds.), *Life-course perspectives on military service* (pp. 119–143). New York, NY: Routledge.

Blank, T., & Schmidt, P. (2003). National identity in a united Germany: Nationalism or patriotism? An empirical test with representative data. *Political Psychology, 24*, 289–312. http://dx.doi.org/10.1111/0162-895X.00329

Bound, J., & Turner, S. (2002). Going to war and going to college: Did World War II and the G.I. Bill increase educational attainment for returning veterans? *Journal of Labor Economics, 20*, 784–815. http://dx.doi.org/10.1086/342012

Coenders, M., & Scheepers, P. (2003). The effect of education on nationalism and ethnic exclusionism: An international comparison. *Political Psychology, 24*, 313–343. http://dx.doi.org/10.1111/0162-895X.00330

Davis, J. A., & Sheatsley, P. B. (1985). *Americans view of the military: A 1984 update* (Report No. 132). Chicago, IL: National Opinion Research Center, University of Chicago.

de Figueiredo, R. J. P., & Elkins, Z. (2003). Are patriots bigots? An inquiry into the vices of in-group pride. *American Journal of Political Science, 47*, 171–188. http://dx.doi.org/10.1111/1540-5907.00012

Dunham, C. C. (1998). Generation units and the life course: A sociological perspective on youth and the anti-war movement. *Journal of Political and Military Sociology, 26*, 137–154.

Elder, G. H., Jr., Shanahan, M. J., & Jennings, J. A. (2015). Human development in time and place. In T. Leventhal & M. Bornstein (Eds.), *Handbook of child psychology and developmental science: Ecological settings and processes in developmental systems* (7th ed., Vol. 4, pp. 6–54). New York, NY: Wiley.

Erikson, R. S., & Stoker, L. (2011). Caught in the draft: The effects of Vietnam draft lottery status on political attitudes. *American Political Science Review, 105,* 221–237.

Faris, J. H. (1984). Economic and non-economic factors in personnel recruitment and retention in the AVF. *Armed Forces and Society, 10,* 251–275. http://dx.doi.org/10.1177/0095327X8401000207

Fredland, J. E., & Little, R. D. (1985). Socioeconomic status of World War II veterans by race: An empirical test of the bridging hypothesis. *Social Science Quarterly, 66,* 533–551.

Frey-Wouters, E., & Laufer, R. S. (1986). *Legacy of a war: The American soldier in Vietnam.* Armonk, NY: M. E. Sharpe.

Grote, N. K., Frieze, I. H., & Schmidt, L. C. (1997). Political attitudes and the Vietnam War: A study of college-educated men of the Vietnam generation. *Journal of Applied Social Psychology, 27,* 1673–1693. http://dx.doi.org/10.1111/j.1559-1816.1997.tb01619.x

Haubert, J., & Fussell, E. (2006). Explaining pro-immigrant sentiment in the U.S.: Social class, cosmopolitanism, and perceptions of immigrants. *The International Migration Review, 40,* 489–507. http://dx.doi.org/10.1111/j.1747-7379.2006.00033.x

Ishio, Y. (2010). Social bases of American patriotism. Examining the effects of dominant social statuses and socialization. *Current Sociology, 58,* 67–93. http://dx.doi.org/10.1177/0011392109348546

Ivie, R. L., Gimbel, C., & Elder, G. H., Jr. (1991). Military experience and attitudes in later life: Contextual influences across forty years. *Journal of Political and Military Sociology, 19,* 101–117.

Jennings, M. K., & Markus, G. B. (1976). Political participation and Vietnam War veterans: A longitudinal study. In N. L. Goldman & D. R. Segal (Eds.), *Social psychology of military service* (pp. 175–199). Beverly Hills, CA: Sage.

Jennings, M. K., & Markus, G. B. (1977). The effect of military service on political attitudes: A panel study. *The American Political Science Review, 71,* 131–147. http://dx.doi.org/10.2307/1956958

Kilburn, M. R., & Klerman, J. A. (1999). *Enlistment decisions in the 1990s: Evidence from individual-level data.* Santa Monica, CA: RAND.

Kosterman, R., & Feshbach, S. (1989). Toward a measure of patriotic and nationalistic attitudes. *Political Psychology, 10,* 257–274. http://dx.doi.org/10.2307/3791647

London, A. S., Wilmoth, J. M., & Dutton, C. (2017). What do we know about veteran status differences in social attitudes? In J. Hicks, E. L. Weiss, & J. F. Coll (Eds.), *The civilian lives of U.S. veterans: Issues and identities* (pp. 577–606). Santa Barbara, CA: Praeger.

Lutz, A. (2013). Race-ethnicity and immigration status in the U.S. military. In J. M. Wilmoth & A. S. London (Eds.), *Life course perspectives on military service* (pp. 68–96). New York, NY: Routledge.

MacLean, A. (2005). Lessons from the Cold War: Military service and college education. *Sociology of Education, 78*, 250–266. http://dx.doi.org/10.1177/003804070507800304

Mettler, S. (2005). *Soldiers to citizens: The G.I. Bill and the making of the greatest generation.* New York, NY: Oxford University Press.

Min, J., Silverstein, M., & Lendon, J. P. (2012). Intergenerational transmission of values over the family life course. *Advances in Life Course Research, 17*, 112–120. http://dx.doi.org/10.1016/j.alcr.2012.05.001

Muthén, L. K., & Muthén, B. O. (2011). *Mplus user's guide* (6th ed.). Los Angeles, CA: Author.

Phillips, N. E. (1973). Militarism and grass roots involvement in the military-industrial complex. *Journal of Conflict Resolution, 17*, 625–655. http://dx.doi.org/10.1177/002200277301700403

Putnam, R. D. (2000). *Bowling alone: The collapse and revival of American community.* New York, NY: Simon & Schuster. http://dx.doi.org/10.1145/358916.361990

Sampson, R. J., & Laub, J. H. (1996). Socioeconomic achievement in the life course of disadvantaged men: Military service as a turning point, circa 1940–1965. *American Sociological Review, 61*, 347–367. http://dx.doi.org/10.2307/2096353

Schreiber, E. M. (1979). Enduring effects of military service? Opinion differences between U.S. veterans and nonveterans. *Social Forces, 57*, 824–839. http://dx.doi.org/10.2307/2577356

Segal, D. R., & Segal, M. W. (1976). The impact of military service on trust in government, international attitudes, and social status. In N. L. Goldman & D. R. Segal (Eds.), *Social psychology of military service* (pp. 201–211). Beverly Hills, CA: Sage.

Stanley, M. (2003). College education and the midcentury GI Bills. *The Quarterly Journal of Economics, 118*, 671–708. http://dx.doi.org/10.1162/003355303321675482

Straughn, J. B., & Andriot, A. L. (2011). Education, civic patriotism, and democratic citizenship: Unpacking the education effect on political involvement. *Sociological Forum, 26*, 556–580. http://dx.doi.org/10.1111/j.1573-7861.2011.01262.x

Truman, H. S. (1948, July 26). *Executive Order 9981.* Retrieved from http://www.trumanlibrary.org/

Turner, S., & Bound, J. (2003). Closing the gap or widening the divide: The effects of the GI Bill and World War II on the educational outcomes of black Americans. *The Journal of Economic History, 63*, 145–177. http://dx.doi.org/10.1017/S0022050703001761

U.S. Code of Federal Regulations. (2014). *38 §3.2, Periods of war.* Retrieved from http://www.ecfr.gov/cgi-bin/text-idx?node=se38.1.3_12&rgn=div8

U.S. Department of Defense. (2011). *January 2011 status of forces survey of active duty members: Leading indicators.* Arlington, VA: Defense Manpower Data Center.

II

HEALTH DYNAMICS

7

MILITARY SERVICE EXPERIENCES AND OLDER MEN'S TRAJECTORIES OF SELF-RATED HEALTH

JANET M. WILMOTH, ANDREW S. LONDON,
AND WILLIAM J. OLIVER

Military service was a normative part of the life course among American men transitioning to adulthood during the middle of the 20th century. Rates of participation in the military were over 50% for each single-year birth cohort from 1915 to 1935, with rates over 70% for those born between 1919 and 1927 (Hogan, 1981). As a result, in 2013, it is estimated that male veterans over the age of 50 represented 67.8% of the 22,299,350 living veterans in the United States (U.S. Department of Veterans Affairs, National Center for Veterans Analysis and Statistics, 2014). Given the high prevalence of military service among older men and the policy relevance of meeting the needs of older veterans (Wilmoth & London, 2011), researchers with interests in aging and the life course have increasingly focused on understanding the enduring effects of military service on health (Settersten, 2006; Wilmoth, London, & Parker, 2010). At the same time, a recent review of all military-related articles published between 1980 and 2013 in seven major aging-related journals suggests

http://dx.doi.org/10.1037/0000061-008
Long-Term Outcomes of Military Service: The Health and Well-Being of Aging Veterans, A. Spiro III,
R. A. Settersten Jr., and C. M. Aldwin (Editors)
Copyright © 2018 by the American Psychological Association. All rights reserved.

that the consequences of military service for later-life health have long been understudied (Wilmoth & London, 2016).

Although there is a substantial literature on the short-term impact of military service on health (MacLean, 2013), studies of long-term outcomes among older veterans are less common. Moreover, many of the published studies of long-term health outcomes are limited by data constraints. Research on older veterans is primarily based on cross-sectional research designs and nonrepresentative samples that focus exclusively on veterans or on users of Department of Veterans Affairs (VA) health care. Furthermore, very few studies directly compare veterans with nonveterans using population-representative data (Wilmoth & London, 2016), and those that do are often unable to adequately address selection into military service, selective mortality, and differential attrition, which must be taken into account to confidently draw conclusions about the causal effect of military service (Wolf, Wing, & Lopoo, 2013).

Research that does use large-scale samples to examine how later-life health varies by veteran status has generally not examined how this variation might reflect differences in military service experiences. However, the inclusion of more detailed measures of military service experiences in recent waves of the Health and Retirement Study (HRS) provides a new opportunity to elaborate on previous studies of the differential consequences of early-adulthood military service on health trajectories in later life (Wilmoth et al., 2010). This chapter uses HRS data to examine whether adverse military service experiences contribute to differences in later-life self-rated health trajectories among older men. We focus on self-rated health because it is a global health indicator that is closely related to diagnosed health conditions, physical functioning, health care use, and mortality (Idler & Benyamini, 1997; Jylhä, 2009; Jylhä, Guralnik, Balfour, & Fried, 2001).

MILITARY SERVICE AND LATER-LIFE HEALTH

There are competing expectations about the influence of military service on later-life health. On the one hand, one might expect that military service in general, and adverse military service experiences in particular, would result in veterans having worse later-life health trajectories than nonveterans. Military service is a risky endeavor that can compromise health through (a) training accidents and overuse injuries (MacLean, 2013), (b) exposure to hazardous environments (e.g., exposure to radiation, environmental toxins, or chemicals) or infectious diseases (Brown et al., 2001; Scott, 1992), and (c) exposure to a culture of substance use (e.g., tobacco, alcohol, and other drugs; Bedard & Deschênes, 2006; London, Herd, Miech, & Wilmoth,

2016; Miech, London, Wilmoth, & Koester, 2013; Teachman, Anderson, & Tedrow, 2015). In addition, combat exposure increases the risk of short-term injury and long-term disability (Elder, Shanahan, & Clipp, 1997; MacLean, 2010, 2013), physical and mental health problems (Card, 1983; Clipp & Elder, 1996; Elder & Clipp, 1989; Vogt, King, King, Savarese, & Suvak, 2004), inadequate sleep (London, Burgard, & Wilmoth, 2014), and mortality (Bedard & Deschênes, 2006; Dobkin & Shabani, 2009; Elder, Clipp, Brown, Martin, & Friedman, 2009).

On the other hand, certain aspects of military service may promote better long-term health outcomes. For example, training programs and exercise regimes that help military personnel to maintain a relatively high level of physical fitness during service can set the stage for lifelong physical activity (MacLean, 2013). Military service involves specialized training that can facilitate occupational attainment, which can lead to health-promoting circumstances, such as improved work environments, increased earnings, and access to high-quality health insurance (Kleykamp, 2013; Street & Hoffman, 2013). Military personnel and veterans also have access to various health care, housing, educational, and retirement benefits designed to reward those who served in the armed forces and ameliorate the negative effects of service-connected injuries (Street & Hoffman, 2013; Wilmoth & London, 2011; Wilmoth, London, & Heflin, 2015). Finally, military experiences can contribute to positive adaptation and resilience that could improve long-term health outcomes (Aldwin, Levenson, & Spiro, 1994; Jennings, Aldwin, Levenson, Spiro, & Mroczek, 2006). Such development may be especially evident among those who were not physically or psychologically harmed by military service, but it may also emerge among those who were. In the latter case, such positive outcomes may result from stress-related or posttraumatic growth (see Spiro, Settersten, & Aldwin, 2016).

The empirical evidence regarding variation in later-life health by veteran status supports the notion that military service is associated with negative long-term health outcomes, while providing some salient caveats about the importance of heterogeneity in military service experiences. In general, veterans are in poorer health and have more functional limitations and disabilities than nonveterans (Aldwin et al., 1994; Beebe, 1975; Centers for Disease Control, 1988; Keehn, 1980; Schnurr, Spiro, & Paris, 2000; Teachman, 2011). These poorer health outcomes have been associated with various aspects of military service, such as late entry into military service (Elder et al., 1997), overseas active duty (Elder et al., 2009), and combat exposure and associated posttraumatic stress disorder (PTSD; Elder et al., 1997; Schnurr & Spiro, 1999). However, veterans' appraisals of their military service experiences, which are remarkably consistent over the life course, may be more important in shaping long-term outcomes than stressful combat exposure per se (Jennings et al.,

2006; Settersten, Day, Elder, & Waldinger, 2012; see also Chapter 1, this volume). Positive appraisals of military service mitigate the effects of combat exposure on later-life PTSD (Aldwin et al., 1994) and are associated with resilience, wisdom, and successful aging (Elder & Clipp, 1989; Jennings et al., 2006; Pietrzak, Tsai, Kirwin, & Southwick, 2014).

When considering the implications of military service for long-term health outcomes, it is important to keep in mind how these effects unfold across the life course. As Teachman (2013) noted:

> The effects of military service may not be proportionate across the life course . . . military service may produce results that vary according to stage in the life course. . . . What may appear to be a null effect of military service at one point in the life course may be very different at earlier or later points in time. (pp. 282–283)

One example of unfolding effects is "later-adulthood trauma reengagement," which can occur among older veterans who successfully avoided or dealt with highly stressful combat exposure in early- and midadulthood. As these veterans confront, rework, and try to make meaning of their wartime memories in later life, some may experience positive personal growth, whereas others may exhibit increased stress-related symptomatology (Davison et al., 2016).

Given the potential for age-related change in the effects of military service on later-life health, we advocate taking a long view and using longitudinal data to model age-related health trajectories, instead of examining health outcomes at a single point in time or changes between two points in time. These models, which are based on repeated, prospective observations of veterans and nonveterans over time, allow the effect of military service on health to change with age. To better isolate the effects of military service, these models should take into account early-life factors that influence selection into service, such as childhood health and family-of-origin socioeconomic status, and mid- to late-life characteristics, such as education, income, marital status, and health behaviors, that potentially mediate the relationship between service and later-life health trajectories (see Wilmoth & London, 2013, for more discussion of this model).

In our research, we have addressed this issue of unfolding effects by examining men's health trajectories across a broad range of ages and outcomes in later life. Using longitudinal data from the HRS, we have found that (a) veterans have better health—based on indicators of number of conditions, functional limitations, self-rated health—around retirement age, but experience greater age-related declines in health than nonveterans; (b) among veterans, men who served during wartime have better health around retirement age but more rapid age-related declines in health than men who did not serve during wartime; and (c) among war veterans, Vietnam veterans are in poorer health around retirement age, but they appear to experience less substantial age-related health declines than men who served during previous wars (Wilmoth et al., 2010). These latter findings are generally consistent with those of Dobkin and Shabani (2009), who found that Vietnam veterans had more activity limitations and worse self-rated health than nonveterans and that, as they aged from their 20s into their mid-50s, functioning and health deteriorated much more rapidly among veterans than among nonveterans.

In addition, we have examined the impact of veteran status on changes in men's body mass index (BMI) and cognition. Across a range of cohorts, Wilmoth, London, and Himes (2015) found that veterans have marginally higher BMI than nonveterans within each cohort. Brown, Wilmoth, and London (2014) reported that veterans have higher cognition scores than nonveterans around retirement age, but their cognition scores decline more rapidly with increasing age, and that veterans who served during the Korean War have lower cognition scores around retirement age, but less steep age-related declines than veterans who served during World War II. We have also documented that veterans have similar or higher mortality in later life than nonveterans, although military service offsets some of the mortality disadvantage experienced by Black men (London & Wilmoth, 2006). Collectively, our research with the HRS suggests that any health advantages veterans may have as they enter later life quickly erode with age. Higher rates of smoking among veterans than nonveterans across the life course may be a contributing factor (London et al., 2016; see also Chapter 10, this volume).

Our research has not yet considered variation in military service experiences, beyond examining variation across cohorts who served during different historical time periods, because of data limitations. Given this, we have been unable to determine how adverse military service experiences, such as combat exposure or service-related disability, which occur relatively early in the adult life course, affect men's later-life health trajectories. On the basis of prior research, we hypothesize that veterans who experienced adverse events during military service will have poorer health and steeper health declines in later life than veterans who did not have such adverse experiences and nonveterans. Furthermore, we expect that veterans who did not have adverse military experiences will have better health around retirement age, but steeper health declines in later life than nonveterans.

DATA

This study uses longitudinal data from the HRS (http://hrsonline.isr. umich.edu/), including (a) the biennial 1992 to 2012 public use files; (b) the 2006, 2008, 2010, and 2012 leave-behind questionnaire, which was given to respondents in randomly selected study households who participated in the enhanced face-to-face interview; and (c) the 2013 Veterans Mail Survey.

Sample

We combined these data sets to construct a single file based on 16,347 men from the HRS who were born from 1890 to 1959 and were ages 51 and older when they entered the study (see Table 7.1). Over the 20 years of the study, these men were interviewed between one and 10 times, depending on the year they entered the study and the number of follow-ups in which they participated. Consequently, the analytic sample in the person–period file used to estimate the models contains a total of 72,161 observations. The analytic sample excludes women because less than 1% of the women in the HRS served in the military.

Measures

The HRS data contain a range of variables that enable us to examine how military service experiences contribute to differences in later-life self-rated health trajectories among older men, net of the effect of key control and mediator variables.

TABLE 7.1
Distribution of Veteran Statuses Among Males in the HRS Sample
(N = 16,347) and the Analytic Sample (N = 72,161)

Veteran status	HRS sample, %	HRS sample, no.	Analytic sample[a], %	Analytic sample[a], no.
Nonveteran	53.4	8,771	47.1	33,959
Veteran	46.3	7,576	52.9	38,202
Veteran, no combat fire[b]	16.1	2,626	26.2	18,921
Veteran, combat fire	7.0	1,138	10.9	7,833
Veteran, combat fire unknown	23.3	3,812	15.8	11,448
Veteran, no service-related disability[b]	39.3	6,432	48.9	35,311
Veteran, service-related disability	7.0	1,144	4.0	2,891
Veteran, no VA SCDR[b]	7.9	1,297	13.4	9,659
Veteran, VA SCDR	1.7	285	2.5	1,834
Veteran, unknown VA SCDR	36.7	5,994	37.0	26,709

Note. HRS = Health and Retirement Study. VA SCDR = Veterans Affairs Service-Connected Disability Rating. [a]The analytic sample is based on a person–period file in which each HRS male respondent contributed up to 10 observations. [b]The percentages and numbers for each veteran subgroup sum to the veteran total.

Dependent Variable

The dependent variable is self-rated health, which is a five-category ordinal measure, with 5 = *excellent*, 4 = *very good*, 3 = *good*, 2 = *fair*, and 1 = *poor health*. Similar to our prior research, we model self-rated health as a continuous variable, with missing observations excluded from the analysis.

Military Service Experience Variables

Military service experiences can be ascertained from questions located in different parts of the HRS survey. On the core questionnaire, respondents retrospectively report whether they have "ever served in the active military of the United States." We use this information to construct a veteran status variable that identifies nonveterans and veterans. Respondents with missing military service information are included in the nonveteran category. Overall, 47% of the men in our analytic sample are nonveterans and 53% are veterans. Given that respondents can contribute different numbers of observations to the person–period file used to estimate the models, the distribution of veteran status in the analytic sample differs from that in the HRS sample. As shown in Table 7.1, the percentage of men in the HRS sample who are veterans is 46%, which is lower than the percentage of veterans in the analytic sample. Our primary interest is assessing the implications of potentially detrimental service-related experiences on later-life health. Therefore, we use the veteran status variable in conjunction with three additional measures as the focal variables in our analyses.

As shown in Table 7.1, the first measure captures whether veterans experienced *combat fire*. The 2006, 2008, 2010, and 2012 leave-behind surveys contained a series of life-event questions that included this item. Respondents were asked to indicate whether they had "ever fired a weapon in combat or been fired upon in combat" at any point in their lives. Nearly 11% of the analytic sample is composed of veterans who experienced combat fire, 26% are veterans who did not experience combat fire, and 16% are veterans whose combat fire experience is unknown because they were not in a household that was randomly selected to participate in the enhanced face-to-face interview, chose not to answer the question, did not return the leave-behind questionnaire, or had died or were lost to follow-up by 2006.

The second and third measures capture service-related disability. The second measure is based on a core questionnaire item that asked all respondents who reported military service: "Do you have a disability connected with military service?" Only 4% of the analytic sample consists of veterans with a service-connected disability according to this measure. However, this broad question based on the respondent's perceived source of a disability does not specifically ask whether the disability is certified by the VA. Such a documented service-connected disability rating (SCDR) is used by the VA to determine eligibility for benefits. Our third measure is drawn from the 2013 Veterans Mail Survey, which includes the question "Do you have a VA service-connected disability rating?" This measure is limited because most veterans in the HRS sample did not participate in the 2013 Veterans Mail Survey, and therefore it is unknown whether they have a documented VA SCDR. Only 2.5% of the analytic sample is composed of veterans who responded "yes" to this question, 13% are veterans who responded "no," and 37% are veterans whose SCDR is unknown because they did not answer the question, chose not to participate in the 2013 Veterans Mail Survey, or had died or were lost to follow-up by 2013. Supplemental analysis indicates that younger veterans who served either during the early Cold War or the Vietnam War were more likely to participate in the mail survey than older World War II and Korean War veterans.

Control and Mediator Variables

The analysis includes a first group of control variables and a second group of mediator variables that are potentially related to military service and later-life health. Unless otherwise noted, respondents with missing information are assigned to the modal category of the control and mediator variables. The control variables are retrospectively reported early-life characteristics that occurred prior to military service and could influence selection into military service in different historical periods (Card, 1983; Flynn, 1993; Sackett & Mavor, 2006; Teachman & Tedrow, 2014). These measures are indicators of relative (dis)advantage: race/ethnicity, early-life health (excellent/good/very good/fair vs. poor and missing information), and an early-life socioeconomic disadvantage indicator based on mother's education, father's education and occupation, and family socioeconomic status.

The variables that might mediate the relationship between military service experiences and later-life health are mid- to late-life characteristics measured long after military service ended. These measures include health-related sociodemographic variables (marital status, education, household income, and labor force participation) and health behavior variables (ever smoked, currently drinks alcohol, and body weight). All of these mid- to late-life variables, except education, are time varying across the 20-year study period.

We also include three methodological variables that take into account whether the respondent ever had a proxy interview, dropped out of the study, or died during the 20-year time span of the study. These variables adjust for the potential relationship between sample attrition and self-rated health trajectories. For additional details about the measurement of these variables, see Wilmoth et al. (2010).

Finally, similar to Wilmoth, London, and Himes (2015), we include a measure of birth cohort that takes into account the year when respondents turned age 18. This cohort measure captures, approximately, when the men became eligible to serve in the military, regardless of whether they actually entered the military or served in a given war. This measure situates nonveterans and veterans historically, and takes into account exposure to health-related cultural influences (e.g., norms related to smoking, diet, and exercise) in a formative stage of the life course (see Online Appendix A, available at http://pubs.apa.org/books/supp/spiro/ for additional discussion of the "age-18 birth cohort" measure).

ANALYTIC PLAN

We present a series of conditional growth curve models (estimated with SAS PROC MIXED) examining the impact of combat fire, service-connected disability, and a documented VA SCDR on men's later-life self-rated health trajectories. For each of the service measures, two models are estimated: (a) the first includes only the age and veteran experience variables and (b) the second adds the controls for the early- and mid- to late-life characteristics (the coefficients for the controls are not shown in the tables but are available from the first author on e-mail request). In all of these models, time is defined in terms of mean-centered chronological age. All models include age and age-squared to test for nonlinearity in the relationship between age and self-rated health, and to account for potential nonlinearity in the slopes that estimate age-related changes in health in relation to the military service variables. We focus on interpreting the coefficients for the effect of veteran status on self-rated health at the mean age of 67 and the effect of veteran status on the change in self-rated health over time (see Tables 7.2–7.4).

For illustrative purposes, we present figures showing predicted self-rated health trajectories at ages 50 through 90, based on the fully specified models. To obtain the predicted values, we allow age and military service experience to vary while holding each covariate constant at its modal or mean value. Thus, the predicted values represent "typical" men of the specified age and military service experience group who (a) report good early-life health; (b) are non-Hispanic White, married, high school graduates, out of the labor force, nonsmokers, nondrinkers, normal weight, from the World War II age 18 cohort; (c) have mean early-life disadvantage scores and mean household incomes; and (d) did not have a proxy interview, were not lost to follow-up, and did not die during the study period. Holding constant a different set of characteristics would shift the predicted age trajectories up or down (depending on the covariate values being held constant), but the veteran status differences by age would remain the same.

RESULTS

Table 7.2 presents the results from growth curve models estimating the effect of exposure to combat fire on men's mid- to late-life self-rated health trajectories. The coefficients indicate that veterans who did not experience combat fire, as well as those who did experience it, have significantly higher (i.e., better) self-rated health at the mean-centered age. The magnitude of these differences is attenuated, but is still statistically significant, in Model 2. There are no significant self-rated health differences at the mean-centered age between nonveterans and veterans whose combat fire experience is

TABLE 7.2
Growth Curve Models Estimating the Effect of Combat Fire
on Men's Mid- to Late-Life Self-Rated Health Trajectories

	Model 1[a] b (SE)	Model 2[b] b (SE)
Intercept	2.9955*** (.0126)	3.5628*** (.0294)
Age	−0.0261*** (.0008)	−0.0176*** (.0009)
Age^2	−0.0001 (.000)	−0.0003*** (.000)
Veteran, no combat fire[c]	0.4044*** (.0225)	0.1485*** (.0213)
Veteran, combat fire	0.2981*** (.0321)	0.0631* (0.0287)
Veteran, combat fire unknown	0.0045 (.0229)	0.0324 (.0230)
Age*Veteran, no combat fire	−0.0034* (.0015)	−.00076*** (.0014)
Age^2* Veteran, no combat fire	−0.0004** (.0001)	−0.0004* (.0001)
Age*Veteran, combat fire	−0.0036 (.0022)	−0.0085*** (.0021)
Age^2*veteran, combat fire	−.0003* (.0001)	−0.0003*** (.0001)
Age*Veteran, unknown combat fire	−0.0069*** (.0019)	−0.0107*** (.0018)
Age^2*Veteran, unknown combat fire	−0.0006*** (.0001)	−0.0005*** (.0001)

Note. $N = 72,161$ for both models. b = coefficient. SE = standard error.
[a]Model 1 only includes the variables shown in the table. [b]Model 2 includes controls for age 18 birth cohort, race/ethnicity, childhood disadvantage, childhood health, education, labor force participation, household income, marital status, smoking, drinking alcohol, underweight and overweight, and ever had a proxy respondent, lost to follow-up, or died during the study period. Complete models are available from the first author on request. [c]Nonveteran is the reference category for the combat fire variables.
*$p < .05$, **$p < .01$, ***$p < .001$.

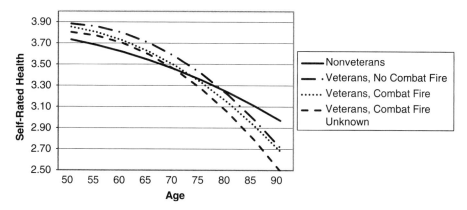

Figure 7.1. Predicted self-rated health trajectories by combat fire status.

unknown. The age and age-squared coefficients indicate that self-rated health decreases at an increasing rate with age, particularly for veterans, regardless of veterans' combat fire experience.

The differences in self-rated health trajectories across the combat fire categories are shown in Figure 7.1. The trajectory for nonveterans (which is indicated by the solid line) is lower than the veteran groups until age 70, when there is a cross-over that results in the nonveterans having higher self-rated health at the most-advanced ages. Veterans who did not experience combat fire (indicated by the line with a dash and dot) have better self-rated health than nonveterans up until age 75, but thereafter, their self-rated health declines substantially faster. Although veterans who did not experience combat fire have worse self-rated health than nonveterans at the most advanced ages, they continue to fare better than the two other veteran groups. Veterans who experienced combat fire (indicated by the dotted line) have a self-rated health trajectory that is similar to veterans who did not experience combat fire, although the overall level of self-rated health at each age is slightly lower. Veterans whose combat fire experience is unknown have the lowest levels of self-rated health at every age over 70.

The models in Table 7.3 estimate the impact of service-related disability on men's mid- to late-life self-rated health trajectories. Compared with nonveterans at the mean-centered age, the fully-specified model indicates that veterans without a service-related disability have significantly higher self-rated health, and veterans with a service-related disability have significantly lower self-rated health. The age and age-square coefficients indicate that self-rated health decreases with age and does so more rapidly among the two veteran groups.

Figure 7.2 shows the predicted self-rated health trajectories by service-related disability status. Prior to age 70, veterans with no service-related

TABLE 7.3
Growth Curve Models Estimating the Effect of Service-Related Disability
on Men's Mid- to Late-Life Self-Rated Health Trajectories

	Model 1[a] b (SE)	Model 2[b] b (SE)
Intercept	2.9954*** (.0127)	3.5724*** (.0291)
Age	−0.0262*** (.0008)	−0.0166*** (.0009)
Age^2	−.0001 (.0001)	−.0003*** (.0001)
Veteran, no service-related disability[c]	0.2498*** (.0180)	0.1214*** (.0172)
Veteran, service-related disability	−0.0639 (.0393)	−0.1093** (.0365)
Age*Veteran, no service-related disability	−0.0071*** (.0013)	−0.0113*** (.0012)
Age^2*Veteran, no service-related disability	−0.0004*** (.0001)	−0.0004*** (.0001)
Age*Veteran, service-related disability	0.0053+ (.0031)	−0.0033 (.0028)
Age^2*Veteran, service-related disability	−0.0007*** (.0002)	−0.0007*** (.0001)

Note. $N = 72,161$ for both models. b = coefficient. *SE* = standard error.
[a]Model 1 only includes the variables shown in the table. [b]Model 2 includes controls for age 18 birth cohort, race/ethnicity, childhood disadvantage, childhood health, education, labor force participation, household income, marital status, smoking, drinking alcohol, underweight and overweight, and ever had a proxy respondent, lost to follow-up, or died during the study period. Complete models are available from the first author on request. [c]Nonveteran is the reference category for the service-related disability categories.
+$p < .10$, *$p < .05$, **$p < .01$, ***$p < .001$.

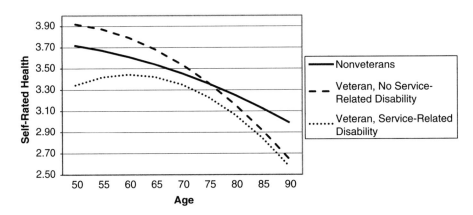

Figure 7.2. Predicted self-rated health trajectories by service-related disability status.

disability have higher self-rated health than nonveterans. However, after age 70, the self-rated health of veterans with no service-related disability rapidly declines such that they have lower self-rated health than non-veterans after age 75. Veterans with a service-related disability have lower self-rated health throughout later life, although the discrepancy between this group and their veteran counterparts who do not have a service-related disability narrows substantially with age.

Table 7.4 presents the findings related to having a documented VA SCDR. Similar to the findings for service-related disability, veterans with no SCDR

TABLE 7.4
Growth Curve Models Estimating the Effect
of VA Service-Connected Disability Rating (SCDR)
on Men's Mid- to Late-Life Self-Rated Health Trajectories

	Model 1[a] b (SE)	Model 2[b] b (SE)
Intercept	2.9956*** (.0126)	3.5622*** (.0292)
Age	−0.0261*** (.0008)	−0.0176*** (.0009)
Age^2	−0.0001 (.0001)	−0.0003*** (.0001)
Veteran, no VA SCDR[c]	0.5852*** (.029)	0.2348*** (.0273)
Veteran, VA SCDR	0.1755** (.0597)	−0.0493 (.0539)
Veteran, unknown VA SCDR	0.1178*** (.0187)	0.0535** (.0181)
Age*Veteran, no VA SCDR	−0.0001 (.0019)	−0.0044* (.0018)
Age^2*Veteran, no VA SCDR	−0.00004 (.0001)	−0.0001 (.0001)
Age*Veteran, VA SCDR	−0.0059 (.0040)	0.0006 (.0038)
Age^2*Veteran, VA SCDR	−0.0002 (.0003)	−0.0004+ (.0003)
Age*unknown VA SCDR	−0.0068*** (.0014)	−0.0108*** (.0013)
Age^2*unknown VA SCDR	−.0006*** (.0001)	−0.0005*** (.0001)

Note. $N = 72,161$ for both models. b = coefficient. SE = standard error.
[a]Model 1 only includes the variables shown in the table. [b]Model 2 includes controls for age 18 birth cohort, race/ethnicity, childhood disadvantage, childhood health, education, labor force participation, household income, marital status, smoking, drinking alcohol, underweight and overweight, and ever had a proxy respondent, lost to follow-up, or died during the study period. Complete models are available from the first author on request. [c]Nonveteran is the reference category for the SCDR categories.
$+p < .10$, $*p < .05$, $**p < .01$, $***p < .001$.

have significantly higher self-rated health than nonveterans at the mean-centered age. However, unlike the findings based on the other measure of service-related disability, veterans with an SCDR are not significantly different than nonveterans at the mean-centered age in the fully specified model. Veterans whose SCDR is unknown have significantly higher self-rated health than nonveterans at the mean-centered age. The downward trend in self-rated health with age is accentuated for veterans with no SCDR and veterans whose SCDR is unknown.

Figure 7.3, which presents the predicted self-rated health trajectories by SCDR status, demonstrates the advantage experienced by veterans without an SCDR. Although their self-rated health declines more rapidly with age than that of nonveterans, this group continues to have better predicted values than nonveterans at every age from 50 through 90. Overall, veterans with an SCDR and whose SCDR rating status is unknown, respectively, are not substantially different from nonveterans across most of the ages, although they appear to have lower self-rated health at the most advanced ages.

CONCLUSION

Overall, the findings demonstrate the enduring effects of military service on men's health. Our prior research using the HRS (Wilmoth et al., 2010) found that veterans overall and war-service veterans in particular tend to have better health around retirement age but subsequently experience more rapid age-related health declines. This chapter extends that research by examining the effects of adverse military experiences on later-life health. The

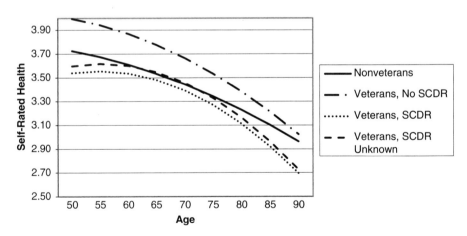

Figure 7.3. Predicted self-rated health trajectories by VA Service-Connected Disability Rating (SCDR) status.

findings suggest that exposure to adverse military experiences does not inevitably lead to negative later-life health outcomes. The results indicate that military service that causes physical or mental harm resulting in disability is associated with poorer later-life health outcomes. Regardless of whether the indicator is a general measure of military service-related disability or a more specific measure of a documented VA SCDR, veterans with a military service-related disability have lower self-rated health throughout later life. These findings underscore the importance of ensuring that adequate medical and social services are available to disabled veterans regardless of age. Contrary to our expectations, from age 50 through the late 70s, men who were exposed to combat fire exhibited better self-rated health than nonveterans and veterans whose combat exposure is unknown. Thereafter, combat fire veterans had worse self-rated health than nonveterans but continued to have better self-rated health than the veterans whose combat exposure is unknown. This suggests service that involves combat exposure may encourage the development of coping skills that facilitate successful aging. Given this, combat fire veterans might not need the same types of services as disabled veterans or use them as extensively in later life. But both groups are likely to require more services at advanced ages than nonveterans. Both groups would probably also benefit during young and middle adulthood from receiving consistent support aimed at ameliorating the negative effects of military service experiences, especially combat-related physical and mental trauma that results in disability. Earlier intervention in the life course might enable younger cohorts of All-Volunteer Force (AVF) veterans to avoid the steep later-life health and cognitive declines, and high later-life mortality, that have been observed among older veteran cohorts (Brown et al., 2014; London & Wilmoth, 2006; Wilmoth et al., 2010).

Unfortunately, the HRS data do not contain indicators of coping skills or appraisals of military service that would enable us to identify the mechanisms through which these effects operate (but see Chapter 1, this volume). The data also do not allow us to test the healthy-warrior effect, in which only the most physically fit are selected to serve in the military and sent into combat (Armed Forces Health Surveillance Center, 2007; Haley, 1998). It is also noteworthy that exposure to adverse military service experiences is unknown for the majority of veterans who did not participate in the 2006 to 2012 leave-behind survey or the 2013 Veterans Mail Survey and that the health trajectories of the veterans whose experiences are unknown are most similar to the veterans who reported experiencing adversity (i.e., combat and service-connected disability). This suggests that the veterans who experienced adversity may be underrepresented in the leave-behind and mail surveys. In addition, as previously mentioned, supplemental analysis indicated that older veterans who served in World War II and the Korean War were less likely to be in those surveys. Consequently, those supplemental surveys probably are not representative of the larger group of veterans included in the HRS.

The results are also conditional on survival to age 51, which is the youngest age of entry into the HRS as a primary respondent. Given this, there is likely unobserved heterogeneity because of midlife mortality that could result in the sampled veterans being healthier than the nonveterans. If so, our results likely underestimate the differences between veteran and nonveterans. Our findings also likely underestimate differences across service-related disability status, given that veterans may not self-identify as being disabled because of the importance of physical fitness in military culture (Griffin & Stein, 2015). Finally, we did not disaggregate the analysis by period of war service. Future research should evaluate the capacity of available samples to support such subgroup analyses.

Despite these limitations, we were able to elaborate on previous findings demonstrating that older veterans have different later-life health trajectories than nonveterans, thus illustrating the importance of taking into account the heterogeneity of military service experiences. Serving in the military has enduring effects on the lives of military personnel that continue into old age. The observed health differences between older nonveterans and various veteran groups cannot be explained by differences in the characteristics of the groups. Our fully specified models indicate early-life and mid-to-late life characteristics explain some, but not all, of the later-life differences between veterans and nonveterans in self-rated health. Some of this variation could be due to other unmeasured aspects related to military service (e.g., draft status, rank, military occupational specialty) and postservice experiences (e.g., use of GI bill benefits or VA services). Future research should consider these factors to the extent possible.

These veteran status differences in self-rated health could also be operating through specific health conditions. Although it is beyond the scope of the present analysis to model specific health outcomes, future research should consider how adverse military service experiences shape the risk of developing chronic conditions like heart disease, stroke, diabetes, arthritis, and cancer and influence veteran status differences in cause-specific mortality and all-cause mortality. It is particularly important to differentiate the detrimental effects of specific service-based events from the subsequent pathways through which these experiences shape the risk of disease and mortality. For example, exposure to environmental toxins or a prosmoking culture during military service (London et al., 2016) might directly increase the risk of certain types of cancer, whereas long-term stress processes stemming from adverse military experiences might be more consequential for heart disease. Isolating the factors contributing to veterans' unique patterns of disease and mortality will provide insight into the most effective interventions.

Overall, we need a more complete understanding of how the relationship between military service and health varies across cohorts. There is some evidence that Korean War and Vietnam War veterans are entering later life in worse health than World War II veterans (Wilmoth et al., 2010). It remains to be seen how the trajectories of these veterans will compare with World War II veterans as they move into more advanced ages. Veterans from the early AVF, who served between 1975 and 1990, are likely to be in better health in later life than veterans who served earlier during the 20th century because they, for the most part, were not subject to military operations involving direct combat. Although military service is less prevalent among more-recent birth cohorts, the physical and mental health needs of veterans who served in the Gulf War and Operations Iraqi Freedom/ Enduring Freedom/New Dawn are substantial. This is due in part to the nature of these recent wars, which have involved numerous short-term rotations in war zones, repeated use of reserve forces, and unconventional warfare with a high risk of injury due to improvised explosive devices. Improvements in military medicine have increased the chances of survival for those who are injured. Consequently, more military personnel have disabilities associated with posttraumatic stress, traumatic brain injuries, and limb amputation. Although veterans from older cohorts also suffered from lifelong service-connected disabilities, their experiences may not be applicable to more recent cohorts. Advances in treatment and rehabilitative technologies are enabling more effective interventions, which could result in veterans from more recent cohorts being in better health around retirement age and exhibiting slower age-related declines in health than veterans from the older cohorts.

Large-scale, nationally representative, longitudinal data are necessary to effectively track cohort differences in age-related health trajectories between veterans with various military service experiences and nonveterans. Data sets such as the HRS and National Longitudinal Surveys (http://www.bls.gov/nls/) provide foundations on which we can build our understanding of aging veterans, and Add Health (http://www.cpc.unc.edu/projects/addhealth) may eventually be able to do so. But often, the measures of military service experiences in these data sets are limited, and there are an insufficient number of veterans to support detailed analyses of differences by gender, race/ethnicity, and class. Extant data also do not adequately capture the potential influence of military service on the lives of those who are connected to military personal, including spouses, children, and parents. Attaining a more complete understanding of the impact of military service on lives will enable policymakers and service providers to more effectively meet the needs of currently aging populations and to plan to meet the needs of future cohorts of older veterans.

REFERENCES

Aldwin, C. M., Levenson, M. R., & Spiro, A., III. (1994). Vulnerability and resilience to combat exposure: Can stress have lifelong effects? *Psychology and Aging, 9,* 34–44. http://dx.doi.org/10.1037/0882-7974.9.1.34

Armed Forces Health Surveillance Center. (2007). Healthy deployers: Nature and trends of health care utilization during the first year prior to deployment to OEF/OIF, active components, U.S. armed forces, January 2002–December 2006. *Medical Surveillance Monthly Report, 14*(5), 2–5.

Beebe, G. W. (1975). Follow-up studies of World War II and Korean War prisoners: II. Morbidity, disability, and maladjustments. *American Journal of Epidemiology, 101,* 400–422. http://dx.doi.org/10.1093/oxfordjournals.aje.a112108

Bedard, K., & Deschênes, O. (2006). The long-term impact of military service on health: Evidence from World War II and Korean War veterans. *The American Economic Review, 96,* 176–194. http://dx.doi.org/10.1257/000282806776157731

Brown, M. T., Wilmoth, J. M., & London, A. S. (2014). Veteran status and men's later-life cognitive trajectories: Evidence from the Health and Retirement Study. *Journal of Aging and Health, 26,* 924–951. http://dx.doi.org/10.1177/0898264314534893

Brown, P., Zavestoski, S., McCormick, S., Linder, M., Mandelbaum, J., & Luebke, T. (2001). A gulf of difference: Disputes over Gulf War-related illnesses. *Journal of Health and Social Behavior, 42,* 235–257. http://dx.doi.org/10.2307/3090213

Card, J. J. (1983). *Lives after Vietnam: The personal impact of military service.* Lexington, MA: Lexington Books.

Centers for Disease Control. (1988). Health status of Vietnam veterans: II. Physical health. *JAMA, 259,* 2708–2714. http://dx.doi.org/10.1001/jama.1988.03720180034029

Clipp, E. C., & Elder, G. H., Jr. (1996). The aging veteran of World War II: Psychiatric and life course insights. In P. E. Ruskin & J. A. Talbott (Eds.), *Aging and post-traumatic stress disorder* (pp. 19–51). Washington, DC: American Psychiatric Press.

Davison, E. H., Pless Kaiser, A., Spiro, A., III, Moye, J., King, L. A., & King, D. W. (2016). From late-onset stress symptomatology to later-adulthood trauma reengagement in aging combat veterans: Taking a broader view. *The Gerontologist, 56,* 14–21. http://dx.doi.org/10.1093/geront/gnv097

Dobkin, C., & Shabani, R. (2009). The health effects of military service: Evidence from the Vietnam draft. *Economic Inquiry, 47,* 69–80. http://dx.doi.org/10.1111/j.1465-7295.2007.00103.x

Elder, G. H., Jr., & Clipp, E. C. (1989). Combat experience and emotional health: Impairment and resilience in later life. *Journal of Personality, 57,* 311–341. http://dx.doi.org/10.1111/j.1467-6494.1989.tb00485.x

Elder, G. H., Jr., Clipp, E. C., Brown, J. S., Martin, L. R., & Friedman, H. W. (2009). The lifelong mortality risks of World War II experiences. *Research on Aging, 31*, 391–412. http://dx.doi.org/10.1177/0164027509333447

Elder, G. H., Jr., Shanahan, M. J., & Clipp, E. C. (1997). Linking combat and physical health: The legacy of World War II in men's lives. *The American Journal of Psychiatry, 154*, 330–336. http://dx.doi.org/10.1176/ajp.154.3.330

Flynn, G. Q. (1993). *The draft 1940–1973.* Lawrence, KS: University Press of Kansas.

Griffin, C. L., Jr., & Stein, M. A. (2015). Self-perception of disability and prospects for employment among U.S. veterans. *Work, 50*, 49–58.

Haley, R. W. (1998). Point: Bias from the "healthy-warrior effect" and unequal follow-up in three government studies of health effects of the Gulf War. *American Journal of Epidemiology, 148*, 315–323. http://dx.doi.org/10.1093/oxfordjournals.aje.a009645

Hogan, D. P. (1981). *Transitions and social change: The early lives of American men.* New York, NY: Academic Press.

Idler, E. L., & Benyamini, Y. (1997). Self-rated health and mortality: A review of twenty-seven community studies. *Journal of Health and Social Behavior, 38*, 21–37. http://dx.doi.org/10.2307/2955359

Jennings, P. A., Aldwin, C. M., Levenson, M. R., Spiro, A., III, & Mroczek, D. K. (2006). Combat exposure, perceived benefits of military service, and wisdom in later life: Findings from the Normative Aging Study. *Research on Aging, 28*, 115–134. http://dx.doi.org/10.1177/0164027505281549

Jylhä, M. (2009). What is self-rated health and why does it predict mortality? Towards a unified conceptual model. *Social Science & Medicine, 69*, 307–316. http://dx.doi.org/10.1016/j.socscimed.2009.05.013

Jylhä, M., Guralnik, J. M., Balfour, J., & Fried, L. P. (2001). Walking difficulty, walking speed, and age as predictors of self-rated health: The women's Health and Aging Study. *The Journals of Gerontology: Series A. Biological Sciences and Medical Sciences, 56*, M609–M617. http://dx.doi.org/10.1093/gerona/56.10.M609

Keehn, R. J. (1980). Follow-up studies of World War II and Korean conflict prisoners: III. Mortality to January 1, 1976. *American Journal of Epidemiology, 111*, 194–211. http://dx.doi.org/10.1093/oxfordjournals.aje.a112887

Kleykamp, M. (2013). Labor market outcomes among veterans and military spouses. In J. M. Wilmoth & A. S. London (Eds.), *Life-course perspectives on military service* (pp. 144–164). New York, NY: Routledge.

London, A. S., Burgard, S. A., & Wilmoth, J. M. (2014). The influence of veteran status, psychiatric diagnosis, and traumatic brain injury on inadequate sleep. *Journal of Sociology and Social Welfare, XLI*(4), 49–67.

London, A. S., Herd, P., Miech, R. A., & Wilmoth, J. M. (2016). The influence of men's military service on smoking across the life course. *Journal of Drug Issues.* Advance online publication. http://dx.doi.org/10.1177/0022042616678617

London, A. S., & Wilmoth, J. M. (2006). Military service and (dis)continuity in the life course: Evidence on disadvantage and mortality from the Health and Retirement Study and the Study of Assets and Health Among the Oldest-Old. *Research on Aging, 28,* 135–159. http://dx.doi.org/10.1177/0164027505281572

MacLean, A. (2010). The things they carry: Combat, disability, and unemployment among U.S. men. *American Sociological Review, 75,* 563–585. http://dx.doi.org/10.1177/0003122410374085

MacLean, A. (2013). A matter of life and death: Military service and health. In J. M. Wilmoth & A. S. London (Eds.), *Life-course perspectives on military service* (pp. 200–220). New York, NY: Routledge.

Miech, R. A., London, A. S., Wilmoth, J. M., & Koester, S. (2013). The effects of the military's antidrug policies over the life course: The case of past-year hallucinogen use. *Substance Use & Misuse, 48,* 837–853. http://dx.doi.org/10.3109/10826084.2013.800120

Pietrzak, R. H., Tsai, J., Kirwin, P. D., & Southwick, S. M. (2014). Successful aging among older veterans in the United States. *The American Journal of Geriatric Psychiatry, 22,* 551–563. http://dx.doi.org/10.1016/j.jagp.2012.11.018

Sackett, P. R., & Mavor, A. S. (Eds.). (2006). *Assessing fitness for military enlistment: Physical, medical, and mental health standards.* Washington, DC: National Academies Press.

Schnurr, P. P., & Spiro, A., III. (1999). Combat exposure, posttraumatic stress disorder symptoms, and health behaviors as predictors of self-reported physical health in older veterans. *Journal of Nervous and Mental Disease, 187,* 353–359. http://dx.doi.org/10.1097/00005053-199906000-00004

Schnurr, P. P., Spiro, A., III, & Paris, A. H. (2000). Physician-diagnosed medical disorders in relation to PTSD symptoms in older male military veterans. *Health Psychology, 19,* 91–97. http://dx.doi.org/10.1037/0278-6133.19.1.91

Scott, W. J. (1992). PTSD and Agent Orange: Implications for a sociology of veterans' issues. *Armed Forces and Society, 18,* 592–612. http://dx.doi.org/10.1177/0095327X9201800409

Settersten, R. A., Jr. (2006). When nations call: How wartime military service matters for the life course and aging. *Research on Aging, 28,* 12–36. http://dx.doi.org/10.1177/0164027505281577

Settersten, R. A., Jr., Day, J., Elder, G. H., Jr., & Waldinger, R. J. (2012). Men's appraisals of their military experiences in World War II: A 40-year perspective. *Research in Human Development, 9,* 248–271. http://dx.doi.org/10.1080/15427609.2012.705558

Spiro, A., III, Settersten, R. A., & Aldwin, C. M. (2016). Long-term outcomes of military service in aging and the life course: A positive re-envisioning. *The Gerontologist, 56,* 5–13. http://dx.doi.org/10.1093/geront/gnv093

Street, D., & Hoffman, J. (2013). Military service, social policy, and later-life financial and health security. In J. M. Wilmoth & A. S. London (Eds.), *Life-course perspectives on military service* (pp. 221–242). New York, NY: Routledge.

Teachman, J. (2011). Are veterans healthier? Military service and health at age 40 in the all-volunteer era. *Social Science Research, 40*, 326–335. http://dx.doi.org/10.1016/j.ssresearch.2010.04.009

Teachman, J. D. (2013). Setting an agenda for future research on military service and the life course. In J. M. Wilmoth & A. S. London (Eds.), *Life-course perspectives on military service* (pp. 254–274). New York, NY: Routledge.

Teachman, J., Anderson, C., & Tedrow, L. M. (2015). Military service and alcohol use in the United States. *Armed Forces and Society, 41*, 460–476. http://dx.doi.org/10.1177/0095327X14543848

Teachman, J., & Tedrow, L. (2014). Delinquent behavior, the transition to adulthood, and the likelihood of military enlistment. *Social Science Research, 45*, 46–55. http://dx.doi.org/10.1016/j.ssresearch.2013.12.012

U.S. Department of Veterans Affairs, National Center for Veterans Analysis and Statistics. (2014). *Veteran population projection model 2014* [VetPop2014]. Retrieved from http://www.va.gov/vetdata/Veteran_Population.asp

Vogt, D. S., King, D. W., King, L. A., Savarese, V. W., & Suvak, M. K. (2004). War-zone exposure and long-term general life adjustment among Vietnam veterans: Findings from two perspectives. *Journal of Applied Social Psychology, 34*, 1797–1824. http://dx.doi.org/10.1111/j.1559-1816.2004.tb02586.x

Wilmoth, J. M., & London, A. S. (2011). Aging veterans: Needs and provisions. In J. L. Angel & R. Settersten (Eds.), *Handbook of the sociology of aging* (pp. 445–461). New York, NY: Springer. http://dx.doi.org/10.1007/978-1-4419-7374-0_28

Wilmoth, J. M., & London, A. S. (Eds.). (2013). *Life course perspectives on military service*. New York, NY: Routledge.

Wilmoth, J. M., & London, A. S. (2016). The influence of military service on aging. In L. George & K. Ferraro (Eds.), *Handbook of aging and the social sciences* (8th ed., pp. 227–250). Boston, MA: Elsevier. http://dx.doi.org/10.1016/B978-0-12-417235-7.00011-1

Wilmoth, J. M., London, A. S., & Heflin, C. M. (2015). The use of VA Disability Compensation and Social Security Disability Insurance among working-aged veterans. *Disability and Health Journal, 8*, 388–396. http://dx.doi.org/10.1016/j.dhjo.2015.02.004

Wilmoth, J. M., London, A. S., & Himes, C. L. (2015). Inter-cohort variation in the consequences of U.S. military service on men's mid- to late-life body mass index trajectories. In C. Burton-Jeangros, S. Cullati, A. Sacker, & D. Blane (Eds.), *A life course perspective on health trajectories and transitions* (pp. 133–154). New York, NY: Springer Science. http://dx.doi.org/10.1007/978-3-319-20484-0_7

Wilmoth, J. M., London, A. S., & Parker, W. M. (2010). Military service and men's health trajectories in later life. *The Journals of Gerontology: Series B. Psychological Sciences and Social Sciences, 65B*, 744–755. http://dx.doi.org/10.1093/geronb/gbq072

Wolf, D. A., Wing, C., & Lopoo, L. M. (2013). Methodological problems in determining the consequences of military service. In J. M. Wilmoth & A. S. London (Eds.), *Life-course perspectives on military service* (pp. 254–274). New York, NY: Routledge.

8

STUDYING LONGITUDINAL LINKS FROM EARLY ADULT ADVERSITY TO LATER-LIFE WELL-BEING: AMERICAN REPATRIATED PRISONERS OF THE VIETNAM WAR

LEWINA O. LEE, AVRON SPIRO III, ANNA L. TYZIK, DANIEL W. KING, AND LYNDA A. KING

Being captured and held as a prisoner of war is among the most excruciating human experiences, with effects that permeate all aspects of life and endure across the lifespan and even generations. The negative physical and mental health consequences of the prisoner-of-war experience have been documented from the Civil War to the Vietnam War (e.g., Nefzger, 1970; Nice, Garland, Hilton, Baggett, & Mitchell, 1996; Pizarro, Silver, & Prause, 2006; Speed, Engdahl, Schwartz, & Eberly, 1989). Although society recognizes and honors the gallantry and remarkable survival of these individuals,

This chapter was supported by National Institute on Aging Grants R24-AG039343 and K08-AG048221, and a Senior Research Career Scientist award from the Clinical Science Research and Development Service, U.S. Department of Veterans Affairs, to Dr. Avron Spiro. Research on the Vietnam RPWs was supported by grants from the Center for Naval Analyses (Terence Keane, PhD, principal investigator) and the R. E. Mitchell Center for Repatriated Prisoner of War Studies (Daniel W. King, principal investigator) to the Boston VA Research Institute, and the Massachusetts Veterans Epidemiology Research and Information Center, VA Boston Healthcare System. The views expressed in this chapter are those of the authors and do not necessarily represent the views of the U.S. Department of Veterans Affairs or other support institutions.

http://dx.doi.org/10.1037/0000061-009
Long-Term Outcomes of Military Service: The Health and Well-Being of Aging Veterans, A. Spiro III, R. A. Settersten Jr., and C. M. Aldwin (Editors)
Copyright © 2018 by the American Psychological Association. All rights reserved.

little research exists on factors that facilitated coping with captivity stress and enabled favorable adaptation following repatriation. In particular, repatriated prisoners of war (RPWs) from the Vietnam era are a unique group who endured lengthier captivity than their World War II and Korean conflict counterparts (Skelton, 1992), yet exhibited tremendous psychological resilience against such adversity.

This chapter documents demographic and other personal and military characteristics that predict health and adjustment among Vietnam RPWs, who were assessed on homecoming in 1973 and again in 2002. We first provide an overview of the population and the research program, followed by a review and synthesis of four empirical studies on the short- and long-term outcomes of these men. We then discuss the findings in relation to the broader literature to highlight key themes regarding stress, coping, and resilience processes gleaned from this population. Our goal is to identify factors that could ameliorate the deleterious effects of exposure to extreme stressors during captivity, as these findings may offer guidance for efforts to enhance resilience. This is especially timely given that these Vietnam veterans are in their later years, when possible long-term and previously latent effects of their war zone or captivity experiences can emerge and interact with the process of normal aging. We also compared RPWs from the Vietnam era with earlier cohorts to gain insight into unique factors that promote resilience in this group. Our findings have relevance for strengthening the knowledge base for future selection and training of military personnel and for efforts to reduce stress-related pathologies as they return to civilian life.

VIETNAM-ERA REPATRIATED PRISONERS OF WAR: AN OVERVIEW

From February to May of 1973, 567 American military personnel were repatriated from Southeast Asia to Clark Air Force Base in the Philippines and subsequently to the United States, following their imprisonment by opposing forces during the Vietnam War. These army, navy, marine, and air force men had endured, on average, about 4.5 years of incarceration in South and/or North Vietnam, with many spending the majority of their captivity in the infamous Hoa Lo ("Hanoi Hilton") prison. As with all RPWs, their stressor experience was multifaceted. In addition to the usual threats associated with combat and war zone exposures, most suffered injuries at the time of capture, illnesses during captivity, isolation from one another, no communication with families, psychological and physical torture, malnutrition, and poor sanitary conditions. Moreover, there was definite ambiguity concerning the length of captivity, uncertainty and distress regarding efforts on the part of their own country to secure their release, and despair over whether friends and family were aware that they were alive.

Vietnam RPWs differed from those taken prisoner in prior conflicts (see Oboler, 1987). Although each branch of the military (except the U.S. Coast Guard) was represented among these men, over 80% were air force pilots or navy aviators who were shot down while conducting aerial combat operations over North Vietnam. In contrast to other wars, when U.S. prisoners were fairly representative of the military, most of the RPWs were officers, career military, older, and college educated. Further, many had received specialized Survival, Evasion, Resistance, and Escape (SERE) resiliency training to prepare them to cope with the challenges and threats of the prisoner-of-war experience. Following their repatriation, many went on to reach the top ranks of military leadership, achieve significant roles in politics and government, or become prominent corporate executives.

The repatriation process began at the conclusion of hostilities between the United States and North Vietnam in 1973, with waves of returnees over several months. At Clark Air Force Base in the Philippines, these RPWs were administered a comprehensive examination by a team of medical, psychiatric, and psychological professionals and underwent military debriefings on their captivity experiences. When deemed medically stable for further travel, they were evacuated to the United States to be reunited with their families, and they received additional evaluations over several weeks at medical centers nearest their home or duty station.

This early collection of information on each RPW, coupled with personal and military information, was later archived within the R. E. Mitchell Center for Prisoner of War Studies, a program within the Navy Medicine Operational Training Center in Pensacola, Florida. The RPWs were followed over time by Mitchell Center staff and associates, with repeated assessments of their physical and mental health, especially during the first years following repatriation. In 2002, our research team collected additional information from the surviving RPWs via a mailed survey, which comprised a retrospective assessment of some aspects of their military service, captivity, and repatriation experiences using standardized measures, as well as an assessment of their current health and well-being. In summary, these two assessment occasions (1973 and 2002) provided data on the RPWs from the time of captivity to later life (see L. A. King et al., 2011, and D. W. King et al., 2015, for detailed descriptions of the study methods).

Because our RPW project relies on archival and longitudinal data, we must acknowledge the methodological impact of incomplete data. Two categories of incomplete data are relevant: one related to branch of service and the other to nonrandom loss of data over time. First, the pattern of available data differs somewhat by military branch. For example, a questionnaire on coping strategies during solitary confinement was administered only to the navy RPWs (Deaton, Berg, Richlin, & Litrownik, 1977). Data on weight change, nutrition, injuries, and illnesses are unavailable for air force RPWs, which limits the sample size of studies and representativeness of findings based on the archival data.

Second, as in all longitudinal research, the impact of nonrandom attrition due to dropout or death may be important. Of the 567 RPWs in the population, 471 were living and accessible through the Mitchell Center in 2002, of whom 292 participated in our follow-up mail survey (response rate = 62%). Respondents to the 2002 survey tended to be older, more educated, and more likely to be officers at the time of capture than nonrespondents, but otherwise the groups were similar on marital status, captivity duration and stressors, and repatriation mental health (D. W. King et al., 2015; Park, Pless Kaiser, Spiro, King, & King, 2012). It is possible that RPWs who were alive and willing to participate had greater resources at captivity and more favorable health in later life, resulting in a nonrandom pattern of missing data because of survival bias. We used full information maximum-likelihood estimation of missing data (Graham, 2012) by including covariates of missingness (e.g., age and education) in our analyses. This strategy assumes the missing data are dependent on the observed data and serves to minimize estimation bias.

DESCRIPTION OF THE POPULATION

Table 8.1 provides descriptive statistics on the RPWs by branch of service. At the time of capture, they were on average 30 years old, nearly 90% were officers, and three quarters were married. Army and marine RPWs tended to be younger, had less education, and were less likely to have officer status and be married than their air force and navy counterparts.

As mentioned previously, RPWs captured in North Vietnam were typically downed aviators. They were often used for propaganda purposes and suffered more systematic brutality and interrogations compared with infantry soldiers captured by the Vietcong in South Vietnam, who experienced less torture but were held in environments with lower chances of survival (e.g., imprisoned in bamboo cages and transported with Vietcong units; L. A. King et al., 2011; Skelton, 1992). These differences are illustrated in Table 8.1 by the greater proportion of time spent in North Vietnam and lengthier durations in captivity and solitary confinement of navy RPWs than army RPWs.

Captivity stressors are indexed by weight change, nutrition, injuries sustained prior to and at the time of capture, injuries and illness attributable to captivity, and physical and psychological torture during captivity. Vietnam RPWs reported an estimated weight loss of 10 to 20 pounds. As noted by

TABLE 8.1
Characteristics of Vietnam RPWs at Repatriation in 1973 and Subsequently in 2002

	Total	Air force	Navy	Army	Marines
Collected in 1973 (n % of total)	567	326 (57)	138 (24)	77 (14)	26 (5)
Demographics at capture:					
Age (SD)	29.90 (5.81)	31.01 (5.57)	30.80 (4.98)	24.91 (5.03)	26.04 (5.95)
Education (SD)	15.10 (1.89)	15.65 (1.34)	15.47 (1.45)	12.60 (2.03)	13.41 (2.68)
% Caucasian	96.1	97.6	99.3	83.1	100
% Married	75.1	83.3	74.6	53.3	46.2
% Officers (vs. enlisted)	89.1	97.2	100	45.5	57.7
General captivity descriptors:					
Captivity duration (months)	53.23 (29.54)	50.48 (32.39)	61.71 (26.90)	49.14 (18.82)	54.88 (22.86)
Solitary confinement (weeks)	32.64 (52.23)	n/a	38.87 (55.99)	11.26 (34.13)	52.05 (52.10)
% Captured before 1969	70.3	67.7	81.9	58.5	76.9
% Time in South (vs. North) Vietnam	14.4	n/a	<1	40.9	10.1
Captivity stressors:					
Weight change SD	1.43 (0.92)	n/a	1.35 (0.95)	1.53 (0.89)	1.60 (0.88)
Nutrition (SD)	6.03 (1.88)	n/a	6.15 (1.94)	5.63 (1.73)	6.56 (1.85)
Injuries at time of capture (SD)	2.34 (2.50)	n/a	2.27 (2.37)	2.58 (2.93)	2.09 (1.90)
Captivity injuries and illnesses (SD)	9.45 (5.02)	n/a	8.49 (4.80)	11.56 (4.97)	8.95 (4.71)
Physical torture (SD)	1.05 (0.54)	1.01 (0.51)	1.25 (0.54)	0.84 (0.51)	1.11 (0.71)
Psychological torture (SD)	1.33 (0.57)	1.29 (0.56)	1.52 (0.51)	1.21 (0.54)	1.34 (0.71)

(continues)

TABLE 8.1
Characteristics of Vietnam RPWs at Repatriation in 1973 and Subsequently in 2002 (Continued)

	Total	Air force	Navy	Army	Marines
Collected in 2002 (n, % of n in 1973*)	292 (51.5)	176 (54)	88 (63)	21 (27)	7 (27)
Age	64.88 (6.31)	65.28 (6.61)	65.48 (5.03)	60.22 (6.73)	60.12 (6.28)
% College graduate or more education	92.1	92.0	92.1	60.0	71.4
% Married	90.4	94.3	84.1	81.0	100
% Retired	62.3	64.2	38.1	38.1	71.4
SF-12 physical health functioning (T-score)	40.64 (9.97)	41.08 (9.60)	41.26 (10.70)	34.06 (6.87)	41.41 (12.33)
SF-12 mental health functioning (T-score)	50.65 (10.80)	51.43 (10.72)	51.29 (9.6)	42.77 (13.40)	46.94 (11.07)
PTSD symptoms	24.81 (10.07)	24.13 (9.35)	24.04 (9.28)	33.48 (15.11)	25.29 (8.32)
BSI anxiety symptoms (T-score)	52.12 (11.23)	51.08 (10.59)	50.91 (10.51)	62.71 (13.32)	56.86 (10.76)
BSI depressive symptoms (T-score)	54.79 (11.03)	54.24 (10.61)	53.22 (10.33)	64.43 (12.09)	57.00 (12.73)
Life satisfaction	20.35 (6.51)	20.76 (6.00)	21.19 (6.34)	13.62 (8.10)	19.86 (5.34)
Positive appraisal of military experiences	32.11 (6.18)	32.20 (6.46)	32.48 (5.46)	29.40 (6.88)	33.43 (3.87)

Note. RPW = repatriated prisoners of war; n/a = information not available. Weight change indicates difference in weight during captivity and on repatriation (range: 0 = none to 4 = within 40–60 lb). Nutrition indexes the number of food types endorsed as received at least once a week or more often (range: 0–11). Injuries at time of capture refers to the number of situational domains in which physical injuries incurred just prior to or around the time of capture (range: 0–6). Captivity injuries and illnesses refers to the number of bodily systems in which physical health problems were endured during captivity (range: 0–11). Physical torture indicates the frequency of exposure to incidents of physical abuse (e.g., deprivations, withdrawal of sustenance; range: 0–3). Psychological torture indicates exposure to incidents of psychological abuse (e.g., threats of nonrepatriation, attempts to elicit guilt for role in war; range 0–4.5). Physical and mental health functioning is based on the physical health component and mental health component scores, respectively, as assessed by the VR-12 (Ware, Kosinski, & Keller, 1994). Higher scores represent better functioning. PTSD symptoms were measured with the PTSD Checklist–Civilian (Weathers, Litz, Herman, Huska, & Keane, 1993; range: 17–85). Anxiety and depressive symptoms were measured with the Brief Symptom Inventory (BSI) and transformed to T-score using male nonpatient norms (Derogatis, 1993). Life satisfaction was measured with the Satisfaction With Life Scale (Diener et al., 1985; range: 5–35). Positive appraisal of military experiences was measured with 11 items on personal gains and growth attributed to combat and military services (King et al., 2007; range 0–44).
* % of n in 1973 does not account for individuals who were deceased or unable to be located for the 2002 mailing, and therefore it is lower than the actual response rate.

L. A. King et al. (2011), this is likely to be an underestimate of true weight loss because it indexes the difference between the estimated lowest weight during captivity and the actual weight on repatriation in 1973, following some improvement in diet and medical care prior to release. Readers should be cautious in comparing this index of weight change in Vietnam RPWs with that in the literature on World War II or Korean-era RPWs because the latter typically conceptualized weight change as the difference between weight at military induction or estimated precaptivity weight and estimated lowest weight during captivity (e.g., Sutker & Allain, 1996). The nutrition variable in Table 8.1 suggests a somewhat varied diet during captivity, with the RPWs receiving six out of 11 food types on a weekly or more frequent basis. The Vietnam RPWs had suffered just over two injuries at the time of capture and reported enduring injuries and illnesses in over nine bodily systems on average during their prolonged captivity. RPWs noted that both physical and psychological torture occurred occasionally to fairly often during captivity.

In 2002, the Vietnam RPWs were on average 65 years old. Over half (62%) were fully retired, and another 10% were semiretired. Most (90%) were married. Compared with 1973, when 65% had attained at least college education, 92% had done so by 2002. The aftermath of captivity remained visible in their physical health, as evidenced by scores on the SF-12 measure of health-related quality of life (Ware, Kosinski, & Keller, 1994), which were on average one standard deviation below the U.S. population mean. However, their mental health was on par with the general population. Fewer than 5% ($n = 13$) of the 2002 sample met criteria for probable posttraumatic stress disorder (PTSD), based on the cutoff score of 50 (Weathers, Litz, Herman, Huska, & Keane, 1993). Anxiety and depressive symptom mean scores were close to normative levels, except for the army RPWs, whose symptoms were on average 1.3–1.4 standard deviations above the norm. Air force and navy RPWs scored close to the slightly satisfied range (21–25) in life satisfaction (Diener, Emmons, Larsen, & Griffin, 1985), although the army RPWs scored in the dissatisfied range (10–14). The RPWs generally agreed or strongly agreed with statements on the benefits of their experiences, such as learning to get along with others and learning a lot about oneself.

RESEARCH STUDIES AND FINDINGS

Here, we review a series of four studies investigating the immediate and more enduring impacts of captivity on the Vietnam RPWs as they entered their later years, as well as factors that moderated or mediated the effects of captivity on later-life adjustment.

Captivity Stressors and Postrepatriation Mental Health

L. A. King et al. (2011) were the first to document the captivity experiences and mental health outcomes on repatriation for navy, army, and marine personnel. Repatriation mental health was indexed by measures of posttraumatic stress symptomatology (PTSS), general distress, and interpersonal negativity assessed within weeks after release from captivity. Being an officer was associated with better repatriation mental health compared with enlisted personnel. Men with more education, lengthier service at the time of capture, and a smaller proportion of captivity time in South Vietnam had better repatriation mental health. Greater physical torture was more strongly linked to PTSS in enlisted men than officers. Psychological torture was minimally related to PTSS and interpersonal negatively among officers, reflecting their preparedness, but a negative association was observed for enlisted personnel, such that those reporting higher levels of psychological torture endorsed less distress on repatriation than those reporting lower levels of psychological torture. This seemingly paradoxical association (greater torture, less distress) may reflect the diminishing efficacy of psychological torture when used frequently over time, arising from a greater sense of predictability and acclimation among its recipients.

Captivity Stressors and Later-Life Mental Health

Park and colleagues (2012) evaluated the associations of demographic factors, captivity stressors, and repatriation distress with mental health outcomes in later life using data from the 2002 survey. The associations of demographic factors and captivity stressors with mental health outcomes (Park et al., 2012) paralleled those reported for repatriation mental health outcome assessed in 1973 by L. A. King et al. (2011). Older age and officer status were linked to lower levels of PTSD, anxiety, and depressive symptoms in 2002; greater physical torture was related to higher levels of PTSD symptoms. Older age at captivity and lower levels of repatriation PTSS were consistently associated with lower levels of PTSD, anxiety, and depressive symptoms when the RPWs were on average 65 years old. Additionally, greater physical torture was linked to more severe PTSD symptoms, but not anxiety or depression, in later life, which speaks to the traumatizing nature of the stressor.

Tracing the Lifespan Effects of Captivity on Positive Adjustment in Later Life

Adopting a lifespan developmental perspective, D. W. King et al. (2015) examined direct and indirect pathways from demographic factors and torture during captivity, via repatriation mental distress, to later-life stressful events and psychosocial resources, and ultimately to later-life positive adjustment (mastery, life satisfaction, and mental health) in the 567 Vietnam RPWs. Paths in the structural equation model reflected a developmental sequence, beginning with "fixed" demographic characteristics at capture, continuing to the captivity experience and the postrepatriation period, and culminating with self-assessments of well-being in later life.

Older age and more education were resources that buffered against mental distress at repatriation; being married was no longer important after accounting for the effects of age and education. The effects of older age were mediated by lower levels of repatriation mental distress, fewer retirement concerns, and greater social support in later life, whereas education also indirectly facilitated later-life adjustment via less repatriation mental distress.

Although greater physical torture was associated with more mental distress on repatriation, it was also linked to more positive appraisal of military experiences in later life. In contrast, psychological torture was unrelated to repatriation mental distress and had marginal associations with later-life variables. Age, education, and physical torture were associated with repatriation mental distress, which, in turn, was linked to lower levels of positive adjustment in later life. D. W. King et al. (2015) proposed that repatriation mental distress served as an index of low psychological resources and integrity as RPWs emerged from a prolonged period of extreme suffering. RPWs in high distress on repatriation were depleted of resources, leading to a downward spiral and worse adjustment in later years, which could not be explained by social support and positive appraisal of military experiences in later life. On the other hand, RPWs who were psychologically resilient on homecoming were better able to parlay their resources into other accomplishments and positive adjustment over time.

Finally, normative later-life stressors were associated with lower levels of positive adjustment both directly and indirectly through greater retirement concerns and less social support in later life. Thus, late-life stressors such as widowhood and cognitive decline can predispose RPWs to anticipate retirement with anxiety and apprehension, thus reducing positive adjustment. This chapter takes a developmental perspective, considering factors that attenuate or exacerbate the long-term impact of captivity on subsequent well-being.

Role of Coping Strategies in the Long-Term Health Impact of Captivity Stressors

A coping measure was administered by mail to 69 naval aviator RPWs in 1974. The Solitary Confinement Questionnaire was developed to assess strategies used to "kill time" during solitary confinement (Deaton et al., 1977). Pless Kaiser et al. (2011) created an approach-based coping subscale, active engagement with solitary confinement (e.g., communicating with fellow RPWs by tap code), and an avoidance-based coping subscale, disengagement from the stressor (e.g., daydreaming, recalling past events). They assessed whether coping strategy use modified the association between four captivity stressors and five health outcomes measured in 2002. Captivity stressors included injuries sustained at or prior to capture, injuries and illness experienced during captivity, and physical and psychological torture; health outcomes included physical and mental health functioning, PTSD, and depressive and anxiety symptoms.

The associations between the coping strategies and long-term health outcomes were conditional on the magnitude of captivity stress. Among RPWs who suffered less physical torture than others, those who found approach strategies more useful and avoidance strategies less useful in coping with solitary confinement reported better physical functioning in later life. In contrast, among RPWs who suffered more severe physical torture, lower endorsement of approach strategies was linked to better physical health functioning in later life. A similar pattern was observed for mental health outcomes: Among RPWs who sustained fewer injuries at or prior to capture, those who found approach strategies helpful had more favorable mental health in later life; however, among RPWs who sustained more injuries, lower endorsement of approach strategies was linked to better subsequent mental health.

KEY THEMES FROM VIETNAM RPW STUDIES

Lower Levels of Psychopathology in Vietnam RPWs

A notable finding from these four studies is the low level of later-life psychopathology among RPWs from the Vietnam era (Park et al., 2012; Pless Kaiser et al., 2011), especially compared with RPWs from World War II and the Korean conflict. Table 8.2 summarizes the prevalence of PTSD among older RPW samples from World War II, the Korean conflict, and the Vietnam War. Caution is warranted when considering findings from small samples, such as the Korean War sample of Sutker and Allain (1996). Methodological considerations affecting prevalence estimates include somewhat higher rates obtained from use of questionnaires rather than diagnostic interviews, as seen in the MFUA study (Page, 1992), recruitment strategies, and time since repatriation. Turning points such as retirement and institutionalization as RPWs transition into the end of life can trigger a resurgence of PTSD symptoms (Davison et al., 2006, 2016; Rintamaki, Weaver, Elbaum, Klama, & Miskevics, 2009), suggesting higher rates of PTSD among old-old than young-old RPWs. Nonetheless, it appears that methodological factors alone

TABLE 8.2
Prevalence of Current PTSD Among Older RPW Samples by Era and Assessment Method

Era (M)	Year and age at assessment	PTSD prevalence	Instrument/PTSD criteria	Source(s)
Assessed by diagnostic interviews:				
WWII (475)	1984–1985, typical age 65–75	12–19%	DSM–III–R by SCID[a]	Page (1992)
WWII (188)	Mean age = 71 (SD = 4)	54–76%	DSM–III–R by DIS[b]	Sutker & Allain (1996)
Korea (408)	1984–1985, typical age 55–65	38%	DSM–III–R by SCID	Page (1992)
Korea (26)	Mean age = 72 (SD = 4)	88%	DSM–III–R by DIS	Sutker & Allain (1996)
WWII & Korea (426)	1984–1987	35%	Clinician-diagnosed DSM–III PTSD[c]	Eberly & Engdahl (1991)
Assessed by self-report questionnaires:				
WWII (352)	1984–1985, typical age 65–75	22–38%	Mississippi PTSD Scale[d] ≥89	Page (1992)
WWII (157)	2000–2005, age 70–90	12–34%	Mississippi PTSD Scale ≥91	Rintamaki et al. (2009)
WWII (442)	Age 58–78, mean age = 64 (SD = 4)	56%	Probable DSM–III PTSD based on a questionnaire constructed by the authors	Zeiss & Dickman (1989)
Korea (268)	1984–1985, typical age 55–65	45%	Mississippi PTSD Scale ≥89	Page (1992)
Vietnam (292)	2002, mean age = 65 (SD = 6)	4.5%	PCL-C > 50	Current chapter

Note. PTSD = posttraumatic stress disorder; WWII = World War II; RPW = repatriated prisoners of war; PCL–C = PTSD Checklist–Civilian; DSM–III–R = Diagnostic and Statistical Manual of Mental Disorders (3rd ed., rev.; American Psychiatric Association, 1987). [a]Abbreviated version of the Structured Clinical Interview for DSM–III–R, Non-patient Version (Spitzer et al., 1986). [b]National Institute of Mental Health Diagnostic Interview Schedule, computerized (Robins, Helzer, Croughan, & Ratcliff, 1981). [c]Clinician ratings were based on the Research Diagnostic Criteria for the Schedule for Affective Disorders and Schizophrenia–Lifetime (SADS-L; Spitzer, Endicott, & Robins, 1978) and a PTSD symptom checklist based on DSM–III criteria (65% of sample), or a review of records to derive the SADS-L and PTSD diagnoses. [d]The Mississippi PTSD Scale (Keane, Malloy, & Fairbank, 1984) is a paper-and-pencil measure that roughly approximates DSM–III criteria for PTSD.

cannot fully account for the large discrepancy in PTSD prevalence between RPWs from the Vietnam era and earlier conflicts.

Indirect evidence suggests lower levels of depressive symptoms among Vietnam RPWs compared with earlier cohorts. For example, when Vietnam RPWs were assessed in 2002, the Brief Symptom Inventory depression and anxiety subscale scores were lower than psychiatric norms and much closer to community norms (Derogatis & Melisaratos, 1983). On the other hand, estimated current prevalence rates of depression were noticeably higher among World War II and Korean conflict RPWs when assessed in 1994–1995 (Page, Engdahl, & Eberly, 1991). One factor that may account for the lower levels of later-life psychopathology among the Vietnam RPWs than earlier cohorts is the favorable reception that Vietnam RPWs received on homecoming. Most remained in the military, many made appearances as honored guests or speakers at public events, and some ran for public office (Sledge, Boydstun, & Rabe, 1980).

Maturity as a Resilience Factor

A prominent theme across the four studies of Vietnam RPWs is the protective effect of maturity against negative outcomes of captivity, both at repatriation and nearly 30 years later. D. W. King et al. (2015) found that older age and more education at capture enhanced psychological well-being in later life by attenuating repatriation mental distress; older age at capture was also linked to greater social support in later life. Park et al. (2012) reported that older age at capture was associated with lower levels of PTSD, anxiety, and depressive symptoms in later life. In the broader prisoner-of-war literature, older age at capture has also been related to less severe PTSD and depressive symptoms among older RPWs from World War II and the Korean conflict (Dikel, Engdahl, & Eberly, 2005; Engdahl, Page, & Miller, 1991; but see Zeiss & Dickman, 1989).

There is a strong correlation of officer status with age and education. Most Vietnam RPWs were pilots or aviators and therefore tended to be older and more educated than general military personnel (D. W. King et al., 2015). Air force and navy RPWs, who were predominantly (> 95%) officers, were on average 5 to 6 years older than army and marine RPWs, of whom about half were officers (see Table 8.1). Aircrew personnel received SERE training, which emphasized skills for enduring torture and solitary confinement, and provided psychological preparation and survival skills to navigate the captivity experience. Army RPWs were youngest, with the least education and the lowest proportion of officers at captivity, and fared worse on physical and mental health outcomes than the rest of the group when assessed in 2002.

Greater education may be a proxy for general resources to cope with hardship and promote long-term adaptation. The positive association between education and physical health is well established (Montez & Friedman, 2015). Premilitary education has been consistently linked to lower likelihood of PTSD (Brewin, Andrews, & Valentine, 2000). Among Vietnam theater veterans, higher premilitary education protected against both the onset and maintenance of PTSD (Schnurr, Lunney, & Sengupta, 2004). Education may facilitate coping with captivity and postcaptivity life challenges by promoting problem-solving skills and self-efficacy. It may help cultivate cognitive resources that mitigate the traumatic impact of captivity, such as verbal ability to create a coherent account of the stressful experience (Sloan, Marx, Bovin, Feinstein, & Gallagher, 2012), mental flexibility to reevaluate core beliefs, and complex cognitive skills to assign meaning to the experience (Monson et al., 2006; Resick, Monson, & Chard, 2014).

The Silver Lining of Physical Torture

That greater physical torture was linked to more severe mental distress at repatriation (L. A. King et al., 2011; D. W. King et al., 2015) is consistent with a large literature on the detrimental mental health effects of captivity (e.g., Speed et al., 1989). However, physical torture was also related to greater positive appraisal of military service in later life (D. W. King et al., 2015). This finding resonates with those of Sledge et al. (1980): RPWs were more likely to report desirable changes in interpersonal (e.g., valuing communication) and cultural (e.g., greater interest in politics) domains as a result of captivity than were non-RPW controls who served as military pilots/navigators in Southeast Asia. RPWs captured before 1969 (i.e., those subjected to more systematic torture) were also more likely to report desirable changes about themselves, such as increased optimism and ability to discriminate important from trivial; 73% of RPWs endorsed having favorable "significant mental changes" attributable to their captivity experience. Compared with RPWs who did not endorse favorable mental changes, the "benefited" subgroup reported more conflict with captors over their physical treatment and more severe problems in prison (Sledge et al., 1980), which mirror D. W. King et al.'s (2015) finding of an association between more physical torture and greater positive appraisals of their military experience.

Posttraumatic growth, or positive psychological change emerging in the aftermath of stressful experiences (Tedeschi & Calhoun, 1996), is particularly relevant to understanding the long-term adaptation of RPWs. Despite mixed findings on the relation between PTSD and posttraumatic growth, one review noted a weak but positive association when posttraumatic growth was assessed using standardized measures (Zoellner & Maercker, 2006). For example, Solomon and Dekel (2007) found higher levels of posttraumatic growth among RPWs than combat veterans of the Yom Kippur War. The coupling of distress and growth resonates with Elder and Clipp's (1989) observations of greater psychological disturbance, but also greater endorsement of benefits, from their military service, and more pronounced gains in goal orientation, assertiveness, and ego resiliency among middle-aged World War II and Korean veterans who survived heavy combat compared with those reporting no/low combat. Thus, combat's legacy is reflected both in its destructiveness and its "comradeship, exhilaration, and lessons for living" (Elder & Clipp, 1989, p. 332), a perspective reiterated by others (e.g., Aldwin, Levenson, & Spiro, 1994; Settersten, Day, Elder, & Waldinger, 2012).

Feder et al. (2008) observed moderate or higher levels of posttraumatic growth in 19 out of 30 Vietnam RPWs assessed in 2003 to 2005. Longer captivity was associated with greater growth, consistent with findings of a positive association between event severity and posttraumatic growth (Aldwin et al., 1994; Settersten et al., 2012). Future work should examine whether perceived benefits of the captivity (or military) experience are related to other dimensions of well-being, particularly those more closely related to posttraumatic growth, such as purpose in life and personal growth.

Importance of Goodness of Fit in the Use of Coping Strategies

Much can be learned about coping from survivors of extreme adversity, such as being held as a prisoner of war. One early study, based on the Vietnam-era air force RPWs, found no association between coping during captivity and psychiatric diagnoses at repatriation and at 5-year follow-up (Ursano, Wheatley, Sledge, Rahe, & Carlson, 1986). Coping was operationalized by peer ratings of performance during captivity and whether one received any decoration on repatriation. However, this measure reflects little of the RPWs' actual coping strategies and is more an outcome of coping. Among RPWs who experienced more severe stressors, better coping outcome was related to repression, denial, and defensiveness.

The stress and coping literature has emphasized goodness of fit between coping efforts and other situational (e.g., stressor severity) or personal (e.g., appraisal) variables in determining coping effectiveness (Lazarus & Folkman, 1984). Among Gulf War veterans, greater use of approach-based coping with the most stressful combat stressor was associated with lower PTSD symptoms, particularly for those with greater combat exposure (Sharkansky et al., 2000). Among Vietnam veterans, problem-focused coping with Vietnam-related war zone experiences was related to optimal levels of postdeployment adjustment at moderate (but not low or high) levels of combat exposure (Suvak, Vogt, Savarese, King, & King, 2002).

In our work, Pless Kaiser et al. (2011) evaluated the goodness-of-fit hypothesis among Vietnam RPWs dealing with a prolonged and extreme stressor in relation to later-life well-being. Active problem-solving was most beneficial when the RPWs were more physically capable and situated in a less extreme (lower torture) context. RPWs who had less control over the environment because of torture or injuries benefited most from avoidance-based strategies. Being able to accurately read and anticipate the consequences of a low-control situation might have enabled them to conserve energy for recovery, accept the circumstances, and avoid unnecessary risks. Thus, personal characteristics and available resources determine the best possible course of action. The significant longitudinal associations that spanned 3 decades suggest that the RPWs likely generalized the coping strategies used successfully in captivity to other challenges as they reintegrated to postcaptivity lives.

IMPLICATIONS FOR POLICY AND PRACTICE

There has been significant recent interest in interventions, such as the Comprehensive Soldier Fitness program (CSF; Casey, 2011; Seligman & Fowler, 2011), to enhance psychological resilience among U.S. soldiers and returning troops. The Institute of Medicine (2014), however, found little support for the effectiveness of the CSF and similar programs. Our Vietnam RPW studies have led us to several recommendations for mitigating the burden of deployment stressors on our soldiers. First, there are individual differences in immediate outcomes and developmental trajectories among military personnel who share the same combat and deployment experiences (Spiro, Settersten, & Aldwin, 2016). Predictors of PTSD differ across populations, and even a relatively "universal" set of predictors varies in strength across groups that differ in demographic and/or stressor characteristics (Brewin et al., 2000). Interventions must be tailored to match the attributes and stress history of the recipients.

Second, maturity factors that bolster resilience suggest that there are long-term gains from providing greater training to younger military recruits prior to deployment. Military training programs should promote coping strategies that match simulated situations with varying levels of resources and differing situational demands.

Third, PTSD and posttraumatic growth can co-occur. Although significant resources are dedicated to enhance posttraumatic growth among returning veterans (Tedeschi & McNally, 2011), ongoing screening for psychopathology is equally important in the decades following homecoming. Even among asymptomatic individuals, life transitions or major life events could rekindle combat-related flashbacks and intrusive memories (Davison et al., 2016; Rintamaki et al., 2009). Health care providers should be encouraged to inquire about military service and screen for clinically significant distress among combat veterans.

In summary, our findings have implications for developing interventions to prepare younger cohorts of military personnel for potential hardship. Interventions should both mitigate symptoms and promote resilience.

REFERENCES

Aldwin, C. M., Levenson, M. R., & Spiro, A., III. (1994). Vulnerability and resilience to combat exposure: Can stress have lifelong effects? *Psychology and Aging, 9*, 34–44. http://dx.doi.org/10.1037/0882-7974.9.1.34

Brewin, C. R., Andrews, B., & Valentine, J. D. (2000). Meta-analysis of risk factors for posttraumatic stress disorder in trauma-exposed adults. *Journal of Consulting and Clinical Psychology, 68*, 748–766. http://dx.doi.org/10.1037/0022-006X.68.5.748

Casey, G. W., Jr. (2011). Comprehensive soldier fitness: A vision for psychological resilience in the U.S. Army. *American Psychologist, 66*, 1–3. http://dx.doi.org/10.1037/a0021930

Davison, E. H., Pless, A. P., Gugliucci, M. R., King, L. A., King, D. W., Salgado, D. M., . . . Bachrach, P. (2006). Late-life early emergence of early-life trauma: The phenomenon of late-onset stress symptomatology among aging combat veterans. *Research on Aging, 28*, 84–114. http://dx.doi.org/10.1177/0164027505281560

Davison, E. H., Pless Kaiser, A., Spiro, A., III, Moye, J., King, L. A., & King, D. W. (2016). From late-onset stress symptomatology to later-adulthood trauma reengagement in aging combat veterans: Taking a broader view. *The Gerontologist, 56*, 14–21. http://dx.doi.org/10.1093/geront/gnv097

Deaton, J. E., Berg, S. W., Richlin, M., & Litrownik, A. J. (1977). Coping activities in solitary confinement of U.S. Navy POWs in Vietnam. *Journal of Applied Social Psychology, 7*, 239–257. http://dx.doi.org/10.1111/j.1559-1816.1977.tb00749.x

Derogatis, L. R. (1993). *Brief Symptom Inventory (BSI): Administration, scoring and procedures manual* (4th ed.). Minneapolis, MN: National Computer Systems.

Derogatis, L. R., & Melisaratos, N. (1983). The Brief Symptom Inventory: An introductory report. *Psychological Medicine, 13*, 595–605. http://dx.doi.org/10.1017/S0033291700048017

Diener, E., Emmons, R. A., Larsen, R. J., & Griffin, S. (1985). The satisfaction with life scale. *Journal of Personality Assessment, 49*, 71–75. http://dx.doi.org/10.1207/s15327752jpa4901_13

Dikel, T. N., Engdahl, B., & Eberly, R. (2005). PTSD in former prisoners of war: Prewar, wartime, and postwar factors. *Journal of Traumatic Stress, 18*, 69–77. http://dx.doi.org/10.1002/jts.20002

Eberly, R. E., & Engdahl, B. E. (1991). Prevalence of somatic and psychiatric disorders among former prisoners of war. *Psychiatric Services, 42*, 807–813. http://dx.doi.org/10.1176/ps.42.8.807

Elder, G. H., Jr., & Clipp, E. C. (1989). Combat experience and emotional health: Impairment and resilience in later life. *Journal of Personality, 57,* 311–341. http://dx.doi.org/10.1111/j.1467-6494.1989.tb00485.x

Engdahl, B. E., Page, W. F., & Miller, T. W. (1991). Age, education, maltreatment, and social support as predictors of chronic depression in former prisoners of war. *Social Psychiatry and Psychiatric Epidemiology, 26,* 63–67. http://dx.doi.org/10.1007/BF00791528

Feder, A., Southwick, S. M., Goetz, R. R., Wang, Y., Alonso, A., Smith, B. W., . . . Vythilingam, M. (2008). Posttraumatic growth in former Vietnam prisoners of war. *Psychiatry: Interpersonal and Biological Processes, 71,* 359–370. http://dx.doi.org/10.1521/psyc.2008.71.4.359

Graham, J. W. (2012). *Missing data: Analysis and design.* New York, NY: Springer Science & Business Media. http://dx.doi.org/10.1007/978-1-4614-4018-5

Institute of Medicine. (2014). *Preventing psychological disorders in service members and their families: An assessment of programs.* Washington, DC: National Academies Press.

Keane, T. M., Malloy, P. F., & Fairbank, J. A. (1984). Empirical development of an MMPI subscale for the assessment of combat-related PTSD. *Journal of Consulting and Clinical Psychology, 62,* 888–891.

King, L. A., King, D. W., Schuster, J., Park, C. L., Moore, J. L., Kaloupek, D. G., & Keane, T. M. (2011). Captivity stressors and mental health consequences among repatriated U.S. Navy, Army, and Marine Vietnam-era prisoners of war. *Psychological Trauma: Theory, Research, Practice, and Policy, 3,* 412–420. Advance online publication. http://dx.doi.org/10.1037/a0021411

King, L. A., King, D. W., Vickers, K., Davison, E. H., & Spiro A, III. (2007). Assessing late-onset stress symptomatology among aging male combat veterans. *Aging & Mental Health, 11,* 175–191.

King, D. W., King, L. A., Park, C. L., Lee, L. O., Kaiser, A. P., Spiro, A., III, . . . Keane, T. M. (2015). Positive adjustment among American repatriated prisoners of the Vietnam War: Modeling the long-term effects of captivity. *Clinical Psychological Science, 3,* 861–876. http://dx.doi.org/10.1177/2167702614554448

Lazarus, R. S., & Folkman, S. (1984). *Stress, appraisal, and coping.* New York, NY: Springer.

Monson, C. M., Schnurr, P. P., Resick, P. A., Friedman, M. J., Young-Xu, Y., & Stevens, S. P. (2006). Cognitive processing therapy for veterans with military-related posttraumatic stress disorder. *Journal of Consulting and Clinical Psychology, 74,* 898–907. http://dx.doi.org/10.1037/0022-006X.74.5.898

Montez, J. K., & Friedman, E. M. (2015). Educational attainment and adult health: Under what conditions is the association causal? *Social Science & Medicine, 127,* 1–7. http://dx.doi.org/10.1016/j.socscimed.2014.12.029

Nefzger, M. D. (1970). Follow-up studies of World War II and Korean War prisoners: I. Study plan and mortality findings. *American Journal of Epidemiology, 91,* 123–138. http://dx.doi.org/10.1093/oxfordjournals.aje.a121120

Nice, D. S., Garland, C. F., Hilton, S. M., Baggett, J. C., & Mitchell, R. E. (1996). Long-term health outcomes and medical effects of torture among U.S. Navy prisoners of war in Vietnam. *JAMA, 276,* 375–381. http://dx.doi.org/10.1001/jama.1996.03540050035020

Oboler, S. (1987). American prisoners of war: An overview. In T. Williams (Ed.), *Post-traumatic stress disorders: A handbook for clinicians* (pp. 131–143). Cincinnati, OH: Disabled American Veterans.

Page, W. F. (1992). *The health of former prisoners of war: Results from the Medical Examination Survey of former POWs of World War II and the Korean conflict.* Washington, DC: National Academies Press.

Page, W. F., Engdahl, B. E., & Eberly, R. E. (1991). Prevalence and correlates of depressive symptoms among former prisoners of war. *Journal of Nervous and Mental Disease, 179,* 670–677. http://dx.doi.org/10.1097/00005053-199111000-00004

Park, C. L., Pless Kaiser, A., Spiro, A., III, King, D. W., & King, L. A. (2012). Does wartime captivity affect late-life mental health? A study of Vietnam-era repatriated prisoners of war. *Research in Human Development, 9,* 191–209. http://dx.doi.org/10.1080/15427609.2012.705554

Pizarro, J., Silver, R. C., & Prause, J. (2006). Physical and mental health costs of traumatic war experiences among Civil War veterans. *Archives of General Psychiatry, 63,* 193–200. http://dx.doi.org/10.1001/archpsyc.63.2.193

Pless Kaiser, A., Park, C. L., King, L. A., King, D. W., Schuster, J., Spiro, A., III, . . . Keane, T. M. (2011). Long-term effects of coping with extreme stress: Longitudinal study of Vietnam-era repatriated prisoners of war. *Journal of Traumatic Stress, 24,* 680–690.

Resick, P. A., Monson, C. M., & Chard, K. M. (2014). *Cognitive processing therapy: Veteran/military version: Therapist and patient materials manual.* Washington, DC: Department of Veterans Affairs.

Rintamaki, L. S., Weaver, F. M., Elbaum, P. L., Klama, E. N., & Miskevics, S. A. (2009). Persistence of traumatic memories in World War II prisoners of war. *Journal of the American Geriatrics Society, 57,* 2257–2262. http://dx.doi.org/10.1111/j.1532-5415.2009.02608.x

Robins, L. N., Helzer, J. E., Croughan, J., & Ratcliff, K. S. (1981). National Institute of Mental Health Diagnostic Interview Schedule: Its history, characteristics, and validity. *Archives of General Psychiatry, 38,* 381–389.

Schnurr, P. P., Lunney, C. A., & Sengupta, A. (2004). Risk factors for the development versus maintenance of posttraumatic stress disorder. *Journal of Traumatic Stress, 17,* 85–95. http://dx.doi.org/10.1023/B:JOTS.0000022614.21794.f4

Seligman, M. E. P., & Fowler, R. D. (2011). Comprehensive Soldier Fitness and the future of psychology. *American Psychologist, 66,* 82–86. http://dx.doi.org/10.1037/a0021898

Settersten, R. A., Jr., Day, J., Elder, G. H., Jr., & Waldinger, R. J. (2012). Men's appraisals of their military experiences in World War II: A 40-year perspective.

Research in Human Development, 9, 248–271. http://dx.doi.org/10.1080/15427609.2012.705558

Sharkansky, E. J., King, D. W., King, L. A., Wolfe, J., Erickson, D. J., & Stokes, L. R. (2000). Coping with Gulf War combat stress: Mediating and moderating effects. *Journal of Abnormal Psychology, 109*, 188–197. http://dx.doi.org/10.1037/0021-843X.109.2.188

Skelton, W. P., III. (1992). Repatriated prisoners of war: Tallying the tolls from each theater. *VA Practitioner, 9*, 69–75.

Sledge, W. H., Boydstun, J. A., & Rabe, A. J. (1980). Self-concept changes related to war captivity. *Archives of General Psychiatry, 37*, 430–443. http://dx.doi.org/10.1001/archpsyc.1980.01780170072008

Sloan, D. M., Marx, B. P., Bovin, M. J., Feinstein, B. A., & Gallagher, M. W. (2012). Written exposure as an intervention for PTSD: A randomized clinical trial with motor vehicle accident survivors. *Behaviour Research and Therapy, 50*, 627–635. http://dx.doi.org/10.1016/j.brat.2012.07.001

Solomon, Z., & Dekel, R. (2007). Posttraumatic stress disorder and posttraumatic growth among Israeli ex-POWs. *Journal of Traumatic Stress, 20*, 303–312. http://dx.doi.org/10.1002/jts.20216

Speed, N., Engdahl, B., Schwartz, J., & Eberly, R. (1989). Posttraumatic stress disorder as a consequence of the POW experience. *Journal of Nervous and Mental Disease, 177*, 147–153. http://dx.doi.org/10.1097/00005053-198903000-00004

Spiro, A., III, Settersten, R. A., & Aldwin, C. M. (2016). Long-term outcomes of military service in aging and the life course: A positive re-envisioning. *The Gerontologist, 56*, 5–13. http://dx.doi.org/10.1093/geront/gnv093

Spitzer, R. L., Endicott, J., & Robins, E. (1978). Research diagnostic criteria: Rationale and reliability. *Archives of General Psychiatry, 35*, 773–782.

Spitzer, R. L., William, J. B., & Gibbon, M. (1986). *Structured Clinical Interview for DSM–III, Non-patient version (SCID-NP-V; 12/1/86)*. New York, NY: Biometrics Research Department, New York State Psychiatric Institute.

Sutker, P. B., & Allain, A. N., Jr. (1996). Assessment of PTSD and other mental disorders in World War II and Korean conflict POW survivors and combat veterans. *Psychological Assessment, 8*, 18–25. http://dx.doi.org/10.1037/1040-3590.8.1.18

Suvak, M. K., Vogt, D. S., Savarese, V. W., King, L. A., & King, D. W. (2002). Relationship of war-zone coping strategies to long-term general life adjustment among Vietnam veterans: Combat exposure as a moderator variable. *Personality and Social Psychology Bulletin, 28*, 974–985. http://dx.doi.org/10.1177/014616720202800710

Tedeschi, R. G., & Calhoun, L. G. (1996). The Posttraumatic Growth Inventory: Measuring the positive legacy of trauma. *Journal of Traumatic Stress, 9*, 455–471. http://dx.doi.org/10.1002/jts.2490090305

Tedeschi, R. G., & McNally, R. J. (2011). Can we facilitate posttraumatic growth in combat veterans? *American Psychologist, 66*, 19–24. http://dx.doi.org/10.1037/a0021896

Ursano, R. J., Wheatley, R., Sledge, W., Rahe, A., & Carlson, E. (1986). Coping and recovery styles in the Vietnam era prisoner of war. *Journal of Nervous and Mental Disease, 174,* 707–714. http://dx.doi.org/10.1097/00005053-198612000-00001

Ware, J. E., Jr., Kosinski, M., & Keller, S. K. (1994). *SF-36 Physical and Mental Health Summary Scales.* Boston, MA: The Health Institute, New England Medical Center.

Weathers, F. W., Litz, B. T., Herman, D. S., Huska, J. A., & Keane, T. M. (1993, October). *The PTSD Checklist: Reliability, validity, and diagnostic utility.* Paper presented at the annual meeting of the International Society for Traumatic Stress Studies, San Antonio, TX.

Zeiss, R. A., & Dickman, H. R. (1989). PTSD 40 years later: Incidence and person-situation correlates in former POWs. *Journal of Clinical Psychology, 45,* 80–87. http://dx.doi.org/10.1002/1097-4679(198901)45:1<80::AID-JCLP2270450112>3.0.CO;2-V

Zoellner, T., & Maercker, A. (2006). Posttraumatic growth in clinical psychology—a critical review and introduction of a two component model. *Clinical Psychology Review, 26,* 626–653. http://dx.doi.org/10.1016/j.cpr.2006.01.008

9

THE IMPACT OF MILITARY SERVICE ON STRESS, HEALTH, AND WELL-BEING IN LATER LIFE

CAROLYN M. ALDWIN, CRYSTAL L. PARK, SOYOUNG CHOUN, AND HYUNYUP LEE

Military service and combat exposure can have lifelong effects, both negative and positive, on the health and well-being of veterans (Aldwin, Levenson, & Spiro, 1994; Spiro & Settersten, 2012; Spiro, Settersten, & Aldwin, 2016; see also Introduction, this volume). As of 2012, there were over 21 million veterans, with an average age of 64; most (63.9%) were over the age of 55 (U.S. Department of Veterans Affairs, 2015). A third of all veterans have experienced combat exposure (U.S. Department of Veterans Affairs, 2010). Military service and combat exposure are two distinct and potentially important determinants of physical health and psychological well-being in many older adults, especially men.

In spite of a considerable amount of research, the influence of military service on health and well-being in later life remains unclear (MacLean & Elder, 2007). Some studies have found that military service or combat

Preparation of this chapter was supported by Grant R24-AG039343 from the National Institute on Aging.

http://dx.doi.org/10.1037/0000061-010

Long-Term Outcomes of Military Service: The Health and Well-Being of Aging Veterans, A. Spiro III, R. A. Settersten Jr., and C. M. Aldwin (Editors)

experiences have an adverse impact on health and well-being, whereas others suggest positive effects (see S. Kang, Aldwin, Choun, & Spiro, 2016; Spiro et al., 2016).

Clearly, the effect of veteran status on well-being in later life is a function of a multitude of factors. For example, the specific conflict (e.g., Bedard & Deschênes, 2006), military rank (Dechter & Elder, 2004), age at entry into military service (Wright, Carter, & Cullen, 2005), and social ties after returning home (S. Kang et al., 2016) have been shown to influence these associations. In addition, selection effects (those who served were healthier) and survivor effects (some had higher death rates and are not included in current studies) render seemingly simple associations difficult to interpret. For example, the military selects those who satisfy minimum physical and mental aptitude criteria, but these criteria may change over time (Bedard & Deschênes, 2006).

This chapter examines positive and negative effects of military service on later-life health and well-being in two ways.

First, it is likely that many of the contradictory findings in the literature are due to variations across studies in health-related constructs such as stress and psychological well-being. Because the effects of military service on physical and mental health are not uniform, it is necessary to better understand differences among groups that may ultimately affect health outcomes.

Second, it is likely that the effects differ depending on whether veterans experienced combat. We contrasted civilian older adults with two types of veterans: noncombat and combat. We suspect that noncombat veterans will report better health than civilians, given the selection criteria for entry into the military, but that adverse effects will be seen for combat veterans, whom we hypothesize will have lower levels of physical health and psychological well-being. Given the research on stress-related growth and psychological outcomes in military samples (Moore, Varra, Michael, & Simpson, 2010; see also Chapter 3, this volume), it is also possible that combat veterans may have higher scores on some types of well-being.

VETERAN STATUS AND PSYCHOLOGICAL WELL-BEING

We divided psychological well-being into three categories: stress, hedonic, and eudaimonic. Hedonic well-being reflects happiness or pleasure, while eudaimonic well-being is based on meaning and the actualization of human potential (Ryan & Deci, 2001).

Stress

Although stress is often perceived to be caused by military service, preexisting stress may also affect not only the decision to serve, but also how to serve. For example, although military service and combat exposure can give rise to both acute and chronic stress, the decision to serve in the military could be influenced by childhood adversity. Thus, it is necessary to disentangle the relationships among veteran status, preexisting and subsequent stress, and well-being in later life.

Individuals with very stressful childhoods may enter military service to escape adverse family and neighborhood environments (Stellman, Stellman, & Koenen, 2000; Werner & Smith, 2001) and may be more likely to serve in combat (Cabrera, Hoge, Bliese, Castro, & Messer, 2007). S. Kang et al. (2016) found that adverse childhood environments were more likely to engender negative appraisals of military service, which in turn were associated with poorer homecoming experiences, more stressful life events, and higher levels of posttraumatic stress disorder (PTSD).

Given that previous exposure to stressful events is a well-established predictor of subsequent exposure (e.g., Breslau, Davis, & Andreski, 1995), it is also possible that military service may increase lifetime exposure to future stressful events, particularly for those exposed to combat. In the Normative Aging Study, for example, combat veterans often became police officers or firefighters in their civilian life, which could have exposed them to further trauma (Schnurr, Spiro, Aldwin, & Stukel, 1998). Stressful events may affect health and well-being by leading to poor health behaviors (Gidycz, Orchowski, King, & Rich, 2008). Thus, combat exposure could increase the risk for future stress. Further, both trauma exposure and PTSD can also initiate kindling processes, whereby heightened sympathetic nervous system sensitivity may create startle responses and overreaction to minor stressors (Mroczek & Almeida, 2004). Thus, it is also possible that such individuals may report more microstressors. To our knowledge, however, no studies have examined these latter two types of stress as sequelae of military service and combat exposure.

Further complicating the links between military service and later-life health and well-being are the actual experiences that service members had while in the military—some are exposed to high levels of combat and other types of trauma, whereas others served in relative safety. Combat predicts poorer physical and mental health for many years following exposure (O'Toole, Catts, Outram, Pierse, & Cockburn, 2009). Combat exposure is related to higher levels of poorer physical health and higher mortality (Levy & Sidel, 2009), as well as mental health problems, particularly PTSD, anxiety, and depression (Prigerson, Maciejewski, & Rosenheck, 2002).

Combat exposure can increase future susceptibility to experiencing increased stress levels. For example, trauma-related PTSD can lead to impaired abilities to concentrate and to attend to potential dangers, information-processing deficits, inability to disengage from risky situations, high-risk behaviors, or substance abuse (Messman-Moore & Long, 2003; Orcutt, Erickson, & Wolfe, 2002). Similarly, military service can also lead individuals to experience heightened levels of chronic stress (Lazar, 2014). The impact of military service and combat exposure on subsequent stressors may be key to understanding their long-term effects on health and well-being in later life.

Hedonic and Eudaimonic Well-Being

The *hedonic* perspective focuses on happiness, generally defined as the presence of positive affect and the absence of negative affect, and life satisfaction. In contrast, the *eudaimonic* perspective emphasizes living life in a full and deeply satisfying way, including purpose and meaning in life, mastery, and spirituality (Ryan & Deci, 2000, 2001). Although related, these are distinct constructs with different correlates. Thus, military service and combat exposure may be associated with lower levels of hedonic but higher levels of eudaimonic well-being.

Relatively little research exists on the long-term associations between military service and hedonic well-being. One study reported inverse relations between combat exposure, as assessed in 1984, and later-life happiness and life satisfaction among Vietnam veterans at a follow-up 14 years later (Stellman et al., 2000). However, another study with a nationally representative sample found that veterans were more likely to be satisfied with life than were nonveterans (Britton, Ouimette, & Bossarte, 2012).

Little empirical research exists on the long-term effects of military service and combat exposure on eudaimonic factors, such as purpose in life, mastery, and religiousness/spirituality. Using life histories from longitudinal studies, Elder and Clipp (1989) developed a scale that documents the positive aspects of military service. Following their work, Aldwin and colleagues (1994) found that military service was associated with higher levels of mastery, spirituality, and coping skills in later life (see also Introduction, this volume). This finding was later replicated in a sample of British veterans (Aldwin & Levenson, 2005). Further, purpose in life was a significant predictor of global quality of life and positive aging in older veterans (Pietrzak, Tsai, Kirwin, & Southwick, 2014). Similarly, a sense of mastery was significantly related to life satisfaction as a protective factor against later-life stressors (Seligowski et al., 2012). Research on veterans with combat-related PTSD found that religiousness and spirituality were significantly associated with better recovery as a resource for positive adaptation (Currier, Holland, & Drescher, 2015). However, more studies are needed that examine the important roles of these existential factors in various aspects of health and well-being in late-life veterans.

Veteran Status and Health

The relationship between veteran status and physical health is complex. On the one hand, some literature suggests that older veterans have poorer health (see Wilmoth, London, & Parker 2010; see also Chapter 7, this volume); however, there is also the complication of selection effects, as veterans are typically in better health than nonveterans at entry to service (Sackett & Mayer, 2006). And there is a "healthy warrior" effect, in which combat soldiers are further selected for excellent physical and mental health (Larson, Highfill-McRoy, & Booth-Kewley, 2008).

As Wilmoth et al. (2010; see also Chapter 8, this volume) pointed out, most studies simply correlate aspects of military service, such as severity of exposure, with health outcomes and do not explicitly compare veterans with nonveterans, or different types of veterans (e.g., combat vs. noncombat). Further, there may be complex relations depending on the type of health outcome, the ages of the veterans, as well as the era in which they served. We examined two types of health outcomes in this study, global self-reported health and biomarkers.

Self-Reported Health

Surprisingly few studies have examined self-reported health by veteran status. Former prisoners of war often have very poor mental and physical health (Solomon, Johnson, Travis, & McBride, 2004; but see Chapter 9, this volume), as do combat veterans (Schnurr & Spiro, 1999). Male veterans exposed to both combat and noncombat trauma had greater increases in physical symptoms in later life (Schnurr et al., 1998). Wilmoth et al. (2010) reported complex patterns depending on age, veteran status, and location of service. In general, at age 62, veterans had more health conditions than did nonveterans, but fewer physical limitations and better self-rated health. Among veterans, those with war service had poor health on all measures. The differences shifted over time, with some groups showing better health in midlife but worse in late life, and vice versa. Thus, it is also important to focus on objective indicators of health.

Biomarkers

Only a handful of studies have examined biomarkers in veteran populations. Most of those are focused on the relationship between PTSD and stress-linked biomarkers, such as cortisol (Lehrner & Yehuda, 2014), as well as metabolic indicators of stress, such as low-density lipoprotein (LDL), and the findings are decidedly mixed. For example, Karlović, Martinac, Buljan, and Zoricić (2004) examined serum lipid levels in a small sample of Croatian

War veterans, about half of whom had PTSD. The combat veterans with PTSD had significantly higher levels of total LDL, and triglycerides, and lower levels of high-density lipoprotein (HDL) than those without. In contrast, Jendričko and colleagues (2009) compared serum lipid levels among small samples of combat veterans, combat veterans with PTSD, and healthy volunteers, and found no differences. However, these analyses controlled for age, body mass index (BMI), and smoking levels. Nonetheless, levels of homocysteine, a general measure of inflammation, were higher in combat veterans with PTSD, compared with both combat veterans without PTSD and healthy controls. Another inflammatory measure, C-reactive protein (CRP), may predict subsequent PTSD among soldiers who were about to be deployed to a war zone (Eraly et al., 2014). Given that stress can increase inflammation (Finch, 2011), it is important to examine the roles of stress and biomarkers among veterans. In this study, we also examine the relationship between biomarkers and positive aspects of well-being.

The Present Study

In the present study, we examined differences in health and well-being among three groups: combat veterans (CVs), noncombat veterans (NCVs), and civilians (CIVs). We examined how these groups differed in physical health, using both subjective and objective indicators, as well as health behavior habits. We were also interested in the amount of stress they might have experienced, including major life events, chronic stress, and micro-stressors, as well as their psychological well-being. We hypothesized that NCVs would be at an advantage over both CIVs and CVs in terms of their physical health, health behavior habits, and hedonic well-being, given that they were selected for good health (H. K. Kang & Bullman, 1996). However, CVs would have more stress, worse physical health and health behavior habits, and lower hedonic well-being than the other groups, given their higher level of trauma exposure during service (MacLean & Elder, 2007). However, such exposure can induce psychological growth; thus, they could have higher levels of eudaimonic well-being.

METHODS

Sample and Procedure

We used data from the Health and Retirement Study (HRS), an ongoing biennial longitudinal survey founded in 1992. Data were collected using the Psychosocial Questionnaire (PQ) from samples of the core panel participants who completed the enhanced face-to-face interview in 2004. The PQ was administered in either 2006 or 2008; response rates were about 90% at both occasions (see Smith et al., 2013). Our sample consisted of 3,412 men aged 50+ in 2006 (mean age = 67.7, SD = 8.9, range = 50–95) who completed the PQ in 2006 or 2008 and had biomarker data from these years. Only 103 (2%) HRS women served in the military, and thus they were omitted (see Table 9.1 for sample characteristics).

We divided the men into three groups: CIVs (n = 1,537, 45%), NCVs (n = 1,152, 34%), and CVs (n = 723, 21%). Using the dates provided in Online Appendix A (available at http://pubs.apa.org/books/supp/spiro/), 40% of the CVs served in the Vietnam War; 19% in World War II and 17% in the Korean War; 12% served in multiple wars, and 2% served during peacetime.

TABLE 9.1
Summary Statistics of Study Variables (N = 3,412)

	Variables	Mean	SD	Possible range
Demographics	Age	67.66	8.87	50–95
	Ethnicity[a]	.17	.37	0, 1
	Education	13.1	3.1	0–17
	Marital status[b]	.81	.39	0, 1
Health and health behaviors	Smoking	13.33	10.48	0–50
	Drinking	2.26	1.76	0–18
	Self-rated health	3.34	1.05	1–5
	Body mass index	28.46	5.02	10.61–61.01
Major stressors	Stressful life events	.24	.57	0–4
	Lifetime trauma	1.13	1.11	0–6
	Childhood adversity	.42	.65	0–3
Chronic stress	Discrimination	1.70	.75	1–6
	Treated unfairly	.57	.95	0–6
	Financial strain	1.83	.92	1–5
Hedonic well-being	Life satisfaction	5.18	1.37	1–7
	Depressive symptoms	1.39	1.84	0–9
	Positive affect	.08	.95	−3.66 to 2.03
	Negative affect	−.17	.87	−1.20 to 4.75
Eudaimonic well-being	Purpose in life	4.66	.90	1–6
	Mastery	4.88	1.03	1–6
	Religiousness	4.70	1.50	1–6
	Prayer	5.14	2.76	1–8
Biomarkers*	TC	193.36	39.26	89.1–349.54
	HDL	48.96	13.75	12.52–96.17
	HbA1c	5.86	.98	4.08–13.99
	CRP	3.73	8.47	.02–75.84

Note. TC = total cholesterol; HDL = high-density-lipoprotein cholesterol; HbA1c = hemoglobin A1C; CRP = C-reactive protein.
[a]Ethnicity (0 = non-Hispanic White, 1 = minority); [b]Marital status (0 = not married, 1 = married).
*Actual ranges are provided for these variables.

Measures

Means and standard deviations for study variables are provided in Table 9.1.

Demographics

Age, ethnicity, marital status, and education were assessed as potential covariates relevant to military experience. *Age* was assessed in 2006. *Education* was assessed by the number of years of schooling. Participants reported on *marital status* in 2006 (1 = married); *ethnicity* was also assessed (1 = minority).

Physical Health and Health Behavior Habits

Self-rated health was assessed on a 5-point Likert scale from *poor* (1) to *excellent* (5). *Body mass index* (BMI) was estimated using height and weight. *Health behaviors* included a dichotomous variable assessing current smoking status as well as the number of cigarettes smoked/day. Drinking status was derived from a question that asked whether they had consumed any alcohol in the past 2 years. The quantity of alcohol consumption indicated the number of drinks per day.

Major Stressors

Stressful life events (SLEs) in the past 5 years (Turner, Wheaton, & Lloyd, 1995) were assessed by summing five items, such as job loss, unemployment of self or family members, moved to worse residence/neighborhood, and robbery victimization. *Lifetime trauma* was measured with six dichotomous items (Krause, Shaw, & Cairney, 2004), including death of child, natural disasters, a life-threatening illness or accident (we omitted the combat item), which were summed. *Early childhood adversity* was assessed using three items that asked about lifetime traumatic events before the age of 18 (Krause et al., 2004) and scored by summing.

Chronic Stressors

Discrimination (Williams, Yu, Jackson, & Anderson, 1997) assessed the hassles and chronic stress related to perceived everyday discrimination. Six items were scored on a 6-point Likert scale, *never* (1) to *almost every day* (6). The items included being treated with less courtesy, receiving poorer service, people thinking you are not smart, people acting as if they are afraid of you, or being threatened or harassed ($\alpha = .80$). *Treated unfairly* was measured with six summed dichotomous items (Williams et al., 1997) that assess major experiences of unfair treatment (i.e., being denied housing, bank loans, jobs, promotions, or being unfairly treated by the police). *Financial strain* was assessed by an item asking "How difficult is it for (you/your family) to meet monthly payments on (your/your family's) bills?" (Campbell, Converse, & Rodgers, 1976). Responses were *not at all difficult* (1) to *completely difficult* (5).

Hedonic Well-Being

Life satisfaction was measured with the Satisfaction With Life Scale (Diener, Emmons, Larsen, & Griffin, 1985); five items were rated on a 7-point Likert scale: *strongly disagree* (1) to *strongly agree* (7) ($\alpha = .88$). *Depressive symptoms during the past week* were assessed using a nine-item dichotomous version of the CES-D (Center for Epidemiologic Studies Depression Scale; Radloff, 1977). *Positive and negative affect* were evaluated by 12 items in 2006 (Almeida, 1996) and 25 items in 2008 from the *Positive and Negative Affect Schedule–Expanded Form* (PANAS-X; Watson & Clark, 1994). Items were rated on a 5-point scale ranging from 1 (*none of the time*) to 5 (*all of the time*) and organized into two subscales: positive affect (six items in 2006, $\alpha = .91$, and 13 items in 2008, $\alpha = .92$) and negative affect (six items in 2006, $\alpha = .87$, and 12 items in 2008, $\alpha = .89$). These scales were z-scored to provide comparable scores for the samples measured in 2006 and 2008.

Eudaimonic Well-Being

Purpose in life was assessed with the Ryff (1989) Measures of Psychological Well-Being. Seven items were scored on a 6-point Likert scale, *strongly disagree* (1) to *strongly agree* (6) ($\alpha = .75$). *Mastery* was measured with five items of perceived mastery (Lachman & Weaver, 1998) rated on a 6-point Likert scale, *strongly disagree* (1) to *strongly agree* (6) ($\alpha = .90$). *Religiousness* was evaluated by four items from the Brief Multidimensional Measure of Religiousness/Spirituality (Fetzer Institute, 2003) rated on a 6-point Likert scale, *strongly disagree* (1) to *strongly agree* (6) ($\alpha = .92$). In addition, *frequency of prayer* was assessed by one item, "How often do you pray privately in places other than at church or synagogue?" Responses were *never* (1) to *more than once a day* (8).

Biomarkers

The HRS collected dried blood spot (DBS) samples by dripping spots of blood from participants' finger onto cards (Crimmins et al., 2013). Four biomarkers were assayed: *total cholesterol* (TC), *HDL cholesterol* (HDL, the so-called good cholesterol), *hemoglobin A1c* (HbA1c), a measure of blood glucose regulation, and *CRP*, an inflammatory indicator. We used the NHANES equivalent assay values for analysis after adjusting for between-lab differences (Crimmins et al., 2013).

RESULTS

CIVs were younger and less educated than the veteran groups (see Table 9.2), reflecting the greater mobilization among the World War II veterans and their access to education via the GI Bill. CVs were less likely to be married than NCVs, but the latter did not differ from civilians. We controlled for variables on which CIVs differed from veterans: age, ethnicity, and education.

As hypothesized, CVs were the worst off of the groups on most of the measures (see Table 9.2). They were more likely to smoke and had poorer self-rated health than the other two groups, as well as higher levels of SLEs, chronic stress, and lifetime trauma. They were more likely to report being discriminated against and being treated unfairly, and had higher levels of financial strain, although the NCVs did not differ from the CIVs. NCVs also reported more life events and lifetime trauma than the CIVs, who had less childhood adversity than the veterans.

CIVs' hedonic well-being also suffered (see Table 9.2). They had the lowest levels of life satisfaction and positive affect, and the highest levels of depressive symptoms. As hypothesized, the NCVs had the lowest levels of negative affect and the highest levels of positive affect, although the CIVs and CVs reported similar affect. Contrary to our expectations, there were no significant differences among the groups in purpose in life, mastery, religiousness, and prayer.

Despite the CVs' higher levels of smoking, poorer self-rated health, greater stress levels, and more psychological distress, there were no significant differences in biomarkers across the groups. They had comparable levels of total cholesterol and HDL, nearly identical levels of HbA1c, and comparable levels of CRP.

These findings were surprising. The CVs' worse physical and psychological profiles should have been reflected in their biomarkers. Thus, we conducted some exploratory analyses to make certain that the biomarkers correlated in the expected ways with the other variables in the study. The biomarkers were related to the other study variables in the expected ways, although the correlations were modest (see Table 9.3). Age was associated with lower levels of both HDL and TC, as well as higher CRP. Drinking was associated with higher levels of both TC and HDL. Ethnicity and BMI were associated with poorer HbA1c. Several of the stress variables, including SLEs and the chronic stress measures, were also associated with worse HbA1c. Hedonic well-being was associated in the expected directions with HbA1c and CRP. Even the eudaimonic variables were associated to varying degrees with the cholesterol, metabolic, and inflammatory measures. Thus, it is very surprising that the combat veterans did not have worse objective

TABLE 9.2
Multivariate Analysis of Variance by Veteran Status ($N = 3,412$)

	Study variable	Mean (SE)			Univariate test $F(df)$	Multivariate test
		CIVs	NCVs	CVs		
Demographics	Age	65.02(.22)[a]	69.25(.25)[b]	71.01(.32)[c]	(2, 3369) = 148.46***	Wilk's λ = .895, F(8, 6732) = 47.98, p < .05
	Ethnicity	.24(.01)[a]	.11(.01)[b]	.14(.01)[b]	(2, 3369) = 44.10***	
	Education	12.80(.08)[a]	13.27(.09)[b]	13.26(.12)[b]	(2, 3369) = 9.39**	
	Marital status	.80(.01)[a]	.83(.01)[a]	.78(.02)[b]	(2, 3369) = 3.42*	
Health and health behaviors	Smoking	.16(.01)[a]	.14(.01)[a]	.22(.02)[b]	(2, 2235) = 5.62**	Wilk's λ = .991, F(8, 4464) = 2.46, p < .05
	Drinking	.65(.02)	.64(.02)	.66(.02)	(2, 2235) = .23	
	Self-rated health	3.25(.03)[a]	3.31(.04)[a]	3.15(.04)[b]	(2, 2235) = 3.96*	
Major stressors	BMI	28.55(.17)	28.75(.18)	28.47(.22)	(2, 2235) = .57	Wilk's λ = .987, F(6, 6674) = 7.06, p < .001
	SLEs	.25(.02)[a]	.21(.02)[b]	.29(.02)[c]	(2, 3360) = 5.29**	
	Lifetime trauma	1.04(.03)[a]	1.16(.03)[b]	1.27(.04)[c]	(2, 3339) = 9.88***	
	Childhood adversity	.37(.02)[b]	.45(.02)[b]	.49(.02)[b]	(2, 3360) = 8.54***	
Chronic stress	Discrimination	1.63(.02)[a]	1.66(.02)[a]	1.81(.03)[b]	(2, 3299) = 10.05***	Wilk's λ = .987, F(6, 6594) = 7.01, p < .001
	Treated unfairly	.51(.03)[a]	.57(.03)[a]	.69(.04)[b]	(2, 3299) = 8.42***	
	Financial strain	1.82(.02)[a]	1.77(.03)[a]	1.95(.03)[b]	(2, 3299) = 9.25***	

(continues)

TABLE 9.2

Multivariate Analysis of Variance by Veteran Status (N = 3,412) (Continued)

Study variable	Mean (SE)			Univariate test F(df)	Multivariate test
	CIVs	NCVs	CVs		
Hedonic well-being					
Life satisfaction	5.25(.04)ᵃ	5.21(.04)ᵃ	5.01(.05)ᵇ	(2, 3345) = 7.62***	*Wilk's* λ = .989, F(8, 6684) = 4.61, p < .001
Depressive symptoms	1.38(.05)ᵃ	1.23(.05)ᵃ	1.64(.07)ᵇ	(2, 3345) = 11.85***	
Positive affect	.09(.03)ᵇ	.12(.03)ᵃ	.02(.04)ᵇ	(2, 3345) = 2.80†	
Negative affect	−.17(.02)ᵇ	−.25(.03)ᵃ	−.10(.03)ᵇ	(2, 3345) = 7.54**	
Eudaimonic well-being					
Purpose in life	4.67(.02)	4.67(.03)	4.64(.03)	(2, 3245) = .44	*Wilk's* λ = .997, F(8, 6484) = 1.32, *ns.*
Mastery	4.89(.03)	4.93(.03)	4.83(.04)	(2, 3245) = 2.12	
Religiousness	4.68(.04)	4.75(.04)	4.70(.06)	(2, 3245) = .77	
Prayer	5.23(.07)	5.10(.08)	5.15(.11)	(2, 3245) = .74	
Biomarkers					
TC	197.5(1.1)	195.7(1.3)	194.6(1.6)	(2, 2677) = 1.13	*Wilk's* λ = .997, F(8, 5348) = .95, *ns.*
HDL	48.96(.40)	48.84(.47)	49.17(.58)	(2, 2677) = .10	
HbA1c	5.86(.03)	5.83(.03)	5.83(.04)	(2, 2677) = .34	
CRP	3.50(.24)	3.64(.28)	4.33(.35)	(2, 2677) = 1.94	

Note. All analyses (except for demographics) control for age, ethnicity, and education. SE = standard error; CIVs = combat veterans; TC = total cholesterol; HDL = high-density-lipoprotein cholesterol; HbA1c = hemoglobin A1C; CRP = C-reactive protein; BMI = body mass index; SLEs = stressful life events; ethnicity (0 = non-Hispanic White, 1 = minority); marital status (0 = not married, 1 = married); ns. = nonsignificant.
a,b,cMeans with different superscript letters are significantly different from each other using Bonferroni's post-hoc analysis.
†p < .10. *p < .05. **p < .01. ***p < .001.

TABLE 9.3
Correlations of Biomarkers With Study Variables ($N = 3{,}412$)

	Variables	TC	HDL	HbA1c	CRP
Demographics	Age	−.180***	−.049**	.025	.048**
	Ethnicity[a]	.022	.015	.129***	.030
	Education	−.006	.077***	−.096***	−.076***
	Marital status[b]	−.020	−.024	−.028	−.029
Health and health behaviors	Smoking	.028	.105	−.058	−.026
	Drinking	.113***	.103***	−.026	.016
	Self-rated health	.102***	.102***	−.201***	−.106***
	Body mass index	−.035*	−.195***	.219***	.102***
Major stressors	Stressful life events	.047**	−.024	.060***	.016
	Lifetime trauma	−.049**	−.044*	.032	.030
	Childhood adversity	−.009	−.042*	.044*	.006
Chronic stress	Discrimination	.013	−.030	.058***	.031
	Treated unfairly	.029	.021	.055**	.004
	Financial strain	.044*	−.045*	.092***	.027
Hedonic well-being	Life satisfaction	.003	.028	−.100***	−.044*
	Depressive symptoms	−.019	−.062**	.078***	.076***
	Positive affect	.015	.052**	−.081***	−.050**
	Negative affect	−.002	−.026	.054**	.047**
Eudaimonic well-being	Purpose in life	.049**	.067***	−.091***	−.063***
	Mastery	.026	.020	−.041*	−.018
	Religiousness	−.008	−.043*	.050**	.049**
	Prayer	−.029	−.034	.024	.022

Note. TC = total cholesterol; HDL = high-density-lipoprotein cholesterol; HbA1c = hemoglobin A1C; CRP = C-reactive protein.
[a]Ethnicity (0 = non-Hispanic White, 1 = minority); [b]Marital status (0 = not married, 1 = married).
*$p < .05$; **$p < .01$; ***$p < .001$.

physical health, despite clearly having higher behavioral and psychological risk factors.

DISCUSSION

This study examined both positive and negative effects of military service on health and well-being in later life, as well as the complex interplay between stress and military service. The noncombat veterans were lower on SLEs and negative affect, but higher on positive affect, than civilians or combat veterans. In contrast, the combat veterans were more likely to smoke, often had higher levels of both acute and chronic stress, and had lower levels of hedonic well-being. However, there were no differences between the groups on either eudaimonic well-being or the biomarkers, which is puzzling.

Military Service and Optimal Aging

As mentioned earlier, veterans are an excellent group in which to examine different ways of aging, from optimal to impaired (Spiro et al., 2016). On the one hand, veterans are selected for good health. After completing their service, they are also eligible for resources via the GI Bill, which allows them better access to higher education and housing. Those with low resources may turn to the medical care provided by the VA system. Thus, veterans may have an advantage over civilians for optimal aging. Pietrzak et al. (2014) found that 82% of veterans said they were aging optimally, versus 10% to 60% among general older adult samples (Aldwin & Igarashi, 2015).

Pietrzak et al.'s (2014) results were supported by the pattern of findings in this study. The noncombat veterans were more educated and more likely to be married than the civilians, and they had more positive affect and less negative affect. They also had lower numbers of SLEs than civilians but higher levels of lifetime trauma and childhood adversity. This latter finding supports Werner and Smith's (2001) observation that military service provides a turning point for children growing up in adverse circumstances. It provides an opportunity for young adults to escape difficult environments or families characterized by conflict, and provides training and other resources to achieve higher levels of education and better paying jobs.

Military Service and Impaired Aging

Veteran populations also provide an opportunity to examine impaired or vulnerable aging, especially among combat veterans, who may have higher levels of health problems, disabilities, and mental health problems (Asnaani, Reddy, & Shea, 2014). This assertion was also supported by our results. Compared with noncombat veterans, the combat veterans were less likely to be married and had higher smoking levels and poorer self-rated health. They also had higher levels of SLEs, lifetime trauma, and chronic stress, including discrimination, being treated unfairly, and financial strain, even though they were less likely to be minorities. Combat veterans also had more depressive symptoms and negative affect, the lowest life satisfaction, and less positive affect. Thus, being a combat veteran increases the risk for vulnerable aging. One third of the homeless are veterans; a third of these served in a war zone (National Coalition for the Homeless, 2009).

Military Service and Resilient Aging

Analyses of the biomarkers told a different story. There were no differences among the civilian and veteran groups on cholesterol, metabolic control, inflammatory factors, or BMI. Perhaps the history of physical fitness ingrained from military service compensated for the higher risk factors among the CVs. Physical fitness is one of the best predictors of optimal aging (Aldwin & Gilmer, 2013).

An alternative interpretation lies in the results seen with eudaimonic well-being. We had hypothesized that combat veterans would have higher levels of meaning in life, mastery, and the like, given the opportunities that trauma may afford for personal growth (Jennings, Aldwin, Levenson, Spiro, & Mroczek, 2006; Moore et al., 2010; see also Chapter 8, this volume). However, there were no differences among the three groups on eudaimonic well-being. Given the positive association between the eudaimonic measures and the biomarkers, perhaps the ability of the combat veterans to maintain eudaimonia was also protective and may reflect a type of resilience.

Study Limitations

There were several limitations to this study. Despite the large, national sample, it is likely that the veterans who were most vulnerable (e.g., homeless veterans, those with serious mental and physical health problems) may not have responded to this survey. Thus, we may have overestimated the health of the combat veterans (although the same caveats might apply to the other two groups as well). We were also unable to include women, as few in our sample were veterans. Thus, it is unclear how well these results might generalize to women veterans.

In addition, veterans from more recent wars have faced a different set of stressors. They have been exposed to different types of toxins as well as a greater preponderance of improvised explosive devices, resulting in more maiming and traumatic brain injury. Further, enhanced medical treatment has assured a much higher survival rate but also a much more disabled group of veterans. As Spiro et al. (2016) pointed out, different wars and cohorts may have very different service and homecoming experiences, so caution needs to be used in generalizing these results. Research is needed to replicate these results in veterans of more recent conflicts.

CONCLUSION

To our knowledge, this is the first study to compare such a wide range of outcomes across large samples of civilians, noncombat veterans, and combat veterans. Clearly, veteran samples afford an unparalleled opportunity to examine optimal and impaired aging. Future research should examine longitudinal trajectories in aging veteran populations and the mechanisms by which these experiences may influence outcomes, to better understand how aspects of military service impact later life.

REFERENCES

Aldwin, C. M., & Gilmer, D. F. (2013). *Health, illness, and optimal aging: Biological and psychosocial perspectives* (2nd ed.). New York, NY: Springer.

Aldwin, C. M., & Igarashi, H. (2015). Successful, optional, and resilient aging: A psychosocial perspective. In B. T. Mast, P. A. Lichtenberg, & B. D. Carpenter (Eds.), *APA handbook of clinical geropsychology: Vol. 1. History and status of the field and perspectives on aging* (pp. 331–359). Washington, DC: American Psychological Association.

Aldwin, C. M., & Levenson, M. R. (2005). Military service and emotional maturation: The Chelsea Pensioners. In K. W. Warner & G. Elder, Jr. (Eds.), *Historical influences on lives and aging* (pp. 255–281). New York, NY: Plenum Press.

Aldwin, C. M., Levenson, M. R., & Spiro, A., III. (1994). Vulnerability and resilience to combat exposure: Can stress have lifelong effects? *Psychology and Aging, 9,* 34–44. http://dx.doi.org/10.1037/0882-7974.9.1.34

Almeida, D. M. (1996). *National Survey of Midlife Development in the United States (MIDUS I) National Study of Daily Experiences (NSDE), 1996–1997.* Ann Arbor, MI: Inter-university Consortium for Political and Social Research.

Asnaani, A., Reddy, M. K., & Shea, M. T. (2014). The impact of PTSD symptoms on physical and mental health functioning in returning veterans. *Journal of Anxiety Disorders, 28,* 310–317. http://dx.doi.org/10.1016/j.janxdis.2014.01.005

Bedard, K., & Deschênes, O. (2006). The long-term impact of military service on health: Evidence from World War II and Korean War veterans. *The American Economic Review, 96,* 176–194. http://dx.doi.org/10.1257/000282806776157731

Breslau, N., Davis, G. C., & Andreski, P. (1995). Risk factors for PTSD-related traumatic events: A prospective analysis. *The American Journal of Psychiatry, 152,* 529–535. http://dx.doi.org/10.1176/ajp.152.4.529

Britton, P. C., Ouimette, P. C., & Bossarte, R. M. (2012). The effect of depression on the association between military service and life satisfaction. *Quality of Life Research, 21,* 1857–1862. http://dx.doi.org/10.1007/s11136-011-0104-4

Cabrera, O. A., Hoge, C. W., Bliese, P. D., Castro, C. A., & Messer, S. C. (2007). Childhood adversity and combat as predictors of depression and post-traumatic stress in deployed troops. *American Journal of Preventive Medicine, 33,* 77–82. http://dx.doi.org/10.1016/j.amepre.2007.03.019

Campbell, A., Converse, P. E., & Rodgers, W. L. (1976). *The quality of American life: Perceptions, evaluations, and satisfactions.* New York, NY: Russell Sage Foundation.

Crimmins, E., Faul, J., Kim, J. K., Guyer, H., Langa, K., Ofstedal, M. B., . . . Weir, D. (2013). *HRS documentation report: Documentation of biomarkers in the 2006 and 2008 Health and Retirement Study.* Ann Arbor: University of Michigan Survey Research Center. Retrieved from http://hrsonline.isr.umich.edu/index.php?p=userg

Currier, J. M., Holland, J. M., & Drescher, K. D. (2015). Spirituality factors in the prediction of outcomes of PTSD treatment for U.S. military veterans. *Journal of Traumatic Stress, 28,* 57–64. http://dx.doi.org/10.1002/jts.21978

Dechter, A. R., & Elder, G. H., Jr. (2004). World War II mobilization in men's work lives: Continuity or disruption for the middle class? *American Journal of Sociology*, *110*, 761–793. http://dx.doi.org/10.1086/422662

Diener, E., Emmons, R. A., Larsen, R. J., & Griffin, S. (1985). The Satisfaction With Life Scale. *Journal of Personality Assessment*, *49*, 71–75. http://dx.doi.org/10.1207/s15327752jpa4901_13

Elder, G. H., Jr., & Clipp, E. C. (1989). Combat experience and emotional health: Impairment and resilience in later life. *Journal of Personality*, *57*, 311–341. http://dx.doi.org/10.1111/j.1467-6494.1989.tb00485.x

Eraly, S. A., Nievergelt, C. M., Maihofer, A. X., Barkauskas, D. A., Biswas, N., Agorastos, A., . . . Marine Resiliency Study Team. (2014). Assessment of plasma C-reactive protein as a biomarker of posttraumatic stress disorder risk. *JAMA Psychiatry*, *71*, 423–431. http://dx.doi.org/10.1001/jamapsychiatry.2013.4374

Fetzer Institute. (2003). Brief Multidimensional Measure of Religiousness/Spirituality: 1999. In N. W. Group (Ed.), *Multidimensional measurement of religiousness/spirituality for use in health research* (2nd ed., pp. 85–88). Kalamazoo, MI: John E. Fetzer Institute. Retrieved from https://www.gem-measures.org/Public/MeasureDetail.aspx?mid=1155&cat=2

Finch, C. E. (2011). Inflammation in aging processes: An integrative and ecological perspective. In E. J. Masoro & S. N. Anstad (Eds.), *Handbook of the biology of aging* (7th ed., pp. 275–296). San Diego, CA: Academic Press. http://dx.doi.org/10.1016/B978-0-12-378638-8.00012-9

Gidycz, C. A., Orchowski, L. M., King, C. R., & Rich, C. L. (2008). Sexual victimization and health-risk behaviors: A prospective analysis of college women. *Journal of Interpersonal Violence*, *23*, 744–763. http://dx.doi.org/10.1177/0886260507313944

Jendričko, T., Vidović, A., Grubisić-Ilić, M., Romić, Z., Kovacić, Z., & Kozarić-Kovacić, D. (2009). Homocysteine and serum lipids concentration in male war veterans with posttraumatic stress disorder. *Progress in Neuro-Psychopharmacology & Biological Psychiatry*, *33*, 134–140. http://dx.doi.org/10.1016/j.pnpbp.2008.11.002

Jennings, P., Aldwin, C. M., Levenson, M. R., Spiro, A., III, & Mroczek, D. M. (2006). Combat exposure, perceived benefits of military service, and wisdom in later life: Findings from the Normative Aging Study. *Research on Aging*, *28*, 115–134. http://dx.doi.org/10.1177/0164027505281549

Kang, H. K., & Bullman, T. A. (1996). Mortality among U.S. veterans of the Persian Gulf War. *The New England Journal of Medicine*, *335*, 1498–1504. http://dx.doi.org/10.1056/NEJM199611143352006

Kang, S., Aldwin, C. M., Choun, S., & Spiro, A., III (2016). A life-span perspective on combat exposure and PTSD symptoms in later life: Findings from the VA Normative Aging Study. *The Gerontologist*, *56*, 22–32. http://dx.doi.org/10.1093/geront/gnv120

Karlović, D., Martinac, M., Buljan, D., & Zoricić, Z. (2004). Relationship between serum lipid concentrations and posttraumatic stress disorder symptoms in soldiers with combat experiences. *Acta Medica Okayama*, *58*, 23–27.

Krause, N., Shaw, B. A., & Cairney, J. (2004). A descriptive epidemiology of lifetime trauma and the physical health status of older adults. *Psychology and Aging, 19,* 637–648. http://dx.doi.org/10.1037/0882-7974.19.4.637

Lachman, M. E., & Weaver, S. L. (1998). The sense of control as a moderator of social class differences in health and well-being. *Journal of Personality and Social Psychology, 74,* 763–773. http://dx.doi.org/10.1037/0022-3514.74.3.763

Larson, G. E., Highfill-McRoy, R. M., & Booth-Kewley, S. (2008). Psychiatric diagnoses in historic and contemporary military cohorts: Combat deployment and the healthy warrior effect. *American Journal of Epidemiology, 167,* 1269–1276. http://dx.doi.org/10.1093/aje/kwn084

Lazar, S. G. (2014). The mental health needs of military service members and veterans. *Psychodynamic Psychiatry, 42,* 459–478. http://dx.doi.org/10.1521/pdps.2014.42.3.459

Lehrner, A., & Yehuda, R. (2014). Biomarkers of PTSD: Military applications and considerations. *European Journal of Psychotraumatology, 5.* Retrieved from https://www.ncbi.nlm.nih.gov/pmc/articles/PMC4138702/pdf/EJPT-5-23797.pdf; http://dx.doi.org/10.3402/ejpt.v5.23797

Levy, B. S., & Sidel, V. W. (2009). Health effects of combat: A life-course perspective. *Annual Review of Public Health, 30,* 123–136. http://dx.doi.org/10.1146/annurev.publhealth.031308.100147

MacLean, A., & Elder, G. H., Jr. (2007). Military service in the life course. *Annual Review of Sociology, 33,* 175–196. http://dx.doi.org/10.1146/annurev.soc.33.040406.131710

Messman-Moore, T. L., & Long, P. J. (2003). The role of childhood sexual abuse sequelae in the sexual revictimization of women: An empirical review and theoretical reformulation. *Clinical Psychology Review, 23,* 537–571. http://dx.doi.org/10.1016/S0272-7358(02)00203-9

Moore, S. A., Varra, A. A., Michael, S. T., & Simpson, T. L. (2010). Stress-related growth, positive reframing, and emotional processing in the prediction of post-trauma functioning among veterans in mental health treatment. *Psychological Trauma: Theory, Research, Practice, and Policy, 2,* 93–96. http://dx.doi.org/10.1037/a0018975

Mroczek, D. K., & Almeida, D. M. (2004). The effect of daily stress, personality, and age on daily negative affect. *Journal of Personality, 72,* 355–378. http://dx.doi.org/10.1111/j.0022-3506.2004.00265.x

National Coalition for the Homeless. (2009). *Homeless veterans.* Retrieved from www.nationalhomeless.org/factsheets/veterans.html#fn

Orcutt, H. K., Erickson, D. J., & Wolfe, J. (2002). A prospective analysis of trauma exposure: The mediating role of PTSD symptomatology. *Journal of Traumatic Stress, 15,* 259–266. http://dx.doi.org/10.1023/A:1015215630493

O'Toole, B. I., Catts, S. V., Outram, S., Pierse, K. R., & Cockburn, J. (2009). The physical and mental health of Australian Vietnam veterans 3 decades after the war and its relation to military service, combat, and post-traumatic stress disorder. *American Journal of Epidemiology, 170*, 318–330. http://dx.doi.org/10.1093/aje/kwp146

Pietrzak, R. H., Tsai, J., Kirwin, P. D., & Southwick, S. M. (2014). Successful aging among older veterans in the United States. *The American Journal of Geriatric Psychiatry, 22*, 551–563. http://dx.doi.org/10.1016/j.jagp.2012.11.018

Prigerson, H. G., Maciejewski, P. K., & Rosenheck, R. A. (2002). Population attributable fractions of psychiatric disorders and behavioral outcomes associated with combat exposure among US men. *American Journal of Public Health, 92*, 59–63. http://dx.doi.org/10.2105/AJPH.92.1.59

Radloff, L. S. (1977). The CES-D Scale: A self-report depression scale for research in the general population. *Applied Psychological Measurement, 1*, 385–401. http://dx.doi.org/10.1177/014662167700100306

Ryan, R. M., & Deci, E. L. (2000). The darker and brighter sides of human existence: Basic psychological needs as a unifying concept. *Psychological Inquiry, 11*, 319–338. http://dx.doi.org/10.1207/S15327965PLI1104_03

Ryan, R. M., & Deci, E. L. (2001). On happiness and human potentials: A review of research on hedonic and eudaimonic well-being. *Annual Review of Psychology, 52*, 141–166. http://dx.doi.org/10.1146/annurev.psych.52.1.141

Ryff, C. (1989). Happiness is everything, or is it? Explorations on the meaning of psychological well-being. *Journal of Personality and Social Psychology, 57*, 1069–1081. http://dx.doi.org/10.1037/0022-3514.57.6.1069

Sackett, P. R., & Mayer, A. S. (Eds.). (2006). *Assessing fitness for military enlistment: Physical, medical, and mental health standards.* Washington, DC: National Academies Press.

Schnurr, P. P., & Spiro, A., III. (1999). Combat exposure, posttraumatic stress disorder symptoms, and health behaviors as predictors of self-reported physical health in older veterans. *Journal of Nervous and Mental Disease, 187*, 353–359. http://dx.doi.org/10.1097/00005053-199906000-00004

Schnurr, P. P., Spiro, A., III, Aldwin, C. M., & Stukel, T. A. (1998). Physical symptom trajectories following trauma exposure: Longitudinal findings from the normative aging study. *Journal of Nervous and Mental Disease, 186*, 522–528. http://dx.doi.org/10.1097/00005053-199809000-00002

Seligowski, A. V., Pless Kaiser, A., King, L. A., King, D. W., Potter, C., & Spiro, A., III. (2012). Correlates of life satisfaction among aging veterans. *Applied Psychology: Health and Well-Being, 4*, 261–275. http://dx.doi.org/10.1111/j.1758-0854.2012.01073.x

Smith, J., Fisher, G., Ryan, L., Clarke, P. House, J, & Weir, D. (2013). *HRS Psychosocial and Lifestyle Questionnaire 2006–2010: Documentation report.* Ann Arbor: Institute for Social Research, University of Michigan, Ann Arbor. Retrieved from: http://hrsonline.isr.umich.edu/sitedocs/userg/HRS2006-2010SAQdoc.pdf

Solomon, A., Johnson, K., Travis, J., & McBride, E. (2004). *From prison to work: The employment dimensions of prisoner reentry* (Report of the Reentry Roundtable). Washington, DC: Urban Institute, Justice Policy Center.

Spiro, A., III, & Settersten, R. A., Jr. (2012). Long-term implications of military service for late-life health and well-being. *Research in Human Development, 9*, 183–190. http://dx.doi.org/10.1080/15427609.2012.705551

Spiro, A., III, Settersten, R. A., Jr., & Aldwin, C. M. (2016). Long-term outcomes of military service in aging and the life course: A positive re-envisioning. *The Gerontologist, 56*, 5–13. http://dx.doi.org/10.1093/geront/gnv093

Stellman, S., Stellman, J., & Koenen, K. (2000). Enduring social and behavioral effects of exposure to military combat in Vietnam. *Annals of Epidemiology, 10*, 480. http://dx.doi.org/10.1016/S1047-2797(00)00161-7

Turner, R. J., Wheaton, B., & Lloyd, D. A. (1995). The epidemiology of social stress. *American Sociological Review, 60*, 104–125. http://dx.doi.org/10.2307/2096348

U.S. Department of Veterans Affairs. (2010, October). *National survey of veterans, active duty service members, demobilized National Guard and reserve members, family members, and surviving spouses: Final report.* Retrieved from https://www.va.gov/survivors/docs/nvssurveyfinalweightedreport.pdf

U.S. Department of Veterans Affairs. (2015, June). Profile of veterans: 2012. *Data from the American Community Survey.* Retrieved from https://www.va.gov/vetdata/docs/SpecialReports/Profile_of_Veterans_2012.pdf

Watson, D., & Clark, L. A. (1994). *The PANAS-X: Manual for the positive and negative affect schedule-expanded form.* Unpublished manuscript, University of Iowa, Iowa City.

Werner, E., & Smith, R. S. (2001). *Journeys from childhood to midlife: Risk, resilience, and recovery.* Ithaca, NY: Cornell University Press.

Williams, D. R., Yu., Y., Jackson, J. S., & Anderson, N. B. (1997). Racial differences in physical and mental health: Socio-economic status, stress and discrimination. *Journal of Health Psychology, 2*, 335–351. http://dx.doi.org/10.1177/135910539700200305

Wilmoth, J. M., London, A. S., & Parker, W. M. (2010). Military service and men's health trajectories in later life. *The Journals of Gerontology: Series B. Psychological Sciences and Social Sciences, 65B*, 744–755. http://dx.doi.org/10.1093/geronb/gbq072

Wright, J. P., Carter, D. E., & Cullen, F. T. (2005). A life-course analysis of military service in Vietnam. *Journal of Research in Crime and Delinquency, 42*, 55–83. http://dx.doi.org/10.1177/0022427804270436

10

EXPLORING THE VETERAN MORTALITY DIFFERENTIAL: THE INFLUENCE OF WAR ERA AND SMOKING BEHAVIOR

SCOTT D. LANDES, MONIKA ARDELT, AND ANN T. LANDES

Because the military screens the health of incoming recruits, veterans can be expected to have better health than the general population. In theory, this would result in a positive mortality selection effect, often termed a "healthy veteran" effect (Liu, Engel, Kang, & Cowan, 2005), with veterans having a lower mortality risk than nonveterans. On the other hand, veterans typically are exposed to greater occupational hazards during their time of service than the general population, including threats posed by war. As a consequence, veterans may have a higher postservice mortality risk than nonveterans. Indeed, both of these mortality differentials have been confirmed. Some studies have reported that veterans in general have a lower mortality risk than their peers in the general population (Dalager & Kang, 1997; Kang & Bullman, 1996), but older veterans (over the age of 70) have a higher mortality risk than nonveterans (Liu et al., 2005).

We thank the leaders and members of the NIA R24 Military Research Network for their feedback on this project.

http://dx.doi.org/10.1037/0000061-011
Long-Term Outcomes of Military Service: The Health and Well-Being of Aging Veterans, A. Spiro III, R. A. Settersten Jr., and C. M. Aldwin (Editors)

These mixed findings indicate the possibility of a veteran mortality differential, that is, the mortality differential between veterans and nonveterans. This veteran mortality differential likely reflects both a healthy veteran effect due to the health screening of military recruits, as well as the hazards of serving in the military. However, this differential also could be due to a range of psychosocial or behavioral issues, including smoking behavior (MacLean, 2013; Wilmoth, London, & Parker, 2010). Smoking harms almost every organ in the body; is linked to increased incidence of cardiovascular disease, cancer, and chronic obstructive pulmonary disease; and is the single greatest cause of avoidable morbidity and mortality in the United States (Brown, 2010; Jacobs et al., 1999; Lakier, 1992; U.S. Department of Health and Human Services, 2014). Unfortunately, smoking is more prevalent among veterans than nonveterans (Bastian & Sherman, 2010; Feigelman, 1994; Klevens et al., 1995; McKinney, McIntire, Carmody, & Joseph, 1997). Although this finding is expected among older veterans whose years of service occurred during a time when the military provided free cigarettes to soldiers (E. A. Smith, Blackman, & Malone, 2007), it is unfortunately also the case among younger veterans. Indeed, Brown (2010) found that younger veterans are not only more likely to smoke than their peers in the general population, but that smoking rates for veterans born between 1975 and 1989 were comparable to the higher smoking rates in the general population in the 1960s and 1970s.

In general, smoking is a maladaptive behavior linked to coping with greater stress, such as exposure to combat (B. Smith et al., 2008). In addition to veterans having higher rates of smoking than nonveterans in general, both smoking prevalence and the amount of smoking increase for veterans during times of deployment (Bastian & Sherman, 2010; Cunradi, Moore, & Ames, 2008; Forgas, Meyer, & Cohen, 1996; Poston et al., 2008; Talcott et al., 2013). This is not surprising as the U.S. military has either deliberately or inadvertently fostered a culture where smoking is conceptualized as a way to deal with the increased stress presented by military service and war (Jahnke et al., 2011; McKinney et al., 1997; Offen, Arvey, Smith, & Malone, 2011; E. A. Smith & Malone, 2009a).

Early studies linking smoking behavior to increased mortality risk among veterans were based on the predominantly White, male veterans who served in the military between 1917 and 1940. For example, Dorn (1959) and Kahn (1966) showed that veterans who currently smoked had a higher mortality risk than former smokers or nonsmokers, and that veterans who were former smokers had a higher mortality risk than nonsmokers. Subsequent studies confirmed that life expectancy was lower for veterans who had ever smoked, and that current smokers had a higher mortality risk for all causes of death, cardiovascular disease, cancer, and respiratory disease (Rogot, 1978; Rogot & Murray, 1980).

In a study comparing male veterans to nonveterans from the 1920 to 1939 birth cohorts included in the Current Population Survey (CPS), Bedard and Deschênes (2006) found that veterans had a higher mortality risk for ischemic heart disease and lung cancer after age 40. However, they showed that smoking behavior accounted for 64% to 79% of the increased veteran mortality risk due to heart disease, and 35% to 58% of the increased veteran mortality risk due to lung cancer, for those ages 40 to 75. As they explained, smoking may be the key to understanding the veteran mortality differential because the increased health risk related to military service may reflect both exposure to service-related hazards and the development of smoking behavior.

To summarize, research has shown that an age-related veteran mortality differential may exist, with younger veterans having a lower mortality risk than their nonveteran peers, whereas older veterans have a higher mortality risk. Although this veteran mortality differential could result from both a healthy soldier selection effect (which is protective of mortality) and the increased risks of mortality associated with military service in general, and with deployment in particular, it could also result from the increased smoking behavior of veterans. We expand on these findings to further clarify the association between smoking behavior and the veteran mortality differential. Using data from the 1997–2004 National Health Interview Survey (NHIS) that were linked to National Death Index (NDI) mortality data through 2006, we first clarified whether a veteran mortality differential existed for the entire sample, and whether veterans who participated in the NHIS had a higher prevalence of smoking than nonveterans. We then asked whether controlling for smoking reduced the veteran mortality differential for the entire sample. To account for the possible effects of serving during wartime in addition to smoking behavior, we repeated the analyses separately for specific cohorts that did/did not serve during times of war. This study is unique because it accounts for both smoking behavior and membership in a war-era cohort when comparing mortality risks for veterans and nonveterans.

The following hypotheses were tested in this study:

- *Hypothesis 1:* A veteran mortality differential exists, that is, veterans have a higher mortality risk than nonveterans for the entire sample.
- *Hypothesis 2:* Veterans have a higher prevalence of smoking behavior.
- *Hypothesis 3:* Controlling for smoking behavior eliminates the veteran mortality differential.
- *Hypothesis 4:* Results vary by war-era cohort, with the veteran mortality risk only present for those cohorts who served during a time of war.

METHODS

Data and Sample

Data were from the 1997–2004 NHIS, linked to the 1997–2006 NDI. Created by the National Center on Health Statistics (NCHS), the NHIS-NDI Linked Mortality Files use the unique person identifier from NHIS data as a linkage to NDI death certificate data. Only cases with a known mortality status were included. The sample comprised 92,459 men ages 25 to 84 from the NHIS 1997–2004 sample adult-level data files. Women were excluded because there were not enough female veterans in the sample to permit quantitative analyses.

For the NHIS Survey, veteran status was self-identified. Survey respondents who were over 18 years of age were asked whether they had "ever been honorably discharged from active duty in the U.S. Army, Navy, Air Force, Marine Corps, or Coast Guard." Hence, this study does not include veterans who reported receiving any other discharge—general, other than honorable, bad conduct, or dishonorable. Further, the NHIS data only include respondents from the noninstitutionalized, civilian population. Therefore, no data are available in the NHIS for those currently serving in the military or those who live in long-term care facilities (Harris, Hendershot, & Stapleton, 2005). Nonetheless, the NHIS sample adult-level data provide a sizeable nationally representative sample of veterans and nonveterans in the U.S. noninstitutionalized population, with ample measures detailing health and health behavior.

The dependent variable was mortality status and was coded 1 if the NHIS survey participant was deceased prior to December 31, 2006; otherwise, mortality status was coded 0. Several covariates were included in the models. Age was coded in single years ranging from 25 to 84. Black was a dichotomous variable measuring race and was coded 1 for those respondents who identified their race as Black and 0 for all other races. Education was measured based on threshold levels of education (1 = *1–8 years of education*; 2 = *9–12 years of education without the completion of a high school diploma*; 3 = *achievement of a high school diploma or GED*; 4 = *completion of some college courses or an AA degree*; 5 = *completion of a bachelor's degree*; 6 = *completion of a master's degree or doctoral degree*). Family income < $20K is a dichotomous variable (1 = *combined family income less than $20,000 per year*; 0 = *family income greater than or equal to $20,000 per year*). In the NHIS, marital status was originally a nine-category nominal variable; it was recoded as a three-category variable measuring: married; widowed, divorced, or separated; and never married. For survival analysis, marital status was entered as two binary variables, with married designated as the reference category.

Health status was measured with two separate variables. The first dichotomous variable, fair–poor health, was constructed from a 5-point scale of reported health (1 = *fair or poor overall health*; 0 = *excellent, very good, or good overall health*). A further measure captured whether the respondent reported prior diagnosis of any of three medical conditions associated with smoking and higher mortality risk—circulatory disease, respiratory disease, or cancer. Smoking behavior was a three-level ordinal variable in the NHIS data that measured cigarette smoking behavior and was coded for never smoked, former smoker, and current smoker. For survival analysis, it was measured with three separate dichotomous variables, with current smoker designated as the reference category.

Analytic Plan

We used Cox regression models, a common method of survival analysis that allows analysis of the effect of predictor variables on the time-to-event for binary outcomes such as mortality, and censoring at the end of the observation period. Because the NHIS uses a complex, multistage sample design involving stratification and clustering, SPSS Version 22 Complex Sample Cox Regression was used for analysis. This allowed for variance estimation using NHIS design variables and weights provided for the linked NHIS-NDI data (National Center for Health Statistics, 2009). Because the 1997–2004 NHIS questionnaires had a similar structure, the pooled data were treated as one large sample, per suggestions from the NCHS. We calculated hazard rates for mortality risk on the basis of time in the study and occurrence of mortality, accounting for the study design features. Men who were alive at the end of the study period in 2006 were censored. Multiple imputations were used to impute missing data for education, family income, marital status, fair–poor health, and smoking status.

We began by testing whether a veteran mortality differential was present in the entire sample (Hypothesis 1). After analyzing differences in smoking behavior between veterans and nonveterans (Hypothesis 2), we tested whether including smoking behavior in regression models eliminated the veteran mortality differential in the entire sample (Hypothesis 3). We tested Hypothesis 4 by repeating prior analyses separately for each war-era cohort. For all models, we report hazard ratios (HR) and confidence intervals (CI) for risk of mortality. The HR provides the risk for dying during the study period; values equal to 1.0 indicate no increased or decreased risk of mortality, values above 1.0 indicate increased risk of mortality, and values below 1.0 indicate decreased risk of mortality. Loosely interpreted, the CI informs that we are 95% confident that the "true" HR is contained within the confidence interval.

To identify the war-era cohorts, we used the dates from the U.S. Code of Federal Regulations (2014). The NHIS does not provide information on dates of military service or whether a veteran experienced combat. Instead, war-era cohorts were constructed on the basis of the men's birth dates. The first war era analyzed in this study was World War II, which in the United States had an official start date of December 7, 1941. A November 11, 1942, amendment to the Selective Training and Service Act required all men ages 18 to 37 to register for military service. Therefore, we reasoned that veterans who turned 18 during a time of war were, on average, more likely to have wartime service, and to experience the stressors related to war, than veterans who turned 18 during a period when the United States was at peace.

On the basis of this reasoning, the war era cohorts were determined by subtracting 18 years from the start and end years of each war and grouping the men by associated years of birth (see Online Appendix A, available at http:// pubs.apa.org/books/supp/spiro/). Although it is likely true that some veterans born after 1972 served in the Gulf War or Iraq and/or Afghanistan, the low number of deaths among these younger men in the NHIS data prevented the analysis of these war-era cohorts. Therefore, these younger veterans and nonveterans were included in the post-Vietnam-era cohort.

RESULTS

Bivariate Comparison of Veterans and Nonveterans

Table 10.1 compares categorical variables between veterans and non-veterans. In the sample, 27% of the men were veterans and 73% of the men were nonveterans. The mortality rate for the veterans in the study was 14.4%, whereas the mortality rate for nonveterans was 5.1%, $\chi^2(1, n = 92,457) = 2,239.61, p < .001$. This difference was likely a result of the age difference between the two groups; veterans averaged 59 years of age, whereas the nonveterans averaged 44 years, $t(92,457) = 143.57, p < .001$. Possibly further reflecting the age difference in the two groups, veterans in the sample reported poorer health than nonveterans. Seventeen percent of veterans and 12% of nonveterans reported fair to poor health, $\chi^2(1, n = 92,379) = 554.51, p < .001$. In addition, 11% of veterans, compared with only 5% of nonveterans, had a life-threatening disease, $\chi^2(1, n = 92,457) = 1,245.87, p < .001$. This health difference could have also been a reflection of the stark differences in smoking behavior between veterans and nonveterans. Only 31% of veterans reported they had never smoked, compared with 50% of nonveterans. A much higher percentage of veterans (44%) than nonveterans (23%) were former smokers. The rates of current smoking for veterans (25%) and nonveterans (27%) were similar. A chi-square test revealed that overall differences in smoking behavior were significant, $\chi^2(2, n = 91,890) = 4,428.84, p < .001$. Analysis of standardized residuals clarified that differences in all three types of smoking behavior were significant contributors to

TABLE 10.1
Comparisons Between Veterans and Nonveterans on Study Variables

	% Veterans n = 25,267 (27.3%)	% Nonveterans n = 67,192 (72.7%)	χ^2	df	p
Mortality—dead	14.4	5.1	2,239.62	1	< .001
Black	11.4	12.4	17.00	1	< .001
Education			1,280.55	5	< .001
0–8 years	5.2	9.8			
9–12 years	8.7	11.8			
High school diploma/GED	32.1	27.0			
Some college/AA degree	31.0	24.0			
Bachelor's degree	13.9	17.3			
Master's degree or PhD	9.1	10.1			
Family income <20K	20.1	21.4	19.73	1	< .001
Marital status			2,252.94	2	< .001
Married	63.4	62.3			
Widowed/divorced/ separated	27.5	17.4			
Never married	9.1	20.3			
Fair–poor health	17.4	11.6	554.51	1	< .001
Life-threatening disease	11.2	4.7	1,245.87	1	< .001
Smoking status			4,428.84	2	< .001
Never	30.6	50.0			
Former	44.4	23.1			
Current	25.0	26.9			

the chi-square relationship; however, the primary difference was between never smokers and former smokers.

Survival Analysis for All Veterans and Nonveterans

Results of survival analyses for the full sample of veterans and nonveterans are shown in Table 10.2. When controlling for age, race, and socioeconomic status in Model 1, veterans had a 14% higher mortality risk than nonveterans (95% CI [1.07, 1.21]). Controlling for smoking behavior in Model 2, the veteran mortality differential decreased, as veterans only had a 7% higher mortality risk than nonveterans (95% CI [1.01, 1.14]). Both smoking status measures predicted mortality outcomes at the $p < .001$ level and highlighted the effect of differences in smoking behavior between veterans and nonveterans. Those who never smoked, a characteristic more indicative of nonveterans than veterans, had a 56% lower mortality risk than current smokers (95% CI [0.40, 0.47]). However, the mortality risk for former

TABLE 10.2
Predictors of Mortality, Full Sample

Predictor variables	Model 1		Model 2		Model 3	
	HR	95% CI	HR	95% CI	HR	95% CI
Demographics and socioeconomic status						
Veteran	1.14***	1.07–1.21	1.07*	1.01–1.14	1.07*	1.00–1.13
Age	1.08***	1.08–1.09	1.09***	1.09–1.09	1.08***	1.08–1.09
Black	1.30***	1.20–1.39	1.29***	1.19–1.39	1.18***	1.09–1.27
Education	.88***	0.86–0.90	.91***	0.89–0.92	.95***	0.93–0.97
Family income <20K	1.38***	1.29–1.47	1.34***	1.25–1.43	1.12***	1.05–1.20
Marital status						
Married (ref)						
Widowed/divorced/separated	1.34***	1.27–1.42	1.28***	1.21–1.35	1.29***	1.22–1.37
Never married	1.60***	1.46–1.76	1.62***	1.47–1.78	1.68***	1.53–1.86
Smoking status						
Current smoker (ref)						
Never smoked			.44***	0.40–0.47	.48***	0.44–0.52
Former smoker			.61***	0.57–0.65	.62***	0.57–0.66
Health status						
Fair–poor health					1.93***	1.80–2.07
Life-threatening health condition					2.03***	1.90–2.17

Note. N = 92,459. HR = hazard ratio; CI = confidence interval.
*p < .05. ***p < .001.

194 LANDES, ARDELT, AND LANDES

smokers, a characteristic more indicative of veterans than nonveterans, was only 38% lower than for current smokers (95% CI [0.57, 0.65]).

The addition of the health status variables in Model 3 did not reduce the veteran mortality differential from Model 2, as veterans had a 7% higher mortality risk than nonveterans (95% CI [1.00, 1.13]). However, even with the introduction of health status to the model, the predictive effect of smoking behavior remained consistent, as the reduction in mortality risk was greater for those who never smoked than for former smokers.

Survival Analysis by War-Era Cohort

Survival analysis was conducted for all combined nonwar-era cohorts, then separately for each war-era cohort to further elucidate the trend between the veteran mortality differential and smoking behavior. Analyses reported in Table 10.3 indicate that a veteran mortality differential was not present in the combined nonwar-era cohorts and was not present in each nonwar-era cohort. However, a veteran mortality differential was present in each of the war-era cohorts: World War II era, Korean War era, and Vietnam War era. Prior to survival analysis, differences in smoking behavior were tested for each war-era cohort.

World War II–Era Cohort

In the World War II–era cohort, 69% of the men were veterans, and 31% were nonveterans. On the basis of a chi-square test of smoking behavior, 25% of veterans had never smoked, compared with 39% of nonveterans; 64% of veterans were former smokers, and 48% of nonveterans were former smokers; and 11% of veterans were current smokers, and 13% of nonveterans were current smokers. Although the overall chi-square test was significant for these differences, $\chi^2(2, n = 5,069) = 115.68$, $p < .001$, analysis of standardized residuals showed that only the differences in never smoked and former smoker contributed to the chi-square relationship.

Survival analysis for the World War II–era cohort demonstrated the mitigating effect of differential smoking behavior when comparing mortality risk between veterans and nonveterans. As reported in Model 1 of Table 10.4, World War II–era veterans had a 28% higher mortality risk than nonveterans from the same era (95% CI [1.80, 2.07]), controlling for demographic and socioeconomic measures. However, controlling for smoking behavior (Model 2) reduced the veteran mortality differential from 28% to 23% (95% CI [1.07, 1.41]). The addition of health status (Model 3) further reduced the veteran mortality differential, but veterans' mortality risk remained 20% higher (95% CI [1.04, 1.38]) than nonveterans. Using Model 3 to summarize

TABLE 10.3
Predictors of Mortality, Combined Nonwar Eras

Predictor variables	All nonwar eras n = 360,329		WWI–WWII interim n = 21,266		WWII–Korea interim n = 17,159		Korea–Vietnam interim n = 69,346		Post-Vietnam n = 252,558	
	HR	95% CI	HR	95% CI	HR	95% CI	HR	95% CI	HR	95% CI
Veteran	1.06	0.99–1.15	0.95	0.85–1.06	1.08	0.89–1.31	1.10	0.96–1.26	0.98	0.71–1.36
Age	1.09***	1.08–1.09	1.06***	1.04–1.08	0.98	0.94–1.02	1.03**	1.01–1.05	1.08**	1.06–1.10
Black	1.22***	1.10–1.35	1.01	0.84–1.21	1.23	0.98–1.55	1.28*	1.05–1.57	1.50*	1.15–1.95
Education	.89***	0.86–0.91	.94**	0.91–0.98	.84***	0.79–0.90	.87***	0.83–0.91	.77***	0.71–0.83
Family income <20K	1.34***	1.22–1.37	1.13	1.00–1.21	1.12	0.90–1.38	1.80***	1.53–2.14	1.71***	1.32–2.21
Marital status										
Married (ref)										
Widowed/ divorced/ separated	1.23***	1.14–1.33	1.02	0.91–1.14	1.23*	1.01–1.49	1.54***	1.31–1.81	1.83***	1.37–2.40
Never married	1.54***	1.35–1.75	.84	0.64–1.11	1.21	0.86–1.71	1.72***	1.35–1.19	2.06***	1.62–2.62

Note. WWI = World War I; WWII = World War II; HR = hazard ratio; CI = confidence interval.
*p < .05. **p < .01. ***p < .001.

TABLE 10.4
Predictors of Mortality, World War II Era

Predictor variables	Model 1 HR	Model 1 95% CI	Model 2 HR	Model 2 95% CI	Model 3 HR	Model 3 95% CI
Demographics and socioeconomic status						
Veteran	1.28***	1.12–1.47	1.23**	1.07–1.41	1.20*	1.04–1.38
Age	1.02	0.99–1.04	1.02	1.00–1.04	1.00	0.98–1.02
Black	1.24*	1.04–1.48	1.23*	1.03–1.48	1.06	0.89–1.28
Education	.88***	0.84–0.92	.89***	0.86–0.93	.94**	0.90–0.98
Family income <20K	1.18*	1.03–1.35	1.16*	1.01–1.32	1.04	0.90–1.19
Marital status						
Married (ref)						
Widowed/divorced/separated	1.37***	1.21–1.54	1.33***	1.18–1.50	1.39***	1.23–1.57
Never married	1.48**	1.17–1.87	1.49***	1.18–1.89	1.56***	1.23–1.99
Smoking status						
Current smoker (ref)						
Never smoked			.46***	0.38–0.56	.49***	0.40–0.59
Former smoker			.65***	0.55–0.76	.64***	0.55–0.76
Health status						
Fair–poor health					1.81***	1.57–2.07
Life-threatening health condition					1.99***	1.75–2.27

Note. $N = 5,098$. HR = hazard ratio; CI = confidence interval.
*$p < .05$. **$p < .01$. ***$p < .001$.

the effect of smoking behavior in the World War II sample, when compared with current smokers, the reduction in mortality risk was greater for never smokers than for former smokers. Those who never smoked, more characteristic of nonveterans, had a 51% lower mortality risk than current smokers (95% CI [0.40, 0.59]). Former smokers, more characteristic of veterans, had a 36% lower mortality risk than current smokers (95% CI [0.55, 0.76]).

Korean War–Era Cohort

In the Korean War–era cohort, 53% of the men were veterans and 47% were nonveterans. Results from a chi-square test showed that among the Korean War–era cohort, 28% of veterans had never smoked, compared with 36% of nonveterans; 54% of veterans were former smokers, compared with 46% of nonveterans; and the rates of current smoking among veterans (18%) and nonveterans of the Korean War–era cohort (19%) were similar. Although the overall chi-square test was significant for these differences, $\chi^2(2, n = 5,207) = 45.86, p < .001$, analysis of standardized residuals showed that only the differences in never smoked and former smoker contributed to the chi-squared relationship.

Survival analysis of the Korean War–era cohort showed a weak veteran mortality differential. As reported in Model 1 of Table 10.5, veterans had a 22% higher mortality risk than nonveterans after controlling for demographic and socioeconomic status variables (95% CI [1.05, 1.43]). This veteran mortality differential was no longer significant, $p > .05$, when controlling for smoking behavior (Model 2), but again reached statistical significance, $p = .042$, when adding health status to the analysis (Model 3). Therefore, although controlling for smoking status eliminated the weak veteran mortality differential in the Korean War–era cohort, some of the effects of smoking were explained by health status. On the basis of Model 3, those who never smoked and former smokers had lower mortality risk than current smokers. Men who never smoked, more characteristic of nonveterans, had a 48% lower mortality risk (95% CI [0.42, 0.64]) than current smokers. Men who were former smokers, more characteristic of veterans, had a 43% lower mortality risk (95% CI [0.47, 0.70]) than current smokers.

Vietnam War–Era Cohort

Among the Vietnam War–era cohort 27% of the men were veterans, and 73% were nonveterans. A chi-square test of smoking differences for the Vietnam War–era cohort revealed a slight difference in smoking behavior compared with the World War II–era and Korean War–era cohorts. Similar to the earlier war-era cohorts, among the Vietnam War–era cohort, 29% of veterans reported they had never smoked, compared with 45% of nonveterans. However, less

TABLE 10.5
Predictors of Mortality, Korean War Era

Predictor variables	Model 1		Model 2		Model 3	
	HR	95% CI	HR	95% CI	HR	95% CI
Demographics and socioeconomic status						
Veteran	1.22*	1.05–1.43	1.17	1.00–1.37	1.18*	1.01–1.38
Age	.97	0.94–1.00	.98	0.95–1.01	.97	0.94–1.00
Black	1.33**	1.08–1.63	1.30*	1.03–1.48	1.21	0.94–1.48
Education	.90***	0.85–0.95	.92**	0.87–0.98	.99	0.93–1.05
Family income <20K	1.55***	1.27–1.91	1.48***	1.21–1.81	1.15	0.93–1.42
Marital status						
Married (ref)						
Widowed/divorced/separated	1.51***	1.27–1.79	1.40***	1.18–1.66	1.39***	1.17–1.64
Never married	1.36*	1.00–1.83	1.34	0.99–1.80	1.32	0.97–1.78
Smoking status						
Current smoker (ref)						
Never smoked			.46***	0.38–0.57	.52***	0.42–0.64
Former smoker			.59***	0.49–0.71	.57***	0.47–0.70
Health status						
Fair–poor health					2.07***	1.69–2.54
Life-threatening health condition					2.12***	1.75–2.57

Note. $N = 5,239$. HR = hazard ratio; CI = confidence interval.
*$p < .05$. **$p < .01$. ***$p < .001$.

than half of both veterans (35%) and nonveterans (27%) were former smokers. Yet, unlike the World War II–era and Korean War–era cohorts, a difference was present in current smoking behavior among the Vietnam War–era cohort. Thirty-six percent of veterans in the Vietnam War–era cohort were current smokers, whereas only 28% of nonveterans were current smokers. The overall chi-square test was significant for these differences, $\chi^2(2, n = 21,390) = 429.42$, $p < .001$, and analysis of standardized residuals showed that all three smoking behaviors contributed to the chi-square relationship.

Similar to the World War II–era and Korean War–era cohorts, a veteran mortality differential was also present in the Vietnam War–era cohort. The survival analyses (see Table 10.6) demonstrated that veterans had a 21% higher mortality risk (95% CI [1.01, 1.45]) than nonveterans, controlling for demographic characteristics and socioeconomic status (Model 1). However, the veteran mortality differential was fully eliminated when controlling for smoking behavior (Model 2) and smoking behavior and health status (Model 3). These results highlight the negative outcome of former and current smoking behavior among veterans. On the basis of results from Model 3, compared with current smokers, men who never smoked had a 48% lower mortality risk (95% CI [0.41, 0.65]), and men who were former smokers had a 31% lower mortality risk (95% CI [0.57, 0.84]).

CONCLUSION

Results from this study confirmed a veteran mortality differential in the full sample. However, further analysis revealed that a higher mortality risk was only present for those veterans who came of age during a time of war. Veterans who turned 18 during World War II, the Korean War, or the Vietnam War had a higher mortality risk than nonveterans who turned 18 during these war eras. By contrast, veterans who came of age when the United States was not involved in an official war did not have a higher mortality risk than nonveterans. This finding lends credence to the contention that the increased hazards surrounding wartime deployment lead to a mortality disadvantage for veterans (London & Wilmoth, 2006). In essence, though veterans have a health selection effect and start healthier than their nonveteran peers, the combination of wartime service and smoking behavior leads to an increased mortality risk.

The veteran mortality differential present in the war-era cohorts was partially to fully explained by smoking behavior. Though a similar percentage of veterans and nonveterans were current smokers, a higher percentage of veterans were former smokers. In other words, more nonveterans than veterans had never smoked, and this difference in smoking behavior contributed to the veteran mortality differential. For the World War II–era cohort,

TABLE 10.6
Predictors of Mortality, Vietnam War Era

Predictor variables	Model 1 HR	Model 1 95% CI	Model 2 HR	Model 2 95% CI	Model 3 HR	Model 3 95% CI
Demographics and socioeconomic status						
Veteran	1.21*	1.01–1.45	1.11	0.92–1.33	1.10	0.92–1.32
Age	1.04***	1.02–1.06	1.04***	1.02–1.06	1.02*	1.00–1.04
Black	1.58***	1.29–1.92	1.57***	1.28–1.92	1.42***	1.15–1.74
Education	.83***	0.78–0.88	.87***	0.81–0.93	.93*	0.87–1.00
Family income <20K	1.89***	1.56–2.29	1.78***	1.47–2.16	1.19	0.96–1.46
Marital status						
Married (ref)						
Widowed/divorced/separated	1.77***	1.49–2.11	1.66***	1.38–1.96	1.61***	1.35–1.92
Never married	1.99***	1.59–2.49	1.97***	1.58–2.47	2.07***	1.65–2.60
Smoking status						
Current smoker (ref)						
Never smoked			.47***	0.38–0.58	.52***	0.41–0.65
Former smoker			.68***	0.55–0.83	.69***	0.57–0.84
Health status						
Fair–poor health					2.34***	1.90–2.88
Life-threatening health condition					2.17***	1.14–3.46

Note. N = 21,547. HR = hazard ratio; CI = confidence interval.
*p < .05. ***p < .001.

controlling for smoking reduced the veteran mortality differential. For the Korean war–era and Vietnam War–era cohorts, controlling for smoking fully eliminated the veteran mortality differential. These findings call attention to the negative health effects of ever smoking and the possibility of an age or cohort effect.

It is important to note that results from this study confirm that quitting smoking does decrease mortality risk (Jacobs et al., 1999; Lakier, 1992; U.S. Department of Health and Human Services, 2014). However, the lowest mortality risk was among those who never smoked, indicative of 50% of nonveterans in our overall sample but only of 31% of veterans. Therefore, although it is beneficial for the Veterans Affairs (VA) Healthcare System to continue smoking cessation efforts, it would be even better for the U.S. military to actively campaign against smoking by service members. Although the U.S. military has historically viewed smoking as a panacea to the stresses encountered by service members during times of war (E. A. Smith & Malone, 2009b), the military's attitude toward smoking has evolved over the years. In 1975, the military ceased providing cigarettes as part of rations for deployed personnel (Bedard & Deschênes, 2006; E. A. Smith & Malone, 2009a). In 1986, the U.S. Department of Defense banned tobacco use during basic training, and in 1994 passed a smoke-free workplace policy for military bases (Jahnke et al., 2011; McKinney et al., 1997; Offen et al., 2011; E. A. Smith & Malone, 2009a). Yet the military continues to subsidize the price of cigarettes on bases, with cigarettes priced 5% less than the lowest price in the surrounding community, and state and local taxes are not collected in on-base military retail stores (Bedard & Deschênes, 2006; Haddock, Jahnke, Poston, & Williams, 2013).

E. A. Smith et al. (2007), E. A. Smith and Malone (2009a, 2009b), and Offen and colleagues (2011) reported that the military's efforts to reduce or eliminate smoking have been thwarted at the Congressional level by tobacco lobbyists. In addition, tobacco companies have purposefully targeted deployed troops by directly advertising cigarettes through military channels and mailing free cigarettes to deployed service members (E. A. Smith & Malone, 2009a). To their credit, through Operation Live Well and the Healthy Base Initiative, the military is attempting to increase tobacco-free areas on U.S. military bases and to brand tobacco use as a health risk that negatively affects troop health and readiness (Bondurant & Wedge, 2009; National Prevention Council, 2014).

Another interesting finding of the present study is that the veteran mortality differential was lower for men from the Korean War and Vietnam War eras than for men from the World War II era. This variation could be related to the age difference between war-era cohorts, indicating that the negative effects of war and increased smoking behavior among veterans manifest in later life. However, variation in the experience of war and postmilitary service may also inform this finding. For instance, there were differences in the benefits available through the GI Bill among World War II, Korean War, and Vietnam War veterans. This variation has been linked to differential outcomes in educational attainment for veterans' postmilitary service (Bound & Turner, 2002). In addition, developments in medical technology that occurred during the 20th century may have resulted in improved diagnosis and treatment of disease through the Veterans Health Administration for those serving in later war cohorts (Miller, 2012).

The primary limitation of this study regards the NHIS data on military service, which provide information only on whether an individual was honorably discharged from the U.S. military; start and stop dates for military service are not available. Therefore, we do not know for certain whether a veteran did or did not serve in specific war eras. Furthermore, the NHIS does not include data on age at time of service, or whether the veteran experienced combat during military service, both of which are related to life course disruption and mortality risk (Elder, 1987; Elder, Clipp, Brown, Martin, & Friedman, 2009; London & Wilmoth, 2006). Although this lack of data on military service limited our analysis, the combined NHIS–NDI data nonetheless offered a sizable sample of veterans and nonveterans for analysis of the effects of veteran status on mortality. Furthermore, the estimate of war era by year of birth provided the opportunity to analyze the effect of war eras on the veteran mortality differential.

In considering the veteran mortality differential, Bedard and Deschênes (2006) demonstrated that it is necessary to attend not only to differences between veterans and nonveterans but also to the smoking behavior of these groups. Findings from the present study support this contention, as the veteran mortality differential among men who participated in the 1997–2004 NHIS was partially explained by the fact that a higher percentage of veterans than nonveterans were ever cigarette smokers. Yet, beyond this confirmation of prior research, our study contributes the finding that the veteran mortality differential is only present among those veterans who came of age during a war era. It was only the veterans who turned 18 during World War II, the Korean War, and the Vietnam War who had a higher mortality risk than nonveterans of the same war-era cohort. On the basis of these findings, it is essential that future studies of the veteran mortality differential attend not only to the associations between mortality and smoking behavior but also to possible differences among war-era cohorts.

REFERENCES

Bastian, L. A., & Sherman, S. E. (2010). Effects of the wars on smoking among veterans. *Journal of General Internal Medicine, 25*, 102–103. http://dx.doi.org/10.1007/s11606-009-1224-1

Bedard, K., & Deschênes, O. (2006). The long-term impact of military service on health: Evidence from World War II and Korean War veterans. *The American Economic Review, 96*, 176–194. http://dx.doi.org/10.1257/000282806776157731

Bondurant, S., & Wedge, R. (Eds.). (2009). *Combating tobacco use in military and veteran populations.* Washington, DC: National Academies Press.

Bound, J., & Turner, S. (2002). Going to war and going to college: Did World War II and the G.I. Bill increase education attainment for returning veterans? *Journal of Labor Economics, 20*, 784–815. http://dx.doi.org/10.1086/342012

Brown, D. W. (2010). Smoking prevalence among US veterans. *Journal of General Internal Medicine, 25*, 147–149. http://dx.doi.org/10.1007/s11606-009-1160-0

Cunradi, C. B., Moore, R. S., & Ames, G. (2008). Contribution of occupational factors to current smoking among active-duty U.S. Navy careerists. *Nicotine & Tobacco Research, 10*, 429–437. http://dx.doi.org/10.1080/14622200801889002

Dalager, N. A., & Kang, H. K. (1997). Mortality among Army Chemical Corps Vietnam veterans. *American Journal of Industrial Medicine, 31*, 719–726. http://dx.doi.org/10.1002/(SICI)1097-0274(199706)31:6<719::AID-AJIM8>3.0.CO;2-L

Dorn, H. F. (1959). Tobacco consumption and mortality from cancer and other diseases. *Public Health Reports, 74*, 581–593. http://dx.doi.org/10.2307/4590516

Elder, G. H., Jr. (1987). War mobilization and the life course: A cohort of World War II veterans. *Sociological Forum, 2*, 449–472. Retrieved from https://link.springer.com/article/10.1007/BF01106621

Elder, G. H., Jr., Clipp, E. C., Brown, J. S., Martin, L. R., & Friedman, H. W. (2009). The lifelong mortality risks of World War II experiences. *Research on Aging, 31*, 391–412. http://dx.doi.org/10.1177/0164027509333447

Feigelman, W. (1994). Cigarette smoking among former military service personnel: A neglected social issue. *Preventive Medicine, 23*, 235–241. http://dx.doi.org/10.1006/pmed.1994.1032

Forgas, L. B., Meyer, D. M., & Cohen, M. E. (1996). Tobacco use habits of naval personnel during Desert Storm. *Military Medicine, 161*, 165–168.

Haddock, C. K., Jahnke, S. A., Poston, W. S. C., & Williams, L. N. (2013). Cigarette prices in military retail: A review and proposal for advancing military health policy. *Military Medicine, 178*, 563–569. http://dx.doi.org/10.7205/MILMED-D-12-00517

Harris, B. H., Hendershot, G., & Stapleton, D. C. (2005). *A guide to disability statistics from the National Health Interview Survey.* Ithaca, NY: Rehabilitation Research and Training Center on Disability Demographics and Statistics, Cornell University.

Jacobs, D. R., Jr., Adachi, H., Mulder, I., Kromhout, D., Menotti, A., Nissinen, A., & Blackburn, H. (1999). Cigarette smoking and mortality risk: Twenty-five-year follow-up of the Seven Countries Study. *Archives of Internal Medicine, 159*, 733–740. http://dx.doi.org/10.1001/archinte.159.7.733

Jahnke, S. A., Hoffman, K. M., Haddock, C. K., Long, M. A. D., Williams, L. N., Lando, H. A., & Poston, W. S. C. (2011). Military tobacco policies: The good, the bad, and the ugly. *Military Medicine, 176*, 1382–1387. http://dx.doi.org/10.7205/MILMED-D-11-00164

Kahn, H. A. (1966). The Dorn study of smoking and mortality among U.S. veterans: Report on eight and one-half years of observation. *National Cancer Institute Monograph, 19,* 1–125.

Kang, H. K., & Bullman, T. A. (1996). Mortality among U.S. veterans of the Persian Gulf War. *The New England Journal of Medicine, 335,* 1498–1504. http://dx.doi.org/10.1056/NEJM199611143352006

Klevens, R. M., Giovino, G. A., Peddicord, J. P., Nelson, D. E., Mowery, P., & Grummer-Strawn, L. (1995). The association between veteran status and cigarette-smoking behaviors. *American Journal of Preventive Medicine, 11,* 245–250.

Lakier, J. B. (1992). Smoking and cardiovascular disease. *The American Journal of Medicine, 93*(1, Suppl. 1), S8–S12. http://dx.doi.org/10.1016/0002-9343(92)90620-Q

Liu, X., Engel, C., Jr., Kang, H., & Cowan, D. (2005). The effect of veteran status on mortality among older Americans and its pathways. *Population Research and Policy Review, 24,* 573–592. http://dx.doi.org/10.1007/s11113-005-5056-3

London, A. S., & Wilmoth, J. M. (2006). Military service and (dis)continuity in the life course: Evidence on disadvantage and mortality from the Health and Retirement Study and the Study of Assets and Health Dynamics Among the Oldest-Old. *Research on Aging, 28,* 135–159. http://dx.doi.org/10.1177/0164027505281572

MacLean, A. (2013). A matter of life and death: Military service and health. In J. M. Wilmoth & A. S. London (Eds.), *Life course perspectives on military service* (pp. 200–220). New York, NY: Routledge.

McKinney, W. P., McIntire, D. D., Carmody, T. J., & Joseph, A. (1997). Comparing the smoking behavior of veterans and nonveterans. *Public Health Reports, 112,* 212–217.

Miller, T. W. (2012). *The Praeger handbook of veterans' health: History, challenges, issues, and developments.* Santa Barbara, CA: Praeger.

National Center for Health Statistics. (2009). *Variance estimation and other analytic issues in the 1997–2005 NHIS.* Atlanta, GA: Centers for Disease Control and Prevention.

National Prevention Council. (2014). *Annual status report.* Washington, DC: U.S. Department of Health and Human Services, Office of the Surgeon General. Retrieved from https://www.surgeongeneral.gov/priorities/prevention/2014-npc-status-report.pdf

Offen, N., Arvey, S. R., Smith, E. A., & Malone, R. E. (2011). Forcing the Navy to sell cigarettes on ships: How the tobacco industry and politicians torpedoed Navy tobacco control. *American Journal of Public Health, 101,* 404–411. http://dx.doi.org/10.2105/AJPH.2010.196329

Poston, W. S. C., Taylor, J. E., Hoffman, K. M., Peterson, A. L., Lando, H. A., Shelton, S., & Haddock, C. K. (2008). Smoking and deployment: Perspectives of junior-enlisted U.S. Air Force and U.S. Army personnel and their supervisors. *Military Medicine, 173,* 441–447. http://dx.doi.org/10.7205/MILMED.173.5.441

Rogot, E. (1978). Smoking and life expectancy among U.S. veterans. *American Journal of Public Health, 68*, 1023–1025. http://dx.doi.org/10.2105/AJPH.68.10.1023

Rogot, E., & Murray, J. L. (1980). Smoking and causes of death among U.S. veterans: 16 years of observation. *Public Health Reports, 95*, 213–222.

Smith, B., Ryan, M. A. K., Wingard, D. L., Patterson, T. L., Slymen, D. J., & Macera, C. A., & the Millennium Cohort Study Team. (2008). Cigarette smoking and military deployment: A prospective evaluation. *American Journal of Preventive Medicine, 35*, 539–546. http://dx.doi.org/10.1016/j.amepre.2008.07.009

Smith, E. A., Blackman, V. S., & Malone, R. E. (2007). Death at a discount: How the tobacco industry thwarted tobacco control policies in US military commissaries. *Tobacco Control, 16*, 38–46. http://dx.doi.org/10.1136/tc.2006.017350

Smith, E. A., & Malone, R. E. (2009a). "Everywhere the soldier will be": Wartime tobacco promotion in the US military. *American Journal of Public Health, 99*, 1595–1602. http://dx.doi.org/10.2105/AJPH.2008.152983

Smith, E. A., & Malone, R. E. (2009b). Tobacco promotion to military personnel: "The plums are here to be plucked." *Military Medicine, 174*, 797–806. http://dx.doi.org/10.7205/MILMED-D-04-4108

Talcott, G. W., Cigrang, J., Sherrill-Mittleman, D., Snyder, D. K., Baker, M., Tatum, J., . . . Heyman, R. E. (2013). Tobacco use during military deployment. *Nicotine & Tobacco Research, 15*, 1348–1354. http://dx.doi.org/10.1093/ntr/nts267

U.S. Code of Federal Regulations. (2014). Periods of War, 38 C.F.R. § 3. Retrieved from http://www.ecfr.gov/cgi-bin/text-idx?rgn=div5&node=38:1.0.1.1.4#se38.1.3_12

U.S. Department of Health and Human Services. (2014). *The health consequences of smoking—50 years of progress: A report of the Surgeon General.* Atlanta, GA: U.S. Department of Health and Human Services, Centers for Disease Control and Prevention, National Center for Chronic Disease Prevention and Health Promotion, Office on Smoking and Health.

Wilmoth, J. M., London, A. S., & Parker, W. M. (2010). Military service and men's health trajectories in later life. *The Journals of Gerontology: Series B. Psychological Sciences and Social Sciences, 65B*, 744–755. http://dx.doi.org/10.1093/geronb/gbq072

11

MILITARY SERVICE AND CHANGES IN MEMORY PERFORMANCE DURING LATER LIFE

ROBERT S. STAWSKI, MEGHANN L. FENN, CHENKAI WU, AND GWENITH G. FISHER

Decline in episodic memory, memory of information and experiences in place and time, is often the most noted change experienced by individuals as they advance into the aging years (Hoyer & Verhaeghen, 2006). Despite the robustness and ubiquity of aging-related declines in episodic memory, there is considerable heterogeneity in the rate of aging-related decline (Dixon et al., 2004). Although psychological sciences have long attempted to identify cognitive mechanisms (e.g., processing speed; Salthouse, 1996) accounting for aging-related changes, the social and behavioral sciences more broadly have become increasingly interested in identifying and understanding psychosocial and life course factors associated with cognitive aging (Kremen, Lachman, Pruessner, Sliwinski, & Wilson, 2012). The life course perspective suggests that an individual's life comprises a set of roles and events that take place over time throughout life. Although previous research has examined

This work was supported by National Institute on Aging (NIA) Grant R03-AG042919.

http://dx.doi.org/10.1037/0000061-012

Long-Term Outcomes of Military Service: The Health and Well-Being of Aging Veterans, A. Spiro III, R. A. Settersten Jr., and C. M. Aldwin (Editors)

the effects of broader social and life course factors, such as birth cohort and socioeconomic position, on later-life cognition (Dodge, Zhu, Lee, Chang, & Ganguli, 2014; Horvat et al., 2014), there is a paucity of research linking a history of military service to cognitive function. We draw on the life course perspective, aiming to expand this literature by examining the effects of military service on later-life changes in episodic memory.

Military service has long been identified as a significant life course factor shaping later-life outcomes (MacLean & Elder, 2007). Veteran status is granted to all who served in a branch of the armed forces irrespective of duration, timing, or type of service. However, variations in veterans' experiences and exposures differentially impact their health and well-being in later life. Duration of service, active duty, wartime service, combat exposure, and even era served have been shown to impact the lives of older veterans (Wilmoth & London, 2013). Institutional supports afforded during and after service (e.g., health care, education, physical training) represent health-promoting dimensions of military service, whereas exposures to extreme situations such as combat represent health-compromising dimensions of service. Consistent with this, recent research has demonstrated that history of military service, and particularly service during wartime, can place individuals at risk for accelerated aging-related declines in physical and functional health (Wilmoth, London, & Parker, 2010). Comparatively less research has focused on the impact of military service on cognitive function in adulthood and old age, with most of the research focusing on combat exposure and posttraumatic stress disorder (PTSD).

Among the most voluminous literature on military service and cognition in later life is the literature examining the effects of combat exposure and PTSD. Combat exposure reflects an extremely stressful experience associated with PTSD and reduced hippocampal volume due to chronic exposure to stress hormones (Sapolsky, 1996). Given that the hippocampus governs episodic memory performance, and is known to shrink with age (Raz, Rodrigue, Head, Kennedy, & Acker, 2004; see also Chapter 12, this volume), episodic memory is an important domain to study in the context of military service and cognitive aging. Previous research has shown that combat veterans exhibit significantly poorer performance across multiple domains of cognitive function, including attention, learning, memory, motor speed, and general intellectual ability (Toomey et al., 2009; Vasterling et al., 2002). Sullivan, Griffiths, and Sohlberg (2014) observed a slightly different pattern of results, that memory recall accuracy among those exposed to combat was comparable with that of civilians, although the veterans took significantly longer to analyze the paragraph presented and significantly longer to respond during recall. Such patterns suggest that the observed differences in memory performance reflect deficiencies in the processing, comprehension, and encoding of information rather than simply retrieval of information (Naveh-Benjamin, Kilb, & Fisher, 2006). Together, these studies suggest that veterans who experienced combat exhibit compromised attention and memory function.

In comparison with research on combat exposure and PTSD, little research exists linking military service more generally to later-life cognition. One notable exception is a recent article by Brown, Wilmoth, and London (2014), who examined the impact of veteran status on trajectories of cognitive function among older men born between 1895 and 1941 from the Health and Retirement Study (HRS). Using a measure of global cognitive function, Brown and colleagues found that after adjustment for multiple social, demographic, and health-related covariates, veterans exhibited overall better cognitive function, particularly during the midlife years (~60–65), but subsequently exhibited significantly steeper aging-related decline, compared with nonveterans. Additionally, veterans who served during wartime, particularly World War II or multiple wars, exhibited accelerated aging-related declines in cognitive function. Another exception is a longitudinal study of United Kingdom veterans with wartime service (Wessely et al., 2003). The authors found that veterans were more likely to have difficulty with long-term memory recall and recognition of wartime events. The results of these studies indicate that military service is an important factor related to declining later-life cognition. Additionally, service during wartime, although not necessarily combat exposure, is an important dimension of service conferring risk for later-life cognition. Although the results of these studies are intriguing and suggestive of the importance of military service on later-life cognition, some questions remain.

The measure of cognitive function used by Brown and colleagues (2014) reflects general cognitive status across multiple domains, rather than specific cognitive abilities (McArdle, Fisher, & Kadlec, 2007). As such, it adequately qualifies as global cognitive status but lacks depth and specificity for determining whether the observed effects of military service exist for all domains of cognition, or whether certain performance domains are differentially impacted. The study by Wessely et al. (2003) focused on memory of wartime experiences, providing limited insight into the impacts of wartime service on general, or decontextualized, memory performance. Thus, examination of military service impacting later-life memory would help extend the combat exposure/PTSD, general military service, and life course cognitive aging literatures. Additionally, given the effects of military service on mental and physical health (Wilmoth, London, & Parker, 2010), adjusting for such factors when considering the impact of military service on memory is warranted. Furthermore, additional research on military service and later-life cognitive function is needed in the simple interest of replication and extension.

THE CURRENT STUDY

This study examines two research questions regarding the relationship between military service and memory performance during later life. First, is military service related to level and rate of change in memory performance? Second, do characteristics of military service, including duration of service in the military and service during wartime, moderate the effect of military service on level and rate of change in memory performance? Consistent with previous literature, we predicted that military service would be associated with accelerated aging-related declines in memory performance and that declines would be much steeper among veterans who served during wartime.

METHOD

We examined data from the HRS, which is an ongoing U.S. nationally representative longitudinal panel study that began in 1992 (Sonnega et al., 2014). Data from HRS are collected biennially using mixed mode assessments (i.e., telephone and face-to-face interviews) and provide comprehensive information about health, economics, finances, employment, cognition, family networks, and social relations. The baseline assessment of the initial sample (the HRS cohort) was conducted from 1992 to 1993 among adults born 1931–1941 (age 50 and older). Beginning in 1998, the Assets and Health Dynamics among the Oldest Old (AHEAD) study, which was begun in 1993 and consisted of adults born in 1923 and earlier, was merged with the HRS sample into a single interview schedule and study. In 1998, two additional samples, including participants born 1924–1930 (Children of the Depression Age [CODA]) and 1942–1947 (War Babies [WB]), were incorporated to fill the generational gap between the HRS and the AHEAD samples, and to replenish the younger sample that had aged since 1992. Every 6 years a new sample of adults ages 51 to 56 is added to maintain a sample frame of older adults ages 51 and older; thus, the Early Baby Boomer (EBB) sample (born 1948–1953) and the Mid Baby Boomer (MBB) sample (born 1954–1959) were added into the HRS in 2004 and 2010, respectively.

Data Selection

For the current study, we used data from the 1998–2010 waves of data collection, as the memory assessment was revised from 20- to a 10-item recall test in 1998, making this the historical point in the study when the assessment of memory became consistent across assessments. We draw only on participants from the HRS, AHEAD, CODA, and WB samples, as respondents in the EBB and MBB samples had limited longitudinal information (one to three assessments). The HRS, AHEAD, CODA, and WB samples provide up to seven assessments or 12 years of longitudinal data. Last, we restricted the focus of this study to men, as there were few female veterans (2% of veterans). Data provided by a proxy respondent were also excluded.

Participants

The analytic sample for the current study consisted of 7,020 men age 50 and above at their 1998 assessment (considered baseline for the current study). At baseline, the sample had an average age of 62.38 ($SD = 9.66$, range = 50–96), 12.33 years of education ($SD = 3.46$, range = 0–17), was 85.9% Caucasian (of European American decent), and 59.60% self-identified as veterans. On average, respondents participated in 6.87 waves of the HRS, corresponding to almost 13 years of longitudinal data. Sample descriptive statistics are provided in Table 11.1.

Outcomes

Episodic memory performance was measured using a list of 10 words, which interviewers read aloud to participants, one word at a time (McArdle et al., 2007). Participants then recalled as many words as possible immediately thereafter (*immediate recall*) and again after a 5-minute delay (*delayed recall*). Immediate and delayed recall scores were calculated as the total number of words recalled during each of the two periods, respectively. An index of *forgetting* was also calculated by subtracting the number of words recalled during delayed recall from the number of words recalled during immediate recall.

Military Service Measures

Veteran status was determined by self-report from a single-item whereby participants indicated whether they served in the active military of the United States; it was coded dichotomously (1 = veteran, 0 = nonveteran). *Tenure* (or duration) of service was measured by subtracting the respondent's self-reported start year from the end year. *Wartime era* was defined using methods described by Wilmoth et al. (2010; see also Online Appendix A, available at http://pubs.apa.org/books/supp/spiro/) based on a respondent's indication of serving during wartime years: World War II (1941–1946), Korean War (1950–1955), or Vietnam War (1964–1975).

TABLE 11.1
Descriptive Statistics for Demographic, Health,
and Military Service–Related Variables

	Full sample	HRS	AHEAD	CODA	WB
Age	62.38 (9.66)	56.9 (4.67)	75.47 (5.13)	70.98 (2.01)	53.45 (3.05)
Range	50–96	50–82.5	55–96	60.5–79	50–74
Years of education	12.33 (3.46)	12.45 (3.34)	11.57 (3.75)	12.06 (3.61)	13.39 (2.93)
Range	0–17	0–17	0–17	0–17	0–17
Minority	14.10%	15.30%	12.10%	11.80%	15.00%
Self-rated health	3.16 (1.16)	3.19 (1.13)	2.88 (1.11)	3.12 (1.20)	3.52 (1.19)
Depressive symptoms	1.35 (1.77)	1.32 (1.76)	1.62 (1.83)	1.11 (1.61)	1.26 (1.76)
Chronic conditions	1.60 (1.25)	1.57 (1.23)	1.93 (1.25)	1.79 (1.27)	1.00 (1.08)
Range	0–7	0–7	0–7	0–7	0–6
Veterans	59.60%	58.40%	60.98%	72.96%	50.20%
Duration of service	4.29 (5.24)	4.54 (5.57)	4.30 (5.05)	3.42 (4.33)	4.31 (5.15)
Range	0–54	0–37	0–54	0–32	0–31
Wartime service	83.01%	70.36%	95.90%	98.08%	92.09%
World War II	37.89%	10.18%	93.33%	72.68%	1.62%
Korean War	28.78%	47.94%	2.56%	26.99%	1.62%
Vietnam War	19.66%	16.11%	1.84%	4.47%	89.25%
No. of assessments	6.87 (2.60)	8.30 (2.17)	3.54 (2.12)	4.76 (2.21)	5.72 (1.93)
Range	1–7	1–7	1–7	1–7	1–7

Note. HRS = Initial Health and Retirement Study cohort (born 1931–1941); AHEAD = Assets and Health Dynamics among the Oldest Old (born before 1924); CODA = Children of the Depression Era (born 1924–1930); WB = War Babies (born 1942–1947).

Covariates

Education was indexed as the number of years of education attained by the participant. *Minority status* was indexed by self-report and defined dichotomously (Caucasian vs. non-Caucasian). *Physical health-related covariates* included a single item where participants were asked to rate their overall health on a 5-point Likert scale (1 = *poor*, 2 = *fair*, 3 = *good*, 4 = *very good*, 5 = *excellent*) and a count of the number of eight chronic conditions including hypertension, diabetes, cancer, lung disease, heart problems, stroke, arthritis, and psychiatric problems. *Depressive symptoms* were measured using the sum of eight dichotomous (1 = *yes*, 0 = *no*) items from the Center for Epidemiologic Studies Depression Scale (Steffick, 2000). Education and minority status were measured at baseline, whereas self-rated health, chronic conditions, and depressive symptoms were assessed at each wave.

Analytic Strategy

We used linear growth curve models using SAS PROC MIXED to examine levels (intercepts) and change (slopes) in memory performance. Specifically, this approach identifies sample average levels and slopes in performance, as well as time-invariant (e.g., race, education) and time-varying (e.g., mental and physical health indicators) moderators. The basic growth curve model consists of an intercept, which reflects memory performance at the first wave of assessment (i.e., 1998), and a slope parameter (called "wave" in tabled results) reflecting linear changes in performance per 2 years (as HRS assessments are biennial). Age at baseline (centered at the sample mean [63]) is included as a predictor of both intercept and slope, allowing both to vary as a function of the participant's age at the first assessment. This specification allows for disambiguation of longitudinal, aging-related changes and cross-sectional, age/cohort-related differences in memory.

We included veteran status as a person-level predictor of both intercepts and slopes to provide the critical comparison of differences between veterans and nonveterans in their level and change in memory performance. Restricting analyses to veterans exclusively allows us to examine the same growth model and moderation by person-level characteristics of veterans' service, including duration of service and service during wartime. The former provides a test of whether level and change in memory performance vary based on how long veterans served, whereas the latter tests whether level and change in memory performance differ between veterans who served during wartime and those who did not. Interactions between the military service indicators and age at baseline were also examined to determine whether military service effects differed across men who were relatively younger versus older at the baseline.

Person-level covariates, including race and education, were included to adjust for potential confounds when evaluating the effects of military service on level and change in memory. Time-varying covariates, including self-rated health, number of chronic conditions, and depressive symptoms, were included using person-mean centering (Hoffman & Stawski, 2009), which separates the occasion-specific (time-varying) and person-specific (time-invariant) effects of these variables. We estimated all models using full information maximum likelihood (to account for missing data), and random effects and their covariances were freely estimated.

RESULTS

The results are presented here in three sections: (a) differences in primary memory performance outcomes and covariates by veteran status, (b) differences in level and change in memory performance by veteran status, and (c) effects of service duration and wartime service on veterans' memory performance.

Baseline Differences by Veteran Status

At baseline, veterans—compared with nonveterans—recalled significantly more words during immediate recall performance (5.48 vs. 5.17, $p < .001$, Cohen's $d = 0.12$), and delayed recall performance (4.32 vs. 4.03, $p < .001$, Cohen's $d = 0.10$), but the two groups exhibited comparable rates of forgetting (-1.16 vs. -1.14, $p = .44$, Cohen's $d = 0.01$). Considering study covariates, veterans were significantly older (62.98 vs. 61.50, $p < .001$, Cohen's $d = 0.11$); they had more years of education (12.91 vs. 11.47, $p < .001$, Cohen's $d = 0.29$), better self-rated health (3.23 vs. 3.05, $p < .001$, Cohen's $d = 0.11$), more chronic health conditions (1.63 vs. 1.56, $p < .01$, Cohen's $d = 0.04$), and fewer depressive symptoms (1.23 vs. 1.53, $p < .001$, Cohen's $d = 0.12$); and fewer were racial/ethnic minorities (10% vs. 20%, $p < .001$, Cohen's $d = 0.20$), but completed comparable number of assessment waves (4.99 vs. 4.89, $p = .07$, Cohen's $d = 0.03$).

Level and Change in Memory Performance by Veteran Status

Table 11.2 presents results of multilevel models examining the effects of military service on levels (top portion of table) and rates of change (middle portion of table) for immediate recall (left column), delayed recall (middle column), and forgetting (right column). Preliminary results indicated that

TABLE 11.2
Results of Multilevel Models Examining Effects of Military Service on Episodic Memory Performance

Fixed effects	Immediate recall			Delayed recall			Forgetting		
	Estimate	SE	p	Estimate	SE	p	Estimate	SE	p
Intercept	5.058	.028	<.001	3.989	.033	<.001	-1.071	.022	<.001
Age at baseline	-.063	.003	<.001	-.074	.003	<.001	-.012	.002	<.001
Veteran status	.150	.036	<.001	.109	.042	.01	-.037	.028	.19
Age at baseline*Veteran status	-.001	.003	.75	-.003	.004	.50	-.001	.003	.70
Education	.072	.005	<.001	.177	.006	<.001	.005	.004	.16
Minority status	-.423	.049	<.001	-.645	.057	<.001	-.220	.038	<.001
Wave	-.073	.004	<.001	-.089	.005	<.001	-.010	.004	.004
Wave*Baseline age	-.001	.000	.18	-.001	.000	.01	-.000	.000	.11
Wave*Veteran status	-.017	.005	<.001	-.003	.006	.53	.012	.004	.005
Wave*Baseline age*Veteran status	-.001	.000	.005	-.001	.001	.20	.000	.000	.22
Wave*Education	-.000	.000	.16	-.002	.001	.01	-.001	.001	.12
Wave*Minority status	.009	.006	.10	.003	.007	.66	-.007	.005	.18
Random effects	Estimate	SE	p	Estimate	SE	p	Estimate	SE	p
Intercept	1.033	.033	<.001	1.491	.046	<.001	.289	0.021	<.001
Wave	.004	.000	<.001	.006	.001	<.001	.001	.000	<.001
Covariance (Intercept, Wave)	-.030	.003	<.001	-.047	.005	<.001	-.009	0.003	<.001
Residual	1.353	0.013	<.001	1.771	.017	<.001	1.377	.013	<.001

Note. SE = standard error.

none of the quadratic terms representing nonlinear change in memory indices were statistically significant. As such, we present results of models examining linear change.

For immediate recall, poorer recall at baseline was associated with being older at baseline (Est. = –.063, p < .001), minority status (Est. = –.423, p < .001), and having fewer years of education (Est. = .172, p < .001). It is important to note that veterans exhibited significantly better immediate recall performance at baseline compared to nonveterans (Est. = .150, p < .001). Furthermore, the impact of veteran status on baseline levels of immediate recall performance did not interact with age at baseline (p = .75). With respect to change in immediate recall, we did observe significant declines in performance across waves (Est. = –.073, p < .001), and rate of decline was significantly steeper among veterans (Est. = –.017, p < .001). Furthermore, age at baseline and veteran status did interact to predict rate of decline in immediate recall performance (Est. = –.001, p = .005). Figure 11.1 shows that the older veterans exhibited the fastest rate of decline in immediate recall performance.

For delayed recall, poorer recall at baseline was associated with being older at baseline (Est. = –.074, p < .001), minority status (Est. = –.645, p < .001), and having fewer years of education (Est. = .177, p < .001). It is important to note that veterans exhibited significantly better delayed recall performance at baseline than nonveterans (Est. = .109, p < .01). However, in contrast to immediate recall, age and veteran status did not interact to predict baseline levels of delayed recall performance (p = .50). With respect

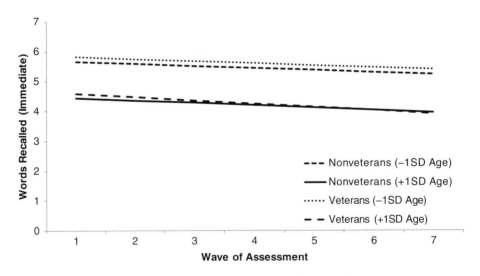

Figure 11.1. Level and change in immediate recall performance by veteran status and age at baseline (–1SD Age ~52; +1SD Age ~74).

to change in delayed recall, we observed significant declines in performance across waves (Est. = −.089, $p < .001$), and this rate of decline was amplified among individuals who were older at baseline (Est. = −.001, $p < .01$) and had fewer years of education (Est. = −.002, $p = .05$). Rate of decline in delayed recall did not differ by veteran status ($p = .53$).

For forgetting, being older (Est. = −.012, $p < .001$) and minority status (Est. = −.220, $p < .001$) were associated with higher levels of forgetting at baseline. There was, however, no difference in forgetting between veterans and nonveterans ($p = .19$). With respect to change, forgetting increased across waves (Est. = −.010, $p = .004$), and the only moderator of change in forgetting was veteran status (Est. = −.012, $p = .005$). Simple slopes indicated that forgetting increased over time in nonveterans (Est. = −.010, standard error [SE] = .004, $p = .004$), whereas veterans' forgetting remained relatively stable (Est. = .002, $SE = .003$, $p = .48$).

Effects of Veterans' Service Duration and Wartime Service on Memory Performance

Adjusting for age at baseline, years of education and race, neither duration of service nor service during wartime were associated with level or rate of change in immediate recall, delayed recall, or forgetting (all $ps > .07$; results not shown). We also explored whether duration of service and service during wartime interacted to predict level or rate of change in memory performance across our three indices, but none of these interactions was statistically significant (all $ps > .30$). Last, we further considered differences in service during wartime by war (i.e., World War II, Korean War, Vietnam War), but we observed no differences in levels or change in any index of memory performance (all $ps > .25$).

Supplemental Analyses

We reran all models from Table 11.2 adjusting for both the time-varying and time-invariant effects of self-rated health, number of chronic health conditions, and depressive symptoms. Results indicated that none of the time-varying effects were significant for any of the memory outcomes. As such, we only report estimates for the time-invariant, person-level effects.

With respect to baseline levels of performance, individual differences in depressive symptoms were negatively associated with immediate (Est. = −.143, $SE = .015$, $p < .001$) and delayed (Est. = −.158, $SE = .018$, $p < .001$) recall performance, whereas individual differences in self-rated health were positively associated with immediate (Est. = .087, $SE = .029$, $p = .003$) and delayed (Est. = .141, $SE = .034$, $p < .001$) recall performance. Number of chronic health conditions was not associated with baseline levels of performance, nor were any of these health-related covariates related to forgetting (all $ps > .10$). Similarly, with respect to longitudinal change in performance, individual differences in self-rated health were positively associated with rates of change for immediate (Est. $= .015$, $SE = .004$, $p < .001$) and delayed (Est. $= .016$, $SE = .005$, $p = < .001$) recall performance, indicating that better self-rated health was associated with less steep decline in both immediate and delayed recall. Neither depressive symptoms nor number of chronic health conditions were predictive of longitudinal change in any index of memory performance. It is important to note that despite these significant associations among self-rated health, depressive symptoms, and memory performance, all veteran status differences in memory performance remained unchanged in terms of direction of effect and statistical significance (results not shown, but available on request to the first author).

DISCUSSION

We investigated whether military service was related to level and rate of change in memory performance, and whether characteristics of veterans' service, including duration of service and wartime service, moderate such effects. Consistent with predictions, veterans exhibited higher levels of immediate and delayed recall performance at baseline compared with nonveterans. Additionally, veterans exhibited significantly steeper aging-related declines in immediate recall, particularly among the oldest veterans. Contrary to predictions, veterans' duration of service and wartime service were unrelated to levels of change in episodic memory performance. Finally, all observed veteran status differences in episodic memory performance remained after adjustment for covariates including physical and mental health.

Our findings that veterans exhibited better immediate and delayed recall performance at earlier ages, and accelerated aging-related declines, are broadly consistent with the results reported by Brown et al. (2014), who examined similar changes in cognitive status using HRS data. However, Brown and colleagues observed curvilinear changes indicating that declines became faster over time, whereas we observed strictly linear changes, indicating that declines were constant over time. There are several notable distinctions between our study and that of Brown and colleagues that potentially contribute to this difference. First, although both studies used data from the HRS, our study included a larger and broader sample in terms of age ranges and restricted analysis to assessments from 1998 on. Second, the cognition measure used by Brown was a composite indicator of global cognitive function, whereas we examined a specific indicator of function—episodic memory. Although we were able to focus on aging-related changes more specific to memory, variation in the rate of aging-related changes across the different dimensions of cognitive function that are captured with a composite index could reveal a more complex pattern of change.

Another explanation for the observed differences between our study and that of Brown et al. (2014) could be differences in how aging-related changes were modeled. For example, Brown and colleagues used an age-based model and observed accelerated decline in cognitive function. We used a time-in-study-based model, with moderation by age at baseline and observed linear declines in memory performance that were slightly, albeit significantly, steeper among those who were older at baseline. We did explore nonlinear change in all indices of memory performance, but none of the quadratic effects were significant (results not shown). Previous research has shown that longitudinal data with heterogeneous ages at baseline can result in the detection of more complex functions that are driven by mean differences as a function of age or birth cohort/year leading to a blending of age-related differences and aging-related changes (Hofer & Sliwinski, 2001). Furthermore, differences in the observed shape of change can lead to potentially different interpretations. Understanding whether observed declines in memory and cognition among veterans are exacerbated by getting older (i.e., acceleration over time) and/or being older (i.e., steeper linear decline relative to other veterans who are younger), will help identify when and for whom potential support is warranted. Despite differences in outcome measures and in modeling approaches, current and previous results suggest the need for continued research of veterans' cognitive aging.

We did not find duration of service, service during wartime, nor war of service as moderators of levels or rates of change in episodic memory. Failure to observe moderation of veterans' levels and rates of change in episodic memory performance would seem to indicate that military service per se, regardless of duration, is an important life course factor that shapes later-life outcomes, including episodic memory. This pattern of results suggests that veterans could be a homogenous group, and this might require consideration for later-life supports in the face of cognitive decline.

The lack of an effect of wartime service or service by war on levels or rates of change in episodic memory is somewhat surprising. Combat exposure is a known risk factor for compromised episodic memory performance in later life (Vasterling et al., 2002); however, we were only able to qualify participants as having served during wartime, not combat exposure. In contrast to our results, Brown et al. (2014) found that wartime service exacerbated aging-related declines in general cognitive function, particularly among veterans of World War II and multiple wars. As stated before, differences in the outcome under study could account for this discrepancy. The effects of wartime service may affect dimensions of cognitive function, other than episodic memory, that are captured in more general composites of cognitive status, and represent opportunity for future research (Vasterling & Proctor, 2011). Sampling in the HRS is done with respect to birth year, and the relatively narrow range of birth years represented in each of the study cohorts confounded age, birth year, and war in which these veterans served. Thus, the ability to detect differences by war of service is potentially impacted by how and whether aging and cohort effects are disambiguated (Hofer & Sliwinski, 2001). Nonetheless, continued investigation of general impacts of wartime service and specific impacts of service during different wars warrants continued investigation.

Interestingly, the impact of veteran status on levels and rates of change in episodic memory differed by index of episodic memory, suggesting that the effects of military service on memory are specific, not general. Although we observed that veterans exhibited less steep aging-related declines in forgetting, we consider this finding cautiously. Because forgetting is simply the difference between delayed and immediate recall scores, the observed veteran status effect reflects that the longitudinal rates of decline for immediate and delayed recall are not the same for veterans and nonveterans. Inspection of the rates of decline in words per wave for immediate and delayed recall indicates similarity for veterans (Immediate = −.087, Delayed = −.089), but not for nonveterans (Immediate = −.079, Delayed = −.090). Thus, the effect observed likely reflects differences in the military service effects on the constituent scores, not the difference score, and underscores the specificity of differences in memory performance by veteran status.

Although both immediate and delayed recall scores indicate the number of words recalled, immediate recall involves particularly effortful attentional processes for encoding, consolidating and retrieving new information. Veterans exhibited compromised performance when more attentionally demanding complex processing, comprehension, and encoding of information were required, as opposed to more strictly retrieval of information (Naveh-Benjamin et al., 2006). This pattern is consistent with the literature on combat exposure, PTSD, and cognitive function, which shows compromised cognitive function in terms of memory, particularly attention and working memory (Vasterling et al., 2002). Taken together, the impact of military service on specific domains of cognitive function may be general, but modified by more extreme aspects of service. As such, continued examination of the domains of cognitive function that are uniquely sensitive to the impact of military service-related factors is needed.

Previous research, including some using data from the HRS, has shown that military service is associated with aging-related declines in self-rated functional health (activities of daily living and instrumental activities of daily living) and increases in chronic conditions (Wilmoth et al., 2010).

Given associations between physical and cognitive health, particularly in advanced age (Spiro & Brady, 2008), it is essential to identify whether the effects of military service on cognitive aging are driven by, or independent of, physical and mental health (see Chapters 7, 9, 12, this volume). Our results revealed that the effects of military service on levels and rates of change in episodic memory were virtually unchanged when we adjusted for self-rated health, number of chronic conditions, and depressive symptoms. Thus, veterans' aging-related declines in memory are not simply a by-product of declines in mental and physical health.

Military service represents a potentially health-promoting context with supports related to medical care, employment, education and skill training, cognitive job complexity, and social interaction and connectedness, all of which can facilitate cognitive function (Rohwedder & Willis, 2010). Transition out of military service may represent a phase whereby such supports are no longer a stable and constant part of life and contribute to increased risk of cognitive decline among veterans. Examining the type and nature of work performed by veterans is potentially important for understanding how military service supports later-life cognitive health (e.g., Fisher et al., 2014). Taken together, both current and prior results suggest that military service is an important factor shaping physical, mental, *and* cognitive health in later life. Future research would benefit from continued examination of the supports that military service provides for maintaining later-life health, as well as bidirectional associations among physical, mental, *and* cognitive health in later life that impact veterans' daily function and quality of life.

Limitations

First, because of historical and cohort effects reflected in the data, our conclusions are restricted to men. Second, it is unclear whether the current findings provide an accurate picture of the impact of various dimensions of military service (e.g., duration, deployment schedules, wartime service) on long-term health and well-being for those currently or recently on active duty. Additionally, our examination was limited to a single measure of episodic memory, word list recall. Advances in the technology (e.g., Internet and smart phone-based assessments) and instrumentation will allow for more thorough explications of the dimensions of cognitive function impacted by military service.

Summary and Conclusion

The results of the current study indicate that military service is related to memory performance in later life. Although this study provides evidence that military service impacts later-life cognitive health, it is clear that this area of inquiry is ripe for additional research. The specificity of effects of military service on immediate but not delayed recall suggests the need to further understand the dimensions of cognitive aging that are exacerbated among veterans; the mechanisms responsible for the accelerated aging-related decline; and candidate lifestyle and health targets for intervention, maintenance, and promotion of cognitive health among veterans (Yaffe, Hoang, Byers, Barnes, & Friedl, 2014). Furthermore, the results of this study, in concert with previous research, underscore the importance of continued examination of life course influences on later-life mental, physical, and cognitive health.

REFERENCES

Brown, M. T., Wilmoth, J. M., & London, A. S. (2014). Veteran status and men's later-life cognitive trajectories: Evidence from the Health and Retirement Study. *Journal of Aging and Health, 26,* 924–951. http://dx.doi.org/10.1177/0898264314534893

Dixon, R. A., Wahlin, A., Maitland, S. B., Hultsch, D. F., Hertzog, C., & Bäckman, L. (2004). Episodic memory change in late adulthood: Generalizability across samples and performance indices. *Memory & Cognition, 32,* 768–778. http://dx.doi.org/10.3758/BF03195867

Dodge, H. H., Zhu, J., Lee, C. W., Chang, C. C. H., & Ganguli, M. (2014). Cohort effects in age-associated cognitive trajectories. *The Journals of Gerontology: Series A. Biological Sciences and Medical Sciences, 69,* 687–694. http://dx.doi.org/10.1093/gerona/glt181

Fisher, G. G., Stachowski, A., Infurna, F. J., Faul, J. D., Grosch, J., & Tetrick, L. E. (2014). Mental work demands, retirement, and longitudinal trajectories of cognitive functioning. *Journal of Occupational Health Psychology, 19,* 231–242. http://dx.doi.org/10.1037/a0035724

Hofer, S. M., & Sliwinski, M. J. (2001). Understanding ageing: An evaluation of research designs for assessing the interdependence of ageing-related changes. *Gerontology, 47,* 341–352. http://dx.doi.org/10.1159/000052825

Hoffman, L., & Stawski, R. S. (2009). Persons as contexts: Evaluating between-person and within-person effects in longitudinal analysis. *Research in Human Development, 6,* 97–120. http://dx.doi.org/10.1080/15427600902911189

Horvat, P., Richards, M., Malyutina, S., Pajak, A., Kubinova, R., Tamosiunas, A., . . . Bobak, M. (2014). Life course socioeconomic position and mid-late life cognitive function in Eastern Europe. *The Journals of Gerontology: Series B. Psychological Sciences and Social Sciences, 69,* 470–481. http://dx.doi.org/10.1093/geronb/gbu014

Hoyer, W. J., & Verhaeghen, P. (2006). Memory aging. In J. Birren & K. W. Schaie (Eds.), *Handbook of the psychology of aging* (6th ed., pp. 209–232). San Diego, CA: Elsevier.

Kremen, W. S., Lachman, M. E., Pruessner, J. C., Sliwinski, M., & Wilson, R. S. (2012). Mechanisms of age-related cognitive change and targets for intervention: Social interactions and stress. *The Journals of Gerontology: Series A. Biological Sciences and Medical Sciences, 67*, 760–765. http://dx.doi.org/10.1093/gerona/gls125

MacLean, A., & Elder, G. H., Jr. (2007). Military service in the life course. *Annual Review of Sociology, 33*, 175–196. http://dx.doi.org/10.1146/annurev.soc.33.040406.131710

McArdle, J. J., Fisher, G. G., & Kadlec, K. M. (2007). Latent variable analyses of age trends of cognition in the Health and Retirement Study, 1992–2004. *Psychology and Aging, 22*, 525–545. http://dx.doi.org/10.1037/0882-7974.22.3.525

Naveh-Benjamin, M., Kilb, A., & Fisher, T. (2006). Concurrent task effects on memory encoding and retrieval: Further support for an asymmetry. *Memory & Cognition, 34*, 90–101. http://dx.doi.org/10.3758/BF03193389

Raz, N., Rodrigue, K. M., Head, D., Kennedy, K. M., & Acker, J. D. (2004). Differential aging of the medial temporal lobe: A study of a five-year change. *Neurology, 62*, 433–438. http://dx.doi.org/10.1212/01.WNL.0000106466.09835.46

Rohwedder, S., & Willis, R. J. (2010). Mental retirement. *The Journal of Economic Perspectives, 24*, 119–138. http://dx.doi.org/10.1257/jep.24.1.119

Salthouse, T. A. (1996). The processing-speed theory of adult age differences in cognition. *Psychological Review, 103*, 403–428. http://dx.doi.org/10.1037/0033-295X.103.3.403

Sapolsky, R. M. (1996). Why stress is bad for your brain. *Science, 273*, 749–750. http://dx.doi.org/10.1126/science.273.5276.749

Sonnega, A., Faul, J. D., Ofstedal, M. B., Langa, K. M., Phillips, J. W., & Weir, D. R. (2014). Cohort profile: Health and Retirement Study (HRS). *International Journal of Epidemiology, 43*, 576–585. http://dx.doi.org/10.1093/ije/dyu067

Spiro, A., III, & Brady, C. B. (2008). Integrating health into cognitive aging research and theory: Quo vadis? In S. M. Hofer & D. F. Alwin (Eds.), *Handbook of cognitive aging: Interdisciplinary perspectives* (pp. 260–283). Thousand Oaks, CA: Sage. http://dx.doi.org/10.4135/9781412976589.n16

Steffick, D. E. (2000). *Documentation of affective functioning measures in the Health and Retirement Study* (HRS Documentation Report DR-005). Ann Arbor: University of Michigan, Survey Research Center. Retrieved from http://hrsonline.isr.umich.edu/sitedocs/userg/dr-005.pdf

Sullivan, M. P., Griffiths, G. G., & Sohlberg, M. M. (2014). Effect of posttraumatic stress on study time in a task measuring four component processes underlying text-level reading. *Journal of Speech, Language, and Hearing Research, 57*, 1731–1739. http://dx.doi.org/10.1044/2014_JSLHR-L-13-0238

Toomey, R., Alpern, R., Vasterling, J. J., Baker, D. G., Reda, D. J., Lyons, M. J., . . . Murphy, F. M. (2009). Neuropsychological functioning of U.S. Gulf War veterans 10 years after the war. *Journal of the International Neuropsychological Society, 15*, 717–729. http://dx.doi.org/10.1017/S1355617709990294

Vasterling, J. J., Duke, L. M., Brailey, K., Constans, J. I., Allain, A. N., Jr., & Sutker, P. B. (2002). Attention, learning, and memory performances and intellectual resources in Vietnam veterans: PTSD and no disorder comparisons. *Neuropsychology, 16*, 5–14. http://dx.doi.org/10.1037/0894-4105.16.1.5

Vasterling, J., & Proctor, S. (2011). Understanding the neuropsychological consequences of deployment stress: A public health framework. *Journal of the International Neuropsychological Society, 17*(1), 1–6. http://dx.doi.org/10.1017/S1355617710001116

Wessely, S., Unwin, C., Hotopf, M., Hull, L., Ismail, K., Nicolaou, V., & David, A. (2003). Stability of recall of military hazards over time. Evidence from the Persian Gulf War of 1991. *The British Journal of Psychiatry, 183*, 314–322. http://dx.doi.org/10.1192/bjp.183.4.314

Wilmoth, J. M., & London, A. S. (Eds.). (2013). *Life course perspectives on military service.* New York, NY: Routledge.

Wilmoth, J. M., London, A. S., & Parker, W. M. (2010). Military service and men's health trajectories in later life. *The Journals of Gerontology: Series B. Psychological Sciences and Social Sciences, 65B*, 744–755. http://dx.doi.org/10.1093/geronb/gbq072

Yaffe, K., Hoang, T. D., Byers, A. L., Barnes, D. E., & Friedl, K. E. (2014). Lifestyle and health-related risk factors and risk of cognitive aging among older veterans. *Alzheimer's & Dementia, 10*(3, Suppl.), S111–S121. http://dx.doi.org/10.1016/j.jalz.2014.04.010

12

LONG-TERM INFLUENCES OF COMBAT EXPOSURE AND POSTTRAUMATIC STRESS SYMPTOMS ON BRAIN STRUCTURE, HEALTH, AND FUNCTIONING: THE VIETNAM ERA TWIN STUDY OF AGING

CAROL E. FRANZ, MICHAEL J. LYONS, AND WILLIAM S. KREMEN

As Vietnam-era veterans enter late midlife, for some the effects of military experience linger. Schnurr, Lunney, Sengupta, and Waelde (2003) reported that 22 years following deployment, 14.7% of Vietnam veterans met criteria for lifetime posttraumatic stress disorder (PTSD). Exposure to combat confers higher risk for PTSD among veterans (Kulka et al., 1990; Lyons, Genderson, & Grant, 2011). Veterans appear to be at higher risk for PTSD than the general population; previous research reported prevalence rates for Vietnam veterans as high as 31% lifetime and 15% in the past year (Kulka et al., 1990). In the general population, PTSD has a lifetime prevalence of approximately 6.8%, 3.5% in the past year (Kessler, Berglund, et al., 2005; Kessler, Chiu, Demler, Merikangas, & Walters, 2005). Posttraumatic stress symptoms (PTSS) are known to persist and are associated with increased morbidity and mortality as well as considerable suffering

http://dx.doi.org/10.1037/0000061-013
Long-Term Outcomes of Military Service: The Health and Well-Being of Aging Veterans, A. Spiro III, R. A. Settersten Jr., and C. M. Aldwin (Editors)

(Elder, Clipp, Brown, Martin, & Friedman, 2009; O'Toole, Catts, Outram, Pierse, & Cockburn, 2009; Wilmoth, London, & Parker, 2010).

Attempts to understand the mechanisms by which PTSS have such long-reaching effects have emphasized two key brain regions implicated in stress neurocircuitry: the hippocampus and the amygdala (Frodl & O'Keane, 2013; McEwen, 2007). Three core features of PTSD implicate the hippocampus: the central role of the hippocampus in the hypothalamic–pituitary–adrenal axis and stress responsivity, neurotoxic effects of traumatic stress, and the role of hippocampal-dependent memory (i.e., reexperiencing traumatic events) in the presentation and persistence of PTSD (Bremner & Vermetten, 2001; McEwen, 2007). Reviews and meta-analyses of this literature have found fairly consistent evidence of smaller hippocampal volume in individuals with PTSD (O'Doherty, Chitty, Saddiqui, Bennett, & Lagopoulos, 2015; van der Werff, van den Berg, Pannekoek, Elzinga, & van der Wee, 2013). Some have interpreted these findings as suggesting that PTSD causes hippocampal shrinkage, yet a causal relationship cannot be inferred from the predominantly cross-sectional data. A recently developed measure of the size of the hippocampus relative to the size of the inferior lateral ventricles—the hippocampal occupancy score—can serve as a proxy for shrinkage or atrophy (Heister, Brewer, Magda, Blennow, & McEvoy, & the Alzheimer's Disease Neuroimaging Initiative, 2011; Jak et al., 2015). However, to our knowledge, no studies have reported on PTSS and hippocampal occupancy. Finally, a review of twin studies found no differences in hippocampal volume in identical twins discordant for PTSD, suggesting that having a small hippocampal volume may be a risk factor for, rather than a sequela of, PTSD (Kremen, Koenen, Afari, & Lyons, 2012).

The amygdala has also been implicated in PTSD because of its role in emotion processing and regulation, fear conditioning, hypervigilance, and memory consolidation (Kim et al., 2011). Amygdala function is closely linked with sensitivity to external cues such as reward, threat, and fearfulness, as well as with both positive and negative appraisals (Adolphs, 2010; Lewis et al., 2014). Adults with trauma exposure or with PTSD have more hyperactive amygdalae during functional magnetic resonance imaging (fMRI) tasks involving emotion processing (Kim et al., 2011; Shin et al., 2005). A meta-analysis, however, found both larger and smaller amygdalae in adults with PTSD compared with others and concluded that the overall pattern of results was inconclusive; overall, very few studies have examined amygdala–PTSD associations (O'Doherty et al., 2015; van der Werff et al., 2013).

Comparisons of these studies are difficult because of their limitations: small and highly selected samples, different methodologies for processing the volumetric data, and wide variation in types and timing of trauma (O'Doherty et al., 2015). In addition, most studies are cross-sectional and focus on adults with current PTSD or on lifetime symptoms reported retrospectively. Finally, research has focused on diagnosed PTSD rather than PTSS. Recent evidence has suggested that continuous measures of symptoms could be as powerful predictors of poor outcomes as the PTSD diagnosis itself (Breslau, Lucia, & Davis, 2004; Goldberg et al., 2014).

Severe PTSS or PTSD appears to be associated with worse functioning across multiple domains in aging adults (Koenen, Stellman, Sommer, & Stellman, 2008). Some studies have found a higher prevalence of aging-related conditions such as heart disease or increased inflammation (Edmondson, Kronish, Shaffer, Falzon, & Burg, 2013; Schnurr, Spiro, & Paris, 2000). Yaffe et al. (2010) and Qureshi et al. (2010) reported higher risk for dementia among veterans with PTSD. Studies have also reported higher rates of marital and social problems, poorer work outcomes, poorer quality of life, and higher rates of comorbid disorders such as depression and anxiety (Franz et al., 2014; Goldberg et al., 2014; O'Toole et al., 2009; Pietrzak, Goldstein, Southwick, & Grant, 2011; Smith, Schnurr, & Rosenheck, 2005; Solomon, Dekel, & Mikulincer, 2008). Given that many of these are also risk factors for poorer aging outcomes, these results suggest that PTSS may be associated with increased risk for accelerated aging.

In this study, we first ask whether combat exposure during military service affects PTSS, and whether these factors in turn influence brain structures associated with stress neurocircuitry nearly 2 decades later. We then examine the extent to which these factors together influence psychological and physical health in late midlife. First, we hypothesize that combat exposure will be associated with PTSS at average age 38. Second, we hypothesize that veterans with higher levels of PTSS will have smaller hippocampal and amygdala volumes, as well as evidence of hippocampal atrophy at average age 56. We then hypothesize that having smaller hippocampal volume and greater hippocampal atrophy at age 56 will be associated with poorer physical health and work outcomes 6 years later because of their associations with stress responsivity. Given the role of the amygdala in emotion processing, we hypothesize that smaller amygdala volumes at age 56 will be associated with poorer psychological and social outcomes, and quality of life, 6 years later. Finally, given findings from previous studies, we predict that PTSS at age 38 will be associated with poorer physical and psychological health, and poorer outcomes, at age 62, even when adjusting for brain measures and other covariates at age 56.

DATA AND DESCRIPTIVE INFORMATION

Sample

Participants were from the Vietnam Era Twin Study of Aging (VETSA), a prospective longitudinal study of risk and protective influences on aging in male

Vietnam-era veterans; the sample comprises community-dwelling veterans, not patients (Kremen, Franz, & Lyons, 2013). In VETSA 1 (baseline), participants were 1,237 individual male twins randomly recruited from 3,322 twin pairs from the nationally representative Vietnam Era Twin Registry (VETR; Eisen, True, Goldberg, Henderson, & Robinette, 1987; Tsuang, Bar, Harley, & Lyons, 2001). The VETR is a research registry created in 1986 of twin brothers who both served in the United States military at some time between 1965 and 1975. The only combat arena during that time was in Southeast Asia. As part of the creation of the VETR, in 1987 participants completed a survey that included PTSS and combat exposure questionnaires. The VETR allows researchers to recruit registry participants for research and maintains a data archive.

VETSA 1 (2002–2008) inclusion criteria were (a) age 51 to 59 years old when recruited and (b) both members of a twin pair agreed to participate. Sampling was age-homogeneous to maximize power to examine within-person differences in change over time. The VETSA 2 (follow-up) assessment occurred approximately 6 years later (2009–2013). More details about the VETSA study are available elsewhere (Kremen, Franz, & Lyons, 2013; Kremen et al., 2010).

Health and lifestyle characteristics of the VETSA 1 sample (average age 56, range 51–60) are comparable to those of men age 55–64 in the general U.S. population: hypertension, 37%/42%; stroke, 2%/4%; heart disease, 13%/20%; diabetes, 12%/16% for VETSA/U.S. statistics, respectively (Centers for Disease Control and Prevention, 2007; Schoenborn & Heyman, 2009). In VETSA 2, 79% of participants were married; 4.6% never married; 2010 U.S. census figures show 72% of men age 50–59 currently married and 10% never married. Median income for households 55–59 years old in the United States was $65,571; for the VETSA 2 men, household median income was $60,000–$69,000. Highlighting their importance for studies of health and aging, Vietnam-era veterans currently account for approximately 24% of adult men over 60, as well as 11% of adults and 47% of all veterans over 60 in the United States (U.S. Department of Veterans Affairs, Office of the Actuary, 2013).

About 25% of VETSA participants were exposed to combat. Participants entered service (on average) in 1968 at age 19.4 ($SD = 1.4$). Approximately 15 years ($SD = 2.8$) elapsed between discharge from service and the age 38 assessment of PTSS. Demographic characteristics of the sample are presented in Table 12.1. We refer to measurement occasions using the mean age at each assessment: age 38 in 1987; 56 at VETSA baseline; and 62 at VETSA follow-up.

Procedure

At age 38, most VETSA participants had completed a mailed VETR survey assessing combat exposure during military service and current PTSS (Goldberg, True, Eisen, & Henderson, 1990). As part of the VETSA, they

TABLE 12.1
Sample Demographics

Variable	Mean (*SE*) or *n* (%)
Lifetime education	13.8 (2.1); associates degree/some college
Own occupation (age 56)	5.6 (2.7); small business owner
Own income (age 56)	5.9 (2.9); $50,000–$59,999 per year
Father occupation	4.7 (1.8); skilled blue collar
Posttraumatic stress symptoms (age 38)	22.7 (7.8) range 13–57
Marital status (age 56)	
Married	396 (80%)
Never married	24 (5%)
Divorced/separated/widowed	78 (15%)
Ethnicity (non-Hispanic White)	434 (89%)
Combat exposures	
Not in Southeast Asia	320 (65%)
In Southeast Asia, no exposure	49 (10%)
1–5 exposures	79 (16%)
6–13 exposures	41 (9%)
Childhood trauma (any)	108 (22%)
Alcohol drinks in past 2 weeks	
None	175 (36%)
> 1 per day	213 (44%)
> 1 but < 2 per day	38 (8%)
2 to < 3 per day	25 (5%)
≥ 3 per day	38 (8%)
Smoking status	
Past	197 (40%)
Current	110 (23%)
Chronic health conditions	
0	186 (38%)
1	180 (37%)
> 1	123 (25%)

Note. *SE* = standard error.

completed at ages 56 and 62 mailed psychosocial questionnaires at home and brought the questionnaire to the test site where they underwent in-depth testing; the following day, eligible participants underwent structural magnetic resonance imaging (MRI; for more details, see Kremen, Fennema-Notestine, et al., 2013; Kremen et al., 2006, 2010). The VETSA 2 assessment took place nearly 6 years after VETSA 1. Although the protocol was similar to that of VETSA 1, MRI data from VETSA 2 were not ready for analysis at the time this chapter was written. Attrition between the two assessments was 18%. Comparisons of demographic measures between follow-up participants and the attrition group showed no differences in most demographics, except that nonreturnees were slightly older and had slightly higher mean incomes than follow-up participants (Franz et al., 2014).

The analytic sample predicting brain outcomes comprises participants with complete data for combat exposure, PTSS at 38, MRI data at age 56 ($n = 469$); analyses predicting functioning and health data at age 62 ($n = 387$) reflect attrition from VETSA 1 to VETSA 2. We focus on individual-level data (not twins) because we are not examining genetic influences. Institutional review board approval was obtained at all sites, and written informed consent was obtained from all participants.

Measures

PTSS and Combat Exposure (Age 38)

At age 38, participants completed the 13-item Vietnam Era Twin Registry PTSD Scale (VETR-PTSDS) based on the *Diagnostic and Statistical Manual of Mental Disorders* (third ed., rev.; *DSM–III–R*; American Psychiatric Association, 1987), the diagnostic standard at the time (Goldberg et al., 1990). Participants indicated how frequently each symptom occurred in the past 6 months (very often, often, sometimes, almost never, or never). The VETR-PTSDS measure had high reliability (alpha = 0.89), strong validity, and correlated .90 with the PTSD Checklist—Civilian Version (PCL-C; Goldberg et al., 1990; Magruder et al., 2015).

As part of the same survey, participants reported on 18 combat-related experiences during military service; reports were validated using military service records (Janes, Goldberg, Eisen, & True, 1991; Lyons et al., 1993). Dohrenwend et al. (2006) found little evidence of bias or falsification in retrospective reports of combat exposure among Vietnam veterans.

Brain Structure Measures (Age 56)

At age 56, structural MRI was conducted on Siemens 1.5 Tesla scanners at one of two sites (260 at University of California, San Diego; 226 at Massachusetts General Hospital). Sagittal T1-weighted MPRAGE sequences were used with a TI = 1,000 ms, TE = 3.31 ms, TR = 2,730 ms, flip angle = 7 degrees, slice thickness = 1.33 mm, voxel size $1.3 \times 1.0 \times 1.3$ mm. Images were automatically corrected for spatial distortion caused by gradient non-linearity and B1 field inhomogeneity. The two T1-weighted images were registered and averaged to improve signal-to-noise. The semiautomated, fully 3D whole-brain segmentation procedure uses a probabilistic atlas and applies a Bayesian classification rule to assign a neuroanatomical label to each voxel; methods were based on FreeSurfer (http://surfer.nmr.mgh.harvard.edu/fswiki, Version 3.0.1b; Fischl et al., 2002; Fischl, Salat, et al., 2004; Fischl, van der Kouwe, et al., 2004). Thirty-four (6.5%) participants were excluded from analyses because of insufficient quality of the parcellation, and an additional 13 participants were missing the VETR-PTSD measure ($n = 469$). This represents 115 monozygotic pairs, 41 monozygotic singletons, 81 dizygotic pairs, 36 dizygotic singletons; the number of singletons (nonpairs) was due to the brother being ineligible for the MRI because of restrictions such as health or claustrophobia.

For analyses of hippocampal and amygdala volume, we created residual variables that adjusted for scanning site and estimated intracranial volume (Kremen et al., 2010). Hippocampal occupancy, a measure of putative hippocampal atrophy, was calculated as bilateral hippocampal volume / (bilateral hippocampal volume + bilateral inferior lateral ventricles) (Heister et al., 2011; Jak et al., 2015).

The following measures of physical, psychological, and functional outcomes were assessed at age 62.

Work and Social Functioning. Occupational status was assessed according to Hollingshead and Redlich criteria (Hollingshead & Redlich, 1955), scored from 0 (*unemployed*) to 9 (*major professional*). Income was reported in 13 $10,000 ranges, ranging from less than $10,000 to $120,000 or more. Social functioning measures included the number of divorces (range 0–5), and the Experiences in Close Relationships Inventory, a measure of adult romantic attachment insecurity such as feelings of overdependence on or avoidance of intimate relationships (Brennan, Clark, & Shaver, 1998).

Psychological Health. Measures of psychological health included the self-report PCL-C based on *DSM–IV* (Weathers, Litz, Herman, Huska, & Keane, 1993), the Center for Epidemiologic Studies Depression Scale (Radloff, 1977), and the Spielberger State-Trait Anxiety Inventory Scale (Spielberger, 2005).

Physical Health. Physical health measures included inflammation (high sensitivity C-reactive protein measured from blood), and the number of major chronic health conditions (Charlson, Szatrowski, Peterson, & Gold, 1994), which summed the number of 16 conditions for which participants responded that a physician told them they had (i.e., diabetes, chronic bronchitis, emphysema, asthma, cancer, osteoarthritis, rheumatoid arthritis, heart attack, heart failure, heart surgery, angina, hypertension, peripheral vascular disease, cirrhosis, AIDS).

Quality of Life. Health-related quality of life was measured with the Short Form 36 Version 1 (SF36); mental and physical component summary scores (MCS/PCS, respectively) were created by standardizing, then averaging, the relevant subscales for each (Ware & Sherbourne, 1992). MCS averages vitality, social functioning, role emotional, and mental health subscales. PCS averages general health, bodily pain, role physical, and physical functioning.

Analytic Plan

We used linear multiple regression models in SAS 9.3 to test predictions of associations among combat exposure, PTSS, and later outcomes. We treated twin pair members as independent. Nonindependence of observations is rarely a problem when the group size is small (M. Neale, personal communication, May 12, 2015). In the case of our twin data, the group size was at most two, and failure to take statistical nonindependence of twin data into account did not alter the results.

We first regressed PTSS symptoms on combat exposure, adjusted for race/ethnicity, socioeconomic status (SES) of family-of-origin, age, and young adult cognitive ability. Young adult cognitive ability was measured with the well-validated 100-item Armed Forces Qualification Test administered at induction into the military (Orme, Brehm, & Ree, 2001).

To test the second hypothesis, the models first examined the extent to which combat exposure and PTSS at age 38 predicted brain outcomes at age 56; models adjusted for race/ethnicity, SES of family-of-origin, age, and young adult cognitive ability. Father's occupation was used to index family-of-origin SES (Hollingshead & Redlich, 1955). Race/ethnicity was coded as non-Hispanic White versus other. In preliminary analyses we examined associations between presence of any apolipoprotein (APOE) *e4* allele and any hard head injury with the brain outcomes. Because neither measure was significantly associated with brain outcomes, they were not included in subsequent analyses. Men who had at least one head injury reported higher levels of PTSS ($r = 0.13$, $p = .01$).

A second set of models added current smoking history, alcohol consumption, and health status at age 56 as covariates. Smoking history was defined by two dummy variables: current cigarette smoker and past smoker. Alcohol consumption in the past 2 weeks was quantified as: never drank/not currently drinking; one or fewer drinks per day; more than one to two drinks per day; more than two drinks per day (Paul et al., 2008). Major chronic health conditions were measured as previously described for age 62. Reported results from the regression models indicate the effect of each measure, adjusting for all other measures in the model. We analyzed models separately for each of the three brain measures.

Finally, we examined the extent to which earlier combat exposure and PTSS, as well as the different brain measures assessed at age 56, predicted age 62 psychological and health outcomes. These models adjusted for young adult cognitive ability, age, father's SES, race, smoking, alcohol consumption, and number of health conditions.

RESULTS

Effects of Combat Exposure on PTSS at Age 38

Combat exposure was significantly associated with PTSS at age 38, $F(4, 464) = 11.09$, $\beta = .01$, standard error $(SE) = .002$, $p < .01$, adjusting for father's SES, age, young adult cognitive ability, and race.

Effects of Combat Exposure and PTSS on Brain Measures at Age 56

PTSS, but not combat exposure, significantly predicted later hippocampal volume and hippocampal occupancy in regression models with the same covariates as previously mentioned (see Table 12.2, Model 1). Men with higher levels of PTSS at age 38 had smaller hippocampi and greater hippocampal atrophy approximately 2 decades later.

A second series of models incorporated current alcohol consumption, smoking, and health conditions into Model 1 as covariates (Table 12.2, Model 2). Accounting for current health risks, age 38 PTSS still predicted hippocampal occupancy, but the association with hippocampal volume was no longer significant. The chronic health conditions index was significantly associated with all three brain measures; having more health conditions was related to smaller hippocampal and amygdala volumes and to greater hippocampal atrophy.

Effects of Combat Exposure, PTSS, and Brain Measures on Age 62 Outcomes

Our final goal was to examine the extent to which combat exposure, PTSS at age 38, and brain measures at age 56 predicted functional outcomes, psychological outcomes, and physical health outcomes at age 62. Regression results reported adjust for all other variables in the models.

More combat exposure during military service was significantly associated with two of 11 outcomes at age 62: higher PTSS on the PCL [$\beta = 0.44$, $SE = .20$, $t(387) = 2.26$, $p = .03$] and more chronic health conditions [$\beta = 0.05$, $SE = .02$, $t(387) = 2.53$, $p = .01$] in late midlife. Models adjusted for age 38 PTSS, age 20 cognitive ability, all three brain measures, race/ethnicity, age, father SES, alcohol consumption, smoking, and health problems at age 56.

PTSS at age 38 significantly predicted worse outcomes on most measures at age 62 in models adjusted for combat exposure, age 20 cognitive ability, all three brain measures, race/ethnicity, age, father SES, alcohol consumption, smoking, and health problems at age 56. All p-values are two-tailed. Higher levels of PTSS were associated with worse social functioning: more divorces [$\beta = 0.01$, $SE = .01$,

TABLE 12.2
Multiple Linear Regressions of PTSS at Age 38 and Combat Exposure Predicting Hippocampal and Amygdala Volume and Hippocampal Atrophy at Age 56

Measure	Hippocampal volume		Hippocampal atrophy		Amygdala volume	
	Model 1 β (SE) p	Model 2 β (SE) p	Model 1 β (SE) p	Model 2 β (SE) p	Model 1 β (SE) p	Model 2 β (SE) p
PTSS	**-.01 (.01) p = .04**	-.01 (.01) p = .10	**-.02 (.01) p < .01**	**-.02 (.01) p < .01**	-.01 (.01) p = .21	-.01 (.01) p = .38
Combat exposure	-.03 (.02) p = .11	-.03 (.02) p = .11	-.02 (.02) p = .34	-.01 (.02) p = .41	-.03 (.02) p = .10	-.03 (.02) p = .08
Race	.20 (.17) p = .22	.18 (.16) p = .24	.25 (.16) p = .12	.24 (.15) p = .13	.09 (.16) p = .60	.07 (.16) p = .66
Age	**-.05 (.02) p = .01**	**-.04 (.02) p = .02**	**-.06 (.02) p < .01**	**-.06 (.02) p < .01**	**-.05 (.02) p = .01**	**-.05 (.02) p = .01**
Father SES	.04 (.03) p = .11	.03 (.03) p = .19	**.07 (.03) p = .01**	**.06 (.03) p = .02**	.02 (.03) p = .51	.01 (.03) p = .67
Cognitive ability	-.08 (.07) p = .23	-.08 (.07) p = .23	-.04 (.07) p = .56	-.05 (.07) p = .49	-.07 (.07) p = .29	-.08 (.07) p = .24
Alcohol consumption		-.03 (.04) p = .48		**-.08 (.04) p = .03**		.00 (.04) p = .97
Smoking status						
Past		-.10 (.10) p = .34		-.22 (.10) p = .04		.03 (.11) p = .80
Current		.05 (.13) p = .71		-.03 (.12) p = .82		-.06 (.13) p = .67
No. major chronic conditions		**-.13 (.04) p < .01**		**-.13 (.04) p < .01**		**-.10 (.05) p = .03**
Overall model:	**F(6, 462) = 3.94, p < .001**	**F(10, 462) = 3.55, p < .01**	**F(6, 462) = 6.61, p < .01**	**F(10, 462) = 6.26, p < .01**	**F(6, 462) = 2.66, p = .02**	**F(10, 462) = 2.13, p = .02**

Note. Covariates of alcohol consumption, smoking, and number of chronic conditions are based on age 56 assessment. Cognitive ability assessed at age 20. PTSS = posttraumatic stress symptoms; *SE* = standard error; SES = socioeconomic status; race: 1 = White, 0 = non-White. Items in bold indicate significant results.

$t(386) = 2.00$, $p = .05$], and more insecure attachment [$\beta = 0.29$, $SE = .06$, $t(386) = 5.12$, $p < .0001$]. Men with greater PTSS earlier in adulthood reported poorer psychological health on all three measures at age 62: higher levels of depressive symptoms and anxiety [$\beta = 0.39$, $SE = .05$, $t(385) = 7.59$, $p < .0001$; $\beta = 0.42$, $SE = .06$, $t(387) = 6.70$, $p < .0001$, respectively], and more symptoms of PTSS on the PCL [$\beta = 0.52$, $SE = .06$, $t(387) = 8.10$, $p < .0001$]. Finally, PTSS predicted higher levels of inflammation [$\beta = 0.01$, $SE = .01$, $t(373) = 2.07$, $p = .04$] and poorer quality of life on both the PCS and MCS SF36 summaries [$\beta = -0.17$, $SE = .05$, $t(387) = -3.61$, $p < .001$; $\beta = -0.33$, $SE = .05$, $t(387) = -6.42$, $p < .0001$, respectively].

Hippocampal volume and hippocampal occupancy at age 56 were associated with occupational status, income, and PCL scores at age 62 (see Table 12.3). As predicted, having a smaller hippocampus or more hippocampal atrophy was associated with lower occupation and income as well as with more symptoms of posttraumatic stress 6 years later.

TABLE 12.3
Age 62 Outcomes Predicted by Hippocampal Volume,
Hippocampal Atrophy, and Amygdala Volume at Age 56

	Hippocampal volume β (SE) p	Hippocampal atrophy β (SE) p	Amygdala volume β (SE) p
Work and social functioning (age 62)			
Occupation	**.38 (.14) p < .01**	**.48 (.14) p < .01**	.01 (.13) p = .94
Income	**.10 (.04) p = .01**	**.14 (.04) p < .01**	.06 (.04) p = .11
No. divorces	−.06 (.04) p = .12	−.07 (.04) p = .12	.05 (.04) p = .22
Insecure attachment	**−.99 (.44) p = .02**	−.62 (.45) p = .17	**−1.08 (.41) p < .01**
Psychological health (age 62)			
Depressive symptoms	−.54 (.41) p = .18	−.58 (.41) p = .16	**−.99 (.37) p = .01**
Anxiety	−.57 (.49) p = .25	−.54 (.50) p = .28	**−.99 (.46) p = .03**
Posttraumatic stress	**−1.06 (.51) p = .04**	**−1.21 (.52) p = .02**	**−1.51 (.47) p < .01**
Physical health and quality of life			
No. chronic conditions	.04 (.05) p = .44	.01 (.05) p = .88	.01 (.05) p = .89
C-reactive protein (inflammation)	−.05 (.05) p = .29	−.06 (.05) p = .21	.03 (.04) p = .56
SF36 PCS	.55 (.38) p = .14	.66 (.39) p = .09	.68 (.35) p = .06
SF36 MCS	.30 (.41) p = .46	.37 (.41) p = .37	**.92 (.37) p = .01**

Note. $N = 387$; p values are two-tailed. In addition to the brain measure, each model included posttraumatic stress symptoms (age 38), combat exposure, cognitive ability (age 20), age, father's socioeconomic status, smoking, alcohol consumption, and number of health conditions. SE = standard error; PCS = Physical Component Summary Scale; MCS = Mental Component Summary Scale. Items in bold indicate significant results.

Finally, participants with smaller amygdala volumes at age 56 reported higher levels of insecure attachment in intimate relationships, as well as greater depression, anxiety, and PTSS 6 years later (Table 12.3). Having a smaller amygdala volume was also significantly associated with poorer mental health quality of life on the SF36 MCS.

CONCLUSIONS/IMPLICATIONS

We examined the long-term influence of military service-related combat exposure and subsequent PTSS on brain structure, and psychological and physical health. First, across the duration of the study, experiencing more combat exposure was associated with higher levels of PTSS at both ages 38 and 62 (even after adjusting for age 38 symptoms). Combat exposure was not significantly associated with later brain volumes. Second, PTSS predicted hippocampal volume and hippocampal atrophy across nearly 2 decades. Finally, PTSS, greater hippocampal atrophy and smaller amygdala volumes at age 56 predicted poorer psychological and physical health outcomes at age 62. Many of these outcomes are associated with increased risk for less successful aging and early cognitive decline.

Combined, these findings partially support our view that brain structures involved in stress neurocircuitry are both risk factors for and sequelae of PTSS. The fact that the brain structure measures at age 56 predicted outcomes at age 62 suggests that they are risk factors for continued symptoms and poorer functioning. It is also possible that hippocampal and amygdala volumes were already smaller when participants were younger, so that the smaller volumes we observed could have been present long before the age 56 assessment. This notion would be consistent with evidence from identical twins discordant for PTSD indicating that a smaller hippocampus is a risk factor for PTSD (Kremen et al., 2012). However, our finding that age 38 symptoms of posttraumatic stress were associated with hippocampal atrophy at age 56, but not with hippocampal volume per se after adjusting for current health, does suggest that continued hippocampal reduction might also be a sequela of PTSS.

Combat experiences were associated with higher symptoms of posttraumatic stress at ages 38 and 62, decades following exposure. It is note-worthy that the effect of combat exposure on PTSS does not appear to be static, given that its association with age 62 PTSS remained significant even controlling for symptoms at age 38. Associations between combat experience and PTSS were modest, suggesting that other factors during military service, or after, might have played a role. We know little, for instance, about mental health treatments these men might have sought or received that may have mitigated PTSS or other symptoms. Combat exposure for the most part did not directly affect most other age 62 outcomes, thereby limiting our ability to conduct mediation models.

Research on the nature of memory in PTSD may help to explain the relationships we found between PTSS and hippocampal atrophy (Brewin, Gregory, Lipton, & Burgess, 2010). Having a smaller hippocampus may be related to reduced efficiency of initial encoding of experiences and a heightened stress response. Poor initial encoding may thereby increase the likelihood and stressfulness of inappropriate responses to cues in daily life, creating a more neurotoxic environment that contributes to hippocampal shrinkage. It may be that as the hippocampus atrophies, whether due to trauma or age, the stress-response system becomes less efficient, although there may be characteristics (e.g., higher cognitive ability, greater self-esteem) and behaviors (good health, not smoking) that could make this decline in efficiency less severe.

In our analyses, amygdala volume at age 56 was a significant predictor of psychological health at age 62. This is consistent with findings, described earlier, indicating that the amygdala can contribute to stress neurocircuitry through emotion processing and regulation (Kim et al., 2011) and that amygdala function is closely linked with sensitivity to external cues such as reward, threat, and fearfulness (Adolphs, 2010; Lewis et al., 2014). Future analyses could elucidate genetic underpinnings of these relationships; Lewis et al. (2014), for instance, found that the association between positive emotionality and amygdala volume was partly explained by shared genetic influences. Similarly, a review of twin studies of combat-exposed veterans demonstrated that trauma-unexposed co-twins of veterans with PTSD also had smaller hippocampal volumes, compared with trauma-unexposed co-twins of veterans without PTSD (Kremen et al., 2012). Recent work also found an interaction between APOE genotype and combat exposure (Lyons et al., 2013); APOE genotype moderated the relationship between combat exposure and PTSD symptoms. Thus a number of features (e.g., hippocampal volume) commonly associated with PTSD could comprise preexisting risk factors, whereas other features (e.g., fear extinction/conditioning and pain) may be sequelae. These results, combined with other findings of genetic overlap between positive emotionality and amygdala volume, suggest that having a relatively larger amygdala could be a protective factor. Some studies have also found shorter telomere length in adults diagnosed with PTSD and/or who have been exposed to trauma (Lindqvist et al., 2015), though findings are mixed. Telomere shortening appears to serve as a genetic index of accelerated cellular aging related to a number of disorders and could contribute to higher risk for poorer health outcomes or early mortality. Future analyses of genotyping data may help shed more light on the role of genetic influences on associations between posttraumatic symptoms and brain outcomes or other risk factors.

The present study has some limitations. The sample included only male veterans, predominantly Caucasian, so we cannot generalize to women or racial/ethnic groups. Only one war was represented by this sample. We did not have data on PTSD symptoms at age 56; thus, it could be argued that the outcomes at age 62 might simply be accounted for by age 56 PTSS. Even if that were the case, the findings would still demonstrate that symptoms of posttraumatic stress and their deleterious effects can be very long-lived and can still have a negative impact on brain and psychological and physical health decades after trauma exposure. Only one aspect of military service—combat exposure—was examined; noncombat exposure related traumatic events could have occurred during service. We also did not include head injury or APOE as covariates in part because of missing data. The head injury question was introduced late into data collection and did not address severity of the injury; 39% of the men reporting having at least one head injury in their lives. Although men with higher levels of PTSS reported more head injuries ($r = .13$, $p = .01$), head injuries were not associated with combat exposure, brain volume measures, or outcomes at age 62. Addition of the head trauma measure and APOE to the mixed models did not change the overall results. Finally, we did not have premorbid brain or other precombat measures, thereby limiting causal inferences. MR imaging was not conducted in 1965–1975 at the time of the participants' years of military service.

In summary, we found long-lasting effects of combat exposure on PTSS. These symptoms were, in turn, predictors of brain structure, functioning, and health over 2 decades or more. This longitudinal study covers a longer interval than most previous studies, and the results showed that the deleterious effects of combat exposure and PTSS are present even at lower levels of symptoms that are below the threshold for a diagnosis of PTSD.

REFERENCES

Adolphs, R. (2010). What does the amygdala contribute to social cognition? *Annals of the New York Academy of Sciences, 1191*, 42–61. http://dx.doi.org/10.1111/j.1749-6632.2010.05445.x

American Psychiatric Association. (1987). *Diagnostic and statistical manual of mental disorders* (3rd ed., revised). Washington, DC: Author.

Bremner, J. D., & Vermetten, E. (2001). Stress and development: Behavioral and biological consequences. *Development and Psychopathology, 13*, 473–489. http://dx.doi.org/10.1017/S0954579401003042

Brennan, K. A., Clark, C. L., & Shaver, P. R. (1998). Self-report measurement of adult romantic attachment: An integrative overview. In J. A. Simpson & W. S. Rholes (Eds.), *Attachment theory and close relationships* (pp. 46–76). New York, NY: Guilford Press.

Breslau, N., Lucia, V. C., & Davis, G. C. (2004). Partial PTSD versus full PTSD: An empirical examination of associated impairment. *Psychological Medicine, 34*, 1205–1214. http://dx.doi.org/10.1017/S0033291704002594

Brewin, C. R., Gregory, J. D., Lipton, M., & Burgess, N. (2010). Intrusive images in psychological disorders: Characteristics, neural mechanisms, and treatment implications. *Psychological Review, 117*, 210–232. http://dx.doi.org/10.1037/a0018113

Centers for Disease Control and Prevention. (2007). *Health data for all ages.* Hyattsville, MD: National Center for Health Statistics.

Charlson, M., Szatrowski, T. P., Peterson, J., & Gold, J. (1994). Validation of a combined comorbidity index. *Journal of Clinical Epidemiology, 47*, 1245–1251. http://dx.doi.org/10.1016/0895-4356(94)90129-5

Dohrenwend, B. P., Turner, J. B., Turse, N. A., Adams, B. G., Koenen, K. C., & Marshall, R. (2006). The psychological risks of Vietnam for U.S. veterans: A revisit with new data and methods. *Science, 313*, 979–982. http://dx.doi.org/10.1126/science.1128944

Edmondson, D., Kronish, I. M., Shaffer, J. A., Falzon, L., & Burg, M. M. (2013). Posttraumatic stress disorder and risk for coronary heart disease: A meta-analytic review. *American Heart Journal, 166*, 806–814. http://dx.doi.org/10.1016/j.ahj.2013.07.031

Eisen, S., True, W., Goldberg, J., Henderson, W., & Robinette, C. D. (1987). The Vietnam Era Twin (VET) Registry: Method of construction. *Acta Geneticae Medicae et Gemellologiae, 36*, 61–66. http://dx.doi.org/10.1017/S0001566000004591

Elder, G. H., Jr., Clipp, E. C., Brown, J. S., Martin, L. R., & Friedman, H. W. (2009). The life-long mortality risks Of World War II experiences. *Research on Aging, 31*, 391–412. http://dx.doi.org/10.1177/0164027509333447

Fischl, B., Salat, D. H., Busa, E., Albert, M., Dieterich, M., Haselgrove, C., . . . Dale, A. M. (2002). Whole brain segmentation: Automated labeling of neuro-anatomical structures in the human brain. *Neuron, 33*, 341–355. http://dx.doi.org/10.1016/S0896-6273(02)00569-X

Fischl, B., Salat, D. H., van der Kouwe, A. J., Makris, N., Ségonne, F., Quinn, B. T., & Dale, A. M. (2004). Sequence-independent segmentation of magnetic resonance images. *NeuroImage, 23*(Suppl. 1), S69–S84. http://dx.doi.org/10.1016/j.neuroimage.2004.07.016

Fischl, B., van der Kouwe, A., Destrieux, C., Halgren, E., Ségonne, F., Salat, D. H., . . . Dale, A. M. (2004). Automatically parcellating the human cerebral cortex. *Cerebral Cortex, 14*, 11–22. http://dx.doi.org/10.1093/cercor/bhg087

Franz, C. E., Lyons, M. J., Spoon, K. M., Hauger, R. L., Jacobson, K. C., Lohr, J. B., . . . Kremen, W. S. (2014). Post-traumatic stress symptoms and adult attachment: A 24-year longitudinal study. *The American Journal of Geriatric Psychiatry, 22*, 1603–1612. http://dx.doi.org/10.1016/j.jagp.2014.02.003

Frodl, T., & O'Keane, V. (2013). How does the brain deal with cumulative stress? A review with focus on developmental stress, HPA axis function and hippocampal structure in humans. *Neurobiology of Disease, 52,* 24–37. http://dx.doi.org/10.1016/j.nbd.2012.03.012

Goldberg, J., Magruder, K. M., Forsberg, C. W., Kazis, L. E., Ustün, T. B., Friedman, M. J., . . . Smith, N. L. (2014). The association of PTSD with physical and mental health functioning and disability (VA Cooperative Study #569: The course and consequences of posttraumatic stress disorder in Vietnam-era veteran twins). *Quality of Life Research, 23,* 1579–1591. http://dx.doi.org/10.1007/s11136-013-0585-4

Goldberg, J., True, W. R., Eisen, S. A., & Henderson, W. G. (1990). A twin study of the effects of the Vietnam War on posttraumatic stress disorder. *JAMA, 263,* 1227–1232. http://dx.doi.org/10.1001/jama.1990.03440090061027

Heister, D., Brewer, J. B., Magda, S., Blennow, K., & McEvoy, L. K., & the Alzheimer's Disease Neuroimaging Initiative. (2011). Predicting MCI outcome with clinically available MRI and CSF biomarkers. *Neurology, 77,* 1619–1628. http://dx.doi.org/10.1212/WNL.0b013e3182343314

Hollingshead, A. B., & Redlich, F. C. (1955). Social mobility and mental illness. *The American Journal of Psychiatry, 112,* 179–185. http://dx.doi.org/10.1176/ajp.112.3.179

Jak, A. J., Panizzon, M. S., Spoon, K. M., Fennema-Notestine, C., Franz, C. E., Thompson, W. K., . . . Kremen, W. S. (2015). Hippocampal atrophy varies by neuropsychologically defined MCI among men in their 50s. *The American Journal of Geriatric Psychiatry, 23,* 456–465. http://dx.doi.org/10.1016/j.jagp.2014.08.011

Janes, G. R., Goldberg, J., Eisen, S. A., & True, W. R. (1991). Reliability and validity of a combat exposure index for Vietnam era veterans. *Journal of Clinical Psychology, 47,* 80–86. http://dx.doi.org/10.1002/1097-4679(199101)47:1<80::AID-JCLP2270470112>3.0.CO;2-9

Kessler, R. C., Berglund, P., Demler, O., Jin, R., Merikangas, K. R., & Walters, E. E. (2005). Lifetime prevalence and age-of-onset distributions of *DSM–IV* disorders in the National Comorbidity Survey Replication. *Archives of General Psychiatry, 62,* 593–602. http://dx.doi.org/10.1001/archpsyc.62.6.593

Kessler, R. C., Chiu, W. T., Demler, O., Merikangas, K. R., & Walters, E. E. (2005). Prevalence, severity, and comorbidity of 12-month *DSM–IV* disorders in the National Comorbidity Survey Replication. *Archives of General Psychiatry, 62,* 617–627. http://dx.doi.org/10.1001/archpsyc.62.6.617

Kim, M. J., Loucks, R. A., Palmer, A. L., Brown, A. C., Solomon, K. M., Marchante, A. N., & Whalen, P. J. (2011). The structural and functional connectivity of the amygdala: From normal emotion to pathological anxiety. *Behavioural Brain Research, 223,* 403–410. http://dx.doi.org/10.1016/j.bbr.2011.04.025

Koenen, K. C., Stellman, S. D., Sommer, J. F., Jr., & Stellman, J. M. (2008). Persisting posttraumatic stress disorder symptoms and their relationship to functioning in Vietnam veterans: A 14-year follow-up. *Journal of Traumatic Stress, 21*, 49–57. http://dx.doi.org/10.1002/jts.20304

Kremen, W. S., Fennema-Notestine, C., Eyler, L. T., Panizzon, M. S., Chen, C. H., Franz, C. E., . . . Dale, A. M. (2013). Genetics of brain structure: Contributions from the Vietnam Era Twin Study of Aging. *American Journal of Medical Genetics: Part B. Neuropsychiatric Genetics, 162*, 751–761. http://dx.doi.org/10.1002/ajmg.b.32162

Kremen, W. S., Franz, C. E., & Lyons, M. J. (2013). VETSA: The Vietnam Era Twin Study of Aging. *Twin Research and Human Genetics, 16*, 399–402. http://dx.doi.org/10.1017/thg.2012.86

Kremen, W. S., Koenen, K. C., Afari, N., & Lyons, M. J. (2012). Twin studies of posttraumatic stress disorder: Differentiating vulnerability factors from sequelae. *Neuropharmacology, 62*, 647–653. http://dx.doi.org/10.1016/j.neuropharm.2011.03.012

Kremen, W. S., Prom-Wormley, E., Panizzon, M. S., Eyler, L. T., Fischl, B., Neale, M. C., . . . Fennema-Notestine, C. (2010). Genetic and environmental influences on the size of specific brain regions in midlife: The VETSA MRI study. *NeuroImage, 49*, 1213–1223. http://dx.doi.org/10.1016/j.neuroimage.2009.09.043

Kremen, W. S., Thompson-Brenner, H., Leung, Y. M., Grant, M. D., Franz, C. E., Eisen, S. A., . . . Lyons, M. J. (2006). Genes, environment, and time: The Vietnam Era Twin Study of Aging (VETSA). *Twin Research and Human Genetics, 9*, 1009–1022. http://dx.doi.org/10.1375/twin.9.6.1009

Kulka, R. A., Schlenger, W. E., Fairbank, J. A., Hough, R. L., Jordan, B. K., Marmar, C. R., & Weiss, D. S. (1990). *Trauma and the Vietnam War generation: Report of findings from the National Vietnam Veterans Readjustment Study.* New York, NY: Brunner/Mazel.

Lewis, G. J., Panizzon, M. S., Eyler, L., Fennema-Notestine, C., Chen, C. H., Neale, M. C., . . . Franz, C. E. (2014). Heritable influences on amygdala and orbitofrontal cortex contribute to genetic variation in core dimensions of personality. *NeuroImage, 103*, 309–315. http://dx.doi.org/10.1016/j.neuroimage.2014.09.043

Lindqvist, D., Epel, E. S., Mellon, S. H., Penninx, B. W., Révész, D., Verhoeven, J. E., . . . Wolkowitz, O. M. (2015). Psychiatric disorders and leukocyte telomere length: Underlying mechanisms linking mental illness with cellular aging. *Neuroscience and Biobehavioral Reviews, 55*, 333–364. http://dx.doi.org/10.1016/j.neubiorev.2015.05.007

Lyons, M. J., Genderson, M., & Grant, M. (2011). Veterans' mental health: The effects of war. In L. Cottler (Ed.), *Mental health in public health* (pp. 79–103). New York, NY: Oxford University Press.

Lyons, M. J., Genderson, M., Grant, M. D., Logue, M., Zink, T., McKenzie, R., . . . Kremen, W. S. (2013). Gene-environment interaction of ApoE genotype and combat exposure on PTSD. *American Journal of Medical Genetics: Part B. Neuropsychiatric Genetics, 162*, 762–769. http://dx.doi.org/10.1002/ajmg.b.32154

Lyons, M. J., Goldberg, J., Eisen, S. A., True, W., Tsuang, M. T., Meyer, J. M., & Henderson, W. G. (1993). Do genes influence exposure to trauma? A twin study of combat. *American Journal of Medical Genetics, 48,* 22–27. http://dx.doi.org/10.1002/ajmg.1320480107

Magruder, K., Yeager, D., Goldberg, J., Forsberg, C., Litz, B., Vaccarino, V., . . . Smith, N. (2015). Diagnostic performance of the PTSD checklist and the Vietnam Era Twin Registry PTSD scale. *Epidemiology and Psychiatric Sciences, 24,* 415–422.

McEwen, B. S. (2007). Physiology and neurobiology of stress and adaptation: Central role of the brain. *Physiological Reviews, 87,* 873–904. http://dx.doi.org/10.1152/physrev.00041.2006

O'Doherty, D. C., Chitty, K. M., Saddiqui, S., Bennett, M. R., & Lagopoulos, J. (2015). A systematic review and meta-analysis of magnetic resonance imaging measurement of structural volumes in posttraumatic stress disorder. *Psychiatry Research: Neuroimaging, 232,* 1–33. http://dx.doi.org/10.1016/j.pscychresns.2015.01.002

Orme, D. R., Brehm, W., & Ree, M. J. (2001). Armed Forces Qualification Test as a measure of premorbid intelligence. *Military Psychology, 13,* 187–197. http://dx.doi.org/10.1207/S15327876MP1304_1

O'Toole, B. I., Catts, S. V., Outram, S., Pierse, K. R., & Cockburn, J. (2009). The physical and mental health of Australian Vietnam veterans 3 decades after the war and its relation to military service, combat, and post-traumatic stress disorder. *American Journal of Epidemiology, 170,* 318–330. http://dx.doi.org/10.1093/aje/kwp146

Paul, C. A., Au, R., Fredman, L., Massaro, J. M., Seshadri, S., Decarli, C., & Wolf, P. A. (2008). Association of alcohol consumption with brain volume in the Framingham study. *Archives of Neurology, 65,* 1363–1367. http://dx.doi.org/10.1001/archneur.65.10.1363

Pietrzak, R. H., Goldstein, R. B., Southwick, S. M., & Grant, B. F. (2011). Medical comorbidity of full and partial posttraumatic stress disorder in US adults: Results from Wave 2 of the National Epidemiologic Survey on Alcohol and Related Conditions. *Psychosomatic Medicine, 73,* 697–707. http://dx.doi.org/10.1097/PSY.0b013e3182303775

Qureshi, S. U., Kimbrell, T., Pyne, J. M., Magruder, K. M., Hudson, T. J., Petersen, N. J., . . . Kunik, M. E. (2010). Greater prevalence and incidence of dementia in older veterans with posttraumatic stress disorder. *Journal of the American Geriatrics Society, 58,* 1627–1633. http://dx.doi.org/10.1111/j.1532-5415.2010.02977.x

Radloff, L. S. (1977). The CES-D scale: A self-report depression scale for research in the general population. *Applied Psychological Measurement, 1,* 385–401. http://dx.doi.org/10.1177/014662167700100306

Schnurr, P. P., Lunney, C. A., Sengupta, A., & Waelde, L. C. (2003). A descriptive analysis of PTSD chronicity in Vietnam veterans. *Journal of Traumatic Stress, 16,* 545–553. http://dx.doi.org/10.1023/B:JOTS.0000004077.22408.cf

Schnurr, P. P., Spiro, A., III, & Paris, A. H. (2000). Physician-diagnosed medical disorders in relation to PTSD symptoms in older male military veterans. *Health Psychology, 19*, 91–97. http://dx.doi.org/10.1037/0278-6133.19.1.91

Schoenborn, C. A., & Heyman, K. M. (2009, July 8). Health characteristics of adults aged 55 years and over: United States, 2004–2007. *National Health Statistics Reports, 16*. Retrieved from http://www.cdc.gov/nchs/data/nhsr/nhsr016.pdf

Shin, L. M., Wright, C. I., Cannistraro, P. A., Wedig, M. M., McMullin, K., Martis, B., . . . Rauch, S. L. (2005). A functional magnetic resonance imaging study of amygdala and medial prefrontal cortex responses to overtly presented fearful faces in posttraumatic stress disorder. *Archives of General Psychiatry, 62*, 273–281. http://dx.doi.org/10.1001/archpsyc.62.3.273

Smith, M. W., Schnurr, P. P., & Rosenheck, R. A. (2005). Employment outcomes and PTSD symptom severity. *Mental Health Services Research, 7*, 89–101. http://dx.doi.org/10.1007/s11020-005-3780-2

Solomon, Z., Dekel, R., & Mikulincer, M. (2008). Complex trauma of war captivity: A prospective study of attachment and post-traumatic stress disorder. *Psychological Medicine, 38*, 1427–1434. http://dx.doi.org/10.1017/S0033291708002808

Spielberger, C. D. (2005). *The State/Trait Anxiety Inventory for Adults.* Redwood City, CA: Mind Garden.

Tsuang, M. T., Bar, J. L., Harley, R. M., & Lyons, M. J. (2001). The Harvard Twin Study of Substance Abuse: What we have learned. *Harvard Review of Psychiatry, 9*, 267–279. http://dx.doi.org/10.1080/10673220127912

U.S. Department of Veterans Affairs, Office of the Actuary. (2013). *The veteran population projection model 2011 (VetPop2011).* Washington, DC: Author.

van der Werff, S. J., van den Berg, S. M., Pannekoek, J. N., Elzinga, B. M., & van der Wee, N. J. (2013). Neuroimaging resilience to stress: A review. *Frontiers in Behavioral Neuroscience, 7*(39). http://dx.doi.org/10.3389/fnbeh.2013.00039

Ware, J. E., Jr., & Sherbourne, C. D. (1992). The MOS 36-Item Short-Form Health Survey (SF-36): I. Conceptual framework and item selection. *Medical Care, 30*, 473–483. http://dx.doi.org/10.1097/00005650-199206000-00002

Weathers, F. W., Litz, B. T., Herman, D. S., Huska, J. A., & Keane, T. M. (1993, October). *The PTSD Checklist (PCL): Reliability, validity, and diagnostic utility.* Paper presented at the 9th Annual Meeting of the International Society for Traumatic Stress Studies, San Antonio, TX.

Wilmoth, J. M., London, A. S., & Parker, W. M. (2010). Military service and men's health trajectories in later life. *The Journals of Gerontology: Series B. Psychological Sciences and Social Sciences, 65B*, 744–755. http://dx.doi.org/10.1093/geronb/gbq072

Yaffe, K., Vittinghoff, E., Lindquist, K., Barnes, D., Covinsky, K. E., Neylan, T., . . . Marmar, C. (2010). Posttraumatic stress disorder and risk of dementia among US veterans. *Archives of General Psychiatry, 67*, 608–613. http://dx.doi.org/10.1001/archgenpsychiatry.2010.61

13

THE EFFECTS OF COMBAT AND POSTTRAUMATIC STRESS DISORDER ON LONGEVITY

GEORGE E. VAILLANT AND DIANE HIGHUM VAILLANT

Relatively few prospective studies of posttraumatic stress disorder (PTSD) risk factors take a lifespan perspective. Three studies have examined PTSD risk factors in the three time frames of data collection: prewar, wartime, and postwar (Foy, Carroll, & Donahoe, 1987; Green, Grace, Lindy, Gleser, & Leonard, 1990; Schnurr, Friedman, & Rosenberg, 1993). Judging from research on Vietnam War veterans, combat exposure per se appears to be the most reliable wartime predictor of PTSD (Foy et al., 1987), especially exposure to atrocities (Fontana & Rosenheck, 1993; Green et al., 1990). However, these studies have only included Vietnam War veterans. To our knowledge, similar prospective studies have not been undertaken of

This work was originally inspired and shaped by Glen Elder. It was supported by Research Grants K05-MH00364 and MH42248 from the National Institute of Mental Health, AG034554 from the National Institute of Aging, AA00299 from the National Institute on Alcohol Abuse and Alcoholism, the Veterans Affairs Merit Review Program (Durham, NC), and the U.S. Army Research Institute.

http://dx.doi.org/10.1037/0000061-014
Long-Term Outcomes of Military Service: The Health and Well-Being of Aging Veterans, A. Spiro III, R. A. Settersten Jr., and C. M. Aldwin (Editors)

World War II veterans (but see Kang, Aldwin, Choun, & Spiro, 2016, for a review).

To examine the predictors and correlates of PTSD, the authors of a previous article (Lee, Vaillant, Torrey, & Elder, 1995) took advantage of the Harvard Study of Adult Development, a 50-year prospective study of 110 World War II veterans who served in combat overseas (Monks, 1957; Vaillant, 1977; cf. Chapters 1 and 2, this volume). On returning to civilian life in 1946, 31 of these 110 veterans reported four or more symptoms of PTSD. Of this group, five men met criteria for PTSD. Of these five men, two committed suicide, one died in a car accident at age 43, one died of alcoholism at age 74, and one cut himself off socially and emigrated to Australia. Interestingly, in college assessments the men who developed PTSD symptoms had not demonstrated any preexisting mental health problems.

In 1988, the surviving men were sent a questionnaire that focused on their military experiences. The questionnaire included a checklist of current PTSD symptoms derived from the *Diagnostic and Statistical Manual of Mental Disorders* (3rd ed.; *DSM–III*; American Psychiatric Association, 1980). Of the 127 veterans who served overseas (not all of whom were in combat) and survived until 1988, 107 (84%) returned questionnaires. Four of the five originally most symptomatic veterans (all with high combat exposure and three of whom were deceased) failed to return the 1988 questionnaire. Of the 32 men with high combat exposure who did return the 1988 questionnaire, only three reported one or more current symptoms of PTSD. However, of the 14 men with two or more PTSD symptoms in 1946, six had died young (four of these deaths were unnatural), one emigrated, and four men remained symptomatic.

Multiple regression analysis revealed that of four potential premorbid predictors of PTSD (bleak childhood, psychological vulnerability in college, physical symptoms with stress experienced prior to wartime, and combat exposure), only combat exposure made a significant statistical contribution to PTSD symptoms, $t(144) = 4.09$, $p = .0001$. In short, our prior study found that only combat exposure predicted symptoms of PTSD in 1988.

In our 1988 report (Vaillant & Schnurr, 1988), we wrote that we suspected that severe combat led to increased mortality, but our cohort was still too young to test the hypothesis adequately. Similarly, Vietnam veterans have not lived long enough for current studies to assess the full effects of severe combat on mortality. However, by the time of this writing, 38 (16%) of our World War II veterans are still alive at age 93 (+/–1 year), but none of the men with more than one symptom of PTSD or exposed to the most severe combat have survived. This chapter is an effort to ascertain why.

METHODS

Between 1939 and 1942, a multidisciplinary team from the Harvard University Health Service selected 268 male college sophomores for intensive study. They were chosen for appearing to be in good physical and mental health (Heath, 1945; Vaillant, 1977) and for being viewed by the college deans as having the potential for success.

Over the last 75 years, these men have been followed by biopsychosocial mail questionnaires every 2 years, by physical exams every 5 years, and by interview every 15 years. Among variables obtained were a 1946 history of combat experiences, prospectively gathered objective physical health data every 5 years by an internist blinded to their status, repeated assessment of alcohol problems, and death certificates.

Sample

Because the original study group was from the classes of 1939 to 1944, after intensive prospective study during their sophomore year, 144 (54%) men had some level of exposure to World War II. Twenty-four men withdrew from the study early or died in combat during World War II. Since the war, the remaining 244 men have been followed by means of biennially mailed questionnaires for 70 years or until death, and since age 45, by means of physical examinations obtained every 5 years.

Measures

Prewar Variables

After a home visit and family interview, the men's family's social class was rated on a 5-point scale (Hollingshead & Redlich, 1958): 5 = *upper,* 4 = *upper/upper-middle,* 3 = *upper-middle,* 2 = *middle,* 1 = *working class/blue collar.*

Wartime Variables

Directly after World War II, an elaborate questionnaire with open-ended questions on their war experiences was mailed to all men who had been inducted into the military. There was a 97% completion rate. In addition, in 1946 the study staff interviewed the men about their wartime experiences (Monks, 1957). Both the questionnaire and the interview focused on the effects of the war, the men's exposure to combat, and their descriptions of thoughts and bodily symptoms if and when "danger stared them in the face." A psychiatrist who was blind to subsequent data scored all wartime variables.

Combat Exposure Scale. To assess combat exposure, we combined data from a sustained danger scale (Monks, 1957) and a scale of combat experiences. Our intent was to tap both the intensity and frequency of combat exposure. We selected those variables thought to be most important in the development of PTSD (Foy et al., 1987; Keane, Caddell, & Taylor, 1988). The Combat Exposure Scale summed the following experiences, scored 0 (*no*) or 1 (*yes*): (1) Being under enemy fire; (2) Firing at the enemy; (3) Killing anyone; (4) Seeing allies killed or wounded; (5) Seeing enemies killed or wounded; and (6) Being wounded. Points for sustained danger were added as follows: 0 = *no days spent in danger level 7* ("In sustained or heavy enemy action") *or level 6* ("In light or sporadic action"); 1 = *1–21 days in danger levels 7 and/or 6*, and 2 = *22 days or more in levels 7 and/or 6*. In addition, each man received one point if level 6 was reported as the highest level of danger, or 2 points if level 7 was the highest level of danger. Thus, the points assigned for combat exposure ranged from 0 to 10.

Physical Symptoms With Danger. In 1946, the men were asked what their bodily symptoms had been "if and when danger stared you straight in the face." Each of 10 individual symptoms was scored 0 = *absent* and 1 = *present*. The items experienced (palpitations, abdominal distress, headaches, diarrhea, constipation, sweating, shaking, general nervousness, fear of going crazy, and feeling paralyzed) were summed.

Posttraumatic Stress Disorder Symptoms. On the basis of the 1946 interview and questionnaire, 16 symptoms, later included in the *DSM–III* (American Psychiatric Association, 1980) definition of PTSD, were rated 0 = *absent* and 1 = *present*. No man reported more than six symptoms. Of the 14 men who reported two or more symptoms of PTSD, 13 also reported Combat Exposure scores of greater than 5.

Severe Combat Exposure (SCE). Twenty-two men had either a combat exposure score greater than 8 or a combat score greater than 5 and two or more symptoms of PTSD. These men were scored 1 for severe combat. The 222 men who did not meet these criteria received a 0.

Postwar Variables

Physical Symptoms With Stress (Ages 20–60). Six times between college and age 60 years, men were asked, "When under stress, what do you now notice about your reactions?" Of 14 symptoms (e.g., insomnia, headaches, abdominal pain, diarrhea, sweating) only "smoke and drink more" was significantly associated with severe combat.

Alcohol Abuse or Dependence (Ages 18–50). Medical and psychiatric records, interviews, and biennial questionnaires regarding alcohol-related problems (20–40 points in time) were reviewed. *DSM–III* criteria (American

Psychiatric Association, 1980) were used to create a scale of alcohol-related legal, medical, social, or occupational problems (Vaillant, 1993): 1 = *social (less than 3 problems over 3 decades)*, 2 = *alcohol abuse*, and 3 = *alcohol dependence (usually more than 8 problems)*.

Smoking. Smoking history was obtained from biennial questionnaires from ages 21 to 47 years and was summarized as pack years.

Psychosocial Adjustment (Ages 30–47). On the basis of all reported behavior since college, the men were rated for the presence or absence of eight variables, including occupational advancement, job satisfaction, marital satisfaction, recreation with others, sick leave, enjoyable vacation, and income greater than $20,000 (Vaillant & Schnurr, 1988).

Major Depression (Ages 20–50). A psychiatrist, blind to other ratings, reviewed the men's complete records (from college until 1970) for nine correlates of depression not explained by concurrent alcoholism (Vaillant, 1993; Vaillant, Orav, Meyer, Vaillant, & Roston, 1996). Men with three or more indicators of depression ($n = 19$) were classified as having probable major depressive disorder. For these depressed men, the mean number of indicators was 5.4 ± 1.8, contrasted with 0.14 ± 0.49 indicators for the remaining 225 men. (In 1970, the *DSM–III* was not yet published.)

Social Support (Ages 50–70). After reviewing 11 biennial questionnaires and interview data, an independent rater assigned social support ratings (Vaillant, Meyer, Mukamal, & Soldz, 1998). The rating was based on the sum of scores on seven items, each scored 0 to 2. The items were: warm marriage, close adult sibling relationships, close to kids, use of confidants, regular recreation with friends, other contact with friends, and religious participation. The intraclass correlation (computed for 3 raters on 30 cases) was .92.

Exercise (Ages 20–60). Exercise between the ages of 20 and 45 and the ages of 45 and 60, as reported on multiple questionnaires and interviews, was rated on a 1-to-3 scale, defined as 1 = *< 500 kcal/week*, 2 = *500–2,000 kcal/week*, or 3 = *> 2,000 kcal/week* (using the tables provided in the Harvard Sports Code; Schnurr, Vaillant, & Vaillant, 1990; Taylor, 1979).

Vascular Risk Factors. The ages at which both hypertension and heart disease occurred were strongly correlated with age of death. Because not all men suffered from these illnesses, a new variable, "vascular risk," was computed. If a man had either hypertension or heart disease before age 70, he received a score of 1; if not, he received a score of 0.

Estimated Age at Death. Forty-four men were almost certainly still alive as of 2014. Because the mean survival of 92-year-old White men (born in 1920; and of the study men's fathers at 92) was roughly 3 years, those years were added to the surviving men's age in 2014. (In December 2015, 28 men were still alive.)

Because many statistical comparisons were being considered and our numbers are small, some comparisons could be significant by chance. The Bonferroni correction was not done because it would have been overly conservative; instead, we elected to use $p < .03$ as the cutoff for significance.

RESULTS

After excluding the 18 dropouts and the six combat deaths, 219 (90%) of the remaining 244 study men entered the U.S. Armed Forces at an average age of 22. As shown in Table 13.1, 110 of these men experienced at least minimal combat. Results have strongly suggested that World War II SCE predicted shorter lifespan. Twice as many men without SCE survived until age 80 as the 22 men with SCE. Only two (9%) of the 22 men with SCE reached their 90th birthday, contrasted with 74 (32%) of the 232 men without such exposure. We also conducted an analysis of variance comparing the age at death across three groups: those with no combat exposure, those with some, and those with SCE. As can be seen in Table 13.1, the men with no or light/moderate exposure had identical estimated ages at death (82), whereas those with SCE died a full decade earlier, at an average age of 72.

TABLE 13.1
Combat Subgroups and Mean Estimated Age of Death ($N = 268$)

Mean estimated groups	n	Age at death
All men remaining in sample	244	81
Men who did not face combat (4F, physicists, did not go overseas, overseas desk jobs, etc.)[+]	134	82
Men with some combat exposure[+]	110	
Men who faced mild combat (score 1–5)	48	82
Men who faced moderate combat (score 6–8)	46	80
Men who faced high combat (score 9–10)[+]	16	70
[+]$F(3, 240) = 3.4$, $p = .019$		
Men with less than 2 symptoms of PTSD	229	81
Men with 2 symptoms of PTSD	5	78
Men with more than 2 symptoms of PTSD	10	71
$F(2, 241) = 2.5$, $p = .081$		
Men with little or no combat	182	82
Men with high or moderate combat but less than 2 symptoms of PTSD	49	79
Men with high or moderate combat and with more than 2 symptoms of PTSD	13	71
$F(2, 241) = 4.0$, $p = .019$		

Note. We excluded 18 dropouts and 6 World War II deaths. PTSD = posttraumatic stress disorder.

Interestingly, a comparison of estimated ages at death between men with two or more PTSD symptoms, versus men with less than two symptoms, showed only marginal differences. However, the last comparison in Table 13.1 suggests that it was the combination of PTSD symptoms and high combat, rather than the exposure to combat per se, that shortened the men's lifespan. The lives of the 49 men with high combat (scores of 6–10) without multiple symptoms of PTSD were shortened by 3 years; the 13 men with combat scores of 6 to 10 and multiple symptoms of PTSD had their lifespan shortened by an average of 11 years.

This shortened lifespan of the men with SCE (combat scores of 6–10 and multiple symptoms of PTSD, or combat scores of 9–10) could be partially explained by the increased number of unnatural deaths. Eleven (5.0%) of the men without SCE, versus 18.2% of the men with SCE, had unnatural deaths. However, when the 15 men with unnatural deaths (alcoholism, murder, suicide, accident) were removed from the analysis, the age of death of the men with SCE was still 3.3 years earlier than the rest of the sample, $F(1, 228) = 4.5, p = .035$.

Table 13.2 examines the correlates of longevity and contrasts the correlations of these variables with severity of combat and with multiple symptoms PTSD. It reveals that in our study of veterans who were preselected for health and education, many of the standard risk factors for PTSD and high morbidity among those exposed to extreme combat were not significant—for example, social disadvantage, unstable childhood, physical symptoms under stress (other than combat), and major depression. In addition, smoking and poor social support, though known to be bad for longevity, were only minimally correlated with combat exposure and multiple symptoms of PTSD.

Besides unnatural deaths, the chief contender for the difference between the longevity of men with SCE and the noncombatants was the fact that symptoms of PTSD were closely linked to causes of increased vascular risk: alcoholism enhanced by inhibition of smoking cessation (Vaillant, 1993) and early onset of heart disease and hypertension. The men with high combat exposure did not die more frequently from heart disease; rather they developed heart disease and hypertension at a younger age. Of the 22 men with SCE, 60% developed hypertension by age 70; this was twice the rate in the 134 men with no combat exposure.

An analytic problem was posed by the fact that the six variables of interest (high combat, multiple symptoms of PTSD, early mortality, age of onset of heart disease and of hypertension, and alcoholism) were significantly ($p < .03$) associated with one other. Multiple regression analysis was used to examine the variance that these competing factors contributed to longevity. Vascular risk factors explained 14% of the variance ($p < .001$), and alcohol abuse explained an additional 4% ($p = .001$). Adding combat exposure and multiple PTSD

TABLE 13.2
Correlates of Combat, PTSD, and Mortality (N = 244)

	Severity of combat exposure (1–10)	2+ symptoms of PTSD	Age at death
Unimportant correlates of longevity			
Social class of parents	.06	.00	.05
Warm childhood environment	.04	−.03	.11
Physical symptoms with stress	−.07	−.00	.05
Major depression	.03	.19 **	−.03
Correlates of severe combat and longevity			
Severity of combat 1–10	—	.33***	−.17**
Combat 6+ and PTSD 2+			−.17**
Killed someone	.62***	.19*	−.19*
Physical symptoms with danger	.63***	.29***	−.16*
"Vascular risk"	.13	.15*	−.44***
Age hypertension began (n = 148)	−.12	−.07	−.58***
Age heart disease began (n = 95)	.01	−.16*	−.54***
Alcohol abuse/dependence	−.03	.22**	−.30***
Psychological soundness in college	−.04	−.17**	.14*
Poor psychosocial adjustment (age 30–47)	−.00	.15*	−.18**
Uncorrelated with severe combat but significantly correlated with longevity			
Regular exercise	.08	.12	.23**
Good social supports (age 50–70)	−.13	.10	.24***
Smoking (in pack years)	.09	.09	−.24***

Note. Spearman correlation coefficients. PTSD = posttraumatic stress disorder.
*p = < .03. **p < .01. ***p < .001.

symptoms explained no additional variance; however, both variables preceded the explanatory variables in time. That is, combat exposure and symptoms of PTSD occurred earlier in the lifespan of the men, and PTSD symptoms likely contributed to the development of alcoholism, hypertension, and early onset of heart disease. Multiple PTSD symptoms explained 2.7% of the variance in vascular risk, $p = .01$, and 2.2% of the variance in alcohol abuse, $p = .02$. In neither model did adding combat exposure explain additional variance.

DISCUSSION

Our findings differ from those gleaned from studies of Vietnam veterans. Although combat was strongly associated in our sample with symptoms of PTSD, SCE did not lead to major depression or to poor psychosocial adjustment. Here, our atypical sample (Caucasian, highly educated, socially privileged, and preselected for mental and physical health) proved an asset, not a liability, because the study controlled for many potential confounders.

Understanding the role of combat in PTSD and postwar mortality in veterans of Vietnam and later wars has been confounded by the fact that in these conflicts, the less educated and the socially disadvantaged were at greater risk for combat exposure. Thus, it has not always been easy to separate the role of combat from the role of predisposing vulnerabilities. In contrast, in our World War II sample, those veterans who were not exposed to combat were evenly matched with those who experienced the heaviest combat, except that the men exposed to the heaviest combat tended to report a stronger urge to join the U.S. Armed Forces, before the war and during the war, and were unusually proud of their military organization (Lee et al., 1995).

Another of our findings that is at variance with some studies of PTSD is that later alcohol abuse measured by negative behavioral effects (social, occupational, medical, and legal; Vaillant, 1993) was only weakly correlated with combat exposure (Table 13.2), but alcoholism was significantly correlated with symptoms of PTSD.

On the one hand, to clarify the enduring effects of wartime stress on mortality, the present study has four serious disadvantages. First, it excludes men with four of the most important predisposing factors for PTSD: low socioeconomic status, minority group membership, poor education, and low military rank (Green et al., 1990; Kahana, Harel, & Kahana, 1988). Thus, in spite of heavy combat exposure, our study group reported having experienced relatively few PTSD symptoms. Second, our original PTSD information had to be derived from information available in 1946 rather than from more recently devised assessments based on *DSM–III* (American Psychiatric Association, 1980; e.g., Mississippi Scale; Keane et al., 1988) or *DSM–IV* (American Psychiatric Association, 1994; the PTSD Checklist). Third, our sample of men with SCE numbered only 22. Fourth, we hypothesize sustained vascular stress due to increased autonomic arousal as a cause for our findings, yet we lack data regarding measured corticosteroid levels.

In an elegant study of 18,583 Vietnam veterans, using Cox regression to control for virtually all confounders, Boscarino (2008) found that PTSD significantly elevated both vascular risk factors and mortality from heart disease. He seriously considered the effect of PTSD on the hypothalamic pituitary axis and hypertension as mediating factors; however, like ours, his study lacked corticosteroid measures to confirm this hypothesis. In future studies, such measures need to be obtained. His study and ours, as well as those by other investigators (Kang et al., 2016), suggest the importance of monitoring veterans with PTSD for early symptoms of heart disease and hypertension, and vigorous treatment if such symptoms are identified.

On the other hand, our study group enjoys three redeeming advantages. First, it provides a means of studying the symptoms of PTSD prospectively over the entire life course, free of the most important confounding variables such as antisocial personality, childhood abuse, and social disadvantage. Second, our community sample was collected without the distorting effects of preexisting mental health problems or potential secondary gain due to disability claim status. Third, we were able to follow our sample for the remainder of their individual lifespan, thus providing a unique perspective on the importance of combat exposure, PTSD, and cardiovascular risk for premature mortality.

REFERENCES

American Psychiatric Association. (1980). *Diagnostic and statistical manual of mental disorders* (3rd ed.). Washington, DC: Author.

American Psychiatric Association. (1994). *Diagnostic and statistical manual of mental disorders* (4th ed.). Washington, DC: Author.

Boscarino, J. A. (2008). A prospective study of PTSD and early-age heart disease mortality among Vietnam veterans: Implications for surveillance and prevention. *Psychosomatic Medicine, 70,* 668–676. http://dx.doi.org/10.1097/PSY.0b013e31817bccaf

Fontana, A., & Rosenheck, R. (1993). A causal model of the etiology of war-related PTSD. *Journal of Traumatic Stress, 6,* 475–500. http://dx.doi.org/10.1002/jts.2490060406

Foy, D. W., Carroll, E. M., & Donahoe, C. P., Jr. (1987). Etiological factors in the development of PTSD in clinical samples of Vietnam combat veterans. *Journal of Clinical Psychology, 43,* 17–27. http://dx.doi.org/10.1002/1097-4679(198701)43:1<17::AID-JCLP2270430104>3.0.CO;2-Q

Green, B. L., Grace, M. C., Lindy, J. D., Gleser, G. C., & Leonard, A. (1990). Risk factors for PTSD and other diagnoses in a general sample of Vietnam veterans. *The American Journal of Psychiatry, 147,* 729–733. http://dx.doi.org/10.1176/ajp.147.6.729

Heath, C. W. (1945). *What people are.* Cambridge, MA: Harvard University Press.

Hollingshead, A. B., & Redlich, F. C. (1958). *Social class and mental illness.* New York, NY: Wiley. http://dx.doi.org/10.1037/10645-000

Kahana, B., Harel, Z., & Kahana, E. (1988). Predictors of psychological well-being among survivors of the Holocaust. In J. P. Wilson, Z. Harel, & B. Kahana (Eds.), *Human adaptation to extreme stress* (pp. 171–192). New York, NY: Plenum. http://dx.doi.org/10.1007/978-1-4899-0786-8_8

Kang, S., Aldwin, C., Choun, S., & Spiro, A., III. (2016). A life-span perspective on combat exposure and PTSD symptoms in later life: Findings from the VA

Normative Aging Study. *The Gerontologist, 56*, 22–32. http://dx.doi.org/10.1093/geront/gnv120

Keane, T. M., Caddell, J. M., & Taylor, K. L. (1988). Mississippi Scale for Combat-Related Posttraumatic Stress Disorder: Three studies in reliability and validity. *Journal of Consulting and Clinical Psychology, 56*, 85–90. http://dx.doi.org/10.1037/0022-006X.56.1.85

Lee, K. A., Vaillant, G. E., Torrey, W. C., & Elder, G. H. (1995). A 50-year prospective study of the psychological sequelae of World War II combat. *The American Journal of Psychiatry, 152*, 516–522. http://dx.doi.org/10.1176/ajp.152.4.516

Monks, J. P. (1957). *College men at war*. Boston, MA: American Academy of Arts and Science.

Schnurr, P. P., Friedman, M. J., & Rosenberg, S. D. (1993). Premilitary MMPI scores as predictors of combat-related PTSD symptoms. *The American Journal of Psychiatry, 150*, 479–483. http://dx.doi.org/10.1176/ajp.150.3.479

Schnurr, P. P., Vaillant, C. O., & Vaillant, G. E. (1990). Predicting exercise in late midlife from young adult personality characteristics. *The International Journal of Aging and Human Development, 30*, 153–160. http://dx.doi.org/10.2190/51BP-NMYV-M3JE-UGYT

Taylor, H. (1979). *Harvard sports code* (Rev. ed.). Cambridge, MA: Harvard University Press.

Vaillant, G. E. (1977). *Adaptation to life*. Boston, MA: Little Brown.

Vaillant, G. E. (1993). *The natural history of alcoholism*. Cambridge, MA: Harvard University Press.

Vaillant, G. E., Meyer, S. E., Mukamal, K., & Soldz, S. (1998). Are social supports in late midlife a cause or a result of successful physical ageing? *Psychological Medicine, 28*, 1159–1168. http://dx.doi.org/10.1017/S0033291798007211

Vaillant, G. E., Orav, J., Meyer, S. E., Vaillant, L., & Roston, D. (1996). Late-life consequences of affective spectrum disorder. *International Psychogeriatrics, 8*, 13–32. http://dx.doi.org/10.1017/S1041610296002463

Vaillant, G. E., & Schnurr, P. (1988). What is a case? A 45-year study of psychiatric impairment within a college sample selected for mental health. *Archives of General Psychiatry, 45*, 313–319. http://dx.doi.org/10.1001/archpsyc.1988.01800280023003

III

IMPLICATIONS FOR
PRACTICE AND POLICY

14

MENTAL HEALTH CONSIDERATIONS AND SERVICE UTILIZATION IN OLDER ADULT NONVETERANS AND VETERANS

ANICA PLESS KAISER, JOAN M. COOK, JOYCE WANG,
EVE DAVISON, AND PAULA P. SCHNURR

The older adult population is growing in both number and proportion in most countries worldwide. It is projected that by 2050 older adults will comprise 20% more of the total population (U.S. Census Bureau, 2010). For the United States, the total older adult population is projected to reach 88.6 million by that date (U.S. Census Bureau, 2010). This changing demographic landscape will likely result in an increased need for mental health services for older adults (Karel, Gatz, & Smyer, 2012). According to the Institute of Medicine (IOM; 2008), 20% of adults aged 55 and older have a mental health condition, most commonly anxiety disorders, mood disorders, or cognitive impairment. A large cross-sectional, nationally representative survey of adults in the United States, the Behavioral Risk Factor Surveillance System (BRFSS), found that in 2006, 10% and 14% of U.S. adults aged 55 or older had been diagnosed

http://dx.doi.org/10.1037/0000061-015
Long-Term Outcomes of Military Service: The Health and Well-Being of Aging Veterans, A. Spiro III,
R. A. Settersten Jr., and C. M. Aldwin (Editors)

with a lifetime anxiety or depressive disorder, respectively (Strine et al., 2008). In this same nationally representative study, 12% of adults aged 65 or older reported that they "rarely" or "never" received the social support they needed, but only 4% reported being dissatisfied or very dissatisfied with their lives overall (BRFSS, 2006). Analyses using the Second Longitudinal Study of Aging (Centers for Disease Control and Prevention [CDC], 2010), conducted by the present authors, indicated that older adults' perception of social engagement and support decreased over the 6-year study interval. Given the prevalence of mental health disorders, as well as factors related to poor mental health functioning (e.g., low social support), it is important to examine mental health service utilization and treatment outcome in older adults.

According to Raue, Schulberg, Heo, Klimstra, and Bruce (2009), older adults tend to prefer psychotherapy over pharmacotherapy. Despite this, there is some evidence that older adults do not typically seek psychotherapy services. Data from the nationally representative 2001 National Survey on Drug Use and Health reported that only 10% of older adults who were classified as having at least one mental health condition indicated receiving any outpatient mental health treatment in the past year, in comparison with 25% of younger adults with a mental health condition (Karlin, Duffy, & Gleaves, 2008). Thus, there appears to be a large group of older adults suffering from mental health conditions who do not seek treatment.

In addition to the impact on individuals, mental health service utilization among older adults also has societal and resource implications (Centers for Disease Control and Prevention and National Association of Chronic Disease Directors, 2008). Adults of the baby-boomer generation use more mental health services than previous older generations (American Psychological Association, 2009), suggesting that mental health service utilization among older individuals is likely to increase as this cohort ages. The workforce needed to address the mental health needs of older adults extends far beyond the infrastructure currently in place (IOM, 2012).

This chapter summarizes the literature on mental health symptoms and diagnoses, patterns of treatment seeking, and types of mental health services utilized among older nonveterans and veterans in the United States. Service needs and utilization, as well as treatment issues for one disorder that is particularly relevant to the aging cohort of veterans, posttraumatic stress disorder (PTSD), are also reviewed. The chapter concludes with a summary of the literature, a call for the collection of longitudinal data to enable researchers to answer important remaining questions from a lifespan developmental perspective, and the provision of recommendations for avenues of future research.

MENTAL HEALTH NEEDS AND SERVICE UTILIZATION
IN OLDER AND YOUNGER ADULTS

Several large epidemiological studies have investigated the prevalence of psychiatric disorders in older adults. The National Comorbidity Study Replication, a population-based probability sample, included 2,575 community-dwelling adults aged 55 and older. This study reported weighted 12-month prevalence of *Diagnostic and Statistical Manual of Mental Disorders* (fourth ed.; American Psychiatric Association, 1994) mood disorders (4.9%), anxiety disorders (11.6%), and comorbid mood and anxiety disorders (2.8%). When examined by age group, it was found that the likelihood of having a mood or anxiety disorder declined with age (Byers, Yaffe, Covinsky, Friedman, & Bruce, 2010). A similar age trend was reported using data from the National Epidemiologic Survey on Alcohol and Related Conditions. This study also reported past-year prevalence of mood disorders (6.8%) and anxiety disorders (11.4%), as well as substance use disorders (3.8%), in a nationally representative sample (N = 12,312) of adults aged 55 and older (Reynolds, Pietrzak, El-Gabalawy, Mackenzie, & Sareen, 2015).

Some studies provide information regarding treatment for specific types of disorders among older adults. The Collaborative Psychiatric Epidemiologic Surveys (conducted 2001–2003) found that 66% of adults aged 65 and older with major depressive disorder and 72% with anxiety disorders had not received any treatment for these disorders in the previous year (Garrido, Kane, Kaas, & Kane, 2011). There are multiple factors that influence service utilization, and some may be age related, suggesting the importance of comparing utilization patterns among older and younger adults.

Several large studies have examined differences between older and younger adults in mental health treatment seeking and access to specialty care. Older adults (aged 65–74) with mental health conditions were much less likely than younger adults (aged 25–64) to receive any type of mental health treatment. (Even among treatment-seeking older adults, very few are seen in specialty clinics [Bogner, de Vries, Maulik, & Unützer, 2009; Karlin et al., 2008; Wang, Berglund, & Kessler, 2000; Wang et al., 2005]). Although older adults have lower levels of diagnosable mental health problems than younger adults, this difference in prevalence may not explain the differential service use. Older adults who could potentially benefit from treatment are both less likely to seek and to be offered treatment than are younger adults (Karlin et al., 2008).

An important caveat should be noted: Available data on service utilization are outdated, as the older veterans and nonveterans surveyed include the World War II and Korean War cohorts, groups that differ in many ways—including having different mental health needs, physical health comorbidities, and perceptions of mental health treatment—from present-day older adult veterans and nonveterans of the Vietnam era (e.g., the baby-boomer cohort). This issue suggests a potential lack of generalizability between the findings presented here and the needs of the current cohort of older adults. The discrepancies apparent between cohorts underscore the importance of studying and understanding period and cohort effects in addition to age effects—a much-needed emphasis within the aging and mental health literature.

There are several possible explanations for the differences in mental health service utilization by age. Some are related to perceptions about mental health treatment, such as stigma, cultural beliefs, and generational views regarding mental health. Others include low Medicare coverage, the possibility that older adults attribute problems such as anxiety or cognitive decline to aging instead of identifying them as mental health issues, transportation difficulties, differential screening practices, the high prevalence of comorbid physical health problems, and the lack of knowledge about treatment availability and options (IOM, 2008, 2012). Some psychiatric problems may lead older adults to seek non–mental health care because of related physical conditions or behaviors. For example, depression in older adults is associated with poor physical health maintenance and habits, higher rates of medical illness and disability, and increased need for long-term care (IOM, 2008). Likely related to one or a combination of these reasons, older adults with mental health conditions often present to primary care or other medical clinics instead of seeking mental health treatment (Vannoy, Powers, & Unützer, 2006). Some advances have been achieved by implementing collaborative care models in which mental health providers are integrated into primary care settings. A model developed for the treatment of depression in older adults—the Improving Mood-Promoting Access to Collaborative Treatment (IMPACT) program—showed increased use of treatment, greater reductions in depressive symptoms and diagnoses, less health-related functional impairment, and greater quality of life in the intervention group compared with the treatment-as-usual (TAU) group (Unützer et al., 2002). These types of integrated care models are critical for reaching older adults in primary care and other health care settings.

Another systems issue involves insurance coverage for treatment. Insurance payments (or lack thereof) for mental health treatment costs can promote and maintain the lower rate of specialty care utilized by older adults. Many insurers do not reimburse for mental health services delivered by non–mental health providers, despite the fact that many agencies train such staff to deliver mental health treatments (Arean, Raue, Sirey, & Snowden, 2012). Additional systems issues relevant to the aging population are the large caseloads of health care providers and the insufficient time providers often have to deliver evidence-based interventions.

MENTAL HEALTH NEEDS AND SERVICE UTILIZATION IN OLDER VETERANS

In fiscal year (FY) 2015, there were 21.7 million living military veterans in the United States. Of those, 9.9 million (46%) were aged 65 or older. The number of veterans aged 85 and older is projected to increase by about 6% over the next 5 years (U.S. Department of Veterans Affairs [VA], Office of the Actuary, 2015). In FY 2011, about 4 million older veterans were enrolled in VA health care and of those, approximately 2.4 million used VA health care services. Of the 2.4 million, about 16% received a diagnosis of one or more mental health disorders (IOM, 2012). The shift toward increasing numbers of older veterans has significant implications for health care service needs. The number of veterans aged 65 and older with a confirmed mental illness (defined as having a mental disorder diagnosis and at least two outpatient clinical encounters or one residential or inpatient stay) increased by as much as 57% between 2005 and 2013 (Wiechers, Karel, Hoff, & Karlin, 2015). In addition, this study noted that use of non–mental health services among older veterans with mental health disorders also increased over this period. Thus, although it is clear that rates of physical health problems will increase, there may also be an overall increase in referrals for mental health services. According to data through 2010, Vietnam veterans have been seeking VA mental health services for PTSD in increasing numbers, some for the first time (Hermes, Rosenheck, Desai, & Fontana, 2012).

In the general VA population, older age is associated with lower use of mental health care (Hunt & Rosenheck, 2011) and reduced likelihood of receiving psychotherapy. Administrative data from VA specialty mental health clinics demonstrated that the likelihood of treatment decreased with age for all major psychiatric and substance use disorders except dementia (Kerfoot, Petrakis, & Rosenheck, 2011). Older veterans had fewer mental health outpatient visits and a lower likelihood of psychiatric hospitalization; however, when they were hospitalized, they incurred more inpatient days per hospitalization. Older patients were more likely to receive group therapy and less likely to receive individual therapy than younger patients (Hunt & Rosenheck, 2011).

Additionally, more detailed data on service utilization among older veterans, especially mental health service utilization, are limited. One source of useful information is the VA's Northeast Program Evaluation Center (NEPEC), which collects administrative data on all veterans seen throughout the VA system, with a particular emphasis on veterans in PTSD treatment programs. NEPEC data showed that older veterans are diagnosed with psychiatric disorders at a lower rate than younger veterans and were also less likely to receive mental health services (table available from the first author on request). In 2015, almost as many veterans aged 65 and older (2,882,340) used VA services as did veterans younger than 65 (2,888,410). Of those who used VA services, 17% of older veterans and 35% of younger veterans had a confirmed mental illness (defined as a listed diagnosis plus specific mental health visits), and 25% of older veterans and 45% of younger veterans had a possible mental illness (defined as a listed diagnosis). Of those with a confirmed mental illness, 78% of older veterans and 90% of younger veterans used mental health services. Of those with possible mental illness, 56% of older veterans and 77% of younger veterans used mental health services. Among those who used VA services, 17% of older veterans and 39% of younger veterans received specialized mental health services (e.g., visits in a PTSD clinic). Overall service utilization, as well as receipt of specialty medical care among those with both confirmed and possible mental illness, was significantly higher in the younger veterans compared with those 65 and older, with younger veterans utilizing more than twice the non–mental health services (e.g., medical outpatient visits, medical inpatient stays, community living center stays) during the same year (Greenberg & Hoff, 2015a, 2015b).

The caveat mentioned at the beginning of this chapter is particularly relevant to the interpretation of veteran health care utilization data. Many factors contribute to the changing demographics of the older veteran population, such as mortality among World War II veterans, an increase in the proportion of women veterans within this age range, and increased ethnoracial diversity within the younger range of current cohorts.

Our review of the literature documents differences between older and younger veterans and nonveterans in areas associated with mental health and service utilization. Given the importance of understanding the long-term consequences of military service and the health differences between veterans and nonveterans (Agha, Lofgren, VanRuiswyk, & Layde, 2000), a focus on long-term health outcomes within the veteran population is essential. Although there are differences among older and younger veterans and nonveterans in mental health treatment seeking and in specialty care use, it is not clear what factors are associated with the physical and mental health problems that prompt individuals to seek care and whether these factors vary with age. One limitation of much of the literature—on treatment outcomes as well as more general mental health research—is that it does not include older veterans, particularly the oldest-old (aged 85 and older).

MENTAL HEALTH NEEDS, SERVICE UTILIZATION, AND TREATMENT OUTCOME RESEARCH AMONG OLDER VETERANS WITH PTSD SYMPTOMS

One way to widen the focal lens is to consider symptom development and utilization in the aftermath of trauma exposure. A majority of adults (70% or more) in the general population have been exposed to at least one traumatic event during their lifetime (Benjet et al., 2016). Among those who are trauma exposed, older and younger adults differ in the expression of mental health symptoms, their beliefs and attributions about mental health problems and treatment, and their experience of physical health problems (Krause, Shaw, & Cairney, 2004). Although a majority of adults who are exposed to traumatic events do not develop PTSD, this disorder is particularly important to understand within an aging context. About 7% of the adult U.S. population has a lifetime diagnosis of PTSD, and a third of these cases are attributable to combat exposure (Kessler et al., 2005). The National Vietnam Veterans Longitudinal Study (NVVLS)— a follow-up to the 1980 National Vietnam Veterans Readjustment Study (NVVRS)—found the current prevalence of PTSD in Vietnam combat veterans to be 11% (Basu, 2014).

PTSD has detrimental effects on the physical and mental health of veterans and nonveterans alike and is associated with increased health care utilization (Schnurr, 2017). Role changes and functional losses that occur with aging—such as retirement, bereavement, increased physical health problems, and cognitive impairment—may be associated with increases in PTSD symptoms (Cook, 2001). Also, PTSD may be associated with increases in physical and mental health symptoms following retirement in older veterans (Schnurr, Lunney, Sengupta, & Spiro, 2005). Even for those veterans who do not develop PTSD, having been deployed to a war zone and experiencing combat can negatively affect physical and mental health in later life (Spiro, Settersten, & Aldwin, 2016). Exposure to combat, the aftermath of war, and environmental hazards are associated with poor later-life functional health outcomes (Taylor, Ureña, & Kail, 2016). PTSD can mediate the relationship between military exposures and physical health problems (Schnurr, 2017), and physical health problems mediate the positive relationship between PTSD symptoms and health care utilization (Ford et al., 2004).

Several studies have examined mental health service use in older veterans. Among patients who screened positive for PTSD in four VA primary care clinics, older veterans had lower rates of adequate treatment compared with veterans younger than 30 years (Lu, Carlson, Duckart, & Dobscha, 2012). It was unclear whether these differences were due to lower base rates of PTSD in older veterans, their treatment preferences, health care provider responses to positive screens, or other age-related barriers to psychotherapy. Using national VA data, Smith, Cook, Pietrzak, Hoff, and Harpaz-Rotem (2016) examined mental health service utilization among veterans aged 50 and older who received a new diagnosis of PTSD between FY 2008 and FY 2011. Almost 75% received some type of mental health treatment, but only 48% of veterans aged 80 and older received any mental health treatment at all. Older adults in VA were less likely to receive psychotherapy and pharmacotherapy, had fewer psychotherapy visits, and longer waiting times.

Among veterans with a new diagnosis of PTSD receiving treatment between FY 2004 and FY 2007, older, Vietnam-era veterans were less likely than younger veterans to drop out of mental health treatment, more likely to attend more mental health appointments, and more likely to remain in treatment for at least a year. However, Korean War veterans were more likely than Vietnam-era veterans to drop out of treatment, suggesting that this finding may be related to war cohort rather than age (Harpaz-Rotem & Rosenheck, 2011).

Practice guidelines for the treatment of PTSD recommend cognitive–behavioral therapies such as cognitive processing therapy (CPT; Resick & Schnicke, 1993), prolonged exposure (PE; Foa, Hembree, & Rothbaum, 2007), eye movement desensitization and reprocessing (EMDR; Bisson & Andrew, 2007), and selected antidepressant medications (Forbes et al., 2012). CPT is a 12-session manualized therapy adapted from cognitive techniques (Beck, Emery, & Greenberg, 1985). It can be delivered in an individual or group format and focuses on feelings, beliefs, and thoughts which directly relate to the trauma. PE is an eight- to 15-session manualized individual therapy with four main components: education about reactions to trauma and PTSD, breathing training, exposure to trauma-related situations that are objectively safe but avoided because of trauma-related distress (in vivo exposure), and exposure to trauma memories through repeated recounting out loud by clients of the details of their most disturbing event (imaginal exposure). EMDR therapy is an eight-phase psychotherapeutic approach in which the client is assisted in accessing the traumatic memory and holding it in mind briefly while exposed to bilateral dual attention stimulation (e.g., eye movements, sound, light). Unfortunately, older adults have historically not been included in sufficient numbers in randomized controlled trials (RCTs) of PTSD treatment to permit comparisons of older and younger adults. Beginning in 2006–2007, the VA implemented nationwide training and consultation in PE and CPT for mental health providers (Karlin et al., 2010); however, there are no systematic data on use of these treatments by older veterans.

Dinnen, Simiola, and Cook (2015) conducted a systematic review of the more rigorous treatment literature on older adult trauma survivors and identified 13 case studies and seven treatment outcome studies that reported at least one outcome assessment. Of the 13 case studies, five focused on older veterans or former prisoners of war. Of these, three reported a reduction in PTSD symptoms following PE, PE and selective serotonin reuptake inhibitor (SSRI) medication, and supportive therapy and EMDR, and two found no significant improvement in PTSD symptoms following supportive group therapy and psychoeducation combined with supportive group therapy. Of the seven treatment studies, four were focused on persons with military trauma; two of these reported positive effects from therapy (virtual reality vs. imaginal exposure; PE) and two had nonsignificant or mixed effects (cognitive–behavioral therapy for a current stressor vs. trauma-focused cognitive–behavioral therapy; PE vs. TAU) for PTSD symptoms.

There are caveats to be noted for the studies that did not indicate significant reductions in PTSD symptoms. For example, in one study, eight World War II former prisoners of war aged 66 to 76 participated in a long-term biweekly psychoeducational and supportive therapy group (Boehnlein & Sparr, 1993). Posttreatment scores at 1 year showed no significant change in symptomatology, but the authors noted positive clinical impressions of veteran well-being and social functioning. Similarly, Cook, O'Donnell, Moltzen, Ruzek, and Sheikh (2006) described a long-term supportive/cognitive–behavioral group therapy for older combat veterans with severe, chronic PTSD. There were no significant changes in psychological symptoms, despite prominent changes in veterans' ability to manage PTSD symptoms and improved interpersonal functioning noted by clinician observation and informal family reports. These authors noted that PTSD symptom measures may not adequately capture the benefits of psychotherapy for older veterans with PTSD (Boehnlein & Sparr, 1993; Cook et al., 2006). Measures of coping, self-efficacy, or quality of life may more accurately illustrate the benefits of mental health interventions in this population. PTSD symptom measures also do not capture potential benefits such as positive appraisals of military experiences, meaning making, or posttraumatic growth.

The use of PE in older veterans has demonstrated some positive results. Thorp, Stein, Jeste, Patterson, and Wetherell (2012) reported preliminary efficacy of PE in 11 male veterans aged 56 to 78 with PTSD, compared with a nonrandomized TAU group ($n = 53$). The dropout rate of 27% was consistent with studies with younger adults, and clinician- and self-report measures indicated a significant decrease in PTSD symptoms in veterans who completed treatment. All veterans in the PE group showed a clinically significant decline, compared with only 40% of veterans in the TAU condition.

At posttreatment, only 13% in the PE condition continued to meet PTSD criteria, versus 85% of those in the TAU condition.

Yoder et al. (2013) studied 66 older (> 60 years) veterans from different eras (World War II, Korea, Vietnam, and Desert Storm) diagnosed with combat-related PTSD who were treated with PE at a VA PTSD clinic. The mean change in PTSD scores from pre- to posttreatment was clinically and statistically significant. PE was effective in reducing PTSD and depressive symptoms in these older veterans. Preliminary findings from the first RCT of PE with older veterans (ClinicalTrials.gov Identifier #: NCT00539279) suggest that veterans who had stable relationships seemed to do particularly well with treatment initiation and completion (Steven Thorp, personal communication, April 22, 2013).

The use of CPT has not been formally examined among older veterans; however, two studies that included older veterans reported positive effects. Chard, Schumm, Owens, and Cottingham (2010) examined differences in therapy dropout and outcome between Vietnam veterans and those who served in Iraq and Afghanistan. The two groups did not differ in dropout rates, but younger veterans attended significantly fewer CPT sessions than did Vietnam veterans. However, in regression analyses, younger veterans reported significantly lower posttreatment PTSD symptoms compared with Vietnam veterans, indicating that they may have less severe PTSD following this evidence-based treatment. The authors suggested that mental health treatment for Vietnam veterans with severe PTSD may need to include motivational techniques or be multifaceted to address aging and retirement issues. It is important to note, however, that very few Vietnam-era veterans in their sample were over the age of 55.

Using a retrospective chart review within a VA specialty clinic among veterans aged 23 to 77, Jeffreys et al. (2014) found a significant decrease in PTSD symptoms from pre- to posttreatment in both CPT and PE. Older veterans who participated in PE had significantly greater reductions in PTSD symptoms than those who participated in CPT. This may be because PE was delivered in individual treatment, whereas CPT was typically delivered in group or combined (individual and group) format. Older veterans were less likely to drop out of both treatments.

CONCLUSION

Our review of the literature indicates that older veterans and nonveterans seek less mental health treatment and are less likely to be seen in specialty mental health clinics than younger veteran and nonveterans. Possible reasons for these discrepancies range from financial to stigma related to lower perception of need for services to less-effective screening to other systems-based issues. Because older veterans and nonveterans alike are less likely to be seen in specialty mental health clinics, they may receive less specialized and effective care for mental health problems. Older veterans are seeking treatment for PTSD from the VA in increasing numbers, some for the first time (Hermes et al., 2012). There has been increasing attention to the treatment of PTSD in older veterans, and evidence is accumulating to support the use of evidence-based psychotherapies. However, few treatment outcome studies include older veterans, and existing ones often have small samples.

More needs to be done to improve referral follow-up and engage older adults in mental health treatment. The VA provides resources to address this need among veterans—for example, with geriatric mental health clinics; geriatric research, education, and clinical care centers; and other interdisciplinary teams across several disciplines, such as within primary care and mental health settings. Indeed, a major priority of VA mental health enhancement efforts in recent years has been the integration of mental health services into the primary care setting (Zeiss & Karlin, 2008). For a helpful discussion of the nature and function of interdisciplinary care teams, and the usefulness of such an approach in addressing the health care needs of older adults, see Zeiss and Steffen (1996). In addition to investigating broad patterns of treatment utilization, future research should focus on the types and quality of interventions older adults with mental health disorders are receiving.

In this chapter, we have presented available information on mental health service utilization among older veterans and nonveterans, as well as data on PTSD treatment outcome studies. Unfortunately, few national surveys focused on prevalence of mental health disorders among older nonveterans and veterans include questions regarding receipt of mental health services. Additionally, mental health treatment data on older adults with PTSD are limited and tend to involve small samples. Thus, the evidence base is insufficient to answer important questions regarding the effects of military service on long-term outcomes among older veterans.

Given the limitations of the literature and available data on older veterans and mental health treatment, several important questions remain unanswered. For example, what are the best predictors of treatment response in older veterans with mental health disorders? Do war cohort, age, role during military service, treatment expectancies, or cognitive flexibility influence psychotherapy outcomes, and if so, in what ways? What factors are tied to age differences versus cohort/period of service effects? What mechanisms (e.g., reduced hypervigilance) account for treatment response? How might delayed symptom onset affect treatment seeking and response in older veterans? How do physical health and mental health comorbidities affect engagement and retention in mental health treatment? How do problems such as depression and cognitive decline or impairment impact treatment? From a systems perspective, will future cohorts of older veterans (from Vietnam, the Persian Gulf, Iraq and Afghanistan, and other contemporary conflicts) over- or underutilize mental health services? To answer these questions, additional research with older veterans is needed. It is also important to continue studying aging among the various age cohorts—as they are affected by war era, sociopolitical agendas, and other factors in the environment that could influence mental health needs, prevalence, and treatment seeking.

As suggested by Settersten (2006), it is important to consider the role of decades-past military service on the current functioning of older veterans. Taking a life course perspective (Settersten, 2006; Spiro et al., 2016) can lead to a greater understanding of how early-life stress and trauma can affect later-life functioning. Research informed by a life course perspective involves collecting longitudinal data and considering developmental factors (environmental and intrapersonal) that affect how individuals respond to stress and trauma occurring at different points in time. It is important to examine response to treatment, indicators of treatment response, and how group status (e.g., war era) may influence outcomes. Future work that integrates this perspective will enhance our understanding of the important factors that influence mental health service utilization and treatment outcomes for aging veterans and nonveterans over time.

REFERENCES

Agha, Z., Lofgren, R. P., VanRuiswyk, J. V., & Layde, P. M. (2000). Are patients at Veterans Affairs medical centers sicker? A comparative analysis of health status and medical resource use. *Archives of Internal Medicine, 160*, 3252–3257. http://dx.doi.org/10.1001/archinte.160.21.3252

American Psychiatric Association. (1994). *Diagnostic and statistical manual of mental disorders* (4th ed.). Washington, DC: Author.

American Psychological Association. (2009). *Psychotherapy and older adults resource guide.* http://www.apa.org/pi/aging/resources/guides/psychotherapy.aspx

Arean, P. A., Raue, P. J., Sirey, J. A., & Snowden, M. (2012). Implementing evidence-based psychotherapies in settings serving older adults: Challenges and solutions. *Psychiatric Services, 63*, 605–607. http://dx.doi.org/10.1176/appi.ps.201100078

Basu, S. (2014, September). PTSD still plagues more than 1 in 10 Vietnam veterans more than 40 years later. *U.S. Medicine.* Retrieved from http://www.usmedicine.com/agencies/department-of-veterans-affairs/ptsd-still-plagues-more-than-1-in-10-vietnam-veterans-40-years-later

Beck, A. T., Emery, G., & Greenberg, R. (1985). *Anxiety disorders and phobias: A cognitive perspective.* New York, NY: Basic Books.

Behavioral Risk Factor Surveillance System. (2006). *Prevalence data and data analysis tools.* Retrieved from: http://www.cdc.gov/brfss/data_tools.htm

Benjet, C., Bromet, E., Karam, E. G., Kessler, R. C., McLaughlin, K. A., Ruscio, A. M., . . . Koenen, K. C. (2016). The epidemiology of traumatic event exposure worldwide: Results from the World Mental Health Survey Consortium. *Psychological Medicine, 46,* 327–343. http://dx.doi.org/10.1017/S0033291715001981

Bisson, J., & Andrew, M. (2007). Psychological treatment of post-traumatic stress disorder (PTSD). *Cochrane Database of Systematic Reviews,* CD003388.

Boehnlein, J. K., & Sparr, L. F. (1993). Group therapy with WWII ex-POW's: Long-term posttraumatic adjustment in a geriatric population. *American Journal of Psychotherapy, 47,* 273–282.

Bogner, H. R., de Vries, H. F., Maulik, P. K., & Unützer, J. (2009). Mental health services use: Baltimore epidemiologic catchment area follow-up. *The American Journal of Geriatric Psychiatry, 17,* 706–715. http://dx.doi.org/10.1097/JGP.0b013e3181aad5c5

Byers, A. L., Yaffe, K., Covinsky, K. E., Friedman, M. B., & Bruce, M. L. (2010). High occurrence of mood and anxiety disorders among older adults: The National Comorbidity Survey Replication. *Archives of General Psychiatry, 67,* 489–496. http://dx.doi.org/10.1001/archgenpsychiatry.2010.35

Centers for Disease Control and Prevention. (2010). *The second longitudinal study of aging (LSOA II).* Hyattsville, MD: National Center for Health Statistics. Retrieved from http://www.cdc.gov/nchs/lsoa/lsoa2.htm

Centers for Disease Control and Prevention and National Association of Chronic Disease Directors. (2008). *The state of mental health and aging in America. Issue Brief 1: What do the data tell us?* Atlanta, GA: Author.

Chard, K. M., Schumm, J. A., Owens, G. P., & Cottingham, S. M. (2010). A comparison of OEF and OIF veterans and Vietnam veterans receiving cognitive processing therapy. *Journal of Traumatic Stress, 23,* 25–32.

Cook, J. M. (2001). Post-traumatic stress disorder in older adults. *PTSD Research Quarterly, 12,* 1–7.

Cook, J. M., O'Donnell, C., Moltzen, J. O., Ruzek, J., & Sheikh, J. (2006). Clinical observations in the treatment of World War II and Korean War veterans with combat-related PTSD. *Clinical Gerontologist, 29,* 81–93. http://dx.doi.org/10.1300/J018v29n02_09

Dinnen, S., Simiola, V., & Cook, J. M. (2015). Post-traumatic stress disorder in older adults: A systematic review of the psychotherapy treatment literature. *Aging & Mental Health, 19,* 144–150. http://dx.doi.org/10.1080/13607863.2014.920299

Foa, E. B., Hembree, E. A., & Rothbaum, B. O. (2007). *Prolonged exposure therapy for PTSD: Emotional processing of traumatic experiences therapist guide.* New York, NY: Oxford University Press. http://dx.doi.org/10.1093/med:psych/9780195308501.001.0001

Forbes, D., Lloyd, D., Nixon, R. D. V., Elliott, P., Varker, T., Perry, D., . . . Creamer, M. (2012). A multisite randomized controlled effectiveness trial of cognitive processing therapy for military-related posttraumatic stress disorder. *Journal of Anxiety Disorders, 26,* 442–452. http://dx.doi.org/10.1016/j.janxdis.2012.01.006

Ford, J. D., Schnurr, P. P., Friedman, M. J., Green, B. L., Adams, G., & Jex, S. (2004). Posttraumatic stress disorder symptoms, physical health, and health care utilization 50 years after repeated exposure to a toxic gas. *Journal of Traumatic Stress, 17,* 185–194. http://dx.doi.org/10.1023/B:JOTS.0000029261.23634.87

Garrido, M. M., Kane, R. L., Kaas, M., & Kane, R. A. (2011). Use of mental health care by community-dwelling older adults. *Journal of the American Geriatrics Society, 59,* 50–56. http://dx.doi.org/10.1111/j.1532-5415.2010.03220.x

Greenberg, G., & Hoff, R. (2015a). *Older adult (65+ on October 1) fact sheet: National, VISN, and VAMC tables.* West Haven, CT: U.S. Department of Veterans Affairs Office of Mental Health Operations, Northeast Program Evaluation Center. [Tables available from the first author.]

Greenberg, G., & Hoff, R. (2015b). *Younger adult (under age 65 on October 1) fact sheet: National, VISN, and VAMC tables.* West Haven, CT: U.S. Department of Veterans Affairs Office of Mental Health Operations, Northeast Program Evaluation Center. [Tables available from the first author.]

Harpaz-Rotem, I., & Rosenheck, R. A. (2011). Serving those who served: Retention of newly returning veterans from Iraq and Afghanistan in mental health treatment. *Psychiatric Services, 62,* 22–27. http://dx.doi.org/10.1176/ps.62.1.pss6201_0022

Hermes, E. D. A., Rosenheck, R. A., Desai, R., & Fontana, A. F. (2012). Recent trends in the treatment of posttraumatic stress disorder and other mental disorders in the VHA. *Psychiatric Services, 63,* 471–476. http://dx.doi.org/10.1176/appi.ps.201100432

Hunt, M. G., & Rosenheck, R. A. (2011). Psychotherapy in mental health clinics of the Department of Veterans Affairs. *Journal of Clinical Psychology, 67,* 561–573. http://dx.doi.org/10.1002/jclp.20788

Institute of Medicine. (2008). *Retooling for an aging America: Building the health care workforce.* Washington, DC: National Academies Press. Retrieved from https://www.nap.edu/catalog/12089/retooling-for-an-aging-america-building-the-health-care-workforce

Institute of Medicine. (2012). *The mental health and substance use workforce for older adults: In whose hands?* Retrieved from http://www.nap.edu/catalog.php?record_id=13400

Jeffreys, M. D., Reinfeld, C., Nair, P. V., Garcia, H. A., Mata-Galan, E., & Rentz, T. O. (2014). Evaluating treatment of posttraumatic stress disorder with cognitive processing therapy and prolonged exposure therapy in a VHA specialty clinic. *Journal of Anxiety Disorders, 28,* 108–114.

Karel, M. J., Gatz, M., & Smyer, M. A. (2012). Aging and mental health in the decade ahead: What psychologists need to know. *American Psychologist, 67,* 184–198.

Karlin, B. E., Duffy, M., & Gleaves, D. (2008). Patterns and predictors of mental health service use and mental illness among older and younger adults in the United States. *Psychological Services, 5,* 275–294. http://dx.doi.org/10.1037/1541-1559.5.3.275

Karlin, B. E., Ruzek, J. I., Chard, K. M., Eftekhari, A., Monson, C. M., Hembree, E. A., . . . Foa, E. B. (2010). Dissemination of evidence-based psychological treatments for posttraumatic stress disorder in the Veterans Health Administration. *Journal of Traumatic Stress, 23,* 663–673. http://dx.doi.org/10.1002/jts.20588

Kerfoot, K. E., Petrakis, I. L., & Rosenheck, R. A. (2011). Dual diagnosis in an aging population: Prevalence of psychiatric disorders, comorbid substance abuse, and mental health service utilization in the Department of Veterans Affairs. *Journal of Dual Diagnosis, 7,* 4–13. http://dx.doi.org/10.1080/15504263.2011.568306

Kessler, R. C., Berglund, P., Demler, O., Jin, R., Merikangas, K. R., & Walters, E. E. (2005). Lifetime prevalence and age-of-onset distributions of *DSM–IV* disorders in the National Comorbidity Survey Replication. *Archives of General Psychiatry, 62,* 593–602. http://dx.doi.org/10.1001/archpsyc.62.6.593

Krause, N., Shaw, B. A., & Cairney, J. (2004). A descriptive epidemiology of lifetime trauma and the physical health status of older adults. *Psychology and Aging, 19,* 637–648. http://dx.doi.org/10.1037/0882-7974.19.4.637

Lu, M. W., Carlson, K. F., Duckart, J. P., & Dobscha, S. K. (2012). The effects of age on initiation of mental health treatment after positive PTSD screens among Veterans Affairs primary care patients. *General Hospital Psychiatry, 34,* 654–659. http://dx.doi.org/10.1016/j.genhosppsych.2012.07.002

Raue, P. J., Schulberg, H. C., Heo, M., Klimstra, S., & Bruce, M. L. (2009). Patients' depression treatment preferences and initiation, adherence, and outcome: A randomized primary care study. *Psychiatric Services, 60,* 337–343. http://dx.doi.org/10.1176/ps.2009.60.3.337

Resick, P. A., & Schnicke, M. (1993). *Cognitive processing therapy for rape victims: A treatment manual.* Newbury Park: Sage.

Reynolds, K., Pietrzak, R. H., El-Gabalawy, R., Mackenzie, C. S., & Sareen, J. (2015). Prevalence of psychiatric disorders in U.S. older adults: Findings from a nationally representative survey. *World Psychiatry; Official Journal of the World Psychiatric Association (WPA), 14,* 74–81. http://dx.doi.org/10.1002/wps.20193

Schnurr, P. P. (2017). Physical health and health services utilization. In S. Gold & J. Cook (Eds.), *APA handbook of trauma psychology* (Vol. 1, pp. 349–370). Washington, DC: American Psychological Association.

Schnurr, P. P., Lunney, C. A., Sengupta, A., & Spiro, A., III. (2005). A longitudinal study of retirement in older male veterans. *Journal of Consulting and Clinical Psychology, 73,* 561–566. http://dx.doi.org/10.1037/0022-006X.73.3.561

Settersten, R. A., Jr. (2006). When nations call: How wartime military service matters for the life course and aging. *Research on Aging, 28,* 12–36. http://dx.doi.org/10.1177/0164027505281577

Smith, N. B., Cook, J. M., Pietrzak, R., Hoff, R., & Harpaz-Rotem, I. (2016). Mental health treatment for older veterans newly diagnosed with PTSD: A national investigation. *The American Journal of Geriatric Psychiatry, 24*, 201–212. http://dx.doi.org/10.1016/j.jagp.2015.02.001

Spiro, A., III, Settersten, R. A., Jr., & Aldwin, C. M. (2016). Long-term outcomes of military service in aging and the life course: A positive re-envisioning. *The Gerontologist, 56*, 5–13. http://dx.doi.org/10.1093/geront/gnv093

Strine, T. W., Mokdad, A. H., Balluz, L. S., Gonzalez, O., Crider, R., Berry, J. T., & Kroenke, K. (2008). Depression and anxiety in the United States: Findings from the 2006 Behavioral Risk Factor Surveillance System. *Psychiatric Services, 59*, 1383–1390. http://dx.doi.org/10.1176/ps.2008.59.12.1383

Taylor, M. G., Ureña, S., & Kail, B. L. (2016). Service-related exposures and physical health trajectories among aging veteran men. *The Gerontologist, 56*, 92–103. http://dx.doi.org/10.1093/geront/gnv662

Thorp, S. R., Stein, M. B., Jeste, D. V., Patterson, T. L., & Wetherell, J. L. (2012). Prolonged exposure therapy for older veterans with posttraumatic stress disorder: A pilot study. *The American Journal of Geriatric Psychiatry, 20*, 276–280.

Unützer, J., Katon, W., Callahan, C. M., Williams, J. W., Jr., Hunkeler, E., Harpole, L., . . . Langston, C., for the IMPACT Investigators. (2002). Collaborative care management of late-life depression in the primary care setting: A randomized controlled trial. *JAMA, 288*, 2836–2845. http://dx.doi.org/10.1001/jama.288.22.2836

U.S. Census Bureau. (2010). *Fact sheet on older Americans.* Retrieved from https://www.census.gov/prod/2010pubs/p25-1138.pdf

U.S. Department of Veterans Affairs, Office of the Actuary. (2015). *Table 1L: VetPop2014 living veterans by age group, gender, 2013–2043.* Available online at http://www.va.gov/vetdata/Veteran_Population.asp

Vannoy, S., Powers, D., & Unützer, J. (2006). Making an IMPACT on late-life depression. *Current Psychiatry, 5*, 85–92.

Wang, P. S., Berglund, P., & Kessler, R. C. (2000). Recent care of common mental disorders in the United States: Prevalence and conformance with evidence-based recommendations. *Journal of General Internal Medicine, 15*, 284–292. http://dx.doi.org/10.1046/j.1525-1497.2000.9908044.x

Wang, P. S., Lane, M., Olfson, M., Pincus, H. A., Wells, K. B., & Kessler, R. C. (2005). Twelve-month use of mental health services in the United States: Results from the National Comorbidity Survey Replication. *Archives of General Psychiatry, 62*, 629–640. http://dx.doi.org/10.1001/archpsyc.62.6.629

Wiechers, I. R., Karel, M. J., Hoff, R., & Karlin, B. E. (2015). Growing use of mental and general health care services among older veterans with mental illness. *Psychiatric Services, 66*, 1242–1244. http://dx.doi.org/10.1176/appi.ps.201400370

Yoder, M. S., Lozano, B., Center, K. B., Miller, A., Acierno, R., & Tuerk, P. W. (2013). Effectiveness of prolonged exposure for PTSD in older veterans. *International Journal of Psychiatry in Medicine, 45,* 111–124. http://dx.doi.org/10.2190/PM.45.2.b

Zeiss, A. M., & Karlin, B. E. (2008). Integrating mental health and primary care services in the Department of Veterans Affairs health care system. *Journal of Clinical Psychology in Medical Settings, 15,* 73–78. http://dx.doi.org/10.1007/s10880-008-9100-4

Zeiss, A. M., & Steffen, A. (1996). Interdisciplinary health care teams: The basic unit of geriatric care. In L. L. Carstensen, B. A. Edelstein, & L. Dornbrand (Eds.), *The practical handbook of clinical gerontology* (pp. 423–450). Thousand Oaks, CA: Sage.

15

AGING VETERANS AND LONG-TERM OUTCOMES OF MILITARY SERVICE: IMPLICATIONS FOR PRACTICE AND POLICY

RICHARD A. SETTERSTEN JR., CAROLYN M. ALDWIN, AND AVRON SPIRO III

The research presented in this book offers new knowledge about the legacies of military service for the health and well-being of aging veterans. In this chapter, we consider the implications of this evidence for practice and policy meant to improve the future welfare of veterans and their families. These include taking a life course perspective on military experiences, fostering the resilience of veterans through strengthening social relationships and networks, promoting veterans' physical health, and intervening at strategic points of transition during the military life course. The needs of veterans can be better gauged and met by building workforce capacity to serve aging veterans and by improving data resources and using them to conduct policy and planning analyses.

Preparation of this chapter was supported by a grant from the National Institute on Aging, R24-AG039343. Avron Spiro was also supported by a Senior Research Career Scientist award from the Clinical Science R&D Service, U.S. Department of Veterans Affairs. The views expressed in this chapter are those of the authors and do not necessarily represent the views of the U.S. Department of Veterans Affairs or other support institutions.

http://dx.doi.org/10.1037/0000061-016
Long-Term Outcomes of Military Service: The Health and Well-Being of Aging Veterans, A. Spiro III, R. A. Settersten Jr., and C. M. Aldwin (Editors)

A LIFE COURSE PERSPECTIVE
ON MILITARY EXPERIENCES

Knowledge about the long-term effects of service on aging is based largely on World War II and Korean veterans, and increasingly on Vietnam veterans. However, Vietnam veterans had very different wartime and postwar experiences than did World War II and Korean War–era veterans, which might lead to adverse effects on their aging. As history continues to make clear, each war differs, as do those who serve in them. The very nature of the military has changed since the introduction of the all-volunteer force at the end of Vietnam. The demographics of the American military and veteran populations have become more diverse in terms of gender, race, and ethnicity, but perhaps less diverse in socioeconomic background. What we have learned, and continue to learn, about veterans based on those who served in Vietnam and earlier conflicts may be less applicable to more recent veterans, who may face different challenges and opportunities as they age.

Cultural interpretations of war, and a nation's involvement in it, provide a larger framework for veterans and others to understand their roles. For example, World War II was a popular war (although antiwar protests occurred), and strong postwar employment and education programs for veterans meant that they were more actively and fully integrated into the civilian labor force or higher education upon their return. World War II and Korean War veterans may have been in a relatively favorable situation compared with veterans of Vietnam and more current conflicts because of high public endorsement, pride in service, and positive reception; economic opportunity; and GI benefits on their return. More recent generations may face less rosy prospects because of the controversial nature of military intervention, as well as targeted recruitment and high representation of soldiers from less privileged socioeconomic backgrounds.

For an individual veteran, coming to terms with wartime service is a developmental issue in its own right, and one that potentially brings benefits and risks, depending on how it is understood. Indeed, Settersten and colleagues (Chapter 1) point to a growing body of evidence demonstrating that "objective" aspects of military experience (e.g., age at or length of service, whether the veteran saw combat, where the veteran served) may not matter as much in shaping aging outcomes as how the veteran assesses and interprets his or her experiences.

The outcomes of service may be mediated not only through these subjective evaluations of service but also through attitudes and values related to nationalism and patriotism that stem from service. For example, veterans who can integrate their experiences into existing attitudes or values may differ from those who see their service as rupturing or transforming the worldviews they had before they entered. As Silverstein and his colleagues (Chapter 6) show, attitudes and values related to nationalism and patriotism can be transmitted intact to the next generation—or they can be the source of resentment, resistance, or rejection on the part of the next generation, thereby creating intergenerational friction within families.

STRENGTHENING SOCIAL RELATIONSHIPS AND NETWORKS

Veterans are more likely to evaluate their service in positive ways if they are embedded in supportive social relationships and networks with family members, friends, and other veterans and if they communicate with others about their experiences (see Chapters 1 and 4). Veteran service organizations could prioritize opportunities that encourage veterans to share their experiences and facilitate continued contact among service mates, which could be avenues for interventions to improve the social integration and health of veterans.

Marriage is particularly important to understand, as demonstrated by MacDermid Wadsworth and her colleagues (Chapter 4). They show that it is not only important to examine how marital ties support veterans, but also how service itself is a supportive or an unsupportive context for marriage. They suggest that service appears to be a more supportive context for marriage for men than women. The expanding opportunities for women in the military today may increase the likelihood of deployment and family separation, which could be problematic for women who are in marriages in which there is a traditional division of labor, especially concerning primary caregiving responsibilities for children. When women marry other service members in large numbers (and service women are 6 times more likely than service men to be married to another service member), military duties may become harder to coordinate as deployments become longer and less predictable. When military women marry civilians, it may be difficult to find partners who are willing or able to tolerate these challenges. Single mothers may find military careers attractive because job security, pay, and benefits surpass those of many private employers—and yet, their pursuit of military careers may create far more discontinuity and disruption in family life relative to employment in other sectors. These issues carry important implications for military family policies and the supports and options of husbands and wives, fathers and mothers.

FOSTERING RESILIENCE IN VETERANS AND THEIR FAMILIES

Many of the chapters emphasize the need to understand coping with trauma and stress—especially in relation to deployment and combat exposure—to foster the resilience of veterans. There is ample evidence that severe military stressors can result in posttraumatic stress disorder (PTSD), which not only may last for decades but is also associated with increased risk of mortality and morbidities (Chapters 9, 12, and 13). PTSD and its effects ripple outward to affect family members and functioning.

However, most who face military-related stressors do not develop PTSD. Prevalence estimates of military-related PTSD range from less than 10% to 30%, depending on the particular war and population (Institute of Medicine [IOM], 2012). Among soldiers, factors that promote resilience include positive emotions and realistic optimism, social support, cognitive flexibility, self-regulation, and physical fitness (Chapter 8). A good example of this comes from Malone and her colleagues (Chapter 2), whose research reveals that conscientiousness allows veterans to better protect themselves against the emotional trauma of combat. Although conscientiousness, in the absence of a stressor, might hinder ego development because it is strongly related to conventionality and conformity, it helps veterans cope with combat because it is associated with better self-organization and self-regulation.

There are many different trajectories of resilience, as noted by Aldwin and her colleagues (Chapter 9). For example, there is ample evidence that "posttraumatic growth" (PTG) can stem from major stressors such as combat exposure, resulting in higher levels of mastery and social support, better coping skills, and better health outcomes. But resilience is also reflected in "normal" levels of well-being in that it keeps veterans functioning at higher levels despite the trauma. In Aldwin and colleagues' study, combat veterans had just as much purpose in life, mastery, and religiousness as the civilian and noncombat veteran groups, despite their higher levels of stressful life events, chronic stress, trauma, poor health behavior habits, higher depressive symptoms, and lower self-rated health. This suggests that they actually might have achieved a type of resilience in being able to function at comparable levels. In addition, it is important to remember that PTSD and PTG can simultaneously occur within an individual.

If the military could better protect its personnel from developing PTSD, and shift the balance toward PTG, this would have positive long-term effects on health. Helping military personnel to develop coping and resilience resources would not only protect them from the effects of military stress but also provide lifelong resources to promote optimal aging. These include repetitively exposing military personnel to realistic scenarios to prepare them for what lies ahead, attempting to promote mastery and coping self-efficacy by increasing perceptions of control, and teaching soldiers to appraise situations as challenges rather than threats and to apply problem-focused coping and better emotional regulation strategies.

The military has been attempting to improve comprehensive soldier fitness, which includes both psychological and physical fitness (Seligman & Fowler, 2011). The Comprehensive Soldier Fitness program focuses on four dimensions—emotional, social, family, and spiritual fitness—as well as resilience training. However, this effort has not been without its critics. Some have expressed concerns about lack of pilot testing and ethical oversight (Eidelson, Pilisuk, & Soldz, 2011). Others have argued that the program has not been independently and critically evaluated, and it is not clear that current assessment instruments will be able to determine whether the program actually increases resilience to PTSD (Steenkamp, Nash, & Litz, 2013). Deployment is also stressful for military families, especially when the veteran returns with psychological or physical injuries. The military conducts resilience training for its families, such as a program called FOCUS (Families OverComing Under Stress), which has been shown to be effective in reducing psychological distress and problematic behaviors among family members (Saltzman, 2016).

For minorities and women, another layer of stress and even trauma may be layered atop the already difficult experience of combat: race- or gender-related discrimination and violence. Kabat and colleagues (Chapter 3) found that combat stress is exacerbated by perceptions of discrimination, which are associated with higher PTSD symptoms in Hispanic and Black veterans. The stressors experienced by members of these groups (e.g., inappropriate or racist language, insults, harassment), coupled with those experienced by women (e.g., unwanted touching, harassment, rape, violence), can create hostile environments. Rather than find camaraderie and support through one's peers, these individuals often feel threatened by others around them. The institutionalized nature of discrimination (e.g., complaining to superiors without any effect, experiencing harassment from superiors) only serves to worsen the perception that peers cannot be trusted and that one has no support in a dangerous environment. This reinforces the need not only for stronger resilience training, as noted earlier, but also for interventions aimed at eliminating informal and formal modes of discrimination. These types of discrimination and sexual trauma, which were remarkably high in Operation Iraqi Freedom (OIF), Operation Enduring Freedom (OEF), and Operation New Dawn (OND) veterans, increase the likelihood of a wide variety of mental disorders (e.g., Kimerling et al., 2010).

One neglected factor related to fostering resilience for veterans is coping with what Litz and colleagues (2009) called "moral injury"—that is, "perpetrating, failing to prevent, bearing witness to, or learning about acts that transgress deeply held moral beliefs and expectations" (p. 697). Injuries like these are among the stronger predictors of PTSD and other mental health problems (Maguen & Litz, 2012). Efforts are underway to treat moral injuries (Drescher et al., 2011), often involving forgiveness and reparations. Resilience training for soldiers should include individual and group sessions in moral courage (Olsthoorn, 2007), with a view toward preventing atrocities. This will protect veterans' well-being and perhaps also promote their successful aging.

PROMOTING THE PHYSICAL HEALTH OF VETERANS

A conundrum in research on veterans' health follows from "healthy soldier" and "healthy warrior" selection effects. *Healthy soldier* denotes that those who enter the military are generally selected to have better mental and physical health than civilians of comparable age. *Healthy warrior* denotes that soldiers who are deployed are further screened for physical and mental health functioning. Both selection effects can create positive health differentials that favor veterans over civilians, and veterans who were deployed over those who were not, at least in the short term. However, deployed soldiers are more likely to be exposed to combat trauma, physical injury, and hazardous exposures, so teasing apart true stress-related growth from preexisting higher levels of psychological resources can be difficult, especially in the absence of data obtained before entry to the military and before deployment.

Physical insults and trauma can result in higher risk for impaired aging. Those who sustain serious psychological or physical injury have higher rates of physical and psychiatric disability, as well as mortality, and these effects can be seen up to 50 years later. The impact of military service on morbidity and mortality is clear in the case of casualties during training, deployment, or combat. But there are less direct ways that service affects mortality and morbidity through the promotion and use of tobacco (Chapter 10); the links between PTSD and greater alcohol use or hypertension (Chapter 13); or conditions like heart disease, stroke, diabetes, arthritis, or cancer (Chapter 7).

Although there is little research on the link between military service and cognition, Stawski and colleagues (Chapter 11) reveal that veteran status is associated with age-related declines in cognition (at least in terms of memory performance and, in particular, immediate recall), but the mechanism is unclear. Further, they note that service can represent a potentially health-promoting context for cognitive function in that it offers supports related to medical care, employment, education and skill training, cognitive job complexity, and social interaction and connectedness, all of which may facilitate cognitive function.

A resounding theme throughout this book is the need to better differentiate the effects of specific *service experiences* from the *subsequent pathways* through which these experiences shape outcomes. In the case of health, this means disentangling the direct and indirect effects of military service on the risk of disease, mortality, and other negative health outcomes. Too much research simply associates veteran or combat status with various outcomes and imputes a causal relation. To design effective interventions, research must better isolate the factors that contribute to veterans' unique patterns of disease and mortality and understand complex causal chains across the life course. For example, as Wilmoth and colleagues (Chapter 7) note, exposure to environmental toxins during service can increase the risk of certain types of cancer, whereas long-term stress processes that stem from adverse military experiences can increase the risk of heart disease. As another example, combat exposure is linked to PTSD, which in turn is linked to brain structure and functioning, even after many decades (Chapter 12).

The example of smoking offers another excellent case in point. As Landes and colleagues (Chapter 10) note, veterans on average smoke more, and are more likely to ever have smoked, than nonveterans; this differential may account for the higher mortality of veterans, especially among men. Reducing smoking behavior among veterans could decrease the veteran mortality differential and increase veteran longevity. The military's antismoking stance has grown stronger over the years, and it is important that the Department of Veterans Affairs (VA) health care system continue its smoking cessation efforts. But it would be even better for the United States military to actively campaign against smoking and prevent its uptake among soldiers. It has historically viewed smoking as a strategy for coping with stress, and the military continues to encourage cigarette use by providing them at low cost.

As Spiro, Settersten, and Aldwin (2016) pointed out, health care costs for current military personnel and for veterans consume a large portion of the federal budget, including about 20% of overall government health care spending. The Department of Defense (DOD) spends about $50 billion a year for health care for current and retired service men and women and their dependents, and the VA spends an additional $50 billion per year for health care, about half of its annual budget. Much of this cost is for physical health. Because many chronic medical conditions are observed long after initial injury or exposure (Stewart et al., 2015; Taylor, Ureña, & Kail, 2016), the costs stretch over decades (Geiling, Rosen, & Edwards, 2012).

A growing proportion of this cost is spent on mental health conditions, which can be acute, short term, or long term, and can go into periods of remission. PTSD, in particular, has high comorbidity rates (Schnurr, Wachen, Green, & Kaltman, 2014) and thus greatly increases health care costs. Combat experience can be dealt with reasonably successfully for some time, but it can lead to sudden negative mental health issues in later life (Davison et al., 2016). Little is known about how traumatic brain injury will affect the aging of recent veterans, although recent evidence suggests that it might accelerate cognitive aging (Trotter, Robinson, Milberg, McGlinchey, & Salat, 2015). Understanding the long-term effects of service on health and well-being is critical to the financial future of the United States and other nations. There is an urgent need for information on veterans' use of, and need for, health care and disability payments provided by the VA and DOD, and the long-term cost implications of providing them.

INTERVENING AT STRATEGIC POINTS OF TRANSITION

At the heart of the overarching model delineated in the Introduction to this volume is the insight that military service must be understood within the context of the life course. A variety of pre-, during-, and postservice factors must be taken into account. Premilitary characteristics include personality, family dynamics, and early childhood stress. Factors during service include branch of service, training and deployment experiences, age and rank at entry into and exit from the military, and military specialty. The specific nature of service experiences is also important, including potentially positive factors such as training, social relationships, and maturational processes, as well as those that are potentially negative, such as war zone deployment, substance abuse, injuries, or trauma. Postmilitary pathways include the effects of service on health, work, and family life, and how receipt of military benefits may affect these. These factors can have both direct and indirect effects on later-life outcomes (Kang, Aldwin, Choun, & Spiro, 2016), and the meanings and effects of service can change over time (Chapter 1).

A life course model suggests that there may be strategic points for intervention. For example, training military personnel to better cope with hardship is important for fostering resilience against negative effects. Training to prevent moral injury may be especially important in advance of deployment, but skills for health and financial literacy and to help families cope with extended deployments would also be helpful.

Building stronger scaffolds as veterans exit the military and return to civilian life is a similarly important juncture for intervention. For example, Lee and colleagues (Chapter 8) highlight the importance of ensuring adequate psychological, family, and employment support as veterans readjust to civilian lives. Mental health assessment at homecoming can help identify individuals at risk for "downward spirals" in readjustment (e.g., the U.S. Army's pre/postdeployment health assessment program). In particular, encouraging veterans to maintain existing or develop new social networks of other veterans could help decrease the social isolation that some veterans experience, as could greater reliance on the family support system (Burland & Lundquist, 2013). Similarly, Stawski and his colleagues (Chapter 11) suggest that exit from service may represent a phase in which supports are weakened and broken, which may contribute to increased risk of cognitive decline.

In later life, negative effects of service may suddenly emerge, even if veterans have for decades managed to cope with them successfully, or existing effects may be exacerbated in the face of normal aging. When veterans are actively pursuing careers or raising families, life may be busy enough to keep adverse memories at bay. In retirement, some veterans may find that memories can reemerge, causing considerable distress, especially if they threaten life stability, relationships, or resources (Davison et al., 2016). Similarly, bereavement in late life may trigger grief for lost comrades. Difficulties in emotion regulation may also accompany declines in cognitive functioning, heightening the risk for psychological distress. Nonetheless, these types of changes may offer opportunities for growth and redirection (Davison et al., 2016).

BUILDING WORKFORCE CAPACITY
TO SERVE AGING VETERANS

There is significant demand for clinical geropsychologists, especially those who conduct psychotherapy. The current cohort of older veterans is less likely to access needed mental health services than are younger veterans. However, as baby boomers age, increasing numbers will likely seek access to mental health services. Given the increasing number of women and minorities in today's military, it is also important to address diversity issues for tomorrow's aging veterans. Those who work with elderly veterans should be trained in cultural sensitivity and in the potential impact of racial and sexual discrimination and harassment on the aging process.

There is a clear need for improved training for clinicians who provide services to older adults (Hoge, Karel, Zeiss, Alegria, & Moye, 2015; IOM, 2012). According to GeroCentral (2016), a clearinghouse for clinical geropsychologists, there is a severe shortage of mental health professionals:

> Currently, we have only 55% of needed psychiatrists, 18% of needed social workers, and 10% of needed psychologists. By 2030, it is estimated that we will only have 27% of needed psychiatrists, 9% of needed social workers, and 5% of needed psychologists. There is a drastic need to prime the pipeline of geriatric mental health professionals!

In addition, very few doctoral programs in clinical geropsychology have more than one clinician on staff to train doctoral students (S. Qualls, personal communication, August 2015). If academic training programs are the gateway to building the health care workforce and supplying personnel, both universities and the federal government must invest more in training.

IMPROVING DATA TO GUIDE POLICY AND PRACTICE

To effectively assess the multiple effects of military service on health and well-being in both the short and the long term, there is a need for large, representative, longitudinal studies. The DOD has initiated the Millennium Cohort Study (https://www.millenniumcohort.org/about), which includes multiple cohorts of military personnel followed longitudinally. The sample is large enough to examine differences in experiences among veterans, but it cannot assess differences between veterans and nonveterans.

There are a number of ongoing longitudinal studies of aging (e.g., Health and Retirement Study, Midlife in the United States), but most include few veterans, and even fewer women or minority veterans. These studies seldom explore military service in sufficient depth—participants are simply asked whether they are veterans and, if so, perhaps when they served. Assessments of subjective aspects of military experiences (e.g., perceptions of the costs and benefits of service or of its role in aging) are generally nonexistent.

The chapters of this volume repeatedly emphasize the multifaceted nature of service, that different aspects of service may bring different kinds of outcomes, and that outcomes can occur in multiple domains (e.g., physical, mental, social, economic) and be positive or null, not just negative. In addition, those who "share" particular military experiences, such as combat or other trauma, do not necessarily share the same long-term outcomes. There are differences among veterans, and there is variability within veterans over time. Thus, a "common" experience can lead to different outcomes for different veterans, and for an individual veteran, that experience could carry positive, null, or negative effects at different points in her or his life course. For these reasons, much can be learned from systematic comparisons across wars and cohorts; between men and women; and by the location, types, duration, and timing of service.

One challenge for research is that it is difficult to ascertain the effects of service if little or nothing is known about the individual before he or she enters. The lack of information in this regard has made it difficult to fully assess the healthy soldier and healthy warrior effects noted previously. Similarly, although a number of studies have data on preservice and immediate postservice experiences, these data are often retrospective, and their links to service can be weakened by the passage of time. Data collection efforts and analytic strategies should address these problems, perhaps by drawing on the experience of researchers who study the transition to adulthood, and recruiting those researchers to begin long-term longitudinal studies. Several existing longitudinal studies provide premilitary data but have a relatively low prevalence of veterans in their samples (e.g., National Longitudinal Study of Youth, Project Talent, Wisconsin Longitudinal Study).

In particular, there is a need for nationally based longitudinal data that would allow for direct lifespan comparisons between veterans and nonveterans. Ideally, such data would include indicators of early-life characteristics that might influence selection into service, indicators of resilience (collected from veterans and nonveterans), and specific information about service experiences (e.g., branch, rank, combat exposure).

The chapters also emphasize the variability in experiences of service among veterans of different eras, given their differential engagement in wars that are distinctly different in location, the nature of warfare, and social reception. There are very few data sets that incorporate information specific to different conflicts or eras. For example, there is a need to develop a checklist of hazards and resources associated with different deployments (e.g., exposure to Agent Orange in Vietnam or to neurotoxins in the Gulf War).

As Spiro and colleagues (2016) indicated, there has been very little research on aging among veterans of the recent conflicts, including the first Persian Gulf War, the Iraq War (OIF), and the Afghanistan conflicts (OEF and the more recent OND). However, PTSD levels are higher in more recent conflicts, with veterans of the Iraq and Afghanistan conflicts having higher levels than Vietnam veterans, who in turn had higher levels than World War II veterans (IOM, 2012; Tanielian & Jaycox, 2008). As Wilmoth and colleagues (Chapter 7) note, more recent veterans have had very different experiences, with more frequent deployments; higher levels of traumatic brain injuries and amputations due to improvised explosive devices; and more life disruption due to the heavy use of Reserves and National Guard, who are usually older and with more established families. Improvements in military medicine mean that fewer veterans in these conflicts have died, and more have survived with injuries and disabilities, greatly increasing the costs to the federal government for veterans' benefits and health care. This makes the need for data all the more pressing, as these veterans move through adulthood, so that we can begin to understand what is unique about their aging experiences relative to earlier cohorts of veterans.

Several chapters in this volume point to underdeveloped areas where more and better data are needed. In social life, these include gathering subjective perspectives, especially how veterans appraise and make meaning from their military experiences, and how much and with whom they communicate about their experiences (Chapter 1); the family careers of military members (Chapter 4), especially how transitions related to marriage, childbearing, childrearing, divorce, and remarriage unfold within military careers; and how military experiences shape interactions across generations in families and societies, especially the transmission or rejection of core attitudes (Chapter 6). These issues underscore the importance of understanding the potential effects of service on the lives of others connected to military personnel.

Other chapters point to the need for data on aspects of physical and psychological health, including discrimination and trauma experiences in the military (Chapter 3), brain aging (Chapter 12), and mental health treatment (Chapter 14). Individuals with high combat exposure and PTSD symptoms are particularly at risk for worse health and higher mortality (Chapters 12 and 13). One can therefore anticipate that the rate of early retirement may increase in future cohorts (Chapter 5), as more recent veterans may also be at higher risk for rapid physical declines (Chapter 7), thereby placing greater strain on retirement systems.

To facilitate research on the long-term outcomes of military service, readers will find in Online Appendix A a set of recommendations for defining periods of service, and in Online Appendix B a short module of items that can be included in new or ongoing studies to better assess service (both appendices are available at http://pubs.apa.org/books/supp/spiro/).

IMPROVING VETERANS' EXPERIENCES IN HEALTH CARE SYSTEMS

Despite its challenges and limitations, the VA is a health care system devoted to veterans, especially the most vulnerable among them. However, many veterans do not receive their care through the VA, whether because they have access to private health care through their or their spouses' insurance or because they use other federal systems such as Medicare. (Military retirees use TRICARE, a DOD-based federal health care system.) There are concerns about the adequacy of care for veterans who use civilian systems, arising largely from the ignorance of many providers about the "unasked question" (Brown, 2012) "Did you ever serve in the military?" and how such service might interact with the veteran's needs.

Because the legacies of service often go undetected, all providers should be encouraged to inquire whether their patients are veterans and, if so, to consider their military and trauma histories, as well as ongoing stressors, as they work with them. Greater recognition among civilian providers of the potential impact of service on the health of aging patients would assist clinicians in better diagnosing problems and providing appropriate care. With the growing number of OIF/OEF/OND veterans returning home and seeking health care, a number of medical organizations have attempted to provide tools for providers (e.g., American Association of Medical Colleges, 2013; Kane, Saperstein, Bunt, & Stephens, 2013; Sessums & Jackson, 2013), including a pocket card for taking a military health history (http://www.va.gov/oaa/pocketcard).

Finally, there is a need to better integrate military and veteran health care around the transition from active duty to retired status (making it a more "seamless" transition) and to develop a national agenda that unites federal, state, and private organizations around veterans' physical, mental, social, and economic well-being (e.g., Institute for Veterans and Military Families, 2013; Social Work Policy Institute, 2013). These challenges will only become more difficult in future decades as increasing numbers of veterans need and seek aging services in an era beset by financial limitations and potential lack of specialized services. VA funding is currently inadequate and will require an infusion of funds to strengthen VA services, better support access to non-VA services, or both. Seeking a more complete understanding of the impact of service on veterans and their families, as we have begun to do here, will enable policymakers and service providers to more effectively meet the needs of current and future cohorts of older veterans. After all they have done for us, it is the least we can do for them.

REFERENCES

American Association of Medical Colleges. (2013). Health care provider awareness of the military status of patients: Asking the question. *Analysis in Brief, 13*(5), 1–2.

Brown, J. L. (2012). The unasked question. *JAMA, 308,* 1869–1870. http://dx.doi.org/10.1001/jama.2012.14254

Burland, D., & Lundquist, J. H. (2013). The best years of our lives: Military service and family relationships: A life course perspective. In J. M. Wilmoth & A. S. London (Eds.), *Life course perspectives on military service* (pp. 165–184). New York, NY: Routledge.

Davison, E. H., Kaiser, A. P., Spiro, A., III, Moye, J., King, L. A., & King, D. W. (2016). From late-onset stress symptomatology to later-adulthood trauma reengagement in aging combat veterans: Taking a broader view. *The Gerontologist, 56,* 14–21. http://dx.doi.org/10.1093/geront/gnv097

Drescher, K. D., Foy, D. W., Kelly, C., Leshner, A., Schutz, K., & Litz, B. (2011). An exploration of the viability and usefulness of the construct of moral injury in war veterans. *Traumatology, 17,* 8–13. http://dx.doi.org/10.1177/1534765610395615

Eidelson, R., Pilisuk, M., & Soldz, S. (2011). The dark side of comprehensive soldier fitness. *American Psychologist, 66,* 643–644. http://dx.doi.org/10.1037/a0025272

Geiling, J., Rosen, J. M., & Edwards, R. D. (2012). Medical costs of war in 2035: Long-term care challenges for veterans of Iraq and Afghanistan. *Military Medicine, 177,* 1235–1244. http://dx.doi.org/10.7205/MILMED-D-12-00031

GeroCentral. (2016). *Training and careers.* Retrieved from http://gerocentral.org/training-career/

Hoge, M. A., Karel, M. J., Zeiss, A. M., Alegria, M., & Moye, J. (2015). Strengthening psychology's workforce for older adults: Implications of the Institute of Medicine's report to Congress. *American Psychologist, 70,* 265–278. http://dx.doi.org/10.1037/a0038927

Institute for Veterans and Military Families. (2013, February). *A national veterans strategy: The economic, social and security imperative.* Syracuse, NY: Syracuse University, Institute for Veterans and Military Families and Institute for National Security and Counter-terrorism. Retrieved from http://vets.syr.edu/research/a-national-veterans-strategy/

Institute of Medicine. (2012). *The mental health and substance use workforce for older adults: In whose hands?* Washington, DC: National Academies Press.

Kane, S. F., Saperstein, A. K., Bunt, C. W., & Stephens, M. B. (2013). When war follows combat veterans home. *The Journal of Family Practice, 62,* 399–407.

Kang, S., Aldwin, C. M., Choun, S., & Spiro, A., III. (2016). A life-span perspective on combat exposure and PTSD symptoms in later life: Findings from the VA Normative Aging Study. *The Gerontologist, 56,* 22–32. http://dx.doi.org/10.1093/geront/gnv120

Kimerling, R., Street, A. E., Pavao, J., Smith, M. W., Cronkite, R. C., Holmes, T. H., & Frayne, S. M. (2010). Military-related sexual trauma among Veterans Health Administration patients returning from Afghanistan and Iraq. *American Journal of Public Health, 100,* 1409–1412. http://dx.doi.org/10.2105/AJPH.2009.171793

Litz, B. T., Stein, N., Delaney, E., Lebowitz, L., Nash, W. P., Silva, C., & Maguen, S. (2009). Moral injury and moral repair in war veterans: A preliminary model and intervention strategy. *Clinical Psychology Review, 29,* 695–706. http://dx.doi.org/10.1016/j.cpr.2009.07.003

Maguen, S., & Litz, B. (2012). Moral injury in veterans of war. *PTSD Research Quarterly, 23,* 1–6. Retrieved from http://www.ptsd.va.gov/professional/newsletters/research-quarterly/v23n1.pdf

Olsthoorn, P. (2007). Courage in the military: Physical and moral. *Journal of Military Ethics, 6,* 270–279. http://dx.doi.org/10.1080/15027570701755471

Saltzman, W. R. (2016). The FOCUS family resilience program: An innovative family intervention for trauma and loss. *Family Process, 55,* 647–659. http://dx.doi.org/10.1111/famp.12250

Schnurr, P., Wachen, J. S., Green, B. L., & Kaltman, S. (2014). Trauma exposure, PTSD, and physical health. In M. J. Friedman, T. M. Keane, & P. A. Resick (Eds.), *Handbook of PTSD: Science and practice* (2nd ed., pp. 502–521). New York, NY: Guilford Press.

Seligman, M. E. P., & Fowler, R. D. (2011). Comprehensive soldier fitness and the future of psychology. *American Psychologist, 66,* 82–86. http://dx.doi.org/10.1037/a0021898

Sessums, L. L., & Jackson, J. L. (2013). Care of returning military personnel. *Annals of Internal Medicine, 159,* ITC1–ITC15. http://dx.doi.org/10.7326/0003-4819-159-1-201307020-01001

Social Work Policy Institute. (2013, June). *Enhancing the well-being of America's veterans and their families: A call to action for a national veterans policy.* Washington, DC: NASW Foundation. http://cir.usc.edu/wp-content/uploads/2013/12/SWPI-RPT-15914.VeteransLo.pdf

Spiro, A., III, Settersten, R. A., Jr., & Aldwin, C. (2016). Long-term outcomes of military service in aging and the life course: A positive re-envisioning. *The Gerontologist, 56,* 5–13. http://dx.doi.org/10.1093/geront/gnv093

Steenkamp, M. M., Nash, W. P., & Litz, B. T. (2013). Post-traumatic stress disorder: Review of the Comprehensive Soldier Fitness program. *American Journal of Preventive Medicine, 44,* 507–512. http://dx.doi.org/10.1016/j.amepre.2013.01.013

Stewart, I. J., Sosnov, J. A., Howard, J. T., Orman, J. A., Fang, R., Morrow, B. D., . . . Chung, K. K. (2015). Retrospective analysis of long-term outcomes after combat injury: A hidden cost of war. *Circulation, 132,* 2126–2133. http://dx.doi.org/10.1161/CIRCULATIONAHA.115.016950

Tanielian, T., & Jaycox, L. H. (2008). *Invisible wounds of war: Psychological and cognitive injuries, their consequences, and services to assist recovery.* Santa Monica, CA: RAND Corporation.

Taylor, M. G., Ureña, S., & Kail, B. L. (2016). Service-related exposures and physical health trajectories among aging veteran men. *The Gerontologist, 56,* 92–103. http://dx.doi.org/10.1093/geront/gnv662

Trotter, B. B., Robinson, M. E., Milberg, W. P., McGlinchey, R. E., & Salat, D. H. (2015). Military blast exposure, ageing and white matter integrity. *Brain: A Journal of Neurology, 138,* 2278–2292. http://dx.doi.org/10.1093/brain/awv139

INDEX

Foreign policy, 108
Fourth U.S. Marine Division, 20

Gender
    discrimination based on. *See*
        Perceived discrimination
        among Vietnam-era veterans
        and PTSD
    as factor in retirement age, 92
    and labor force participation among
        older veterans, 97
    and marriage in military families, 78,
        82, 85
    and posttraumatic stress disorder, 59
    and women in combat, 75
Generational change, 110–111
GeroCentral, 285
Gerontological Society of America, xvi
The Gerontologist (journal), xvi
GI Bill benefits
    and appraisals of wartime experience,
        33
    cohort differences in, 202–203, 278
    and later-life health/well-being, 176
    and nationalism–patriotism, 109
Grant Study (Harvard Study of Adult
    Development), 12, 21, 23, 27, 246
Great Depression, 94
Griffiths, G. G., 208
Gulf War veterans
    captivity experiences of, 160
    and historical time, 74
    research on, 287
    and veteran mortality differential,
        192
    and veteran support for war, 109

Halbwachs, M., 33
Harpaz-Rotem, I., 266
Harvard Study of Adult Development
    (Grant Study), 12, 21, 23, 27, 246
Hazardous exposures, 126, 140
HbA1c (hemoglobin A1c), 175, 176
HDLs (high-density lipoproteins), 172,
    175
Health. *See also specific headings, e.g.:*
    Later-life health and well-being
    promotion of, 282–284
    and retirement, 95, 98, 103

and veteran status, 171–172
in Vietnam Era Twin Study of Aging,
    228, 233
Health and Retirement Study (HRS)
    and later-life health of older male
        veterans, 126, 128, 130–132,
        139–141
    later-life health/well-being in,
        172–173
    and memory performance in later
        life, 209, 220
Health care spending, 5, 283
Health care systems, 288–289
Healthy Base Initiative, 202
"Healthy soldier," 4, 282
"Healthy warrior," 282
Hearing loss, xvi
Heart disease, 252, 253, 282
Hedonic well-being, 170, 175, 176
Hemoglobin A1c (HbA1c), 175, 176
Heo, M., 260
High-density lipoproteins (HDLs), 172,
    175, 176
Himes, C. L., 129, 133
Hippocampal-dependent memory, 226
Hippocampus, 208, 226, 227, 231,
    233–237
Hispanic veterans, 57, 58. *See also*
    Perceived discrimination among
    Vietnam-era veterans and PTSD
Historical time, 73–74
Hoa La prison, 148
Hoff, R., 266
Holocaust, 107
Home-front mobilization, 30, 33
HRS. *See* Health and Retirement Study
Hypertension, 252, 253
Hypothalamic–pituitary–adrenal axis,
    226

Impaired aging, 180
Improving Mood-Promoting Access
    to Collaborative Treatment
    (IMPACT) program, 262
Income, 92, 95, 128. *See also*
    Socioeconomic status
Individual time, 74
Infectious diseases, 126
Inflammation, 180

Training
    accidents during, 126
    specialized military, 127
Trauma. *See also specific headings*
    and appraisals of wartime experience,
        30, 31
    and conscientiousness, 50
    sexual, 281
Traumatic brain injury, 5
TRICARE, 288
Triglycerides, 172
Truman, Harry, 119
Turner, J. B., 58
Turse, N. A., 58

United Service Organizations, 57
U.S. Air Force, 75
U.S. Armed Forces, 4, 76, 250, 253
U.S. Bureau of Labor Statistics, 76
U.S. Census Bureau, 76
U.S. Code of Federal Regulations, 191
U.S. Congress, 92
U.S. Department of Defense
    active duty surveys conducted by, 76
    Advisory Committee on Women in
        the Services, 74
    and Combat Exclusion Rule, 75
    directives on families and children
        from, 71–72
    and family history of military service,
        111
    health care spending by, 5, 283
U.S. Department of Veterans Affairs, 113

VA. *See* Veterans Affairs
Vascular risk factors, 249, 253
Veteran mortality differential, 187–203
    defined, 188
    possible causes of, 188–189
    research study on, 190–200
Veterans Affairs (VA)
    funding for, 289
    and later-life health of older male
        veterans, 126, 131–133
    Northeast Program Evaluation,
        263–264
    and optimal aging, 180
    and research, xv–xvi
    smoking cessation efforts of, 202, 283

utilization of mental health services
    at, 263, 269
Veterans' days, 20
Veterans Mail Survey, 139
Veteran status
    and memory performance in later
        life, 211, 213, 214, 216
    and nationalism–patriotism, 108–109
VETR (Vietnam Era Twin Registry), 228
VETR-PTSDS (Vietnam Era Twin
    Registry PTSD Scale), 230
VETSA. *See* Vietnam Era Twin Study
    of Aging
Vietnam-era repatriated prisoners of
    war, 147–162
    captivity stressors and mental health
        of, 154
    coping strategies of, 155–156
    implications of research on, 161–162
    key themes from studies on, 156–161
    lifespan effects of captivity on,
        154–155
    overview, 148–150
    statistics on, 150–153
Vietnam Era Twin Registry (VETR), 228
Vietnam Era Twin Registry PTSD Scale
    (VETR-PTSDS), 230
Vietnam Era Twin Study of Aging
    (VETSA), 225–238
    data and description information in,
        227–232
    implications of, 236–239
    results of, 233–236
Vietnam War veterans
    cohort characteristics of, 96
    earnings of, 97
    GI Bill benefits for, 203
    labor force participation among, 99
    lack of research on, 3–4
    later-life health of, 128–129, 132, 141
    mental health services utilized by,
        263
    military pensions for, 98
    mortality of, 198, 199
    nationalism–patriotism among,
        108–111
    and predictors of PTSD, 245, 246
    as prisoners of war. *See* Vietnam-era
        repatriated prisoners of war

ABOUT THE EDITORS

Avron (Ron) Spiro III is research professor of epidemiology and psychiatry at Boston University Schools of Public Health and Medicine. He is the director of Psychosocial Research at the VA Normative Aging Study at the VA Boston Healthcare System and is also affiliated with the Massachusetts Veterans Epidemiology Research and Information Center, the National Center for PTSD, and the Center for Healthcare Organization and Implementation Research. He is a recipient of a Senior Research Career Scientist award from the Clinical Science R&D Service of the U.S. Department of Veterans Affairs (VA) and is a fellow of Divisions 5 (Quantitative and Qualitative Methods) and 20 (Adult Development and Aging) of the American Psychological Association and of the Behavior and Social Sciences Section of the Gerontological Society of America. Dr. Spiro has been funded by the National Institutes of Health (NIH) and the VA, and is the author or coauthor of over 250 publications. He was coprincipal investigator (with Carolyn Aldwin) of an NIH grant to establish a research network on Life-span Outcomes of Military Service and coinvestigator on several projects funded by NIH or the VA studying health, personality, cognition, and aging. His current work involves (a) examining the effects of health and disease on cognitive aging, (b) modeling longitudinal changes in personality in relation to health, (c) developing a lifespan approach to health and aging in veterans, and (d) studying mental disorders and their impact on health and functioning.

Richard A. Settersten Jr. is endowed director of the Hallie Ford Center for Healthy Children and Families, and professor of social and behavioral health sciences at Oregon State University. A fellow of the Gerontological Society of America (GSA), he has held leadership roles in the GSA and the American Sociological Association (ASA). His coedited book (with Jacqueline L. Angel), *Handbook of Sociology of Aging*, won the 2012 Outstanding Publication Award of the ASA's Section on Aging and the Life Course, and an earlier book, *Lives in Time and Place*, won the Kalish Award of the GSA. He coedited (with Vern L. Bengtson) the third edition of the *Handbook of Theories of Aging* and is coeditor (with Megan McClelland) of the journal *Research in Human Development*. The MacArthur Foundation and NIH have supported his research. He has also participated in National Academy of Sciences/Institute of Medicine panel discussions on the health and well-being of young adults and on new directions in social demography, social epidemiology, and sociology of aging. He collaborated with Ron Spiro and Carolyn Aldwin on a grant from the National Institutes of Health to establish a research network on Lifespan Outcomes of Military Service.

Carolyn M. Aldwin is the Jo Anne Leonard endowed director for the Center for Healthy Aging Research and professor of human development and family sciences, Oregon State University. She received her doctorate in adult development and aging from the University of California, San Francisco. She is a fellow of the Gerontological Society of America, as well as both Divisions 20 (Adult Development and Aging) and 38 (Health Psychology) of the American Psychological Association. Dr. Aldwin received the 2011 Developmental Health Psychology Award from these divisions and is a former president of Division 20. She has authored or edited eight books and over 125 other publications on stress, stress-related growth, coping, health, and the long-term effects of military service on health in later life. Her work has been funded by the National Institute on Aging, the National Science Foundation, and the Templeton Foundation. She was coprincipal investigator (with Avron Spiro) on a grant from the National Institutes of Health to establish a research network on Lifespan Outcomes of Military Service.